DIABETIC COOKBOOK FOR BEGINNERS

800+ Appetizing & Healthy Recipes to Easily Manage
Type 2 & Pre Diabetes with a Specific Diet
21 Day Meal Plan with Sweet Desserts & Smoothies Included

Catherine B. Reed

First Printing Edition, 2021

Printed in the United States of America

Available from Amazon.com and other retail outlets

Table Of Contents

CHAPTER 5 SNACKS RECIPE 56

CHAPTER 6 SOUP AND STEW RECIPES 74

CHAPTER 7 MEATLESS RECIPES....92

CHAPTER 8 SALADS RECIPE........124

CHAPTER 9 SAUCES, DIPS & DRESSINGS RECIPE....................134

CHAPTER 10 GRAINS, LEGUMES & PASTA RECIPE 146

CHAPTER 11 POULTRY RECIPES.. 152

CHAPTER 12 FISH AND SEAFOOD RECIPES 172

CHAPTER 13 BEEF, PORK & LAMB RECIPES 192

CHAPTER 14 OTHER FAVORITE RECIPES

CHAPTER 15 DESSERT AND SMOOTHIE RECIPES 258

INTRODUCTION

Diabetes mellitus is a group of diseases that impair the body's ability to use sugar (glucose). Since glucose provides energy to the cells that make up your muscles and tissues, it is vital to your health. It is also the brain's primary source of energy.

Type 1 and type 2 diabetes are two different types of diabetes. Prediabetes and gestational diabetes are two reversible diabetes complications. Prediabetes occurs when blood sugar levels are higher than normal but nothigh enough to be classified as diabetes. Prediabetes is often the precursor to diabetes unless adequate measures are taken to prevent progression. Gestational diabetes is a form of diabetes that occurs during pregnancy but can disappear after the baby is born.

Glucose's Role

The cells that makeup muscles and other tissues use glucose, a sugar, as energy sources. Food and the liver are the two main sources of glucose.

Sugar is ingested into the bloodstream and, with insulin, reaches cells. The liver also stores and produces glucose.

Type 1 diabetes has some causes.

Type 1 diabetes has an uncertain etiology. What is understood is that your immune system, which is usually responsible for fighting dangerous bacteria and viruses, attacks and kills your pancreas' insulin producing cells. You would have very little to no insulin as a result of this. Sugar builds up in your bloodstream instead of being transferred to your cells.

A variety of factors can cause prediabetes and type 2 diabetes.

Your cells become resistant to insulin action in prediabetes— which can lead to type 2 diabetes— and type 2 diabetes. The pancreas is unable to make enough insulin to resolve this resistance. Sugar builds up in your bloodstream instead of going into your cells, where it is required for energy.

It's unclear why this occurs, though genetic and environmental factors are thought to play a role in developing type 2 diabetes. While being overweight is closely linked to the development of type 2 diabetes, not everyone who has the disease is obese.

A variety of factors can cause diabetes during pregnancy.

The placenta releases hormones to keep the pregnancy going during pregnancy. Insulin resistance is increased in your cells as a result of these hormone s.

Your pancreas normally reacts by producing enough extra insulin to overcome this resistance. However, the pancreas can't always keep up. When this occurs, too little glucose enters your cells, and too much remains in your blood, causing gestational diabetes.

TYPE 1 DIABETES RISK FACTORS

The following factors may indicate a higher risk:

Environmental factors are significant. Exposure to a viral disease, for example, is likely to play a role in type 1 diabetes.

The existence of immune system cells that are harmful (autoantibodies). The presence of diabetes autoantibodies is also checked in family members of type 1 diabetes. You have a higher chance of having type 1 diabetes if you have these autoantibodies. However, not everyone with these autoantibodies goes on to develop diabetes.

Geographical details. Type 1 diabetes is more common in some countries, such as Finland and Sweden.

PREDIABETES AND TYPE 2 DIABETES RISK FACTORS

Researchers aren't sure why some people get prediabetes and type 2 diabetes while others don't. Certain factors, how- ever, clearly increase the risk, including:

The amount of weight. Your cells become more insulin tolerant as you gain more fatty tissue. Past of the family. Suppose a parent or sibling has type 2 diabetes, the risk increases.

Ethnicity or race. At the same time, it's unclear why some groups of people, such as Black, Hispanic, American Indian, and Asian Americans, are more vulnerable.

Age is a factor. When you get older, the risk increases. This may be because when you get older, you appear to exercise less, lose muscle mass, and gain weight

Diabetes during pregnancy. If you had gestational diabetes while pregnant, you're more likely to develop prediabetes and type 2 diabetes later in life. You're still at risk for type 2 diabetes if your baby weighed more than 9 pounds (4 kilo- grams).

Polycystic ovary syndrome (PCOS) is a form of polycystic ovary syndrome. Polycystic ovary syndrome, a common dis- order marked by irregular menstrual cycles, excessive hair growth, and obesity, raises the risk of diabetes in women.

Blood pressure that is too high. Type 2 diabetes is related to blood pressure levels greater than 140/90 millimeters of mercury (mm Hg).

Cholesterol and triglyceride levels are abnormal. Type 2 diabetes is more likely if you have low levels of high-density lipoprotein (HDL) or "healthy" cholesterol. Triglycerides are a form of fat that circulates in the bloodstream. Type 2 diabetes is more likely in people with elevated triglyceride levels. Your doctor can determine your cholesterol and triglyceride levels.

FACTORS THAT INCREASE THE RISK OF GESTATIONAL DIABETES

Gestational diabetes can affect pregnant women. Some women are more vulnerable than others. The following are some of the risk factors for gestational diabetes:

Age is a factor. Women over the age of 25 are at a higher risk.

Personal or family history If you have prediabetes, which is a precursor to type 2 diabetes, or if a nearby family member, such as a parent or sibling, has type 2 diabetes, the risk increases.

Difficulties

Diabetes complications that last a long time appear progressively. The longer you have diabetes and the less well you regulate your blood sugar, the more likely you are to develop complications. Diabetes problems can become debilitating or even life-threatening in the long run. Complications that could arise include:

Atherosclerosis is a form of cardiovascular disease. Diabetes significantly raises the risk of coronary artery disease (an- gina), heart attack, stroke, and artery narrowing, among other cardiovascular issues (atherosclerosis).

Harm to the nerves (neuropathy). Sugar in excess can harm the walls of the tiny blood vessels (capillaries) that nourish your nerves, especially in your legs. This may result in tingling, numbness, burning, or pain that starts at the toes or fingers' tips and extends upward.

If left untreated, the affected limbs will lose their ability to feel. Nausea, vomiting, diarrhea, and constipation may all be symptoms of nerve damage related to digestion. It can cause erectile dysfunction in men.

Harm to the kidneys (nephropathy). Millions of tiny blood vessel clusters (glomeruli) remove waste from the kidneys' blood. This delicate filtering system can be harmed by diabetes. Kidney failure or permanent end-stage kidney disease can result from severe damage, necessitating dialysis or a kidney transplant.

Harm to the eyes (retinopathy). Diabetic retinopathy causes damage to the eye's blood vessels, which can lead to blindness. Diabetic patients are more likely to develop severe vision problems, including cataracts and glaucoma.

Hearing loss is an issue. Diabetes patients are more likely to have hearing issues.

Alzheimer's disease is a type of dementia. Dementia, such as Alzheimer's disease, is linked to type 2 diabetes. The higher the risk tends to be, the worse your blood sugar regulation is. Although there are hypotheses on how these conditions are related, none has been proven.

Depression is a state of mind. People with type 1 and type 2 diabetes are more likely to experience depression symptoms. Diabetes treatment may be hampered by depression.

Diabetes during pregnancy may cause complications.

The majority of pregnant women with gestational diabetes have healthy infants. Untreated or uncontrolled blood sugar levels, on the other hand, can cause complications for both you and your kid.

As a result of gestational diabetes, your baby can develop complications such as:

Excessive expansion. Extra glucose will cross the placenta, causing your baby's pancreas to produce more insulin. This will result in your baby being too big (macrosomia). C-section births are more likely for very large infants.

Low blood sugar levels. Since their insulin output is high, babies born to mothers with gestational diabetes may experience low blood sugar (hypoglycemia) shortly after birth.The baby's blood sugar level can be brought back to normal

with prompt feedings and, in some cases, an intravenous glucose solution.

Later in life, type 2 diabetes develops. Obesity and type 2 diabetes are more likely to occur in children whose mothers have gestational diabetes.

Death is unavoidable. Untreated, gestational diabetes may lead to a baby's death before or soon after birth. As a result of gestational diabetes, the mother can experience complications such as:

Preeclampsia is a condition that affects pregnant women. High blood pressure, protein in the urine, and swelling of the legs and feet are all symptoms of this disease. Both the mother and the baby will suffer severe or even life-threatening complications due to preeclampsia.

Gestational diabetes develops later. If you've had gestational diabetes during one pregnancy, you're more likely to get it again during the next. When you get older, you're also more likely to develop diabetes — usually type 2 diabetes.

WHAT ARE THE VARIOUS KINDS OF DIABETES?

The following are the different forms of diabetes:

Type 1 diabetes is an autoimmune condition, which means the body is attacking itself. The insulin-producing cells in your pancreas are killed in this situation.Type 1 diabetes affects up to 10% of people with diabetes. It's most commonly seen in children and young adults (but can develop at any age). It used to be called "juvenile" diabetes.

It commonly affects people in their forties and fifties. Type 2 diabetes is also known as adult-onset diabetes or insulin resistant diabetes. It was probably referred to as "having a bit of sugar" by your parents or grandparents.

Prediabetes is the stage before type 2 diabetes develops. While the blood glucose levels are higher than average, they are not yet high enough to be diagnosed with type 2 diabetes.

Forms of diabetes that are less common include:

Monogenic diabetes syndromes are uncommon inherited types of diabetes that account for 4% of all cases. Neonatal diabetes and young-onset diabetes are two such examples.

Drug- or chemical-induced diabetes: This form of diabetes may occur after an organ transplant due to HIV/AIDS treatment or as a result of glucocorticoid steroid use.

Diabetes insipidus is a rare disease in which the kidneys contain excessive urine.

WHAT IS THE PREVALENCE OF DIABETES?

In the United States, 34.2 million people of all ages – about one in ten – have diabetes. 7.3 million people aged 18 and up (roughly 1 in 5) have no idea they have diabetes (just under 3 percent of all U.S. adults). The number of people diagnosed with diabetes rises as they get older. Diabetes affects more than 26% of adults aged 65 and up (roughly 1 in 4).

WHO IS AT RISK OF DEVELOPING DIABETES? WHAT ARE THE FACTORS THAT PUT YOU AT RISK?

The factors that raise your risk vary depending on which form of diabetes you develop. The following are some of the risk factors for type 1 diabetes:

Type 1 diabetes runs in the family (parents or siblings).

Pancreatitis is a condition in which the pancreas is injured (such as by infection, tumor, surgery, or accident). Autoantibodies (antibodies that mistakenly invade your tissues or organs) are present.

Stress on the body (such as surgery or illness). Viruses can cause illness if you are exposed to them.

The following are risk factors for prediabetes and type 2 diabetes:

Prediabetes or type 2 diabetes in the family (parent or sibling).

You are of African, Hispanic, Native American, Asian, or Pacific Islander ancestry. Being overweight is an issue.

Having a high triglyceride level and a low HDL cholesterol (the "healthy" cholesterol). Inactivity in the physical sense.

Being 45 years old or older. Polycystic ovary syndrome (PCOS). Being a cigarette smoker.

The following are some of the risk factors for gestational diabetes:

Prediabetes or type 2 diabetes in the family (parent or sibling).

Being African-American, Hispanic, Native American, or Asian-American has its advantages and disadvantages. Being overweight before conception.

Being over the age of 25.

WHAT ARE THE CAUSES OF DIABETES?

Getting too much glucose circulating in your blood stream is the cause of diabetes, regardless of the form. However, the explanation for your high blood glucose levels varies depending on the type of diabetes you have.

An immune system disorder causes type 1 diabetes. Insulin-producing cells in your pancreas are attacked and destroyed by your body. Glucose builds up in your bloodstream if you don't have enough insulin to allow glucose into your cells. In certain patients, genes can also play a role. A virus can also cause an immune system attack.

The following factors cause type 2 diabetes and prediabetes. Insulin doesn't function as well as it does in allowing glucose into your body's cells. Insulin resistance has developed in your body's cells.

Gestational diabetes occurs as the placenta produces hormones that make the body's cells more resistant to insulin during pregnancy. Your pancreas is unable to produce sufficient insulin to overcome this resistance. There is an excessive amount of glucose in your bloodstream.

The following are some of the complications:

Coronary artery disease, chest pain, heart attack, stroke, high blood pressure, high cholesterol, and atherosclerosis are all cardiovascular problems (narrowing the arteries).

Nerve damage (neuropathy) induces numbness and tingling in the toes and fingers, spreading. Nephropathy is kidney damage that can lead to kidney failure, dialysis, or transplantation.

Cataracts and glaucoma are examples of eye damage (retinopathy) that can lead to blindness.

Nerve injury, inadequate blood flow, and slow healing of cuts and sores are examples of foot damage.

Infections of the skin
Hearing loss is a common problem.
Depression is a state of mind.
Dementia is a form of dementia.
Problems with the teeth.

Gestational diabetes complications include:
Preeclampsia (high blood pressure, excess protein in urine, leg/foot swelling) in the mother, and the possibility of gestational diabetes in subsequent pregnancies and diabetes later in life.
High-than-normal birth weight, low blood sugar (hypoglycemia), increased risk of developing type 2 diabetes over time, and death soon after birth in newborns.
Is it possible to say whether you have diabetes? The majority of early signs are caused by blood glucose levels higher than average.
The signs of type 1 diabetes normally appear rapidly, in a matter of days or weeks. They're also much more serious.

DIABETES WARNING SIGNS

Some of the warning signs of both forms of diabetes are the same.
Hunger and exhaustion. The food you consume is converted into glucose, which your cells use for energy. However, your cells need insulin to absorb glucose. The glucose can't get into your cells if your body doesn't make enough or any insulin or if your cells reject the insulin your body produces. You won't have any energy. This can make you feel more hungry and exhausted than normal.
I'm peeing more often and thirstier. The average person needs to pee four to seven times a day, but people with diabetes can need to pee even more often. What is the reason for this? Normally, when glucose moves through the kidneys, your body reabsorbs it. However, if your blood sugar levels rise as a result of diabetes, your kidneys may not be able to filter it all out. This allows the body to produce more urine, which depletes the body's fluid reserves. As a result, you'll need to go more often. You may also pee more. You can become extremely thirsty as a result of your frequent peeing. You can pee more if you drink more.
Itchy skin and a dry mouth There is less moisture for other things because it uses fluids to produce pee. You may be- come dehydrated, and your mouth will feel dry. Itchy skin is caused by dry skin.
Vision is hazy. The lenses in your eyes can swell due to changes in your body's fluid levels. They change form and are unable to concentrate.

TYPE 2 DIABETES SYMPTOMS

These usually appear after the blood glucose has been elevated for a long time.
Infections caused by yeast. These are available to both men and women with diabetes. Yeast thrives when there is plenty of glucose available. Conditions can develop in any wet, moist skin fold, such as:
Between the toes and fingers
Breasts underarms
sex organs or in the vicinity of sex organs
Numbness or pain in the feet or thighs. Another consequence of nerve damage is this.
Diabetes signs can be subtle at first, making them difficult to detect. Find out which symptoms necessitate a trip to the doctor.
Both genetic and environmental causes trigger diabetes. Find out more about the causes of diabetes by visiting this page.

Pre-diabetes treatment

If you have prediabetes, making healthy lifestyle decisions will help you return to normal blood sugar levels or prevent them from rising to the levels seen in type 2 diabetes. Exercise and a balanced diet will help you maintain a healthy weight. This can be prevented or delayed by exercising at least 150 minutes a week and losing about 7% of the body weight.

If you're at high risk of diabetes, such as if your prediabetes is worsening or if you have cardiovascular disease, fatty liver disease, or polycystic ovary syndrome, drugs like metformin (Glucophage, Glumetza, and others) may be a choice.

In other cases, cholesterol-lowering medications— especially statins— and high-blood-pressure medications are required. If you're at high risk for cardiovascular disease, your doctor can recommend low-dose aspirin therapy to help prevent it. Good lifestyle decisions, on the other hand, remain crucial.

In some trials, a variety of substances have been shown to increase insulin sensitivity, although others have shown little benefit for blood sugar regulation or lowering A1C levels. Because of the contradictory results, no alternative treatments are currently recommended to help everyone control their blood sugar.

Don't avoid taking your doctor-prescribed drugs if you plan to try some kind of alternative therapy. Make sure you consult with to your doctor before using either of these treatments to make sure they won't cause any side effects or interfere with your current treatment.

Furthermore, since there are no drugs — alternative or traditional — that can cure diabetes, it's important that people who are on insulin medication don't stop taking it until their doctors tell them to.

Chapter 1
BASIC INFORMATION TO KNOW ABOUT DIABETES

Diabetes is a long-term illness that affects how your body converts food into energy. The majority of the food you consume is converted to sugar (also known as glucose) and absorbed into your bloodstream. When your blood sugar levels rise, your pancreas is prompted to release insulin. Insulin acts as a key, allowing blood sugar to enter your body's cells and be used as energy.

If you have diabetes, the body either does not produce enough insulin or does not use it as effectively as it can. As a result, too much blood sugar remains in your bloodstream when there isn't enough insulin or when cells stop responding to insulin.

Diabetes is a serious disease characterized by an abnormally elevated blood glucose level. It can occur when your body does not produce enough insulin or none at all.

Types of Diabetes

Diabetes Type 1

An allergic reaction (in which the body mistakenly attacks itself) is thought to be the cause of type 1 diabetes, which prevents the body from producing insulin. About 5-10% of people with diabetes have type 1 diabetes. Symptoms of type 1 diabetes will come out of nowhere. The most vulnerable are children, adolescents, and young adults. To remain alive if you have type 1 diabetes, you must take insulin every day. At the moment, no one knows how to avoid type 1 diabetes.

Type 2 Diabetes

Your body can't hold blood sugar regularly if you have type 2 diabetes because it doesn't use insulin properly. Type 2 diabetes affects 90-95 percent of diabetics. It takes several years to develop and is commonly diagnosed in adults (but more in children, teens, and young adults). Since you may not have any signs, it's crucial to get your blood sugar checked if you're in danger.

What is type 2 diabetes?

Type 2 diabetes is a severe disorder in which the pancreas' insulin does not function properly or does not produce enough insulin. This indicates that the blood glucose (sugar) levels continue to rise.

What factors contribute to the development of type 2 diabetes?

Insulin is needed for our survival. It serves an important purpose. It allows blood glucose to reach our cells and provide energy to our bodies.

Your body also breaks down carbohydrates from food and drinks and converts them to glucose if you have type 2 diabetes. The pancreas then releases insulin in response to this. However, since this insulin cannot function properly, the blood sugar levels continue to rise. More insulin is produced as a result of this.

Is type 2 diabetes a serious condition?

Type 2 diabetes affects approximately 90% of diabetics in the United Kingdom. It is a debilitating illness that can last a lifetime. These are referred to as diabetes complications. However, you can live well with type 2 diabetes and reduce the risk of developing it.

Is type 2 diabetes curable?

While there is no cure for type 2 diabetes, certain people can get remission. This indicates that your blood sugar levels are normal and that you no longer need diabetes medication. Remission may be life-changing, but it isn't always possible.

Type 2 diabetes treatments

Type 2 diabetes can be treated in various ways, including making healthier lifestyle decisions, using insulin, or taking medication. Your healthcare team will assist you in determining the best treatment option for you. This will help you live well with diabetes by lowering the risk of complications.

Type 2 diabetes symptoms and signs

Type 2 diabetes symptoms progress more slowly than type 1 diabetes symptoms, making the disease more difficult to detect. That's why many people don't notice or don't get any symptoms.

Some people do not seek treatment because they believe the symptoms are unimportant. Unfortunately, this means that certain people with type 2 diabetes will go up to ten years without being diagnosed.

Type 2 diabetes risk factors

Type 2 diabetes signs aren't always apparent, it's important to be aware of these risk factors. They may contain the following:

low blood pressure due to your race

being too fat

We have more detail on all of the risk factors and a Know Your Risk test to help you determine the type 2 diabetes risk in minutes.

I've just been diagnosed with type 2 diabetes.

You will meet other people with type 2 diabetes in our Learning Zone, in addition to using the resources on this page to better understand your condition.

Diabetes During Pregnancy

Pregnant women who have never had diabetes experience gestational diabetes. If you have gestational diabetes, your baby might be more susceptible to health issues. While gestational diabetes normally goes away after your baby is born, it raises your risk of developing type 2 diabetes later in life. Obesity is more likely in your baby as an infant or a teen, and type 2 diabetes is more likely later in life.

Prediabetes affects 88 million people in the United States or about one-third of the population. Furthermore, more than 84 percent of them are completely unaware that they have it. Blood sugar levels are higher than average in people with prediabetes but not elevated enough to be diagnosed as type 2 diabetes.

Diabetes During Pregnancy

Pregnancy triggers gestational diabetes. Hormonal changes can harm insulin's ability to function properly during pregnancy. Approximately 4% of all births are affected by this disorder.

Pregnant women who are over 25 years old, are overweight before birth, have a family history of diabetes, or are Hispanic, black, Native American, or Asian have a higher chance of developing gestational diabetes.

During pregnancy, a test for gestational diabetes is performed. Gestational diabetes raises the risk of complications for both the mother and the unborn child if it is not treated.

Within six weeks of childbirth, blood sugar levels usually return to normal. Women who have had gestational diabetes, on the other hand, are more likely to develop type 2 diabetes later in life.

Chapter 2
GUIDE HEALTHY NUTRIENTS

D iabetes is a chronic condition that has spread worldwide, affecting both adults and children. Diabetes that is not well regulated can lead to heart disease, kidney disease, blindness, and other complications.

These conditions have also been related to prediabetes.

Importantly, certain foods can boost blood sugar and insulin levels, as well as promote inflammation, potentially increasing your disease risk.

Why is carbohydrate intake essential for diabetics?

Carbs, by far, have the biggest impact on your blood sugar. Since they're broken down into sugar (glucose) and absorbed into your bloodstream, this is the case.

Starches, sugar, and fiber are all examples of carbohydrates. On the other hand, Fiber isn't digested and is consumed by your body like other carbohydrates, so it doesn't increase your blood sugar.

The digestible or net carb content of a food is calculated by subtracting fiber from the total carbs in a serving. A cup of mixed vegetables, for example, with 10 grams of carbs and 4 grams of fiber has a net carb count of 6 grams.

When people with diabetes eat too many carbohydrates at once, their blood sugar levels can spike dangerously high.

Low carbohydrate consumption can help avoid blood sugar spikes and lower the risk of diabetes complications.

As a result, it's critical to stay away from the foods and beverages mentioned below.

1. Drinks with added sugar

Sugary foods are the toughest drinks for diabetics to consume.

They're heavy in carbohydrates, for starters, with 38.5 grams in a 12-ounce (354-mL) can of cola.

The same amount of sweetened iced tea and lemonade each have about 45 grams of sugar-only carbs.

Furthermore, these beverages are high in fructose, related to insulin resistance and diabetes. In addition, consumption of sugar-sweetened drinks has been linked to an increased risk of diabetes-related disorders such as fatty liver disease, according to reports.

Furthermore, sugary drinks' high fructose content can cause metabolic changes that promote belly fat and potentially harmful cholesterol and triglyceride levels.

In a different research, eating 25% of calories from high fructose drinks on a weight-maintenance diet resulted in increased insulin resistance and belly fat, a lower metabolic rate, and poorer heart health indicators in adults with overweight and obesity.

Instead of sugary drinks, drink water, club soda, or unsweetened iced tea to help regulate blood sugar levels and reduce disease risk.

2. Trans fatty acids

Trans fats that have been synthesized are highly harmful.

They're made by making unsaturated fatty acids more soluble by adding hydrogen.

3. Pasta, white bread, and rice

This reaction isn't limited to refined white flour-based products. For example, gluten-free pasta was also found to increase blood sugar levels in one study, with rice-based varieties having a greater influence.

In another study, high-carbohydrate diets increased blood sugar levels and reduced brain activity in people with type 2 diabetes and mental impairments.

Fiber is scarce in these processed foods. Fiber aids in the slowing of sugar absorption into the bloodstream.

In other studies, replacing low fiber foods with high fiber foods was shown to lower blood sugar levels in diabetics significantly. Furthermore, people with diabetes saw their cholesterol levels drop.

Increased fiber intake strengthened gut microbiota, resulting in a reduction in insulin resistance.

4. Yogurt with fruit flavors

Plain yogurt can be a healthy option for diabetics. Fruit-flavored types, on the other hand, are a different matter.

Flavored yogurts are typically made with nonfat or low-fat milk and are high in carbohydrates and sugar.

In reality, a 1-cup (245-gram) serving of fruit-flavored yogurt could contain nearly 31 grams of sugar, accounting for nearly 61 percent of the calories.

Rather than choosing high-sugar yogurts that can trigger blood sugar and insulin spikes, go for plain whole milk yogurt, which has no added sugar and can help with appetite control, weight loss, and gut health.

5. Breakfast bowls of cereal with added sugar

If you have diabetes, cereal is one of the worst ways to start your day.

Most cereals are highly refined and contain much more carbohydrates than many people know, despite the health statements on their boxes.

Furthermore, they contain very little protein, a nutrient that can help you feel complete and relaxed during the day while keeping your blood sugar levels steady.

Even some "balanced" breakfast cereals aren't recommended for diabetics.

For example, granola has 44 grams of carbs per 1/2-cup serving (about 56 grams), while Grape-Nuts have 47 grams. Furthermore, each serving contains no more than 7 grams of protein.

Miss most cereals favor a protein-based, low-carb breakfast to keep blood sugar and appetite under control.

6. Coffee drinks with different flavors

On the other hand, Flavored coffee drinks can be considered a liquid snack rather than a nutritious beverage.

According to studies, the brain does not handle liquid and solid foods in the same way. So when you consume calories, you don't make up for that later by eating less, leading to weight gain.

Carbohydrates abound in flavored coffee beverages.

For example, a 16-ounce (473-mL) Caramel Frappuccino from Starbucks has 57 grams of carbs, while a Blonde Vanilla Latte of the same size has 30 grams.

Choose straight coffee or espresso with a tablespoon of heavy cream or half-and-half to hold the blood sugar in check and avoid weight gain.

7. Maple syrup, honey, and agave nectar

People with diabetes often avoid white table sugar and sweets like candy, cookies, and pie.

On the other hand, other types of sugar can trigger blood sugar spikes. Even though these sweeteners aren't heavily refined, they have around the same amount of carbohydrates as white sugar. In reality, the majority of them have even more.

The carb counts for a 1-tablespoon serving of common sweeteners are listed below:

sugar (white): 12.6 g honey, 17.3 g agave nectar, 16 g maple syrup, 13.4 g maple syrup

According to one study, people with prediabetes had equal rises in blood sugar, insulin, and inflammatory markers whether they ate 1.7 ounces (50 grams) of white sugar or honey.

8. Fruit that has been dried

Fruit is high in vitamin C and potassium, and other essential vitamins and minerals.

Fruit is dry, which causes a lack of water, resulting in even higher concentrations of these nutrients.

Unfortunately, the amount of sugar in it increases as well.Grapes have 27.3 grams of carbs per cup (151 grams), with 1.4 grams of fiber. One cup (145 grams) of raisins, on the other hand, contains 115 grams of carbohydrates and 5.4 grams of fiber.

As a result, raisins have more than four times the amount of carbohydrates as grapes. The Carbohydrate Content of some varieties of dried fruit is close to that of fresh fruit.

You don't have to give up fruit entirely if you have diabetes. Sticking to low-sugar fruits like fresh berries or a small apple will help you maintain a healthy blood sugar level while staying within the target range.

9. Snack foods in packages

Snacks such as pretzels, crackers, and other processed snacks are not recommended.

The carbohydrate content of a 1-ounce (28-gram) serving of some famous snacks is as follows:

crackers made of saltine Pretzels have 20.7 grams of carbohydrates, including 0.78 grams of fiber: 22.5 g carbohydrates, including 0.95 g fiber

21.7 grams of carbohydrates, including 0.95 grams of fiber in graham crackers

Some of these foods may have even more carbs than their nutrition labels indicate. According to one report, snack foods have 7.7% more carbohydrates on average than the label claims.

If you're hungry in between meals, nuts or a few low-carb vegetables with an ounce of cheese are a better option.

French fries, number eleven

French fries are a snack you can avoid if you have diabetes.

The Carbohydrate content of potatoes is relatively high. For example, one medium potato has 34.8 grams of carbohydrates and 2.4 grams of fiber.

On the other hand, potatoes may do more than spike your blood sugar until peeled and fried in vegetable oil. Deep-frying foods have been shown to contain toxic compounds such as advanced glycation end products (AGEs) and aldehydes in high quantities. These compounds can increase the risk of disease by promoting inflammation.

Indeed, regular french fries and other fried foods have been related to heart disease and cancer in many studies.

If you don't want to completely skip potatoes, a small serving of sweet potatoes is the best choice.

French fries are high in carbohydrates, which raise blood sugar levels, and they're fried in unhealthy oils, which can cause inflammation and raise the risk of heart disease and cancer.

It can be difficult to know which foods to avoid when you have diabetes. It is, however, possible to make it simpler by following a few guidelines.

Avoiding unhealthy fats, liquid sugars, processed grains, and other refined carb-containing foods should be your top priorities.

Avoiding foods that raise blood sugar and cause insulin resistance will help you stay healthy and reduce the risk of diabetes complications in the future.

Reaching out for help from others can also be beneficial. For example, the free T2D Healthline app from Healthline links you with people who have type 2 diabetes.

Chapter 3
DELICIOUS PRODUCT TO ALWAYS KEEP IN THE PANTRY

Eye disease, which can lead to blindness, nerve and vessel disease, which can lead to limb amputation
Vegetables and fruits
This is your chance to go completely insane! Every fruit and vegetable has its unique collection of nutrients and health advantages.

Make them a part of every meal and snack. The calorie and carbohydrate content of nonstarchy vegetables is the lowest. Non-starchy vegetables to try include:

cauliflower broccoli

Brussels sprouts (Brussels sprouts)

beans (green)

asparagus and eggplant

Arugula, kale, or romaine lettuce are examples of celery salad greens.

carrots (carrots)

courgette

Fruits and starchy vegetables have carbohydrates, just like every other carbohydrate food category, keeping track of them. This isn't to say you can stop them. Just make sure how much you eat fits into your overall meal schedule.

Seafood and meat

Fatty fish is good for your heart and your brain. Omega-3 fatty acid-rich seafood, such as salmon or sardines, is a good choice since omega-3 fatty acids help maintain a healthy heart. At least two servings of fish should be planned per week.

A legume is a type of legume.

The following foods belong to the legume family:

legumes

peasants

lentils and peas

At least one to two 1/2-cup servings per day are recommended. These foods are one of the highest-fiber sources you can consume, despite their high carbohydrate content.

This distinguishes them from other carbohydrate options such as rice, white pasta, and bread. Choose your favorite legumes. You should eat any legumes you like because they're all identical in terms of nutrients.

Dairy and dairy substitutes

One to three low-fat servings per day is a good target. According to some research, yogurt is beneficial to people with diabetes and can also help avoid it in those at risk. In addition, Greek yogurt could be a better choice than other yogurts because it contains more protein and fewer carbohydrates than regular yogurt.

Cottage cheese is another low-carb and high-protein low-carb alternative.

Only keep an eye out for sugar added to yogurts. Flavorings and add-ins, such as granola or cookie pieces, will conceal them. Overall, diabetics should choose foods that are lower in calories, added sugar, and saturated fat.

Unsweetened soy, flax, almond, or hemp milk and yogurt made from them are high in protein and low in carbohydrates.

Frozen foods

There's no reason to forego dessert entirely when you're craving something sweet. But, on the other hand, diets that are too restrictive aren't a good long-term option and sometimes do more harm than good.

Instead, make informed food choices. For example, stick to single-serving desserts and just have one form of dessert in your freezer at a time. This keeps you from succumbing to too much temptation.

Frozen fish and shrimp are also excellent options. They cook quickly and last longer than fresh models, according to Weisenberger. On a busy day, she likes to use these to put together a healthy meal.

Cereals for breakfast and snacks

Where possible, restrict the intake of processed foods, but this isn't always possible. If you're looking for healthier breakfast cereal, crackers, or snack bars, those keywords will help you find them. In general, look for the following words on the packaging:

Wishnick advises eating foods containing at least three grams of dietary fiber per serving and less than eight grams of sugar.

Try reaching for some nuts instead of purchasing many packaged snack foods. Some nuts, such as almonds, can help increase insulin sensitivity and heart health benefits. For people with diabetes, this is a positive thing.

Cereals

Blood sugar levels will spike if you consume too many carbohydrates. With these options, you'll want to be extra cautious. Choose whole grains for improved health, whether you're buying bread or pasta. Check the serving sizes and total carbohydrates on the labels. It's easy to consume too many of these foods.

At least half of your grains should be whole, and two to three servings a day are recommended. When calculating serving sizes, remember that one serving equals a slice of bread or 1/2 cup of cooked oatmeal or other grain.

Consider these foods when selecting whole grains since they take longer to digest and can help you avoid cravings:

corn and oats

quinoa buckwheat

You will notice that baked goods and flour-based items, including whole-wheat flour, cause your blood sugar to rise. If this is the case, look for whole grains that have been minimally processed, are naturally higher in fiber, and are still in their whole food shape. Blood sugar levels can be lowered by combining intact whole grains with healthy fats or protein.

Diet as a treatment

Diet is the only natural treatment for people with diabetes. However, since foods may directly impact your blood sugar levels, Wishnick advises that you choose wisely.

Refined carbohydrates and heavily processed or sugary foods, in simple words, often lead to elevated blood sugar levels.

grains in their entirety

foods that are high in fiber

proteins from animals and plants that are lean

fats that are good for you

It takes more than just cutting carbohydrates to keep a diabetes-friendly diet. But don't let that stop you. It's simple to stick to a diabetes-friendly diet, particularly if you prepare your meals ahead of time.

Give yourself a break if cooking every day isn't possible for you. When you have the opportunity, cook in bulk. Make a double batch of one meal and eat the leftovers for dinner or lunch the next day. You should also search for freezer-friendly recipes. This allows you to freeze extra food and plan menus for the coming weeks.

Chapter 4
Breakfast Recipes

Ham & Jicama Hash

Servings: 4
Cooking Time: 15 Minutes
Ingredients:

- 6 eggs, beaten
- 2 cups jicama, grated
- 1 cup low fat cheddar cheese, grated
- 1 cup ham, diced
- What you'll need from store cupboard:
- Salt and pepper, to taste
- Nonstick cooking spray

Directions:

1.   Spray a large nonstick skillet with cooking spray and place over medium-high heat. Add jicama and cook, stirring occasionally, until it starts to brown, about 5 minutes.
2.   Add remaining Ingredients and reduce heat to medium. Cook about 3 minutes, then flip over and cook until eggs are set, about 3-5 minutes more. Season with salt and pepper and serve.

Nutrition Info: Calories 221 Total Carbs 8g Net Carbs 5g Protein 21g Fat 11g Sugar 2g Fiber 3g

Italian Breakfast Bake

Servings: 8
Cooking Time: 1 Hour
Ingredients:

- 19 oz. pkg. mild Italian sausages, remove casings
- 1 yellow onion, diced
- 8 eggs
- 2 cup half-and-half
- 2 cup reduced fat cheddar cheese, grated
- ¼ cup fresh parsley, diced
- 2 tbsp. butter, divided
- What you'll need from store cupboard:
- 1/2 loaf bread, (chapter 14), cut in cubes
- 1 tsp salt
- ¼ tsp pepper
- ¼ tsp red pepper flakes
- Nonstick cooking spray

Directions:

1.   Spray a 9x13-inch baking dish with cooking spray.
2.   Melt 1 tablespoon butter in a skillet over medium heat. Add sausage and cook, breaking up with a spatula, until no longer pink. Transfer to a large bowl.
3.   Add remaining tablespoon butter to the skillet with the onion and cook until soft, 3-5 minutes. Add to sausage with the cheese and bread cubes.
4.   In a separate bowl, whisk together eggs, half-n-half, and seasonings. Pour over sausage mixture, tossing to mix all Ingredients. Pour into prepared baking dish, cover and chill 2 hours, or overnight.
5.   Heat oven to 350 degrees. Remove cover and bake 50-60 minutes, or a knife inserted in center comes out clean. Serve immediately garnished with parsley.

Nutrition Info: Calories 300 Total Carbs 6g Net Carbs 5g Protein 22g Fat 20g Sugar 4g Fiber 1g

Misto Quente

Servings: 4
Cooking Time: 10 Minutes
Ingredients:

- 4 slices of bread without shell
- 4 slices of turkey breast
- 4 slices of cheese
- 2 tbsp. cream cheese
- 2 spoons of butter

Directions:

1.   Preheat the air fryer. Set the timer of 5 minutes and the temperature to 200C.
2.   Pass the butter on one side of the slice of bread, and on the other side of the slice, the cream cheese.

3.   Mount the sandwiches placing two slices of turkey breast and two slices cheese between the breads, with the cream cheese inside andthe side with butter.

4.   Place the sandwiches in the basket of the air fryer. Set the timer of the air fryer for 5 minutes and press the power button.

Nutrition Info: Calories: 340 Fat: 15g Carbohydrates: 32g Protein: 15g Sugar: 0g Cholesterol: 0mg

Zucchini Bread

Servings: 8
Cooking Time: 40 Minutes
Ingredients:
- ¾ cup shredded zucchini
- 1/2 cup almond flour
- 1/4 teaspoon salt
- 1/4 cup cocoa powder, unsweetened
- 1/2 cup chocolate chips, unsweetened, divided
- 6 tablespoons erythritol sweetener
- 1/2 teaspoon baking soda
- 2 tablespoons olive oil
- 1/2 teaspoon vanilla extract, unsweetened
- 2 tablespoons butter, unsalted, melted
- 1 egg, pastured
Directions:
1.   Switch on the air fryer, insert fryer basket, grease it with olive oil, then shut with its lid, set the fryer at 310 degrees F and preheat for 10 minutes.

2.   Meanwhile, place flour in a bowl, add salt, cocoa powder and baking soda and stir until mixed.

3.   Crack the eggs in another bowl, whisk in sweetener, egg, oil, butter, and vanilla until smooth and then slowly whisk in flour mixture until incorporated.

4.   Add zucchini along with 1/3 cup chocolate chips and then fold until just mixed.

5.   Take a mini loaf pan that fits into the air fryer, grease it with olive oil, then pour in the prepared batter and sprinkle remaining chocolate chips on top.

6.   Open the fryer, place the loaf pan in it, close with its lid and cook for 30 minutes at the 310 degrees F until inserted toothpick into thebread slides out clean.

7.   When air fryer beeps, open its lid, remove the loaf pan, then place it on a wire rack and let the bread cool in it for 20 minutes.

8.   Take out the bread, let it cool completely, then cut it into slices and serve.

Nutrition Info: Calories: 356 Cal Carbs: 2 g Fat: 10 g Protein: 8 g Fiber: 2.5 g

Tortilla

Servings: Two
Cooking Time: 20 Minutes
Ingredients:
- 2 eggs
- 2 slices of ham, chopped
- 2 slices of chopped mozzarella
- 1 tbsp. chopped onion soup
- ½ cup chopped parsley and chives tea
- Salt, black pepper and oregano to taste
- Olive oil spread
Directions:
1.   Preheat the air fryer for the time of 5 minutes and the temperature at 200C.

2.   Spread a refractory that fits in the basket of the air fryer and has a high shelf and reserve.

3.   In a bowl, beat the eggs lightly with a fork. Add the fillings and spices. Place the refractory container in the basket of the air fryer and pour the beaten eggs being careful not to fall.

4.   Set the time from 10 to 15 minutes and press the power button. The tortilla is ready when it is golden brown

Nutrition Info: Calories: 41 Fat: 1.01g Carbohydrates: 6.68g Protein: 1.08g Sugar: 0.25g Cholesterol: 0mg

Poached Eggs & Grits

Servings: 4
Cooking Time: 10 Minutes
Ingredients:
- 4 eggs, poached

- 3 cups skim milk
- ¼ cup Colby cheese, grated
- What you'll need from store cupboard:
- 1 cup grits
- 2 tsp reduced fat parmesan cheese, grated

Directions:
1. In a large microwavable bowl, stir together the grits and most of the milk, save a little to stir in later. Cook 8-10 minutes, stirring every couple of minutes.
2. Meanwhile, poach the eggs in a large pot of boiling water.
3. When grits are done, stir in the cheese until melted and smooth. If they seem too stiff, add the remaining milk.
4. Ladle into 4 bowls and top each with a poached egg, serve.

Nutrition Info: Calories 180 Total Carbs 15g Net Carbs 14g Protein 13g Fat 6g Sugar 10g Fiber 1g

Stuffed French Toast

Servings: 1
Cooking Time: 10 Minutes
Ingredients:
- 1 slice of brioche bread,
- 64 mm thick, preferably rancid
- 113g cream cheese
- 2 eggs
- 15 ml of milk
- 30 ml whipping cream
- 38g of sugar
- 3g cinnamon
- 2 ml vanilla extract
- Nonstick Spray Oil
- Pistachios chopped to cover
- Maple syrup, to serve

Directions:
1. Preheat the air fryer, set it to 175°C.
2. Cut a slit in the middle of the muffin.
3. Fill the inside of the slit with cream cheese. Leave aside.
4. Mix the eggs, milk, whipping cream, sugar, cinnamon, and vanilla extract.
5. Moisten the stuffed French toast in the egg mixture for 10 seconds on each side.
6. Sprinkle each side of French toast with oil spray.

7. Place the French toast in the preheated air fryer and cook for 10 minutes at 175°C
8. Stir the French toast carefully with a spatula when you finish cooking.

Nutrition Info: Calories: 159 Fat: 7.5g Carbohydrates: 25.2g Protein: 14g Sugar: 0g Cholesterol:90mg

Sunrise Smoothies

Servings: 3
Cooking Time: 10 Minutes
Ingredients:
- 1 banana, frozen and sliced
- ¾ cup ruby red grapefruit juice
- ½ cup fresh pineapple, cubed
- ½ cup peach slices, unsweetened
- What you'll need from store cupboard:
- 4 ice cubes
- 1 tbsp. Splenda

Directions:
1. Combine all Ingredients in a blender. Process until smooth. Pour into chilled glasses and serve.

Nutrition Info: Calories 97 Total Carbs 24g Net Carbs 22g Protein 1g Fat 0g Sugar 18g Fiber 2g

Strawberry & Ricotta Crepes

Servings: 4
Cooking Time: 15 Minutes
Ingredients:
- 8 eggs
- 1 cup strawberries, sliced
- 1 cup low-fat ricotta cheese
- What you'll need from store cupboard:
- 2 tsp Splenda
- 2 tsp vanilla
- Nonstick cooking spray

Directions:
1. In a small bowl, place strawberries and sprinkle with 1 teaspoon Splenda, set aside.
2. In a large mixing bowl, whisk ½ cup ricotta cheese with remaining Ingredients.
3. Spray a small nonstick skillet with cooking spray and heat over medium heat.
4. Pour ¼ cup batter at a time into hot pan, swirling the pan to cover the bottom. Cook until

bottom is brown, about 1-2 minutes. Flip over and cook 1 minute more.

5.   To serve, spread each crepe with 2 tablespoons ricotta cheese and fold over. Top with strawberries.

Nutrition Info: Calories 230 Total Carbs 10g Net Carbs 8g Protein 17g Fat 14g Sugar 9g Fiber 2g

Apple Cinnamon Scones

Servings: 16
Cooking Time: 25 Minutes
Ingredients:
- 2 large eggs
- 1 apple, diced
- ¼ cup + ½ tbsp. margarine, melted and divided
- 1 tbsp. half-n-half
- What you'll need from store cupboard:
- 3 cups almond flour
- 1/3 cup + 2 tsp Splenda
- 2 tsp baking powder
- 2 tsp cinnamon
- 1 tsp vanilla
- ¼ tsp salt

Directions:
1.   Heat oven to 325 degrees. Line a large baking sheet with parchment paper.
2.   In a large bowl, whisk flour, 1/3 cup Splenda, baking powder, 1 ½ teaspoons cinnamon, and salt together. Stir in apple.
3.   Add the eggs, ¼ cup melted margarine, cream, and vanilla. Stir until the mixture forms a soft dough.
4.   Divide the dough in half and pat into 2 circles, about 1-inch thick, and 7-8 inches around.
5.   In a small bowl, stir together remaining 2 teaspoons Splenda, and ½ teaspoon cinnamon.
6.   Brush the ½ tablespoon melted margarine over dough and sprinkle with cinnamon mixture. Cut each into 8 equal pieces and place on prepared baking sheet.
7.   Bake 20-25 minutes, or until golden brown and firm to the touch.

Nutrition Info: Calories 176 Total Carbs 12g Net Carbs 9g Protein 5g Fat 12g Sugar 8g Fiber 3g

Lemon Glazed Blueberry Bread

Servings: 12
Cooking Time: 50 Minutes
Ingredients:
- 5 eggs
- ½ cup blueberries
- 5 tbsp. half-n-half, divided
- 3 tbsp. butter, soft
- What you'll need from store cupboard:
- 2 cup almond flour, sifted
- ½ cup Splenda
- 2 tbsp. coconut flour
- 2 tbsp. Swerve confectioners
- 1 ½ tsp baking powder
- 1 tsp vanilla
- Butter flavored cooking spray

Directions:
1.   Heat oven to 350 degrees. Spray an 8.5-inch loaf pan with cooking spray.
2.   In a large bowl, beat the eggs, ½ cup Splenda, and vanilla 2-3 minutes or until the eggs look frothy. Add 3 tablespoons half-n-half and mix again.
3.   In a separate bowl, combine flours and baking powder. Add to egg mixture and beat to combine. Beat in the butter then fold inberries.
4.   Transfer to prepared pan and bake 45-50 minutes or it passes the toothpick test.
5.   Let cool 10 minutes in the pan, then invert onto serving plate.
6.   In a small bowl, whisk together remaining 2 tablespoons half-n-half, powdered Splenda and lemon juice. When bread has cooled drizzle glaze over top, letting it drip down the sides. Slice and serve.

Nutrition Info: Calories 185 Total Carbs 14g Net Carbs 11g Protein 5g Fat 12g Sugar 10g Fiber 3g

Simple Grain-free Biscuits

Servings: 4
Cooking Time: 15 Minutes
Ingredients:
- 2 tablespoons unsalted butter
- ¼ cup plain low-fat Greek yogurt
- Pinch salt
- 1½ cups finely ground almond flour

Directions:

1. Preheat the oven to 375°F (190°C). Line a baking sheet with parchment paper and set aside.
2. Place the butter in a microwave-safe bowl and microwave for 15 to 20 seconds, or until it is just enough to soften.
3. Add the yogurt and salt to the bowl of butter and blend well.
4. Slowly pour in the almond flour and keep stirring until the mixture just comes together into a slightly sticky, shaggy dough.
5. Use a ¼-cup measuring cup to mound balls of dough onto the parchment-lined baking sheet and flatten each into a rounded biscuit shape, about 1 inch thick.
6. Bake in the preheated oven for 13 to 15 minutes, or until the biscuits are lightly golden brown.
7. Let the biscuits cool for 5 minutes before serving.

Nutrition Info: calories: 309 fat: 28.1g protein: 9.9g carbs: 8.7g fiber: 5.1g sugar: 2.0g sodium: 31mg

Strawberry Coconut Scones

Servings: 8 Cooking Time: 40 Minutes
Ingredients:
- 1 ½ cup strawberries, chopped
- 1 large egg
- What you'll need from store cupboard:
- 1 ½ cups almond flour
- ¼ cup coconut oil, melted
- ¼ cup Splenda
- ¼ cup unsweetened coconut, grated
- 2 tbsp. cornstarch
- 1 tsp vanilla
- 1 tsp baking powder

Directions:

1. Heat oven to 350 degrees. Line a 9-inch round baking dish with parchment paper.
2. In a large bowl, beat egg, oil, Splenda, and vanilla until smooth. Scrape sides as needed.
3. Turn mixer to low, and add flour, cornstarch, coconut, and baking powder until incorporated.
4. Fold in strawberries. Spread batter evenly in prepared pan. Bake 35-40 minutes.

5. Let cool 15 minutes before removing from pan. Slice into 8 pieces.

Nutrition Info: Calories 225 Total Carbs 14g Net Carbs 11g Protein 5g Fat 17g Sugar 8g Fiber 3g

Blueberry English Muffin Loaf

Servings: 12
Cooking Time: 1 Hour
Ingredients:
- 6 eggs beaten
- ½ cup almond milk, unsweetened
- ½ cup blueberries
- What you'll need from store cupboard:
- ½ cup cashew butter
- ½ cup almond flour
- ¼ cup coconut oil
- 2 tsp baking powder
- ½ tsp salt
- Nonstick cooking spray

Directions:

1. Heat oven to 350 degrees. Line a loaf pan with parchment paper and spray lightly with cooking spray.
2. In a small glass bowl, melt cashew butter and oil together in the microwave for 30 seconds. Stir until well combined.
3. In a large bowl, stir together the dry Ingredients. Add cashew butter mixture and stir well.
4. In a separate bowl, whisk the milk and eggs together. Add to flour mixture and stir well. Fold in blueberries.
5. Pour into the prepared pan and bake 45 minutes, or until it passes the toothpick test.
6. Cook 30 minutes, remove from pan and slice.

Nutrition Info: Calories 162 Total Carbs 5g Net Carbs 4g Protein 6g Fat 14g Sugar 1g Fiber 1g

Cheese Spinach Waffles

Servings: 4
Cooking Time: 20 Minutes
Ingredients:
- 2 strips of bacon, cooked and crumbled
- 2 eggs, lightly beaten
- ½ cup cauliflower, grated

- ½ cup frozen spinach, chopped (squeeze water out first)
- ½ cup low fat mozzarella cheese, grated
- ½ cup low fat cheddar cheese, grated
- 1 tbsp. margarine, melted
- What you'll need from store cupboard:
- ¼ cup reduced fat Parmesan cheese, grated
- 1 tsp onion powder
- 1 tsp garlic powder
- Nonstick cooking spray

Directions:

1. Thaw spinach and squeeze out as much of the water as you, place in a large bowl.
2. Heat your waffle iron and spray with cooking spray.
3. Add remaining Ingredients to the spinach and mix well.
4. Pour small amounts on the waffle iron and cook like you would for regular waffles. Serve warm.

Nutrition Info: Calories 186 Total Carbs 2g Protein 14g Fat 14g Sugar 1g Fiber 0g

Carrot And Oat Pancakes

Servings: 4
Cooking Time: 8 Minutes
Ingredients:

- ¼ cup plain Greek yogurt
- 1 tablespoon pure maple syrup
- 1 cup rolled oats
- 1 cup low-fat cottage cheese
- 1 cup shredded carrots
- ½ cup unsweetened plain almond milk
- 2 eggs
- 1 teaspoon baking powder
- 2 tablespoons ground flaxseed
- ½ teaspoon ground cinnamon
- 2 teaspoons canola oil, divided

Directions:

1. Stir together the yogurt and maple syrup in a small bowl and set aside.
2. Grind the oats in a blender, or until they are ground into a flour-like consistency.
3. Make the batter: Add the cheese, carrots, almond milk, eggs, baking powder, flaxseed, and

cinnamon to the blender, and process until fully mixed and smooth.

4. Heat 1 teaspoon of canola oil in a large skillet over medium heat.
5. Make the pancakes: Pour ¼ cup of batter into the skillet and swirl the pan so the batter covers the bottom evenly. Cook for 1 to 2 minutes until bubbles form on the surface. Gently flip the pancake with a spatula and cook for 1 to 2 minutes more, or until the pancake turns golden brown around the edges. Repeat with the remaining canola oil and batter.
6. Top the pancakes with the maple yogurt and serve warm.

Nutrition Info: calories: 227 fat: 8.1g protein: 14.9g carbs: 24.2g fiber: 4.0g sugar: 7.0g sodium: 403mg

Jicama Hash Browns

Servings: 2
Cooking Time: 20 Minutes
Ingredients:

- 2 cups jicama, peeled and grated
- ½ small onion, diced
- What you'll need from the store cupboard
- 1 tbsp. vegetable oil
- A pinch of salt to taste
- A pinch of pepper to taste

Directions:

1. Add the oil to a large skillet and heat over med-high heat.
2. Add the onion and cook until translucent.
3. Add the jicama and salt and pepper to taste. Cook until nicely browned on both sides. Serve immediately.

Nutrition Info: Calories 113 Total Carbs 12g Net Carbs 6g Protein 1g Fat 7g Sugar 3g Fiber 6g

Spinach & Tomato Egg Muffins

Servings: 6
Cooking Time: 25 Minutes
Ingredients:

- 6 eggs
- 2 green onions, sliced
- 1 avocado, sliced
- ½ cup fresh spinach, diced
- 1/3 cup tomatoes, diced
- 1/3 cup reduced-fat cheddar cheese, grated

- ¼ cup almond milk, unsweetened
- What you'll need from store cupboard:
- Salt and pepper
- Nonstick cooking spray

Directions:
1. Heat oven to 350 degrees. Spray a muffin pan with cooking spray.
2. In a large bowl, beat together eggs, milk, and salt and pepper to taste.
3. Add remaining Ingredients and mix well.
4. Divide evenly between 6 muffin cups. Bake 20-25 minutes or until egg is set in the middle.
5. Remove from oven let cool 5 minutes. Serve topped with sliced avocado.

Nutrition Info: Calories 176 Total Carbs 5g Net Carbs 2g Protein 8g Fat 15g Sugar 1g Fiber 3g

Cinnamon Rolls

Servings: 6
Cooking Time: 20 Minutes
Ingredients:
- 4 eggs
- 1 ripe banana
- What you'll need from store cupboard:
- 2/3 cup coconut flour
- 6 tbsp. honey, divided
- 6 tbsp. coconut oil, soft, divided
- 1 tsp vanilla
- 1 tsp baking soda
- ½ tsp salt
- 1 tbsp. + ½ tsp cinnamon

Directions:
1. Heat oven to 350 degrees. Line a cookie sheet with parchment paper.
2. In a medium bowl, lightly beat eggs. Beat in the banana. Add 2 tablespoons honey, 2 tablespoons melted coconut oil, and vanilla and mix to combine.
3. Mix in flour, salt, baking soda, and ½ teaspoon cinnamon until thoroughly combined. If dough is too sticky add more flour, a little at a time.
4. Line a work surface with parchment paper and place dough on top. Place another sheet of parchment paper on top and roll out into a large rectangle.

5. In a small bowl, combine 2 tablespoons honey, 2 tablespoons coconut oil, and 1 tablespoons of cinnamon and spread on dough.
6. Roll up and cut into 6 equal pieces. Place on prepared pan and bake 15-30 minutes, or until golden brown.
7. Let cool 10 minutes. Stir together the remaining 2 tablespoons of honey and coconut oil and spread over warm rolls. Serve.

Nutrition Info: Calories 247 Total Carbs 23g Protein 4g Fat 17g Sugar 20g Fiber 1g

Strawberry Kiwi Smoothies

Servings: 4
Cooking Time: 3 Minutes
Ingredients:
- 2 kiwi, peel & quarter
- 6 oz. strawberry yogurt
- 1 cup strawberries, frozen
- ½ cup skim milk
- What you'll need from store cupboard:
- 2 tbsp. honey

Directions:
1. Place all Ingredients in a blender and process until smooth.
2. Pour into glasses and serve immediately.

Nutrition Info: Calories 120 Total Carbs 26g Net Carbs 24g Protein 3g Fat 1g Sugar 23g Fiber 2g

Hawaiian Breakfast Bake

Servings: 6
Cooking Time: 20 Minutes
Ingredients:
- 6 slice ham, sliced thin
- 6 eggs
- ¼ cup reduced fat cheddar cheese, grated
- What you'll need from store cupboard:
- 6 pineapple slices
- 2 tbsp. salsa
- ½ tsp seasoning blend, salt-free

Directions:
1. Heat oven to 350 degrees.
2. Line 6 muffin cups, or ramekins with sliced ham. Layer with cheese, salsa, and pineapple.
3. Crack one egg into each cup, sprinkle with seasoning blend.

4.   If using ramekins place them on a baking sheet, bake 20-25 minutes or until egg whites are completely set but yolks are still soft. Serve immediately.

Nutrition Info: Calories 135 Total Carbs 5g Net Carbs 4g Protein 12g Fat 8g Sugar 3g Fiber 1g

Apple Topped French Toast

Servings: 2
Cooking Time: 10 Minutes
Ingredients:

- 1 apple, peel and slice thin
- 1 egg
- ¼ cup skim milk
- 2 tbsp. margarine, divided
- What you'll need from store cupboard:
- 4 slices Healthy Loaf Bread, (chapter 14)
- 1 tbsp. Splenda brown sugar
- 1 tsp vanilla
- ¼ tsp cinnamon

Directions:

1.   Melt 1 tablespoon margarine in a large skillet over med-high heat. Add apples, Splenda, and cinnamon and cook, stirring frequently, until apples are tender.

2.   In a shallow dish, whisk together egg, milk, and vanilla.

3.   Melt the remaining margarine in a separate skillet over med-high heat. Dip each slice of bread in the egg mixture and cook until golden brown on both sides.

4.   Place two slices of French toast on plates, and top with apples. Serve immediately.

Nutrition Info: Calories 394 Total Carbs 27g Net Carbs 22g Protein 10g Fat 23g Sugar 19g Fiber 5g

Pecan-oatmeal Pancakes

Servings: 6
Cooking Time: 15 Minutes
Ingredients:

- 1 cup quick-cooking oats
- 1½ teaspoons baking powder
- 2 eggs
- ⅓ cup mashed banana (about ½ medium banana)
- ⅓ cup skim milk
- ½ teaspoon vanilla extract
- 2 tablespoons chopped pecans

- 1 tablespoon canola oil

Directions:

1.   Pulse the oats in a food processor until they are ground into a powder-like consistency.

2.   Transfer the ground oats to a small bowl, along with the baking powder. Mix well.

3.   Whisk together the eggs, mashed banana, skim milk, and vanilla in another bowl. Pour into the bowl of dry ingredients and stir with a spatula just until well incorporated. Add the chopped pecans and mix well.

4.   In a large nonstick skillet, heat the canola oil over medium heat.

5.   Spoon ¼ cup of batter for each pancake onto the hot skillet, swirling the pan so the batter covers the bottom evenly. Cook for 1 to 2 minutes until bubbles form on top of the pancake. Flip the pancake and cook for an additional 1 to 2 minutes, or until the pancake is browned and cooked through. Repeat with the remaining batter.

6.   Remove from the heat and serve on a plate.

Nutrition Info: (1 Pancake)calories: 131 fat: 6.9g protein: 5.2g carbs: 13.1g fiber: 2.0g sugar: 2.9g sodium: 120mg

Pumpkin Spice French Toast

Servings: 4
Cooking Time: 20 Minutes
Ingredients:

- 6 eggs
- 1 ½ cup skim milk
- What you'll need from store cupboard:
- 8 slices Healthy Loaf Bread, (chapter 15)
- ¼ cup pumpkin
- 1 tsp salt
- 1 tsp pumpkin pie spice
- 1 tsp vanilla
- Butter flavored cooking spray

Directions:

1.   In a large bowl, whisk together all Ingredients, except bread, until combined. Add the bread slices and toss to coat.

2.   Spray a large, nonstick skillet with cooking spray and place over medium heat. Add bread, two slices, or what fits in the pan, at a time and cook 2-3 minutes per side. Serve as is, or with sugar-free maple syrup.

Nutrition Info: Calories 295 Total Carbs 10g net Carbs 8g Protein 17g Fat 20g Sugar 5g Fiber 2g

Tex Mex Breakfast Bake

Servings: 9
Cooking Time: 40 Minutes
Ingredients:
- 2 cups egg substitute
- 4 scallions, sliced
- 1 cup reduced-fat Monterey Jack cheese, grated and divided
- ¾ cup bell pepper, diced - ½ cup fat-free milk
- ½ cup salsa, (chapter 16)
- What you'll need from the store cupboard
- 10 slices light whole-grain bread, cut into 1-inch pieces
- 1 (4-ounce) can green chilies, diced and drained
- ½ tsp chili powder -. ½ tsp garlic powder
- ¼ tsp black pepper - Nonstick cooking spray

Directions:
1. Spray a 9x13-inch baking dish with cooking spray. Place bread evenly on the bottom.
2. Spray a small skillet with cooking spray and place over medium heat. Add bell pepper and cook until tender, about 5 minutes.
3. In a medium bowl, whisk together remaining Ingredients, reserving ½ cup cheese.
4. Place the cooked peppers over the bread, then pour in the egg mixture. Cover and chill at least 2 hours or overnight.
5. Heat oven to 350 degrees. Sprinkle the reserved ½ cheese over the top of casserole and bake, covered, 20 minutes. Remove the cover and bake 15 – 20 minutes more, or until the eggs are firm in the center.
6. Serve immediately topped salsa.

Nutrition Info: Calories 197 Total Carbs 25g Net Carbs 19g Protein 16g Fat 4g Sugar 9g Fiber 6g

Bagels

Servings: 6
Cooking Time: 20 Minutes
Ingredients:
- 2 cups almond flour
- 2 cups shredded mozzarella cheese, low-fat
- 2 tablespoons butter, unsalted
- 1 1/2 teaspoon baking powder
- 1-teaspoon apple cider vinegar
- 1 egg, pastured
- For Egg Wash:
- 1 egg, pastured
- 1-teaspoon butter, unsalted, melted

Directions:
1. Place flour in a heatproof bowl, add cheese and butter, then stir well and microwave for 90 seconds until butter and cheese has melted.
2. Then stir the mixture until well combined, let it cool for 5 minutes and whisk in the egg, baking powder, and vinegar until incorporated and dough comes together.
3. Let the dough cool for 10 minutes, then divide the dough into six sections, shape each section into a bagel and let the bagels rest for 5 minutes.
4. Prepare the egg wash and for this, place the melted butter in a bowl, whisk in the egg until blended and then brush the mixture generously on top of each bagel.
5. Take a fryer basket, line it with parchment paper and then place prepared bagels in it in a single layer.
6. Switch on the air fryer, insert fryer, then shut with its lid, set the fryer at 350 degrees F and cook for 10 minutes at the 350 degrees F until bagels are nicely golden and thoroughly cooked, turning the bagels halfway through the frying.
7. When air fryer beeps, open its lid, transfer bagels to a serving plate and cook the remaining bagels in the same manner.

Nutrition Info: Calories: 408.7 Cal Carbs: 8.3 g Fat: 33.5 g Protein: 20.3 g Fiber: 4 g

Cornbread

Servings: 8
Cooking Time: 25 Minutes
Ingredients:
- 3/4 cup almond flour
- 1-cup white cornmeal
- 1-tablespoon erythritol sweetener
- 1 1/2 teaspoons baking powder
- 1/4 teaspoon salt
- 1/2 teaspoon baking soda
- 6 tablespoons butter, unsalted; melted
- 2 eggs; beaten

• 1 1/2 cups buttermilk, low fat

Directions:

1. Switch on the air fryer, insert fryer pan, grease it with olive oil, then shut with its lid, set the fryer at 360 degrees F and preheat for 5 minutes.

2. Meanwhile, crack the egg in a bowl and then whisk in butter and milk until blended.

3. Place flour in another bowl, add remaining ingredients, stir until well mixed and then stir in egg mixture until incorporated.

4. Open the fryer, pour the batter into the fryer pan, close with its lid and cook for 25 minutes at the 360 degrees F until nicely goldenand crispy, shaking halfway through the frying.

5. When air fryer beeps, open its lid, take out the fryer pan, and then transfer the bread onto a serving plate.

6. Cut the bread into pieces and serve.

Nutrition Info: Calories: 138 Cal Carbs: 2 g Fat:3 g Protein: 5 g Fiber: 2 g

Ham & Broccoli Breakfast Bake

Servings: 8

Cooking Time: 35-40 Minutes

Ingredients:

• 8-10 eggs, beaten

• 4-6 cup small broccoli florets, blanch for 2 minutes, then drain well . 1-2 cup ham, diced

• 1 cup mozzarella cheese, grated

• 1/3 cup green onion, sliced thin

• What you'll need from store cupboard:

• 1 tsp all-purpose seasoning

• Fresh-ground black pepper, to taste

• Nonstick cooking spray

Directions:

1. Heat oven to 375. Spray a 9x12-inch baking dish with cooking spray.

2. Layer broccoli, ham, cheese and onions in the dish. Sprinkle with seasoning and pepper. Pour eggs over everything.

3. Using a fork, stir the mixture to make sure everything is coated with the egg.

4. Bake 35-40 minutes, or until eggs are set and top is starting to brown. Serve immediately.

Nutrition Info: Calories 159 Total Carbs 7g Net Carbs 5g Protein 15g Fat 9g Sugar 2g Fiber 2g

Muffins Sandwich

Servings: 1

Cooking Time: 10 Minutes

Ingredients:

• Nonstick Spray Oil

• 1 slice of white cheddar cheese

• 1 slice of Canadian bacon

• 1 English muffin, divided

• 15 ml hot water

• 1 large egg

• Salt and pepper to taste

Directions:

1. Spray the inside of an 85g mold with oil spray and place it in the air fryer.

2. Preheat the air fryer, set it to 160°C.

3. Add the Canadian cheese and bacon in the preheated air fryer.

4. Pour the hot water and the egg into the hot pan and season with salt and pepper.

5. Select Bread, set to 10 minutes.

6. Take out the English muffins after 7 minutes, leaving the egg for the full time.

7. Build your sandwich by placing the cooked egg on top of the English muffing and serve

Nutrition Info: Calories 400 Fat 26g, Carbohydrates 26g, Sugar 15 g, Protein 3 g, Cholesterol 155 mg

Cauliflower Potato Mash

Servings: 4

Cooking Time: 30 Minutes

Ingredients:

• 2 cups potatoes, peeled and cubed

• 2 tbsp. butter

• ¼ cup milk

• 10 oz. cauliflower florets

• ¾ tsp. salt

Directions:

1. Add water to the saucepan and bring to boil.

2. Reduce heat and simmer for 10 minutes.

3. Drain vegetables well. Transfer vegetables, butter, milk, and salt in a blender and blend until smooth.

Nutrition Info: Calories 128 Fat 6.2 g, Carbohydrates 16.3 g, Sugar3.3 g, Protein 3.2 g, Cholesterol 17 mg

Apple Cheddar Muffins

Servings: 12Cooking Time: 20 Minutes
Ingredients:

- 1 egg
- ¾ cup tart apple, peel & chop
- 2/3 cup reduced fat cheddar cheese, grated
- 2/3 cup skim milk
- What you'll need from store cupboard:
- 2 cup low carb baking mix
- 2 tbsp. vegetable oil
- 1 tsp cinnamon.

Directions:
1. Heat oven to 400 degrees F. Line a 12 cup muffin pan with paper liners.
2. In a medium bowl, lightly beat the egg. Stir in remaining Ingredients just until moistened. Divide evenly between prepared muffin cups.
3. Bake 17-20 minutes or until golden brown. Serve warm.

Nutrition Info: Calories 162 Total Carbs 17g Net Carbs 13g Protein 10g Fat 5g Sugar 8g Fiber 4g

Mini Mushroom Egg Stacks

Servings: 3Cooking Time: 25 Minutes
Ingredients:

- 6 mini Portobello mushrooms, rinse and remove stems
- 4 cup of mixed baby kale
- 4 eggs, beaten
- 3 green onions, diced
- 3 slices bacon, cooked crisp and crumbled
- ½ red pepper, diced
- 6 tbsp. low fat cheddar cheese, grated
- What you'll need from store cupboard:
- 3 tbsp. olive oil, divided
- Salt and pepper

Directions:
1. Heat oven to 350 degrees.
2. Lay mushrooms on baking sheet and brush with 1 tablespoon oil. Sprinkle with salt and pepper and bake 10-15 minutes, or until tender but firm enough to hold their shape.
3. Heat 1 tablespoon oil in a large skillet over med-high heat. Add vegetables and salt and pepper to taste. Cook, stirring frequently until kale has wilted and peppers are tender. Transfer to a bowl.
4. Wipe skillet clean and heat remaining tablespoon oil. Add eggs and scramble to desired doneness.
5. To assemble, top each mushroom with the kale mixture, then eggs. Sprinkle one tablespoon cheese on top then the bacon. One serving is 2 mushroom stacks.

Nutrition Info: Calories 256 Total Carbs 10g Net Carbs 8g Protein 21g Fat 15g Sugar 2g Fiber 2g

Savory Breakfast Egg Bites

Servings: 8Cooking Time: 20 To 25 Minutes
Ingredients:

- 6 eggs, beaten
- ¼ cup unsweetened plain almond milk
- ¼ cup crumbled goat cheese
- ½ cup sliced brown mushrooms
- 1 cup chopped spinach
- ¼ cup sliced sun-dried tomatoes
- 1 red bell pepper, diced
- Salt and freshly ground black pepper, to taste
- Nonstick cooking spray
- Special Equipment :
- An 8-cup muffin tin

Directions:
1. Preheat the oven to 350°F (180°C). Grease an 8-cup muffin tin with nonstick cooking spray.
2. Make the egg bites: Mix together the beaten eggs, almond milk, cheese, mushroom, spinach, tomatoes, bell pepper, salt, and pepperin a large bowl, and whisk to combine.
3. Spoon the mixture into the prepared muffin cups, filling each about three-quarters full.
4. Bake in the preheated oven for 20 to 25 minutes, or until the top is golden brown and a fork comes out clean.
5. Let the egg bites sit for 5 minutes until slightly cooled. Remove from the muffin tin and serve warm.

Nutrition Info: (1 Egg Bite)calories: 68 fat: 4.1g protein: 6.2g carbs: 2.9g fiber: 1.1g sugar: 2.0g sodium: 126mg

Scallion Sandwich

Servings: 1Cooking Time: 10 Minutes
Ingredients:

- 2 slices wheat bread
- 2 teaspoons butter, low fat
- 2 scallions, sliced thinly
- 1 tablespoon of parmesan cheese, grated
- 3/4 cup of cheddar cheese, reduced fat, grated

Directions:
1. Preheat the Air fryer to 356 degrees.
2. Spread butter on a slice of bread. Place inside the cooking basket with the butter side facing down.
3. Place cheese and scallions on top. Spread the rest of the butter on the other slice of bread Put it on top of the sandwich and sprinkle with parmesan cheese.
4. Cook for 10 minutes.
Nutrition Info: Calorie: 154Carbohydrate: 9g Fat: 2.5g Protein: 8.6g Fiber: 2.4g

Zucchini And Walnut Cake With Maple Flavor Icing

Servings: 5Cooking Time: 35 Minutes
Ingredients:

- 1 9-ounce package of yellow cake mix
- 1 egg
- ⅓ cup of water
- ½ cup grated zucchini
- ¼ cup chopped walnuts
- ¾ tsp. of cinnamon
- ¼ tsp. nutmeg
- ¼ tsp. ground ginger
- Maple Flavor Glaze

Directions:
1. Preheat the fryer to a temperature of 350°F. Prepare an 8 x 3⅞ inch loaf pan. Prepare the cake dough according to package directions, using ⅓ cup of water instead of ½ cup. Add zucchini, nuts, cinnamon, nutmeg, and ginger.
2. Pour the dough into the prepared mold and put it inside the basket. Bake until a toothpick inserted in the middle of the cake is clean when removed for 32 to 34 minutes.

3. Remove the cake from the fryer and let it cool on a grill for 10 minutes. Then, remove the cake and place it on a serving plate. Stop cooling just warm. Spray it with maple flavor glaze.
Nutrition Info: Calories: 196 Carbohydrates: 27gFat: 11g Protein: 1g Sugar: 7g Cholesterol: 0mg

Easy Turkey Breakfast Patties

Servings: 8Cooking Time: 10 Minutes
Ingredients:

- 1 pound (454 g) lean ground turkey
- ½ teaspoon dried thyme
- ½ teaspoon dried sage
- ½ teaspoon salt
- ½ teaspoon freshly ground black pepper
- ¼ teaspoon ground fennel seeds
- 1 teaspoon extra-virgin olive oil

Directions:
1. Mix the ground turkey, thyme, sage, salt, pepper, and fennel in a large bowl, and stir until well combined.
2. Form the turkey mixture into 8 equal-sized patties with your hands.
3. In a skillet, heat the olive oil over medium-high heat. Cook thepatties for 3 to 4 minutes per side until cooked through.
4. Transfer the patties to a plate and serve hot.
Nutrition Info: (1 Patty)calories: 91 fat: 4.8g protein: 11.2g carbs: 0.1g fiber: 0.1g sugar: 0g sodium: 155mg

Sweet Nuts Butter

Servings: 5Cooking Time: 25 Minutes
Ingredients:

- 1½ pounds sweet potatoes, peeled and cut into ½ inch pieces (2 medium)
- ½ tbsp. olive oil
- 1 tbsp. melted butter
- 1 tbsp. finely chopped walnuts
- ½ tsp. grated one orange
- ⅛ tsp. nutmeg
- ⅛ tsp. ground cinnamon

Directions:
1. Put sweet potatoes in a small bowl and sprinkle with oil. Stir until covered and then pour into the basket, ensuring that they are in a single layer. Cook at a temperature of 350°F for 20 to 25

minutes, stirring or turning halfway through cooking.

2. Remove them to the serving plate. Combine the butter, nuts, orange zest, nutmeg, and cinnamon in a small bowl and pour the mixture over the sweet potatoes.

Nutrition Info: Calories: 141 Fat: 1.01g Carbohydrates: 6.68g Protein: 1.08g Sugar: 0.25g Cholesterol: 7mg

Apple Walnut Pancakes

Servings: 18 Cooking Time: 30 Minutes
Ingredients:

- 1 apple, peeled and diced
- 2 cup skim milk
- 2 egg whites - 1 egg, beaten
- What you'll need from store cupboard:
- 1 cup flour
- 1 cup whole wheat flour
- ½ cup walnuts, chopped
- 2 tbsp. sunflower oil
- 1 tbsp. Splenda brown sugar
- 2 tsp baking powder
- 1 tsp salt
- Nonstick cooking spray

Directions:

1. In a large bowl, combine dry Ingredients.
2. In a separate bowl, combine egg whites, egg, milk, and oil and add to dry Ingredients. Stir just until moistened. Fold in apple and walnuts.
3. Spray a large griddle with cooking spray and heat. Pour batter, ¼ cup on to hot griddle. Flip when bubbles form on top. Cook until second side is golden brown. Serve with sugar free syrup.

Nutrition Info: Calories 120 Total Carbs 15g Net Carbs 13g Protein 4g Fat 5g Sugar 3g Fiber 2g

Blueberry Muffins

Servings: 14 Cooking Time: 30 Minutes
Ingredients:

- 1-cup almond flour
- 1 cup frozen blueberries
- 2 teaspoons baking powder
- 1/3 cup erythritol sweetener
- 1 teaspoon vanilla extract, unsweetened
- ½-teaspoon salt - ¼ cup melted coconut oil
- 1 egg, pastured
- ¼ cup applesauce, unsweetened
- ¼ cup almond milk, unsweetened

Directions:

1. Switch on the air fryer, insert fryer basket, grease it with olive oil, then shut with its lid, set the fryer at 360 degrees F and preheat for 10 minutes.
2. Meanwhile, place flour in a large bowl, add berries, salt, sweetener, and baking powder and stir until well combined.
3. Crack the eggs in another bowl, whisk in vanilla, milk, and applesauce until combined and then slowly whisk in flour mixture until incorporated.
4. Take fourteen silicone muffin cups, grease them with oil, and then evenly fill them with the prepared batter.
5. Open the fryer; stack muffin cups in it, close with its lid and cook for 10 minutes until muffins are nicely golden brown and set.
6. When air fryer beeps, open its lid, transfer muffins onto a serving plate and then remaining muffins in the same manner.

Nutrition Info: Calories: 201 Cal Carbs: 27.3 g Fat: 8.8 g Protein: 3 g

Blueberry Buns

Servings: 6 Cooking Time: 12 Minutes
Ingredients:

- 240g all-purpose flour
- 50g granulated sugar
- 8g baking powder
- 2g of salt
- 85g chopped cold butter
- 85g of fresh blueberries
- 3g grated fresh ginger
- 113 ml whipping cream
- 2 large eggs
- 4 ml vanilla extract
- 5 ml of water

Directions:

1. Put sugar, flour, baking powder and salt in a large bowl.
2. Put the butter with the flour using a blender or your hands until the mixture resembles thick crumbs.

3.	Mix the blueberries and ginger in the flour mixture and set aside

4.	Mix the whipping cream, 1 egg and the vanilla extract in a different container.

5.	Put the cream mixture with the flour mixture until combined.

6.	Shape the dough until it reaches a thickness of approximately 38 mm and cut it into eighths.

7.	Spread the buns with a combination of egg and water. Set aside Preheat the air fryer set it to 180°C.

8.	Place baking paper in the preheated inner basket and place the buns on top of the paper. Cook for 12 minutes at 180°C, until golden brown

Nutrition Info: Calories: 105 Fat: 1.64g Carbohydrates: 20.09gProtein: 2.43g Sugar: 2.1g Cholesterol: 0mg

Cafe Mocha Smoothies

Servings: 3Cooking Time: 5 Minutes
Ingredients:

- 1 avocado, remove pit and cut in half
- 1 ½ cup almond milk, unsweetened
- ½ cup canned coconut milk
- What you'll need from store cupboard:
- 3 tbsp. Splenda
- 3 tbsp. unsweetened cocoa powder
- 2 tsp instant coffee - 1 tsp vanilla

Directions:

1.	Place everything but the avocado in the blender. Process until smooth.

2.	Add the avocado and blend until smooth and no chunks remain. - Pour into glasses and serve.

Nutrition Info: Calories 109 Total Carbs 15g Protein 6g Fat 1g Sugar 13g Fiber 0g

Baked Eggs

Servings: 2
Cooking Time: 17 Minutes
Ingredients:

- 2 tablespoons frozen spinach, thawed
- ½-teaspoon salt
- ¼-teaspoon ground black pepper
- 2 eggs, pastured
- 3 teaspoons grated parmesan cheese, reduced-fat
- 2 tablespoons milk, unsweetened, reduced-fat

Directions:

1.	Switch on the air fryer, insert fryer basket, grease it with olive oil, then shut with its lid, set the fryer at 330 degrees F and preheat for 5 minutes.

2.	Meanwhile, take two silicon muffin cups, grease them with oil, then crack an egg into each cup and evenly add cheese, spinach, and milk.

3.	Season the egg with salt and black pepper and gently stir the ingredients, without breaking the egg yolk. Open the fryer, add muffin cups in it, close with its lid and cook for 8 to 12 minutes until eggs have cooked to desired doneness.

4.	When air fryer beeps, open its lid, take out the muffin cups and serve.

Nutrition Info: Calories: 161 Cal Carbs: 3 g Fat: 11.4 g Protein: 12.1 g Fiber: 1.1

Blueberry Stuffed French Toast

Servings: 8Cooking Time: 20 Minutes
Ingredients:

- 4 eggs
- 1 ½ cup blueberries
- ½ cup orange juice
- 1 tsp orange zest
- What you'll need from store cupboard:
- 16 slices bread, (chapter 14)
- 3 tbsp. Splenda, divided
- 1/8 tsp salt
- Blueberry Orange Dessert Sauce, (chapter 15)
- Nonstick cooking spray

Directions:

1.	Heat oven to 400 degrees. Spray a large baking sheet with cooking spray.

2.	In a small bowl, combine berries with 2 tablespoons of Splenda. Lay 8 slices of bread on work surface. Top with about 3 tablespoons of berries and place second slice of bread on top. Flatten slightly. In a shallow dish, whisk remaining Ingredients together. Carefully dip both sides of bread in egg mixture and place on prepared pan.

3.	Bake 7-12 minutes per side, or until lightly browned. Heat up dessert sauce until warm. Plate the French toast and top with 1-2 tablespoons of the sauce. Serve.

Nutrition Info: Calories 208 Total Carbs 20g Net Carbs 18g Protein 7g Fat 10g Sugar 14g Fiber 2g

Hot Maple Porridge

Servings: 1
Cooking Time: 1 Minute
Ingredients:
- 1 tsp margarine
- What you'll need from store cupboard:
- 1/2 cup water
- 2 tbsp. flax meal
- 1 tbsp. almond flour
- 1 tbsp. coconut flour
- 1 tsp Splenda
- ¼ tsp maple extract
- Pinch salt

Directions:
1.   In a microwave safe bowl, combine all Ingredients, except margarine, and mix thoroughly.
2.   Microwave on high for one minute.
3.   Stir in margarine and serve.

Nutrition Info: Calories 143 Total Carbs 9g Net Carbs 2g Protein 5g Fat 1g Sugar 0g Fiber 7g

Cottage Cheese Pancakes

Servings: 2
Cooking Time: 5 Minutes
Ingredients:
- 1 cup low-fat cottage cheese
- 4 egg whites
- What you'll need from the store cupboard
- ½ cup oats
- 1 tbsp. Stevia, raw, optional
- 1 tsp vanilla
- Nonstick cooking spray

Directions:
1.   Place all Ingredients into a blender and process until smooth.
2.   Spray a medium skillet with cooking spray and heat over medium heat.
3.   Pour about ¼ cup batter into hot pan and cook until golden brown on both sides.
4.   Serve with sugar-free syrup, fresh berries, or topping of your choice.

Nutrition Info: Calories 250 Total carbs 25g Net Carbs 23g Protein 25g Fat 4g Sugar 7g Fiber 2g

Scotch Eggs

Servings: 4
Cooking Time: 15 Minutes
Ingredients:
- 1-pound pork sausage, pastured
- 2 tablespoons chopped parsley
- 1/8 teaspoon salt
- 1/8 teaspoon grated nutmeg
- 1 tablespoon chopped chives
- 1/8 teaspoon ground black pepper
- 2 teaspoons ground mustard and more as needed
- 4 eggs, hard-boiled, shell peeled
- 1 cup shredded parmesan cheese, low-fat

Directions:
1.   Switch on the air fryer, insert fryer basket, grease it with olive oil, then shut with its lid, set the fryer at 400 degrees F and preheat for 10 minutes.
2.   Meanwhile, place sausage in a bowl, add salt, black pepper, parsley, chives, nutmeg, and mustard, then stir until well mixed andshape the mixture into four patties.
3.   Peel each boiled egg, then place an egg on a patty and shape the meat around it until the egg has evenly covered.
4.   Place cheese in a shallow dish, and then roll the egg in the cheese until covered completely with cheese; prepare remaining eggs in the same manner.
5.   Then open the fryer, add eggs in it close with its lid and cook for 15 minutes at the 400 degrees F until nicely golden and crispy, turning the eggs and spraying with oil halfway through the frying.
6.   When air fryer beeps, open its lid, transfer eggs onto a serving plate and serve with mustard.

Nutrition Info: Calories: 533 Cal Carbs: 0.6 g Fat: 7 g Protein: 6.3 g Fiber: 0 g

Breakfast Pizza

Servings: 8
Cooking Time: 30 Minutes
Ingredients:
- 12 eggs
- ½ lb. breakfast sausage
- 1 cup bell pepper, sliced
- 1 cup red pepper, sliced
- 1 cup cheddar cheese, grated

- ½ cup half-n-half
- What you'll need from store cupboard:
- ½ tsp salt
- ¼ tsp pepper

Directions:

1. Heat oven to 350 degrees.
2. In a large cast iron skillet, brown sausage. Transfer to bowl.
3. Add peppers and cook 3-5 minutes or until they begin to soften. Transfer to a bowl.
4. In a small bowl, whisk together the eggs, cream, salt and pepper. Pour into skillet. Cook 5 minutes or until the sides start to set.
5. Bake 15 minutes.
6. Remove from oven and set it to broil. Top "crust" with sausage, peppers, and cheese. Broil 3 minutes, or until cheese is melted andstarts to brown.
7. Let rest 5 minutes before slicing and serving.

Nutrition Info: Calories 230 Total Carbs 4g Protein 16g Fat 17g Sugar 2g Fiber 0g

French Toast In Sticks

Servings: 4Cooking Time: 10 Minutes
Ingredients:

- 4 slices of white bread, 38 mm thick, preferably hard
- 2 eggs- 60 ml of milk
- 15 ml maple sauce
- 2 ml vanilla extract
- Nonstick Spray Oil
- 38g of sugar
- 3ground cinnamon
- Maple syrup, to serve
- Sugar to sprinkle

Directions:

1. Cut each slice of bread into thirds making 12 pieces. Place sideways
2. Beat the eggs, milk, maple syrup and vanilla.
3. Preheat the air fryer, set it to 175°C.
4. Dip the sliced bread in the egg mixture and place it in the preheated air fryer. Sprinkle French toast generously with oil spray.
5. Cook French toast for 10 minutes at 175°C. Turn the toast halfway through cooking.

6. Mix the sugar and cinnamon in a bowl.
7. Cover the French toast with the sugar and cinnamon mixture when you have finished cooking.

Nutrition Info: Calories 128 Fat 6.2 g, Carbohydrates 16.3 g, Sugar 3.3 g, Protein 3.2 g, Cholesterol 17 mg

Mango Strawberry Smoothies

Servings: 2
Cooking Time: 10 Minutes
Ingredients:

- ½ mango, peeled and diced
- ¾ cup strawberries, halved
- ½ cup skim milk
- ¼ cup vanilla yogurt
- What you'll need from store cupboard:
- 3 ice cubes
- 2 tsp Splenda

Directions:

1. Combine all Ingredients in a blender. Process until smooth. Pour into chilled glasses and serve immediately.

Nutrition Info: Calories 132 Total Carbs 26g Net Carbs 24g Protein 5g Fat 1g Sugar 23g Fiber 2g

Fried Egg

Servings: 1
Cooking Time: 4 Minutes
Ingredients:

- 1 egg, pastured
- 1/8 teaspoon salt
- 1/8 teaspoon cracked black pepper

Directions:

1. Take the fryer pan, grease it with olive oil and then crack the egg in it.
2. Switch on the air fryer, insert fryer pan, then shut with its lid, and set the fryer at 370 degrees F.
3. Set the frying time to 3 minutes, then when the air fryer beep, open its lid and check the egg; if egg needs more cooking, then air fryer it for another minute.
4. Transfer the egg to a serving plate, season with salt and black pepper and serve.

Nutrition Info: Calories: 90 Cal Carbs: 0.6 g Fat: 7 g Protein: 6.3 g Fiber: 0 g

Tofu Scramble

Servings: 3
Cooking Time: 18 Minutes
Ingredients:
- 12 ounces tofu, extra-firm, drained, ½-inch cubed
- 1 teaspoon garlic powder
- 1 teaspoon onion powder
- 1 teaspoon paprika
- 1/2 teaspoon ground black pepper
- 1/2 teaspoon salt
- 1 tablespoon olive oil
- 2 teaspoon xanthan gum

Directions:
1. Switch on the air fryer, insert fryer basket, grease it with olive oil, then shut with its lid, set the fryer at 220 degrees F and preheat for 5 minutes.
2. Meanwhile, place tofu pieces in a bowl, drizzle with oil, and sprinkle with xanthan gum and toss until well coated.
3. Add remaining ingredients to the tofu and then toss until well coated.
4. Open the fryer, add tofu in it, close with its lid and cook for 13 minutes until nicely golden and crispy, shaking the basket every 5 minutes.
5. When air fryer beeps, open its lid, transfer tofu onto a serving plate and serve.

Nutrition Info: Calories: 94 Cal Carbs: 5 g Fat: 5 g Protein: 6 g Fiber: 0 g

Scrumptious Orange Muffins

Servings: 8Cooking Time: 15 Minutes
Ingredients:
- Dry Ingredients
- 2½ cups finely ground almond flour
- ½ teaspoon baking powder
- ½ teaspoon ground cardamom
- ¾ teaspoon ground cinnamon
- ¼ teaspoon salt
- Wet Ingredients
- 2 large eggs
- 4 tablespoons avocado or coconut oil
- 1 tablespoon raw honey
- ¼ teaspoon vanilla extract
- Grated zest and juice of 1 medium orange
- Special Equipment :
- An 8-cup muffin tin

Directions:
1. Preheat the oven to 375°F (190°C) and line an 8-cup muffin tin with paper liners.
2. Stir together the almond flour, baking powder, cardamon, cinnamon, and salt in a large bowl. Set aside.
3. Whisk together the eggs, oil, honey, vanilla, zest and juice in a medium bowl. Pour the mixture into the bowl of dry ingredients and stir with a spatula just until incorporated.
4. Pour the batter into the prepared muffin cups, filling each about three-quarters full.
5. Bake in the preheated oven for 15 minutes, or until the tops are golden and a toothpick inserted in the center comes out clean.
6. Let the muffins cool for 10 minutes before serving.

Nutrition Info: calories: 287 fat: 23.5g protein: 7.9g carbs: 15.8g fiber: 3.8g sugar: 9.8g sodium: 96mg

Cauliflower Hash Browns

Servings: 6Cooking Time: 25 Minutes
Ingredients:
- 1/4 cup chickpea flour
- 4 cups cauliflower rice
- 1/2 medium white onion, peeled and chopped
- 1/2 teaspoon garlic powder
- 1-tablespoon xanthan gum
- 1/2 teaspoon salt
- 1-tablespoon nutritional yeast flakes
- 1-teaspoon ground paprika

Directions:
1. Switch on the air fryer, insert fryer basket, grease it with olive oil, then shut with its lid, set the fryer at 375 degrees F and preheat for10 minutes.
2. Meanwhile, place all the ingredients in a bowl, stir until well mixed and then shape the mixture into six rectangular disks, each about ½-inch thick.
3. Open the fryer, add hash browns in it in a single layer, close with its lid and cook for 25 minutes at the 375 degrees F until nicely golden and crispy, turning halfway through the frying.
4. When air fryer beeps, open its lid, transfer hash browns to a serving plate and serve.

Nutrition Info: Calories: 115.2 Cal Carbs: 6.2 g Fat: 7.3 g Protein: 7.4 g Fiber: 2.2 g

Grilled Sandwich With Three Types Of Cheese

Servings: TwoCooking Time: 8 Minutes
Ingredients:
- 2 tbsp. mayonnaise
- ⅛ tsp. dried basil
- ⅛ tsp. dried oregano
- 4 slices of whole wheat bread
- 2 slices of ½ to 1-ounce cheddar cheese
- 2 slices of Monterey Jack cheese
- ½ to 1 ounce
- 2 thin slices of tomato
- 2 slices of ½ to 1 oz. provolone cheese Soft butter

Directions:
1. Mix mayonnaise with basil and oregano in a small bowl and then spread the mixture on each side of the slice. Cover each slice with a slice of each cheese and tomato, and then the other slice of bread.
2. Lightly brush each side of the sandwich and put the sandwiches in the basket. Cook at a temperature of 400°F for 8 minutes, turning halfway through cooking.
Nutrition Info: Calories: 141 Fat: 1.01g Carbohydrates: 68g Protein: 1.08g Sugar: 0.25g Cholesterol: 33mg

Holiday Strata

Servings: 8Cooking Time: 1 Hour
Ingredients:
- 8 eggs
- 6 slices bacon, diced
- 4 breakfast sausages, casings removed and meat crumbled
- 1 onion, diced fine
- 1 pint cherry tomatoes
- 4 cup spinach
- 3 cup skim milk
- 1 cup reduced fat cheddar cheese, grated
- What you'll need from store cupboard:
- ½ loaf Italian bread, cut in 2-inch cubes
- 2 tsp Dijon mustard
- 1 tsp salt
- ¼ tsp pepper

- Butter flavored cooking spray
Directions:
1. Spray a 13x9-inch baking dish with cooking spray.
2. Heat a large non-stick skillet over medium heat. Add bacon and sausage and cook until bacon is crisp, and sausage is cooked through, about 5-7 minutes. Transfer to paper towel lined plate. Drain all but 1 tablespoon of fat from the pan.
3. Add onion and cook until soft and golden brown, about 6 minutes.
4. Add tomatoes and spinach and cook until tomatoes start to soften and spinach wilts, about 2 minutes. Remove from heat and set aside to cool.
5. In a large bowl, beat eggs with milk, Dijon, salt and pepper. Mix in cheese, bread, bacon, sausage, and spinach mixture. Pour into prepared pan and cover with plastic wrap.
6. Refrigerate for two hours or overnight.
7. Heat oven to 359 degrees. Uncover and bake 1 hour, or until set in the center. Cool slightly before serving.
Nutrition Info: Calories 343 Total Carbs 24g Net Carbs 22g Protein 25g Fat 16g Sugar 7g Fiber 2g

Blueberry Cinnamon Muffins

Servings: 10
Cooking Time: 30 Minutes
Ingredients:
- 3 eggs
- 1 cup blueberries
- 1/3 cup half-n-half
- ¼ cup margarine, melted
- What you'll need from store cupboard:
- 1½ cup almond flour
- ⅓ cup Splenda
- 1 tsp baking powder
- 1 tsp cinnamon
Directions:
1. Heat oven to 350 degrees. Line 10 muffin cups with paper liners.
2. In a large mixing bowl, combine dry Ingredients.
3. Stir in wet Ingredients and mix well.
4. Fold in the blueberries and spoon evenly into lined muffin pan.

5.   Bake 25-30 minutes or they pass the toothpick test.
Nutrition Info: Calories 194 Total Carbs 12g Net Carbs 10g Protein 5g Fat 14g Sugar 9g Fiber 2g

Crab & Spinach Frittata

Servings: 10Cooking Time: 30 Minutes
Ingredients:
- ¾ lb. crabmeat
- 8 eggs
- 10 oz. spinach, frozen and thawed, squeeze dry
- 2 stalks celery, diced
- 2 cup half-n-half
- 1 cup Swiss cheese
- ½ cup onion, diced
- ½ cup red pepper, diced
- ¼ cup mushrooms, diced
- 2 tbsp. margarine
- What you'll need from store cupboard:
- 1 cup bread crumbs
- ½ tsp salt
- ¼ tsp pepper
- ¼ tsp nutmeg
- Nonstick cooking spray
Directions:
1.   Heat oven to 375 degrees. Spray a large casserole, or baking dish with cooking spray.
2.   In a large bowl, beat eggs and half-n-half. Stir in crab, spinach, bread crumbs, cheese, and seasonings.
3.   Melt butter in a large skillet over medium heat. Add celery, onion, rep pepper, and mushrooms. Cook, stirring occasionally, until vegetables are tender, about 5 minutes. Add to egg mixture.
4.   Pour mixture into prepared baking dish and bake 30-35 minutes, or until eggs are set and top is light brown. Cool 10 minutes before serving.
Nutrition Info: Calories 261 Total Carbs 18g Net Carbs 16g Protein 14g Fat 15g Sugar 4g Fiber 2g

Apple Filled Swedish Pancake

Servings: 6Cooking Time: 20 Minutes
Ingredients:
- 2 apples, cored and sliced thin
- ¾ cup egg substitute
- ½ cup fat-free milk
- ½ cup sugar-free caramel sauce
- 1 tbsp. reduced calorie margarine
- What you'll need from the store cupboard
- ½ cup flour
- 1`1/2 tbsp. brown sugar substitute
- 2 tsp water
- ¼ tsp cinnamon
- 1/8 tsp cloves
- 1/8 tsp salt
- Nonstick cooking spray
Directions:
1.   Heat oven to 400 degrees. Place margarine in cast iron, orovenproof, skillet and place in oven until margarine is melted.
2.   In a medium bowl, whisk together flour, milk, egg substitute, cinnamon, cloves and salt until smooth.
3.   Pour batter in hot skillet and bake 20 – 25 minutes until puffed and golden brown.
4.   Spray a medium saucepan with cooking spray. Heat over medium heat.
5.   Add apples, brown sugar and water. Cook, stirring occasionally, until apples are tender and golden brown, about 4 – 6 minutes.
6.   Pour the caramel sauce into a microwave-proof measuring glass and heat 30 – 45 seconds, or until warmed through.
7.   To serve, spoon apples into pancake and drizzle with caramel. Cut into wedges.
Nutrition Info: Calories 193 Total Carbs 25g Net Carbs 23g Protein 6g Fat 2g Sugar 12g Fiber 2g

Apple Cinnamon Muffins

Servings: 12
Cooking Time: 25 Minutes
Ingredients:
- 1 cup apple, diced fine
- 2/3 cup skim milk
- ¼ cup reduced-calorie margarine, melted
- 1 egg, lightly beaten
- What you'll need from the store cupboard
- 1 2/3 cups flour
- 1 tbsp. Stevia
- 2 ½ tsp baking powder

- 1 tsp cinnamon
- ½ tsp sea salt
- ¼ tsp nutmeg
- Nonstick cooking spray

Directions:

1.   Heat oven to 400 degrees F. Spray a 12-cup muffin pan with cooking spray.
2.   In a large bowl, combine dry Ingredients and stir to mix.
3.   In another bowl, beat milk, margarine, and egg to combine.
4.   Pour wet Ingredients into dry Ingredients and stir just until moistened. Gently fold in apples.
5.   Spoon into prepared muffin pan. Bake 25 minutes, or until tops are lightly browned.

Nutrition Info: Calories 119 Total Carbs 17g Net Carbs 16g Protein 3g Fat 4g Sugar 3g Fiber 1g

Santa Fe Style Pizza

Servings: Two
Cooking Time: 10 Minutes
Ingredients:

- 1 tsp. vegetable oil
- ½ tsp. ground cumin
- 2 tortillas 7 to 8 inches in diameter
- ¼ cup black bean sauce prepared
- 4 ounces cooked chicken, in strips or grated
- 1 tbsp. taco seasonings
- 2 tbsp. prepared chipotle sauce, or preferred sauce
- ¼ cup plus 2 tbsp. corn kernels, fresh or frozen (thawed)
- 1 tbsp. sliced scallions
- 1 tsp. chopped cilantro
- ⅔ cup grated pepper jack cheese

Directions:

1.   Put the oil with the cumin in a small bowl; spread the mixture on both tortillas. Then spread the black bean sauce evenly over both tortillas. Put the chicken pieces and taco seasonings in medium bowl; Stir until chicken is covered. Add the sauce and mix it with the covered chicken.
2.   Remove half of the chicken and place it over the bean sauce in one of the tortillas. Put half the corn, chives, and cilantro over the tortilla and then cover with half the cheese. Put the pizza inside the basket and cook it at a temperature of 400°F for 10 minutes. Prepare the other tortilla and cook it after removing the first one.

Nutrition Info: Calories: 41 Fat: 1.01g Carbohydrates: 6.68g Protein: 1.08g Sugar: 0.25g Cholesterol: 0mg

Brussels Sprout With Fried Eggs

Servings: 4
Cooking Time: 15 Minutes
Ingredients:

- 3 teaspoons extra-virgin olive oil, divided
- 1 pound (454 g) Brussels sprouts, sliced
- 2 garlic cloves, thinly sliced
- ¼ teaspoon salt
- Juice of 1 lemon
- 4 eggs

Directions:

1.   Heat 1½ teaspoons of olive oil in a large skillet over medium heat.
2.   Add the Brussels sprouts and sauté for 6 to 8 minutes until crispy and tender, stirring frequently.
3.   Stir in the garlic and cook for about 1 minute until fragrant. Sprinkle with the salt and lemon juice.
4.   Remove from the skillet to a plate and set aside.

5.   Heat the remaining oil in the skillet over medium-high heat. Crack the eggs one at a time into the skillet and fry for about 3 minutes. Flip the eggs and continue cooking, or until the egg whites are set and the yolks are cooked to your liking.
6.   Serve the fried eggs over the crispy Brussels sprouts.

Nutrition Info: calories: 157 fat: 8.9g protein: 10.1g carbs: 11.8g fiber: 4.1g sugar: 4.0g sodium: 233mg

Cauliflower Breakfast Hash

Servings: 2
Cooking Time: 20 Minutes
Ingredients:

- 4 cups cauliflower, grated
- 1 cup mushrooms, diced
- ¾ cup onion, diced - 3 slices bacon
- ¼ cup sharp cheddar cheese, grated

Directions:

1.   In a medium skillet, over med-high heat, fry bacon, set aside.

2.   Add vegetables to the skillet and cook, stirring occasionally, untilgolden brown.

3.   Cut bacon into pieces and return to skillet.

4.   Top with cheese and allow it to melt. Serve immediately.

Nutrition Info: Calories 155 Total Carbs 16g Net Carbs 10g Protein 10g Fat 7g Sugar 7g Fiber 6g

Peanut Butter And Berry Oatmeal

Servings: 2

Cooking Time: 15 Minutes

Ingredients:

- 1½ cups unsweetened vanilla almond milk
- ¾ cup rolled oats
- 1 tablespoon chia seeds
- 2 tablespoons natural peanut butter
- ¼ cup fresh berries, divided (optional)
- 2 tablespoons walnut pieces, divided (optional)

Directions:

1.   Add the almond milk, oats, and chia seeds to a small saucepan and bring to a boil.

2.   Cover and continue cooking for about 10 minutes, stirring often, or until the oats have absorbed the milk.

3.   Add the peanut butter and keep stirring until the oats are thick and creamy.

4.   Divide the oatmeal into two serving bowls. Serve topped with the berries and walnut pieces, if desired.

Nutrition Info: calories: 260 fat: 13.9g protein: 10.1g carbs: 26.9g fiber: 7.1g sugar: 1.0g sodium: 130mg

Quick Breakfast Yogurt Sundae

Servings: 1

Cooking Time: 0 Minutes

Ingredients:

- ¾ cup plain Greek yogurt
- ¼ cup mixed berries (blueberries, strawberries, blackberries)
- 2 tablespoons cashew, walnut, or almond pieces
- 1 tablespoon ground flaxseed
- 2 fresh mint leaves, shredded

Directions:

1.   Pour the yogurt into a tall parfait glass and scatter the top with the berries, cashew pieces, and flaxseed.

2.   Sprinkle the mint leaves on top for garnish and serve chilled.

Nutrition Info: calories: 238 fat: 11.2g protein: 20.9g carbs: 15.8g fiber: 4.1g sugar: 8.9g sodium: 63mg

Olive & Mushroom Frittata

Servings: 4

Cooking Time: 20 Minutes

Ingredients:

- 2 cups fresh spinach, chopped
- 1 cup cremini mushrooms, sliced
- 4 eggs
- 2 egg whites
- 1/3 cup reduced-fat Parmesan cheese, grated
- ¼ cup Kalamata olives, pitted and sliced thin
- 1 large shallot, sliced thin
- What you'll need from the store cupboard
- 1 tbsp. olive oil
- ½ tsp rosemary
- ¼ tsp black pepper
- 1/8 tsp salt

Directions:

1.   Preheat broiler.

2.   In a nonstick, broiler proof skillet, heat oil over medium heat. Add mushrooms and cook 3 minutes, stirring occasionally. Add spinach and shallot and cook until mushrooms and spinach are tender, about 5 minutes.

3.   In a medium bowl, whisk together eggs and seasonings. Pour egg mixture into skillet. Cook, as it cooks, use a spatula around the edge of skillet, lifting the frittata so uncooked eggs flow underneath. Cook until eggs are almost set.

4.   Sprinkle the olives and cheese over the top. Broil 4-inches from heat until top is lightly browned, about 2 minutes. Let stand 5 minutes before cutting into 4 wedges to serve.

Nutrition Info: Calories 146 Total Carbs 3g Protein 10g Fat 11gSugar 0g Fiber 0g

Pumpkin Muffins

Servings: 10 Cooking Time: 20 Minutes
Ingredients:
- 2 eggs
- ¼ cup butter, melted
- What you'll need from store cupboard:
- 2 cup almond flour
- ¾ cup pumpkin
- ⅓ cup Splenda
- 2 tbsp. pumpkin seeds
- 2 tsp baking powder
- 1 tsp cinnamon
- 1 tsp vanilla
- ½ tsp salt

Directions:
1. Heat oven to 400 degrees. Line a muffin pan with paper liners.
2. In a large bowl, combine butter, pumpkin, eggs and vanilla. Whisk until smooth.
3. In another bowl, combine flour, Splenda, baking powder, cinnamon and salt. Add to pumpkin mixture and stir to combine. Divide evenly between muffin cups.
4. Sprinkle the pumpkin seeds on the top and bake 20 minutes, or they pass the toothpick test.
5. Let cool 10 minutes before serving.

Nutrition Info: Calories 212 Total Carbs 13g Net Carbs 10g Protein 6g Fat 16g Sugar 8g Fiber 3g

Vanilla Mango Smoothies

Servings: 3 Cooking Time: 5 Minutes
Ingredients:
- 1 cup mango, frozen chunks
- 6 oz. vanilla yogurt
- ½ cup orange juice, unsweetened
- What you'll need from store cupboard:
- 1 tbsp. honey

Directions:
1. Place all Ingredients in a blender. Process until smooth.
2. Pour into chilled glasses and serve.

Nutrition Info: Calories 112 Total Carbs 22g Net Carbs 21g Protein 4g Fat 1g Sugar 21g Fiber 1g

Cheesy Spinach And Egg Casserole

Servings: 8
Cooking Time: 35 Minutes
Ingredients:
- 1 (10-ounce / 284-g) package frozen spinach, thawed and drained
- 1 (14-ounce / 397-g) can artichoke hearts, drained
- ¼ cup finely chopped red bell pepper
- 8 eggs, lightly beaten
- ¼ cup unsweetened plain almond milk
- 2 garlic cloves, minced
- ½ teaspoon salt
- ½ teaspoon freshly ground black pepper
- ½ cup crumbled goat cheese
- Nonstick cooking spray

Directions:
1. Preheat the oven to 375°F (190°C). Spray a baking dish with nonstick cooking spray and set aside.
2. Mix the spinach, artichoke hearts, bell peppers, beaten eggs, almond milk, garlic, salt, and pepper in a large bowl, and stir to incorporate.
3. Pour the mixture into the greased baking dish and scatter the goat cheese on top.
4. Bake in the preheated oven for 35 minutes, or until the top is lightly golden around the edges and eggs are set.
5. Remove from the oven and serve warm.

Nutrition Info: calories: 105 fat: 4.8g protein: 8.9g carbs: 6.1g fiber: 1.7g sugar: 1.0g sodium: 486mg

Pumpkin Pie Smoothie

Servings: 2
Cooking Time: 5 Minutes
Ingredients:
- 1 ½ cup almond milk, unsweetened
- 4 oz. reduced fat cream cheese, soft
- ½ cup Greek yogurt
- What you'll need from store cupboard:
- ¼ cup pumpkin puree
- 2 tbsp. Splenda
- 1/8 tsp cinnamon
- Pinch ginger

Directions:
1.   Place all Ingredients in a blender. Process until smooth and everything is combined.
2.   Pour into two glasses and garnish with the pinch of ginger on top.
Nutrition Info: Calories 220 Total Carbs 27g Net Carbs 25g Protein 13g Fat 5g Sugar 15g Fiber 2g

Berry Breakfast Bark

Servings: 6
Cooking Time: 2 Hours
Ingredients:
- 3-4 strawberries, sliced
- 1 ½ cup plain Greek yogurt
- ½ cup blueberries
- What you'll need from store cupboard:
- ½ cup low fat granola
- 3 tbsp. sugar free maple syrup
Directions:
1.   Line a baking sheet with parchment paper.
2.   In a medium bowl, mix yogurt and syrup until combined. Pour into prepared pan and spread in a thin even layer.
3.   Top with remaining Ingredients. Cover with foil and freeze two hours or overnight.
4.   To serve: slice into squares and serve immediately. If bark thaws too much it will lose its shape. Store any remaining bark in an airtight container in the freezer.
Nutrition Info:Calories 69 Total Carbs 18g Net Carbs 16g Protein 7g Fat 6g Sugar 7g Fiber 2g

Lean Lamb And Turkey Meatballs With Yogurt

Servings: 4
Cooking Time: 10 Minutes
Ingredients:
- 1 egg white
- 4 ounces ground lean turkey
- 1 pound of ground lean lamb
- 1 teaspoon each of cayenne pepper, ground coriander, red chili paste, salt, and ground cumin
- 2 garlic cloves, minced
- 1 1/2 tablespoons parsley, chopped
- 1 tablespoon mint, chopped
- 1/4 cup of olive oil
- For the yogurt
- 2 tablespoons of buttermilk
- 1 garlic clove, minced
- 1/4 cup mint, chopped
- 1/2 cup of Greek yogurt, non-fat
- Salt to taste
Directions:
1.   Set the Air Fryer to 390 degrees.
2.   Mix all the ingredients for the meatballs in a bowl. Roll and mold them into golf-size round pieces. Arrange in the cooking basket. Cook for 8 minutes.
3.   While waiting, combine all the ingredients for the mint yogurt in a bowl. Mix well.
Nutrition Info: Calorie: 154 Carbohydrate: 9g Fat: 2.5g Protein: 8.6g Fiber: 2.4g

Cocotte Eggs

Servings: 1Cooking Time: 15 Minutes
Ingredients:
- 1 tbsp. olive oil soup
- 2 tbsp. crumbly ricotta
- 1 tbsp. parmesan cheese soup
- 1 slice of gorgonzola cheese
- 1 slice of Brie cheese
- 1 tbsp. cream soup
- 1 egg
- Nutmeg and salt to taste
- Butternut to taste
Directions:
1.   Spread with olive oil in the bottom of a small glass refractory. Place the cheese in the bottom and season with nutmeg and salt. Add the cream.
2.   Break the egg into a cup and gently add it to the refractory mixture.
3.   Preheat the air fryer for the time of 5 minutes and the temperature at 200C. Put the refractory in the basket of the air fryer, set the time to 10 minutes, and press the power button. Remove and serve still hot.
Nutrition Info: Calories: 138 Cal Carbs: 3 g Fat: 33 g Protein: 7.4 g Fiber: 2.2 g

Cream Buns With Strawberries

Servings: 6Cooking Time: 12 Minutes
Ingredients:
- 240g all-purpose flour
- 50g granulated sugar
- 8g baking powder
- 1g of salt
- 85g chopped cold butter
- 84g chopped fresh strawberries
- 120 ml whipping cream
- 2 large eggs
- 10 ml vanilla extract
- 5 ml of water

Directions:
1. Sift flour, sugar, baking powder and salt in a large bowl. Put thebutter with the flour using a blender or your hands until the mixture resembles thick crumbs.
2. Mix the strawberries in the flour mixture. Set aside for the mixture to stand. Beat the whipping cream, 1 egg and the vanilla extract in a separate bowl.
3. Put the cream mixture in the flour mixture until they are homogeneous, then spread the mixture to a thickness of 38 mm.
4. Use a round cookie cutter to cut the buns. Spread the buns with a combination of egg and water. Set aside
5. Preheat the air fryer, set it to 180°C.
6. Place baking paper in the preheated inner basket.
7. Place the buns on top of the baking paper and cook for 12 minutes at 180°C, until golden brown.
Nutrition Info: Calories: 150Fat: 14g Carbohydrates: 3g Protein: 11g Sugar: 8g Cholesterol: 0mg

Yogurt & Granola Breakfast Popsicles

Servings: 6
Cooking Time: 8 Hours
Ingredients:
- 1 ½ cups fresh berries, chopped
- 1 ¼ cups plain low-fat yogurt
- What you'll need from the store cupboard
- 6 tbsp. granola, crumbled
- 4 tsp sugar free maple syrup, divided
- 1 tsp vanilla
- 6 3-oz Popsicle molds

Directions:
1. In a medium bowl, stir together yogurt, berries, 2 teaspoons maple syrup, and vanilla together.
2. Pour evenly into Popsicle molds.
3. In a small bowl, stir together remaining syrup and granola together. Top each Popsicle with 1 tablespoon of the granola mixture. Insert sticks and freeze 8 hours, or overnight. Popsicles can be stored in the freezer up to 1 week.
Nutrition Info: Calories 73 Total Carbs 20g Net Carbs 18g Protein 5g Fat 4g Sugar 7g Fiber 2g

Spinach Cheddar Squares

Servings: 4
Cooking Time: 40 Minutes
Ingredients:
- 10 oz. spinach, frozen, thaw and squeeze dry
- 1 ½ cup egg substitute
- ¾ cup skim milk
- ¾ cup reduced fat cheddar cheese, grated
- ¼ cup red pepper, diced
- What you'll need from store cupboard:
- 2 tbsp. reduced fat parmesan cheese
- 1 tbsp. bread crumbs
- ½ tsp minced onion, dried
- ½ tsp salt
- ¼ tsp garlic powder
- ¼ tsp pepper
- Nonstick cooking spray

Directions:
Heat oven to 350 degrees. Spray an 8-inch square baking dish with cooking spray.
Sprinkle bread crumbs over the bottom of prepared dish. Top with ½ cup cheese, spinach, and red pepper. In a small bowl, whisk together remaining Ingredients. Pour over vegetables.
Bake 35 minutes. Sprinkle with remaining cheese and bake 2-3 minutes more, or until cheese is melted and a knife inserted in the center comes out clean. Let cool 15 minutes before cutting and serving.
Nutrition Info: Calories 159 Total Carbs 7g Net Carbs 5g Protein 22g Fat 5g Sugar 4g Fiber 2g

Peanut Butter Waffles

Servings: 4
Cooking Time: 10 Minutes
Ingredients:
- 4 eggs
- ½ cup low fat cream cheese
- ½ cup half-n-half
- 2 tbsp. margarine
- What you'll need from store cupboard:
- 2/3 cup low fat peanut butter
- 2 tsp Splenda
- 1 tsp baking powder
- Nonstick cooking spray

Directions:
1. Lightly spray waffle iron with cooking spray and preheat.
2. In a medium glass bowl, place peanut butter, margarine, and cream cheese. Microwave 30 seconds and stir to combine.
3. Stir in the cream, baking powder, and Splenda and mix until all the Ingredients are combined. Stir in eggs and mix well.
4. Ladle into waffle iron and cook until golden brown and crisp on the outside. Serve.

Nutrition Info: Calories 214 Total Carbs 9g Net Carbs 8g Protein 9g Fat 15g Sugar 2g Fiber 1g

Bruschetta

Servings: 2
Cooking Time: 10 Minutes
Ingredients:
- 4 slices of Italian bread
- 1 cup chopped tomato tea
- 1 cup grated mozzarella tea
- Olive oil
- Oregano, salt, and pepper
- 4 fresh basil leaves

Directions:
1. Preheat the air fryer. Set the timer of 5 minutes and the temperature to 2000C.
2. Sprinkle the slices of Italian bread with olive oil. Divide the chopped tomatoes and mozzarella between the slices. Season with salt, pepper, and oregano.
3. Put oil in the filling. Place a basil leaf on top of each slice.

4. Put the bruschetta in the basket of the air fryer being careful not to spill the filling. Set the timer of 5 minutes, set the temperature to180C, and press the power button.
5. Transfer the bruschetta to a plate and serve.

Nutrition Info: Calories: 434 Fat: 14g Carbohydrates: 63g Protein: 11g Sugar: 8g Cholesterol: 0mg

Garlic Bread

Servings: 4-5
Cooking Time: 15 Minutes
Ingredients:
- 2 stale French rolls
- 4 tbsp. crushed or crumpled garlic
- 1 cup of mayonnaise
- Powdered grated Parmesan
- 1 tbsp. olive oil

Directions:
1. Preheat the air fryer. Set the time of 5 minutes and the temperature to 2000C.
2. Mix mayonnaise with garlic and set aside.
3. Cut the baguettes into slices, but without separating them completely.
4. Fill the cavities of equals. Brush with olive oil and sprinkle with grated cheese.
5. Place in the basket of the air fryer. Set the timer to 10 minutes, adjust the temperature to 1800C and press the power button.

Nutrition Info: Calories: 340 Fat: 15g Carbohydrates: 32g Protein: 15g Sugar: 0g Cholesterol: 0mg

Coconut Breakfast Porridge

Servings: 4
Cooking Time: 10 Minutes
Ingredients:
- 4 cup vanilla almond milk, unsweetened
- What you'll need from store cupboard:
- 1 cup unsweetened coconut, grated
- 8 tsp coconut flour

Directions:
1. Add coconut to a saucepan and cook over med-high heat until itis lightly toasted. Be careful not to let it burn.

2. Add milk and bring to a boil. While stirring, slowly add flour, cook and stir until mixture starts to thicken, about 5 minutes.

3. Remove from heat, mixture will thicken more as it cools. Ladle into bowls, add blueberries, or drizzle with a little honey if desired.

Nutrition Info: Calories 231 Total Carbs 21g Net Carbs 8g Protein 6g Fat 14g Sugar 4g Fiber 13g

Bacon Bbq

Servings: 2

Cooking Time: 8 Minutes

Ingredients:

- 13g dark brown sugar
- 5g chili powder
- 1g ground cumin
- 1g cayenne pepper
- 4 slices of bacon, cut in half

Directions:

1. Mix seasonings until well combined.

2. Dip the bacon in the dressing until it is completely covered. Leave aside.

3. Preheat the air fryer, set it to 160°C.

4. Place the bacon in the preheated air fryer

5. Select Bacon and press Start/Pause.

Nutrition Info: Calories: 1124 Fat: 72g Carbohydrates: 59g Protein: 49g Sugar: 11g Cholesterol: 77mg

Chapter 5
Snacks Recipe

Almond Cheesecake Bites

Prep time: 5 minutes, chill time: 30 minutes, Serves: 6

Ingredients:

½ cup reduced-fat cream cheese, soft

What you'll need from store cupboard:

½ cup almonds, ground fine

¼ cup almond butter

2 drops liquid stevia

Instructions:

In a large bowl, beat cream cheese, almond butter and stevia on high speed until mixture is smooth and creamy. Cover and chill 30 minutes.

Use your hands to shape the mixture into 12 balls. Place the ground almonds in a shallow plate. Roll the balls in the nuts completely covering all sides. Store in an airtight container in the refrigerator.

Nutrition Facts Per Serving

Calories 68 Total Carbs 3g Net Carbs 2 Protein 5g Fat 5g Sugar 0g Fiber 1g

Almond Coconut Biscotti

Prep time: 5 minutes, Cook time: 50 minutes, Serves: 16

Ingredients:

1 egg, room temperature

1 egg white, room temperature

½ cup margarine, melted

What you'll need from store cupboard:

2 ½ cup flour

1 1/3 cup unsweetened coconut, grated

¾ cup almonds, sliced

2/3 cup Splenda

2 tsp baking powder

1 tsp vanilla

½ tsp salt

Instructions:

Heat oven to 350 degrees. Line a baking sheet with parchment paper.

In a large bowl, combine dry Ingredients .

In a separate mixing bowl, beat other Ingredients together. Add to dry Ingredients and mix until thoroughly combined.

Divide dough in half. Shape each half into a loaf measuring 8x2 ¾-inches. Place loaves on pan 3 inches apart.

Bake 25-30 minutes or until set and golden brown. Cool on wire rack 10 minutes.

With a serrated knife, cut loaf diagonally into ½-inch slices. Place the cookies, cut side down, back on the pan and bake another 20 minutes, or until firm and nicely browned. Store in airtight container. Serving size is 2 cookies.

Nutrition Facts Per Serving

Calories 234 Total Carbs 13g Net Carbs 10g Protein 5g Fat 18g Sugar 9g Fiber 3g

Almond Flour Crackers

Prep time: 5 minutes, Cook time: 15 minutes, Serves: 8

Ingredients:

½ cup coconut oil, melted

What you'll need from the store cupboard

1 ½ cups almond flour

¼ cup Stevia

Instructions:

Heat oven to 350 degrees. Line a cookie sheet with parchment paper.

In a mixing bowl, combine all Ingredients and mix well.

Spread dough onto prepared cookie sheet, ¼-inch thick. Use a paring knife to score into 24 crackers.

Bake 10 – 15 minutes or until golden brown. Separate and store in air-tight container.
Nutrition Facts Per Serving
Calories 281 Total Carbs 16g Net Carbs 14g Protein 4g Fat 23g Sugar 13g Fiber 2g

Asian Chicken Wings

Prep time: 5 minutes, Cook time: 30 minutes, Serves: 3
Ingredients:
24 chicken wings
What you'll need from store cupboard:
6 tbsp. soy sauce
6 tbsp. Chinese 5 spice
Salt & pepper
Nonstick cooking spray
Instructions:
Heat oven to 350 degrees. Spray a baking sheet with cooking spray.
Combine the soy sauce, 5 spice, salt, and pepper in a large bowl. Add the wings and toss to coat.
Pour the wings onto the prepared pan. Bake 15 minutes. Turn chicken over and cook another 15 minutes until chicken is cooked through.
Serve with your favorite low carb dipping sauce
Nutrition Facts Per Serving
Calories 178 Total Carbs 8g Protein 12g Fat 11g Sugar 1g Fiber 0g

Banana Nut Cookies

Prep time: 10 minutes, Cook time: 15 minutes, Serves: 18
Ingredients:
1 ½ cup banana, mashed
What you'll need from store cupboard:
2 cup oats
1 cup raisins
1 cup walnuts
1/3 cup sunflower oil
1 tsp vanilla
½ tsp salt
Instructions:
Heat oven to 350 degrees.
In a large bowl, combine oats, raisins, walnuts, and salt.
In a medium bowl, mix banana, oil, and vanilla. Stir into oat mixture until combined. Let rest 15 minutes.

Drop by rounded tablespoonful onto 2 ungreased cookie sheets. Bake 15 minutes, or until a light golden brown. Cool and store in an airtight container. Serving size is 2 cookies.
Nutrition Facts Per Serving
Calories 148 Total Carbs 16g Net Carbs 14g Protein 3g Fat 9g Sugar 6g Fiber 2g

BLT Stuffed Cucumbers

Prep time: 15 minutes, Serves: 4
Ingredients:
3 slices bacon, cooked crisp and crumbled
1 large cucumber
½ cup lettuce, diced fine
½ cup baby spinach, diced fine
¼ cup tomato, diced fine
What you'll need from store cupboard:
1 tbsp. + ½ tsp fat-free mayonnaise
¼ tsp black pepper
1/8 tsp salt
Instructions:
Peel the cucumber and slice in half lengthwise. Use a spoon to remove the seeds.
In a medium bowl, combine remaining Ingredients and stir well.
Spoon the bacon mixture into the cucumber halves. Cut into 2-inch pieces and serve.
Nutrition Facts Per Serving
Calories 95 Total Carbs 4g Net Carbs 3g Protein 6g Fat 6g Sugar 2g Fiber 1g

Buffalo Bites

Prep time: 5 minutes, Cook time: 10 minutes, Serves: 4
Ingredients:
1 egg
½ head of cauliflower, separated into florets
What you'll need from store cupboard:
1 cup panko bread crumbs
1 cup low-fat ranch dressing
½ cup hot sauce
½ tsp salt
½ tsp garlic powder
Black pepper
Nonstick cooking spray
Instructions:
Heat oven to 400 degrees. Spray a baking sheet with cooking spray.

Place the egg in a medium bowl and mix in the salt, pepper and garlic. Place the panko crumbs into a small bowl.

Dip the florets first in the egg then into the panko crumbs. Place in a single layer on prepared pan.

Bake 8-10 minutes, stirring halfway through, until cauliflower is golden brown and crisp on the outside.In a small bowl stir the dressing and hot sauce together. Use for dipping.

Nutrition Facts Per Serving

Calories 132 Total Carbs 15g Net Carbs 14g Protein 6g Fat 5g Sugar 4g Fiber 1g

Candied Pecans

Prep time: 5 minutes, Cook time: 10 minutes, Serves: 6

Ingredients:

1 ½ tsp butter

What you'll need from store cupboard:

1 ½ cup pecan halves

2 ½ tbsp. Splenda, divided

1 tsp cinnamon

¼ tsp ginger

1/8 tsp cardamom

1/8 tsp salt

Instructions:

In a small bowl, stir together 1 1/2 teaspoons Splenda, cinnamon, ginger, cardamom and salt. Set aside.Melt butter in a medium skillet over med-low heat. Add pecans, and two tablespoons Splenda. Reduce heat to low and cook, stirring occasionally, until sweetener melts, about 5 to 8 minutes.Add spice mixture to the skillet and stir to coat pecans. Spread mixture to parchment paper and let cool for 10-15 minutes. Store in an airtight container. Serving size is ¼ cup.

Nutrition Facts Per Serving

Calories 173 Total Carbs 8g Net Carbs 6g Protein 2g Fat 16g Sugar 6g Fiber 2g

Cauliflower Hummus

Prep time: 5 minutes, Cook time: 15 minutes, serves 6

Ingredients:

3 cup cauliflower florets

3 tbsp. fresh lemon juice

What you'll need from store cupboard:

5 cloves garlic, divided

5 tbsp. olive oil, divided

2 tbsp. water

1 ½ tbsp. Tahini paste

1 ¼ tsp salt, divided

Smoked paprika and extra olive oil for serving

Instructions:

In a microwave safe bowl, combine cauliflower, water, 2 tablespoons oil, ½ teaspoon salt, and 3 whole cloves garlic. Microwave on high 15 minutes, or until cauliflower is soft and darkened. Transfer mixture to a food processor or blender and process until almost smooth. Add tahini paste, lemon juice, remaining garlic cloves, remaining oil, and salt. Blend until almost smooth.

Place the hummus in a bowl and drizzle lightly with olive oil and a sprinkle or two of paprika. Serve with your favorite raw vegetables.

Nutrition Facts Per Serving

Calories 107 Total Carbs 5g Net Carbs 3g Protein 2g Fat 10g Sugar 1g Fiber 2g

Cheese Crisp Crackers

Prep time: 5 minutes, Cook time: 10 minutes, Serves: 4

Ingredients:

4 slices pepper Jack cheese, quartered

4 slices Colby Jack cheese, quartered

4 slices cheddar cheese, quartered

Instructions:

Heat oven to 400 degrees. Line a cooking sheet with parchment paper.

Place cheese in a single layer on prepared pan and bake 10 minutes, or until cheese gets firm.

Transfer to paper towel line surface to absorb excess oil. Let cool, cheese will crisp up more as it cools.

Store in airtight container, or Ziploc bag. Serve with your favorite dip or salsa.

Nutrition Facts Per Serving

Calories 253 Total Carbs 1g Protein 15g Fat 20g Sugar 0g Fiber 0g

Cheesy Onion Dip

Prep time: 5 minutes, Cook time: 5 minutes, Serves: 8

Ingredients:

8 oz. low fat cream cheese, soft

1 cup onions, grated

1 cup low fat Swiss cheese, grated

What you'll need from store cupboard:

1 cup lite mayonnaise
Instructions:
Heat oven to broil.
Combine all Ingredients in a small casserole dish. Microwave on high, stirring every 30 seconds, until cheese is melted and Ingredients are combined.
Place under the broiler for 1-2 minutes until the top is nicely browned. Serve warm with vegetables for dipping.
Nutrition Facts Per Serving
Calories 158 Total Carbs 5g Protein 9g Fat 11g Sugar 1g Fiber 0g

Cheesy Pita Crisps

Prep time: 5 minutes, Cook time: 15 minutes, Serves: 8
Ingredients:
½ cup mozzarella cheese
¼ cup margarine, melted
What you'll need from store cupboard:
4 whole-wheat pita pocket halves
3 tbsp. reduced fat parmesan
½ tsp garlic powder
½ tsp onion powder
¼ tsp salt
¼ tsp pepper
Nonstick cooking spray
Instructions:
Heat oven to 400 degrees. Spray a baking sheet with cooking spray.
Cut each pita pocket in half. Cut each half into 2 triangles. Place, rough side up, on prepared pan.
In a small bowl, whisk together margarine, parmesan and seasonings. Spread each triangle with margarine mixture. Sprinkle mozzarella over top.
Bake 12-15 minutes or until golden brown.
Nutrition Facts Per Serving
Calories 131 Total Carbs 14g Net Carbs 12g Protein 4g Fat 7g Sugar 1g Fiber 2g

Cheesy Taco Chips

Prep time: 15 minutes, Cook time: 40 minutes, Serves: 6
Ingredients:
1 cup Mexican blend cheese, grated
2 large egg whites
What you'll need from store cupboard:
1 1/2 cup crushed pork rinds

1 tbsp. taco seasoning
¼ tsp salt
Instructions:
Heat oven to 300 degrees. Line a large baking sheet with parchment paper.
In a large bowl, whisk egg whites and salt until frothy. Stir in pork rinds, cheese, and seasoning and stir until thoroughly combined.
Turn out onto prepared pan. Place another sheet of parchment paper on top and roll out very thin, about 12x12-inches. Remove top sheet of parchment paper, and using a pizza cutter, score dough in 2-inch squares, then score each square in half diagonally.
Bake 20 minutes until they start to brown. Turn off oven and let them sit inside the oven until they are firm to the touch, about 10-20 minutes.
Remove from oven and cool completely before breaking apart. Eat them as is or with your favorite dip.
Nutrition Facts Per Serving
Calories 260 Total Carbs 1g Protein 25g Fat 17g Sugar 0g Fiber 0g

Chewy Granola Bars

Prep time: 10 minutes, Cook time: 35 minutes, Serves: 36
Ingredients:
1 egg, beaten
2/3 cup margarine, melted
What you'll need from store cupboard:
3 ½ cup quick oats
1 cup almonds, chopped
½ cup honey
½ cup sunflower kernels
½ cup coconut, unsweetened
½ cup dried apples
½ cup dried cranberries
½ cup Splenda brown sugar
1 tsp vanilla
½ tsp cinnamon
Nonstick cooking spray
Instructions:
Heat oven to 350 degrees. Spray a large baking sheet with cooking spray.
Spread oats and almonds on prepared pan. Bake 12-15 minutes until toasted, stirring every few minutes.

In a large bowl, combine egg, margarine, honey, and vanilla. Stir in remaining Ingredients .

Stir in oat mixture. Press into baking sheet and bake 13-18 minutes, or until edges are light brown. Cool on a wire rack. Cut into bars and store in an airtight container.

Nutrition Facts Per Serving

Calories 119 Total Carbs 13g Net Carbs 12g Protein 2g Fat 6g Sugar 7g Fiber 1g

Chili Lime Tortilla Chips

Prep time: 5 minutes, Cook time: 15 minutes, Serves: 10

Ingredients:

12 6-inch corn tortillas, cut into 8 triangles

3 tbsp. lime juice

What you'll need from store cupboard:

1 tsp cumin

1 tsp chili powder

Instructions:

Heat oven to 350 degrees.

Place tortilla triangles in a single layer on a large baking sheet.

In a small bowl stir together spices.

Sprinkle half the lime juice over tortillas, followed by ½ the spice mixture. Bake 7 minutes.

Remove from oven and turn tortillas over. Sprinkle with remaining lime juice and spices. Bake another 8 minutes or until crisp, but not brown. Serve with your favorite salsa, serving size is 10 chips.

Nutrition Facts Per Serving

Calories 65 Total Carbs 14g Net Carbs 12g Protein 2g Fat 1g Sugar 0g Fiber 2g

Chocolate Chip Blondies

Prep time: 5 minutes, Cook time: 20 minutes, Serves: 12

Ingredients:

1 egg

What you'll need from store cupboard:

½ cup semi-sweet chocolate chips

1/3 cup flour

1/3 cup whole wheat flour

¼ cup Splenda brown sugar

¼ cup sunflower oil

2 tbsp. honey

1 tsp vanilla

½ tsp baking powder

¼ tsp salt

Nonstick cooking spray

Instructions:

Heat oven to 350 degrees. Spray an 8-inch square baking dish with cooking spray.

In a small bowl, combine dry Ingredients .

In a large bowl, whisk together egg, oil, honey, and vanilla. Stir in dry Ingredients just until combined. Stir in chocolate chips.

Spread batter in prepared dish. Bake 20-22 minutes or until they pass the toothpick test. Cool on a wire rack then cut into bars.

Nutrition Facts Per Serving

Calories 136 Total Carbs 18g Net Carbs 16g Protein 2g Fat 6g Sugar 9g Fiber 2g

Cinnamon Apple Chips

Prep time: 5 minutes, Cook time: 10 minutes, Serves: 2

Ingredients:

1 medium apple, sliced thin

What you'll need from store cupboard:

¼ tsp cinnamon

¼ tsp nutmeg

Nonstick cooking spray

Instructions:

Heat oven to 375. Spray a baking sheet with cooking spray.

Place apples in a mixing bowl and add spices. Toss to coat.

Arrange apples, in a single layer, on prepared pan. Bake 4 minutes, turn apples over and bake 4 minutes more.

Serve immediately or store in airtight container.

Nutrition Facts Per Serving

Calories 58 Total Carbs 15g Protein 0g Fat 0g Sugar 11g Fiber 3g

Cinnamon Apple Popcorn

Prep time: 30 minutes, Cook time: 50 minutes, Serves: 11

Ingredients:

4 tbsp. margarine, melted

What you'll need from store cupboard

10 cup plain popcorn

2 cup dried apple rings, unsweetened and chopped

½ cup walnuts, chopped

2 tbsp. Splenda brown sugar

1 tsp cinnamon - ½ tsp vanilla

Instructions:

Heat oven to 250 degrees.

Place chopped apples in a 9x13-inch baking dish and bake 20 minutes. Remove from oven and stir in popcorn and nuts.

In a small bowl, whisk together margarine, vanilla, Splenda, and cinnamon. Drizzle evenly over popcorn and toss to coat. Bake 30 minutes, stirring quickly every 10 minutes. If apples start to turn a dark brown, remove immediately. Pout onto waxed paper to cool at least 30 minutes. Store in an airtight container. Serving size is 1 cup.

Nutrition Facts Per Serving Calories 133 Total Carbs 14g Net Carbs 11g Protein 3g Fat 8g Sugar 7g Fiber 3g

Crab & Spinach Dip

Prep time: 10 minutes, Cook time: 2 hours, Serves: 10

Ingredients:

1 pkg. frozen chopped spinach, thawed and squeezed nearly dry

8 oz. reduced-fat cream cheese

What you'll need from store cupboard:

6 ½ oz. can crabmeat, drained and shredded

6 oz.jar marinated artichoke hearts, drained and diced fine

¼ tsp hot pepper sauce

Melba toast or whole grain crackers (optional)

Instructions:

Remove any shells or cartilage from crab.

Place all Ingredients in a small crock pot. Cover and cook on high 1 ½ - 2 hours, or until heated through and cream cheese is melted. Stir after 1 hour.

Serve with Melba toast or whole grain crackers. Serving size is ¼ cup.

Nutrition Facts Per Serving

Calories 106 Total Carbs 7g Net Carbs 6g Protein 5g Fat 8g Sugar 3g Fiber 1g

Cranberry & Almond Granola Bars

Prep time: 15 minutes, Cook time: 20 minutes, Serves: 12

Ingredients:

1 egg

1 egg white

What you'll need from store cupboard:

2 cup low-fat granola

¼ cup dried cranberries, sweetened

¼ cup almonds, chopped

2 tbsp. Splenda

1 teaspoon almond extract

½ tsp cinnamon

Instructions:

Heat oven to 350 degrees. Line the bottom and sides of an 8-inch baking dish with parchment paper.

In a large bowl, combine dry Ingredients including the cranberries.

In a small bowl, whisk together egg, egg white and extract. Pour over dry Ingredients and mix until combined.

Press mixture into the prepared pan. Bake 20 minutes or until light brown.

Cool in the pan for 5 minutes. Then carefully lift the bars from the pan onto a cutting board. Use a sharp knife to cut into 12 bars. Cool completely and store in an airtight container.

Nutrition Facts Per Serving

Calories 85 Total Carbs 14g Net Carbs 13g Protein 3g Fat 3g Sugar 5g Fiber 1g

Crispy Baked Cheese Puffs

Prep time: 5 minutes, Cook time: 10 minutes, Serves: 4

Ingredients:

2 eggs

½ cup cheddar cheese, grated

¼ cup mozzarella, grated

What you'll need from store cupboard:

½ cup almond flour

¼ cup reduced fat Parmesan

½ tsp baking powder

Black pepper

Instructions:

Heat oven to 400 degrees. Line a baking sheet with parchment paper.

In a large bowl, whisk eggs until lightly beaten. Add remaining Ingredients and mix well.

Divide into 8 pieces and roll into balls. Place on prepared baking sheet. Bake 10-12 minutes or until golden brown. Serve as is or with your favorite dipping sauce.

Nutrition Facts Per Serving

Calories 129 Total Carbs 2g Net Carbs 1g Protein 8g Fat 10g Sugar 0g Fiber 1g

Crunchy Apple Fries

Prep time: 15 minutes, Cook time: 10 minutes, Serves: 8

Ingredients:

3 apples, peeled, cored, and sliced into ½-inch pieces

¼ cup reduced fat margarine, melted

2 tbsp. walnuts, chopped

What you'll need from the store cupboard

¼ cup quick oats

3 tbsp. light brown sugar

2 tbsp. whole wheat flour

1 tsp cinnamon

1/8 tsp salt

Instructions:

Heat oven to 425 degrees. Put a wire rack on a large cookie sheet.

Add oats and walnuts to a food processor or blender and process until the mixture resembles flour.

Place the oat mixture in a shallow pan and add brown sugar, flour, cinnamon, and salt, mix well. Pour melted butter in a separate shallow pan.

Dip apple slices in margarine, then roll in oat mixture to coat completely. Place on wire rack.

Bake 10 – 12 minutes or until golden brown. Let cool before serving.

Nutrition Facts Per Serving

Calories 146 Total Carbs 20g Net Carbs 17g Protein 1g Fat 7g Sugar 13g Fiber 3g

Double Chocolate Biscotti

Prep time: 15 minutes, Cook time: 30 minutes, Serves: 27

Ingredients:

3 egg whites, divided

2 eggs

1 tbsp. orange zest

What you'll need from store cupboard:

2 cup flour

½ cup Splenda

½ cup almonds, toasted and chopped

1/3 cup cocoa, unsweetened

¼ cup mini chocolate chips

1 tsp vanilla

1 tsp instant coffee granules

1 tsp water

½ tsp salt

½ tsp baking soda

Nonstick cooking spray

Instructions:

Heat oven to 350 degrees. Spray a large baking sheet with cooking spray.

In a large bowl, combine flour, Splenda, cocoa, salt, and baking soda.

In a small bowl, whisk the eggs, 2 egg whites, vanilla, and coffee. Let rest 3-4 minutes to dissolve the coffee.

Stir in the orange zest and add to dry Ingredients , stir to thoroughly combine. Fold in the nuts and chocolate chips.

Divide dough in half and place on prepared pan. Shape each half into 14x1 ¾-inch rectangle.

Stir water and remaining egg white together. Brush over the top of the dough. Bake 20-25 minutes, or until firm to the touch. Cool on wire racks 5 minutes.

Transfer biscotti to a cutting board. Use a serrated knife to cut diagonally into ½-inch slice. Place cut side down on baking sheetand bake 5-7 minutes per side. Store in airtight container. Serving size is 2 pieces.

Nutrition Facts Per Serving

Calories 86 Total Carbs 13g Net Carbs 12g Protein 3g Fat 3g Sugar 5g Fiber 1g

Fig Cookie Bars

Prep time: 5 minutes, Cook time: 20 minutes, Serves: 12

Ingredients:

½ cup dried figs

1/8 cup reduced-fat cream cheese

3 tbsp. skim milk

What you'll need from store cupboard:

2/3 cup flour

½ cup quick oats

1/3 cup powdered sugar substitute

6 tbsp. hot water

2 tbsp. sunflower oil

1 tbsp. Splenda

¾ tsp baking powder

½ tsp vanilla

¼ tsp salt

Nonstick cooking spray

Instructions:

Heat oven to 400 degrees. Spray a cookie sheet with cooking spray.

Add the figs, water and Splenda to a blender and process until figs are finely chopped.

In a large bowl, stir together flour, oats, baking powder, and salt. Add oil, and milk 1 tablespoon at a time, until mixture forms a ball.

Roll dough out on a lightly floured surface to a 12x9-inch rectangle. Place on prepared pan. Spread fig mixture in a 2 ½-inch wide strip down the middle. At ½ inch intervals, use a sharp knife to cut the dough almost to the figs on both long sides. Fold strips over filling, overlapping and crossing in the middle.

Bake 15-20 minutes or until light brown. Remove from oven and let cool.

In a small bowl, beat cream cheese, powdered sugar substitute, and vanilla until smooth. Drizzle over bars and cut into 12 pieces.

Nutrition Facts Per Serving

Calories 105 Total Carbs 17g Net Carbs 16g Protein 2g Fat 3g Sugar 9g Fiber 1g

Fluffy Lemon Bars

Prep time: 15 minutes, chill time: 2 hours, Serves: 20

Ingredients:

8 oz. low fat cream cheese, soft

1/3 cup butter, melted

3 tbsp. fresh lemon juice

What you'll need from store cupboard:

12 oz. evaporated milk

1 pkg. lemon gelatin, sugar free

1 ½ cup graham cracker crumbs

1 cup boiling water

¾ cup Splenda

1 tsp vanilla

Instructions:

Pour milk into a large, metal bowl, place beaters in the bowl, cover and chill 2 hours.

In a small bowl, combine cracker crumbs and butter, reserve 1 tablespoon. Press the remaining mixture on the bottom of a 13x9-inch baking dish. Cover and chill until set.

In a small bowl, dissolve gelatin in boiling water. Stir in lemon juice and let cool.

In a large bowl, beat cream cheese, Splenda and vanilla until smooth. Add gelatin and mix well.

Beat the chilled milk until soft peaks form. Fold into cream cheese mixture. Pour over chilled crust

and sprinkle with reserved crumbs. Cover and chill 2 hours before serving.

Nutrition Facts Per Serving

Calories 126 Total Carbs 15g Protein 3g Fat 5g Sugar 10g Fiber 0g

Freezer Fudge

Prep time: 15 minutes, chill time: 2 hours, Serves: 16

Ingredients:

¼ cup margarine

¼ cup creamed coconut

What you'll need from store cupboard:

1 ¼ cup coconut oil

1 cup pecans, ground fine

6 tbsp. cocoa powder, unsweetened

2 tbsp. honey

1 tbsp. vanilla

¼ tsp sea salt

Instructions:

Line an 8x8 inch glass baking dish with wax paper. Add the oil and margarine to a glass measuring cup. Fill a medium saucepan about half full of water and bring to a boil.

Place the measuring cup in the pan and stir until they are melted and combined.

Pour into a blender or food processor and add everything but the nuts. Process until smooth. And the nuts and pulse just to combine.

Pour into the prepared pan and freeze until the fudge is set.

Remove from the pan and cut into 32 pieces. Store in a plastic container in the freezer. Serving size is 2 pieces.

Nutrition Facts Per Serving

Calories 254 Total Carbs 7g Net Carbs 6g Protein 1g Fat 26g Sugar 5g Fiber 1g

Fried Zucchini

Prep time: 10 minutes, Cook time: 10 minutes, Serves: 4

Ingredients:

3 zucchinis, slice ¼ - 1/8-inch thick

2 eggs

What you'll need from store cupboard:

½ cup sunflower oil

1/3 cup coconut flour

¼ cup reduced fat Parmesan cheese

1 tbsp. water

Instructions:

Heat oil in a large skillet over medium heat.

In a shallow bowl whisk the egg and water together.

In another shallow bowl, stir flour and parmesan together.

Coat zucchini in the egg then flour mixture. Add, in a single layer, to the skillet. Cook 2 minutes per side until golden brown. Transfer to paper towel lined plate. Repeat.

Serve immediately with your favorite dipping sauce.

Nutrition Facts Per Serving

Calories 138 Total Carbs 6g Net Carbs 4g Protein 6g Fat 11g Sugar 3g Fiber 2g

Gingerbread Cookies

Prep time: 15 minutes, Cook time: 10 minutes, Serves: 10

Ingredients:

1 egg

¼ cup butter, soft

What you'll need from store cupboard:

2 cup almond flour, sifted

¼ cup Splenda

1 tbsp. cinnamon

1 ½ tsp ginger

1 tsp vanilla

½ tsp baking powder

¼ tsp cloves

¼ tsp nutmeg

Instructions:

In a medium bowl, stir together the almond flour, cinnamon, ginger, cloves, nutmeg, and baking powder.

In a large bowl, beat the butter and Splenda for 1-2 minutes, until fluffy. Beat in the egg and vanilla. Beat in the almond flour mixture until a dough forms.

Form the dough into a ball, wrap with plastic wrap and refrigerate for at least 30 minutes.

Heat the oven to 350 degrees. Line a cookie sheet with parchment paper.

Roll the dough out between two sheets of parchment paper to ¼-inch thick. Cut out desired shapes with cookie cutter and place on prepared pan. Or you can drop dough by teaspoonful onto pan.

Bake 10-15 minutes or until edges are golden brown. Remove to wire rack and cool. Store in airtight container. Serving size is 1 large, or 2 small cookies.

Nutrition Facts Per Serving

Calories 181 Total Carbs 9g Net Carbs 7g Protein 5g Fat 15g Sugar 6g Fiber 2g

Homemade Cheetos

Prep time: 10 minutes, Cook time: 30 minutes, Serves: 6

Ingredients:

3 egg whites

½ cup cheddar cheese, grated and frozen

What you'll need from store cupboard:

¼ cup reduced fat parmesan cheese

1/8 tsp cream of tartar

Instructions:

Heat oven to 300 degrees. Line a baking sheet with parchment paper.

Put the frozen cheese in a food processor/blender and pulse, until it's in tiny little pieces.

In a large mixing bowl, beat egg whites and cream of tartar until very stiff peaks from. Gently fold in chopped cheese. Spoon mixture into a piping bag with ½-inch hole. Gently pipe "cheeto" shapes onto prepared pan. Sprinkle with parmesan cheese. Bake 20-30 minutes. Turn off oven and leave the puffs inside another 30 minutes. Let cool completely and store in an airtight container.

Nutrition Facts Per Serving

Calories 102 Total Carbs 1g Protein 9g Fat 7g Sugar 0g Fiber 0g

Honey & Cinnamon Shortbread

Prep time: 15 minutes, Cook time: 20 minutes, Serves: 22

Ingredients:

½ cup margarine, soft

What you'll need from store cupboard:

1 2/3 cup flour

3 ½ tbsp. honey

1 tsp cinnamon

1/8 tsp baking powder

Instructions:

Heat oven to 350 degrees. Line a baking sheet with parchment paper.

In a large bowl, beat margarine and honey until smooth and creamy.

Mix in the flour and baking powder to create a smooth dough. Shape dough into a rectangle, wrap with plastic wrap and chill 15 minutes.

Roll dough out on a lightly floured surface to ¼-inch thick. Cut into rectangles and place on prepared baking sheet. If you like use a fork to make patterns on the dough. Chill 20 minutes.

Bake 15-20 minutes, or until they start to turn golden brown. Transfer to wire rack to cool completely. Store in an airtight container.

Nutrition Facts Per Serving

Calories 82 Total Carbs 10g Protein 1g Fat 4g Sugar 3g Fiber 0g

Honey Roasted Pumpkin Seeds

Prep time: 10 minutes, Cook time: 30 minutes, Serves: 8

Ingredients:

2 cup raw fresh pumpkin seeds, wash and pat dry

1 tbsp. butter

What you'll need from store cupboard:

3 tbsp. honey

1 tbsp. coconut oil

1 tsp cinnamon

Instructions:

Heat oven to 275 degrees. Line a baking sheet with parchment paper, making sure it hangs over both ends.

Place the pumpkin seeds in a medium bowl.

In a small microwave safe bowl, add butter, coconut oil, and honey. Microwave until the butter melts and the honey is runny. Pour the honey mixture over the pumpkin seeds and stir. Add the cinnamon and stir again.

Dump the pumpkin seeds into the middle of the paper and place it in the oven. Bake for 30-40 minutes until the seeds and honey are a deep golden brown, stirring every 10 minutes.

When the seeds are roasted, remove from the oven and stir again. Stir a few times as they cool to keep them from sticking in one big lump.

Enjoy the seeds once they are cool enough to eat. Store uncovered for up to one week. Serving size is ¼ cup.

Nutrition Facts Per Serving

Calories 267 Total Carbs 13g Net Carbs 12g Protein 8g Fat 22g Sugar 7g Fiber 1g

Honeydew & Ginger Smoothies

Prep time: 5 minutes, blend time: 3 minutes, Serves: 3

Ingredients:

1 ½ cup honeydew melon, cubed

½ cup banana

½ cup nonfat vanilla yogurt

¼ tsp fresh ginger, grated

What you'll need from store cupboard:

½ cup ice cubes

Instructions:

Place all Ingredients in a blender and pulse until smooth. Pour into glasses and serve immediately.

Nutrition Facts Per Serving

Calories 68 Total Carbs 16g Net Carbs 15g Protein 2g Fat 0g Sugar 12g Fiber 1g

Hot & Spicy Mixed Nuts

Prep time: 5 minutes, Cook time: 10 minutes, Serves: 6

What you'll need from store cupboard:

½ cup whole almonds

½ cup pecan halves

½ cup walnut halves

1 tsp sunflower oil

½ tsp cumin

½ tsp curry powder

1/8 tsp cayenne pepper

Dash of white pepper

Instructions:

Heat oven to 350 degrees.

Place the nuts in a large bowl. Add the oil and toss to coat. Stir the spices together in a small bowl. Add to nuts and toss to coat. Spread nuts on a large baking sheet in a single layer. Bake 10 minutes. Remove from oven and let cool. Store in airtight container. Serving size is ¼ cup.

Nutrition Facts Per Serving

Calories 257 Total Carbs 5g Net Carbs 1g Protein 6g Fat 25g Sugar 1g Fiber 4g

Italian Eggplant Rollups

Prep time: 10 minutes, Cook time: 25 minutes, Serves: 8

Ingredients:

16 fresh spinach leaves

4 sun-dried tomatoes, rinsed, drained and diced fine

2 medium eggplants
1 green onion, diced fine
4 tbsp. fat-free cream cheese, soft
2 tbsp. fat-free sour cream
What you'll need from store cupboard:
1 cup spaghetti sauce (chapter 16)
2 tbsp. lemon juice
1 tsp olive oil
1 clove garlic, diced fine
¼ tsp oregano
1/8 tsp black pepper
Nonstick cooking spray
Instructions:
Heat oven to 450 degrees. Spray 2 large cookie sheets with cooking spray.
Trim the ends of the eggplant. Slice them lengthwise in ¼-inch slices. Discard the ones that are mostly skin, there should be about 16 slices. Arrange them in a single layer on prepared pans.
In a small bowl, whisk together the lemon juice and oil and brush over both sides of the eggplant. Bake 20-25 minutes or until the eggplant starts to turn a golden brown color. Transfer to a plate to cool.
In a mixing bowl, combine remaining Ingredients , except spinach, until thoroughly combined.
To assemble, spread 1 teaspoon cream cheese mixture evenly over sliced eggplant, leaving ½-inch border around the edges .Top with a spinach leaf and roll up, starting at small end. Lay rolls, seam side down, on serving plate. Serve with warmspaghetti sauce
Nutrition Facts Per Serving
Calories 78 Total Carbs 12g Net Carbs 6g Protein 3g Fat 3g Sugar 6g Fiber 6g

Margarita Chicken Dip

Prep time: 10 minutes, Cook time: 1 hour, Serves: 12
Ingredients:
2 ½ cup Monterrey jack cheese, grated
1 ½ cup chicken, cooked and shredded
1 ½ blocks cream cheese, soft, cut into cubes
¼ cup fresh lime juice
2 tbsp. fresh orange juice
2 tbsp. Pico de Gallo
1 tbsp. lime zest
What you'll need from store cupboard:
¼ cup tequila
2 cloves garlic, diced fine

1 tsp cumin
1 tsp salt
Instructions:
Place the cream cheese on bottom of crock pot. Top with chicken, then grated cheese. Add remaining Ingredients , except the Pico de Gallo. Cover and cook on low 60 minutes. Stir the dip occasionally to combine Ingredients .
When dip is done transfer to serving bowl. Top with Pico de Gallo and serve with tortilla chips.
Nutrition Facts Per Serving
Calories 169 Total Carbs 5g Protein 14g Fat 8g Sugar 1g Fiber 0g

Mini Eggplant Pizzas

Prep time: 10 minutes, Cook time: 35 minutes, Serves: 4
Ingredients:
1 large eggplant, peeled and sliced into ¼ - inch circles
2 cup spaghetti sauce, (chapter 16)
½ cup reduced-fat mozzarella cheese, grated
2 eggs
What you'll need from the store cupboard
1 ¼ cups Italian bread crumbs
1 tbsp. water
¼ tsp black pepper
Nonstick cooking spray
Instructions:
Heat oven to 350 degrees. Line 2 large cookie sheets with foil and spray well with cooking spray.
In a shallow dish, beat eggs, water and pepper. Place the bread crumbs in a separate shallow dish. Dip eggplant pieces in egg mixture, then coat completely with bread crumbs. Place on prepared cookie sheets. Spray the tops with cooking spray and bake 15 minutes.
Turn the eggplant over and spray with cooking spray again. Bake another 15 minutes.
Remove from oven and top each piece with 1 tablespoon spaghetti sauce. Sprinkle cheese over sauce and bake another 4 – 5 minutes, or until sauce is bubbly and cheese is melted.
Nutrition Facts Per Serving
Calories 171 Total Carbs 24g Net Carbs 20g Protein 9g Fat 5g Sugar 6g Fiber 4g

Mozzarella Sticks

Prep time: 1 hour 10 minutes, Cook time: 30 minutes, Serves: 4

Ingredients:

8 string cheese sticks, halved

2 eggs, beaten

What you'll need from store cupboard:

1 cup reduced fat parmesan cheese

½ cup sunflower oil

1 tbsp. Italian seasoning

1 clove garlic, diced fine

Instructions:

Heat oil in a pot over med-high heat.

In a medium bowl, combine parmesan cheese, Italian seasoning and garlic.

In a small bowl, beat the eggs.

Dip string cheese in eggs then in parmesan mixture to coat, pressing coating into cheese.

Place in hot oil and cook until golden brown. Transfer to paper towel lined plate. Serve warm with marinara sauce,

Nutrition Facts Per Serving

Calories 290 Total Carbs 3g Protein 24g Fat 20g Sugar 0g Fiber 0g

Oatmeal Peanut Butter Bars

Prep time: 5 minutes, Cook time: 10 minutes, Serves: 10

Ingredients:

½ cup almond milk, unsweetened

What you'll need from store cupboard:

1 cup oats

¼ cup agave syrup

6tbsp. raw peanut butter

2 tbsp. peanuts, chopped

1 tsp pure vanilla

Instructions:

Heat oven to 325 degrees. Line a cookie sheet with parchment paper.

Place all Ingredients , except the peanuts, into a food processor. Process until you have a sticky dough. Use your hands to mix in the peanuts.

Separate the dough into 10 equal balls on the prepared cookie sheet. Shape into squares or bars. Press the bars flat to ¼-inch thickness.

Bake 8-12 minutes, or until the tops are nicely browned. Remove from oven and cool completely.

The bars will be soft at first but will stiffen as they cool.

Nutrition Facts Per Serving

Calories 125 Total Carbs 14g Net Carbs 12g Protein 4g Fat 6g Sugar 1g Fiber 2g

Onion Rings

Prep time: 5 minutes, Cook time: 15 minutes, Serves: 4

Ingredients:

1 large onion, slice ½-inch thick

1 egg

What you'll need from store cupboard:

¼ cup sunflower oil

2 tbsp. coconut flour

2 tbsp. reduced fat parmesan cheese

¼ tsp parsley flakes

1/8 tsp garlic powder

1/8 tsp cayenne pepper

Salt to taste

Instructions:

Heat oil in a large skillet over med-high heat.

In a shallow bowl, combine flour, parmesan, and seasonings.

Beat the egg.

Separate onion slices into individual rings and place in large bowl, add beaten egg and toss to coat well. Let rest 1-2 minutes.

In small batches, coat onion in flour mixture and add to skillet.

Cook 1-2 minutes per side, or until golden brown. Transfer to paper towel lined cookie sheet.

Serve with sugar free ketchup, (chapter 16), or your favorite dipping sauce.

Nutrition Facts Per Serving

Calories 184 Total Carbs 8g Net Carbs 5g Protein 3g Fat 16g Sugar 2g Fiber 3g

Orange Oatmeal Cookies

Prep time: 10 minutes, Cook time: 10 minutes, Serves: 18 (2 cookies per serving)

Ingredients:

1 orange, zested and juiced

½ cup margarine

1 egg white

1 tbsp. orange juice

What you'll need from the store cupboard

1 cup whole wheat pastry flour

1 cup oats

¼ cup stevia
¼ cup dark brown sugar substitute
¼ cup applesauce, unsweetened
1/3 cup wheat bran
½ tsp baking soda
½ tsp cream of tartar
¼ tsp cinnamon
Instructions:
Heat oven to 350 degrees. Line two cookie sheets with parchment paper.
In a medium mixing bowl, cream butter. Gradually add the sugars and beat 2 -3 minutes.
Add egg white and applesauce and beat just to combine.
Sift the dry Ingredients together in a large mixing bowl. Add the wet Ingredients , the orange juice, and the zest.
Drop the dough by tablespoons onto the prepared cookie sheets. Bake 10 minutes, or until the bottoms are brown. Cool on wire rack. Store in an airtight container.
Nutrition Facts Per Serving
Calories 129 Total Carbs 17g Net Carbs 16g Protein 2g Fat 6g Sugar 8g Fiber 1g

Parmesan Truffle Chips

Prep time: 10 minutes, Cook time: 20 minutes, Serves: 4
Ingredients:
4 egg whites
½ tsp fresh parsley, diced fine
What you'll need from store cupboard:
3 tbsp. reduced fat parmesan cheese, divided
2 tsp water
½ tsp salt
Truffle oil to taste
Nonstick cooking spray
Instructions:
Heat oven to 400 degrees. Spray two muffin pans with cooking spray.
In a small bowl, whisk together egg whites, water, and salt until combined.
Spoon just enough egg white mixture into each muffin cup to barely cover the bottom. Sprinkle a small pinch of parmesan on each egg white.
Bake 10-15 minutes or until the edges are dark brown, be careful not to burn them.
Let cool in the pans 3-4 minutes then transfer to a small bowl and drizzle lightly with truffle oil. Add

parsley and ½ tablespoon parmesan and toss to coat. Serve.
Nutrition Facts Per Serving
Calories 47 Total Carbs 0g Protein 4g Fat 3g Sugar 0g Fiber 0g

Peanut Butter Oatmeal Cookies

Prep time: 5 minutes, Cook time: 30 minutes, Serves: 20
Ingredients:
2 egg whites
½ cup margarine, soft
What you'll need from store cupboard:
1 cup flour
1 cup quick oats
½ cup reduced-fat peanut butter
1/3 cup Splenda
1/3 Splenda brown sugar
½ tsp baking soda
½ tsp vanilla
Instructions:
Heat oven to 350 degrees.
In a large mixing bowl, combine dry Ingredients and stir to combine.
In a separate bowl, beat together the egg whites and margarine. Add to dry Ingredients and mix well.
Drop by teaspoonful onto nonstick cookie sheets. Bake 8-10 minutes or until edges start to brown. Remove to wire rack and cool completely. Store in an airtight container. Serving size is 2 cookies.
Nutrition Facts Per Serving
Calories 151 Total Carbs 17g Net Carbs 16g Protein 3g Fat 7g Sugar 7g Fiber 1g

Pesto Stuffed Mushrooms

Prep time: 5 minutes, Cook time: 20 minutes, Serves: 4
Ingredients:
12 cremini mushrooms, stems removed
4 oz. low fat cream cheese, soft
½ cup mozzarella cheese, grated
What you'll need from store cupboard:
1/3 cup reduced fat Parmesan cheese
6 tbsp. basil pesto
Nonstick cooking spray
Instructions:
Heat oven to 375 degrees. Line a square baking dish with foil and spray with cooking spray.

Arrange the mushrooms in the baking pan. Set aside.

In a medium bowl, beat cream cheese, pesto and parmesan until smooth and creamy. Spoon mixture into mushroom caps. Top with a heaping teaspoon of mozzarella.

Bake 20-23 minutes or until cheese is melted and golden brown. Let cook 5-10 minutes before serving.

Nutrition Facts Per Serving
Calories 76 Total Carbs 4g Protein 8g Fat 3g Sugar 1g Fiber 0g

Pickled Cucumbers

Prep time: 15 minutes, Cook time: 5 minutes, Serves: 10
Ingredients:
2 cucumbers, cut into 1/4-inch slices
½ onion, sliced thin
What you'll need from the store cupboard
1 ½ cups vinegar
2 tbsp. stevia
1 tbsp. dill
2 cloves garlic, sliced thin
1 tsp peppercorns
1 tsp coriander seeds
½ tsp salt
¼ tsp red pepper flakes
Instructions:
In a medium saucepan, combine vinegar and spices. Bring to a boil over high heat. Set aside.

Place the cucumbers, onions, and garlic into a quart-sized jar, or plastic container, with an air tight lid. Pour hot liquid over the vegetables, making sure they are completely covered.

Add the lid and chill at least a day before serving.
Nutrition Facts Per Serving
Calories 33 Total Carbs 6g Net Carbs 0g Protein 0g Fat 0g Sugar 4g Fiber 0g

Pistachio Cookies

Prep time: 5 minutes, Cook time: 15 minutes, Serves: 13-14
Ingredients:
2 eggs, beaten
What you'll need from store cupboard:
1 2/3 cup almond flour - 1 cup + 2 tbsp. Splenda
3/4 cup + 50 pistachio nuts, shelled

Instructions:
Add the ¾ cup nuts and 2 tablespoons Splenda to a food processor. Process until nuts are ground fine.

Pour the ground nuts into a large bowl, and stir in flour and remaining Splenda until combined.

Add eggs and mix Ingredients thoroughly. Wrap dough with plastic wrap and chill at least 8 hours or overnight.

Heat oven 325 degrees. Line a cookie sheet with parchment paper. Roll teaspoonful of dough into small balls, about 1-inch in diameter. Place on prepared sheet. Smash cookie slightly then press a pistachio in the center. Bake 12-15 minutes or until the edges are lightly browned. Transfer to wire rack to cool completely. Store in airtight container. Serving size is 3 cookies.

Nutrition Facts Per Serving Calories 108 Total Carbs 5g Net Carbs 3g Protein 4g Fat 8g Sugar 3g Fiber 2g

Popcorn Style Cauliflower

Prep time: 5 minutes, Cook time: 20 minutes, Serves: 4
Ingredients:
1 head cauliflower, separated into bite-sized florets
What you'll need from the store cupboard
¼ tsp garlic powder
¼ tsp salt
1/8 tsp black pepper
Butter-flavored cooking spray
Instructions:
Heat oven to 400 degrees.

Place cauliflower in a large bowl and spray with cooking spray, making sure to coat all sides. Sprinkle with seasonings and toss to coat.

Place in a single layer on a cookie sheet. Bake 20 – 25 minutes or until cauliflower starts to brown. Serve warm.

Nutrition Facts Per Serving
Calories 53 Total Carbs 11g Net Carbs 6g Protein 4g Fat 0g Sugar 5g Fiber 5g

Raspberry Walnut Parfaits

Prep time: 10 minutes, chill time: 1 hour, Serves: 4
Ingredients:
1 can coconut milk, chilled (not low fat)
½ cup fresh raspberries, rinsed and dried
What you'll need from store cupboard:

¼ cup walnuts, coarsely chopped
1 tbsp. Splenda
1 tsp vanilla
Instructions:
In a medium bowl, combine the berries and walnuts.
In a large bowl, beat coconut milk, Splenda and vanilla until combined. Let rest 5 minutes.
In 4 small mason jars, spoon half the vanilla cream evenly.
Top with berries. Repeat. Screw on the lids and chill at least one hour.
Nutrition Facts Per Serving
Calories 213 Total Carbs 8g Net Carbs 6g Protein 4g Fat 20g Sugar 4g Fiber 2g

Rosemary Potato Chips

Prep time: 10 minutes, Cook time: 20 minutes, Serves: 6
Ingredients:
2 medium red potatoes, unpeeled cut in 1/16-inch slices
1 ¼ cup fat-free sour cream
2 tbsp. fresh rosemary, chopped fine
What you'll need from store cupboard:
1 tbsp. olive oil
¼ tsp garlic salt
1/8 tsp black pepper
Nonstick cooking spray
Instructions:
Heat oven to 450 degrees. Spray 2 baking sheets with cooking spray.
In a small bowl, combine rosemary, garlic salt, and pepper.
Pat potatoes dry with paper towels. Arrange in single layer on prepared pans, spray with cooking spray.
Bake 10 minutes. Flip over, brush with oil and sprinkle with herb mixture.
Bake 5-10 minutes more until golden brown. Cool before serving.
Serving size is about 10 chips with 3 tablespoons sour cream for dipping.
Nutrition Facts Per Serving
Calories 83 Total Carbs 14g Net Carbs 12g Protein 2g Fat 3g Sugar 1g Fiber 2g

Rum Spiced Nuts

Prep time: 5 minutes, Cook time: 10 minutes, Serves: 12
Ingredients:
2 tbsp. Margarine
What you'll need from store cupboard:
3 cups mixed nuts, unsalted
2 tbsp. dark rum
2 tbsp. Splenda
2 tsp curry powder
1 tsp salt
1 tsp ancho chili powder
1 tsp cinnamon
1 tsp cumin
Instructions:
Place a medium, nonstick, skillet over medium heat. Add nuts and cook, stirring frequently, about 3-5 minutes, to lightly toast them.
Add the margarine and rum and cook until most of the liquid evaporates.
Combine the remaining Ingredients in a large bowl. Add the nuts and toss to coat.
Dump out onto a large baking sheet to cool. Store in an airtight container. Serving size is ¼ cup.
Nutrition Facts Per Serving
Calories 254 Total Carbs 10g Net Carbs 8g Protein 6g Fat 22g Sugar 4g Fiber 2g

Soft Pretzel Bites

Prep time: 15 minutes, Cook time: 15 minutes, Serves: 8
Ingredients:
3 cups mozzarella cheese, grated
3 large eggs
½ cup cream cheese
What you'll need from the store cupboard
2 cups almond flour, super fine
1 tbsp. baking powder
1 tbsp. coarse salt
Instructions:
Heat oven to 400 degrees. Line a large cookie sheet with parchment paper.
Stir almond flour and baking powder together in a small bowl.
Place the mozzarella and cream cheese in a large glass bowl. Be sure to surround the cream cheese with the mozzarella. Melt the cheese in 30 second intervals on high, stirring after each interval.

Continue this step until they are completely melted, about 2 – 2 ½ minutes.

Place the cheese, 2 eggs, and flour mixture into a food processor with a dough blade. Pulse on high until the mixture forms a uniform dough.

Wrap a pastry board with plastic wrap making sure it is taut. Lightly coat your hands with vegetable oil and separate dough into 8 equal parts. Roll each into 1-inch thick ropes.

With a sharp knife, cut dough into ¾-inch pieces. Place on prepared cookie sheet.

In a small bowl, whisk the remaining egg. Brush the dough pieces with egg then sprinkle with salt.

Bake 12 minutes, or until lightly browned. Set oven to broil and cook another 2 minutes to crisp up the outside of the pretzels. Serve warm by themselves or dip them in cheese sauce

Nutrition Facts Per Serving

Calories 242 Total Carbs 6g Net Carbs 3g Protein 11g Fat 20g Sugar1g Fiber 3g

Tangy Almond Shortbread Cookies

Prep time: 5 minutes, Cook time: 15 minutes, Serves: 8

Ingredients:

6 tbsp. margarine

1 tsp freshly grated lemon zest

What you'll need from store cupboard:

2 cup almond flour

1/3 cup Splenda

Nonstick cooking spray

Instructions:

1. In a small saucepan, melt margarine over medium heat.

2. Stir in flour, Splenda, and zest until thoroughly combined.

3. Form dough into a "log", wrap with plastic wrap and chill in the freezer for 30 minutes, or the refrigerator for 2 hours.

4. Heat oven to 350 degrees. Spray a cookie sheet with cooking spray.

5. Use a sharp knife to slice dough in ½-inch thick cookies. Place on prepared cookie sheet. Bake 15 minutes or until golden brown and firm.

Cool completely before serving. Serving size is 2 cookies.

Nutrition Facts Per Serving
Calories 254 Total Carbs 13g Net Carbs 10g Protein 5g Fat 20g Sugar 9g Fiber 3g

Tex Mex Popcorn

Prep time: 5 minutes, Cook time: 5 minutes, Serves: 4

Ingredients:

¼ cup cilantro, diced

Refrigerated butter-flavor spray

What you'll need from store cupboard:

4 cup popcorn

1 tsp chili powder

½ tsp salt

½ tsp cumin seeds

½ tsp garlic powder

1/8 tsp smoked paprika

Instructions:

Place popcorn in a large bowl and spritz with butter spray. Add remaining Ingredients and toss to coat. Continue spritzing and tossing until popcorn is well coated.

Store in an airtight container. Serving size is 1 cup.

Nutrition Facts Per Serving

Calories 32 Total Carbs 6g Net Carbs 5g Protein 1g Fat 0g Sugar 0g Fiber 1g

Tortilla Chips

Prep time: 10 minutes, Cook time: 10 minutes, Serves: 4

Ingredients:

2 cup part-skim grated mozzarella cheese, grated

What you'll need from store cupboard:

¾ cup super fine almond flour

½ tsp salt

½ tsp chili powder

Instructions:

1. Heat oven to 375 degrees.

2. Prepare a double boiler. Over high heat, bring the water in the pot to a simmer, then turn heat to low. Add all the Ingredients to the top of the double boiler and stir constantly until cheese melts and mixture holds together in a ball. Turn out onto a large piece of parchment paper and let cool 5 minutes.

3. Knead the dough to thoroughly combine all the Ingredients . Separate into 2 equal portions. Working with one portion at a time, roll dough out

between two pieces of parchment paper into 9x15-inch rectangle.

4.   Remove top piece of parchment and with a pizza cutter, or sharp knife, cut rectangle into squares or triangles. Slide the parchment paper onto a cookie sheet and arrange dough shapes so they have ½-inch space between them. Repeat with second dough portion.

Bake 5-8 minutes, or until centers are golden brown. Remove from oven and transfer to wire rack to cool. Chips will crisp up as they cool. Store in an airtight container.

Nutrition Facts Per Serving

Calories 95 Total Carbs 3g Net Carbs 2g Protein 5g Fat 8g Sugar 0g Fiber 1g

Watermelon & Shrimp Ceviche

Prep time: 20 minutes, chill time: 1hour 30 minutes, Serves: 14

Ingredients:

1 lb. medium shrimp, peeled, deveined and tails removed

1 jalapeño pepper, diced fine

1 cup seedless watermelon, diced fine

½ cup + 2 tbsp. lime juice, divided

½ cup jicama, diced fine

½ cup red onion, diced fine

½ cup fresh cilantro, chopped

What you'll need from store cupboard:

Salt and pepper, to taste

Instructions:

1.   Chop shrimp into small pieces.

2.   In a medium bowl, combine shrimp and ½ cup lime juice. Cover and chill 1 hour or until shrimp turn pink. Drain and discard juice.

3.   In a large mixing bowl, combine all Ingredients . Salt and pepper to taste. Cover and chill at least 30 minutes.

Serve with, or on, your favorite crackers. Serving size is ¼ cup.

Nutrition Facts Per Serving

Calories 47 Total Carbs 3g Protein 8g Fat 1g Sugar 1g Fiber 0g

Zucchini Chips

Prep time: 5 minutes, Cook time: 10 minutes, Serves: 6

Ingredients:

1 large zucchini, sliced into ¼-inch circle

1/4 cup reduced fat, Parmesan cheese, grated fine

3 tbsp. low-fat milk

What you'll need from the store cupboard

1/3 cup whole wheat breadcrumbs

½ tsp garlic powder

1/8 tsp cayenne pepper

Nonstick cooking spray

Instructions:

After slicing zucchini pat dry with paper towels. Let sit for 60 minutes before using. Then pat dry again.

Heat oven to 425 degrees. Spray a wire rack with cooking spray and place on cookie sheet.

In a medium bowl combine all Ingredients except milk and zucchini. Pour milk into a shallow bowl. Dip zucchini into milk the coat with bread crumb mixture. Place on wire rack and bake 10 -15 minutes or until browned and crisp. Serve immediately.

Nutrition Facts Per Serving

Calories 25 Total Carbs 3g Protein 2g Fat 1g Sugar 1g Fiber 0g

Chapter 6
Soup And Stew Recipes

Irish Stew

Servings: 2
Cooking Time: 35 Minutes
Ingredients:
1.5lb diced lamb shoulder
1lb chopped vegetables
1 cup low sodium beef broth
3 minced onions
1tbsp ghee
Directions:
Mix all the ingredients in your Instant Pot.
Cook on Stew for 35 minutes.
Release the pressure naturally.
Nutrition Info: Calories: 330; Carbs: 9; Sugar: 2;
Fat: 12; Protein: 49; GL: 3

Vegetarian Split Pea Soup In A Crock Pot

Servings: 8
Cooking Time: 10 Minutes
Ingredients:
2 chopped ribs celery
2 cubes low-sodium bouillon
8 c. water
2 c. uncooked green split peas
3 bay leaves
2 carrots
2 chopped potatoes
Pepper and salt
Directions:

In your Crock-Pot, put the bouillon cubes, split peas, and water. Stir a bit to break up the bouillon cubes.
Next, add the chopped potatoes, celery, and carrots followed with bay leaves.
Stir to combine well.
Cover and cook for at least 4 hours on your Crock-Pot's lowsetting or until the green split peas are soft.
Add a bit salt and pepper as needed.
Before serving, remove the bay leaves and enjoy.
Nutrition Info: Calories: 149, Fat:1 g, Carbs:30 g, Protein:7 g, Sugars:3 g, Sodium:732 mg

Thai Peanut, Carrot, & Shrimp Soup

Servings: 4
Cooking Time: 10 Minutes
Ingredients:
3 garlic cloves, minced
½ onion, sliced
1 tablespoon Thai red curry paste
1 tablespoon coconut oil
fresh cilantro, minced, for garnish
½ pound shrimp, peeled and deveined
½ cup unsweetened plain almond milk
4 cups of low-sodium vegetable broth
½ cup whole unsalted peanuts
2 cups carrots, chopped
Directions:
In a pan, heat your oil over medium-high heat until shimmering.
Add your curry paste to the pan and cook continually stirring for about 1 minute. Add the garlic, onion, and carrots, along with peanuts to the pan. Continue cooking for 3 minutes or until your onion begins to soften.
Add your broth and bring to a boil. Reduce heat to a low setting and simmer for 6 minutes or until carrots are tender.
Use your immersion blender to puree your soup until smooth and return to pot. With heat setting on low, add the almond milk and stir to combine.

Add your shrimp to the pot and cook for 3 minutes or until cooked.
Garnish soup with cilantro, then serve and enjoy!
Nutrition Info: Carbs per serving: 17g

Ham Asparagus Soup

Servings: 3-4
Cooking Time: 55 Min.
Ingredients:
5 crushed garlic cloves
1 cup chopped ham
4 cups (preferably homemade) chicken broth
2 pounds trimmed and halved asparagus spears
2 tablespoons butter
1 chopped yellow onion
½ teaspoon dried thyme
Salt and freshly (finely ground) black pepper, as per taste preference
Directions:
Arrange Instant Pot over a dry platform in your kitchen. Open its top lid and switch it on.
Find and press "SAUTE" cooking function; add the butter in it and allow it to heat.
In the pot, add the onions; cook (while stirring) until turns translucent and softened for around 4-5 minutes.
Add the garlic, ham bone and broth; stir, and cook for about 2-3 minutes.
Add the other ingredients; gently stir to mix well.
Close the lid to create a locked chamber; make sure that safety valve is in locking position.
Find and press "SOUP" cooking function; timer to 45 minutes with default "HIGH" pressure mode.
Allow the pressure to build to cook the ingredients. After cooking time is over press "CANCEL" setting. Find and press "QPR" cooking function. This setting is for quick release of inside pressure. Slowly open the lid, add the mix in a blender or processor. Blend or process to make a smooth mix. Place the mix in serving bowls and enjoy the keto.
Nutrition Info: Calories - 146 Fat: 7g Saturated Fat: 3g Trans Fat: 0g Carbohydrates: 5g Fiber: 4g Sodium: 262mg Protein: 10g

Cabbage Soup

Servings: 2
Cooking Time: 35 Minutes
Ingredients:
1lb shredded cabbage

1 cup low sodium vegetable broth
1 shredded onion
2tbsp mixed herbs
1tbsp black pepper
Directions:
Mix all the ingredients in your Instant Pot.
Cook on Stew for 35 minutes.
Release the pressure naturally.
Nutrition Info: Calories: 60; Carbs: 2; Sugar: 0; Fat: 2; Protein: 4; GL: 1

Chickpea Soup

Servings: 2
Cooking Time: 35 Minutes
Ingredients:
1lb cooked chickpeas
1lb chopped vegetables
1 cup low sodium vegetable broth
2tbsp mixed herbs
Directions:
Mix all the ingredients in your Instant Pot.
Cook on Stew for 35 minutes.
Release the pressure naturally.
Nutrition Info: Calories: 310; Carbs: 20; Sugar: 3; Fat: 5; Protein: 27; GL: 5

Meatball Stew

Servings: 2
Cooking Time: 25 Minutes
Ingredients:
1lb sausage meat
2 cups chopped tomato
1 cup chopped vegetables
2tbsp Italian seasonings
1tbsp vegetable oil
Directions:
Roll the sausage into meatballs.
Put the Instant Pot on Sauté and fry the meatballs in the oil until brown. Mix all the ingredients in your Instant Pot. Cook on Stew for 25 minutes.
Release the pressure naturally.
Nutrition Info: Calories: 300; Carbs: 4; Sugar: 1; Fat: 12; Protein: 40; GL: 2

Squash Soup

Servings: 6
Cooking Time: 8 Hours
Ingredients:
2 lb butternut squash, peeled, chopped into chunks

1 tsp ginger, minced
1/4 tsp cinnamon
1 Tbsp curry powder
2 bay leaves
1 tsp black pepper
1/2 cup heavy cream
2 cups chicken stock
1 Tbsp garlic, minced
2 carrots, cut into chunks
2 apples, peeled, cored and diced
1 large onion, diced
1 tsp salt
Directions:
Spray a crock pot inside with cooking spray.
Add all ingredients except cream to the crock pot and stir well.
Cover and cook on low for 8 hours.
Purée the soup using an immersion blender until smooth and creamy.
Stir in heavy cream and season soup with pepper and salt.
Serve and enjoy.
Nutrition Info: Calories 170 Fat 4.4 g Carbohydrates 34.4 g Sugar13.4g Protein 2.9 g Cholesterol 14 mg

French Onion Soup

Servings: 2
Cooking Time: 35 Minutes
Ingredients:
6 onions, chopped finely
2 cups vegetable broth
2tbsp oil
2tbsp Gruyere
Directions:
Place the oil in your Instant Pot and cook the onions on Sauté until soft and brown.
Mix all the ingredients in your Instant Pot.
Cook on Stew for 35 minutes.
Release the pressure naturally.
Nutrition Info: Calories: 110; Carbs: 8; Sugar: 3; Fat: 10; Protein: 3; GL: 4

Cherry Stew

Servings: 6
Cooking Time: 10 Minutes
Ingredients:
2 c. water
½ c. powered cocoa

¼ c. coconut sugar
1 lb. pitted cherries
Directions:
In a pan, combine the cherries with all the water, sugar plus the hot chocolate mix, stir, cook over medium heat for ten minutes, divide into bowls and serve cold.
Enjoy!
Nutrition Info: Calories: 207, Fat:1 g, Carbs:8 g, Protein:6 g, Sugars:27 g, Sodium:19 mg

Curried Carrot Soup

Servings: 6
Cooking Time: 5 Minutes
Ingredients:
2 celery stalks, chopped
1 small onion, chopped
1 tablespoon extra-virgin olive oil
1 tablespoon fresh cilantro, chopped
¼ teaspoon freshly ground black pepper
1 cup of canned coconut milk
¼ teaspoon salt
4 cups of low-sodium vegetable broth
6 medium carrots, roughly chopped
1 teaspoon fresh ginger, minced
1 teaspoon ground cumin
1 ½ teaspoon curry powder
Directions:
Heat your Instant Pot to high setting and add the olive oil.
Sauté your celery and onion for 3 minutes. Add the curry powder, ginger, and cumin to the pot and cook for about 30 seconds.
Add the carrots, vegetable broth, and salt to your pot. Close pot and seal and set on high for 5 minutes. Allow the pressure to release naturally.
Pure your soup in batches in a blender jar and transfer back into the pot. Stir in the coconut milk along with pepper and heat through. Top soup with cilantro, then serve and enjoy!
Nutrition Info: Carbs per serving: 13g

Vegan Cream Soup With Avocado & Zucchini

Servings: 2
Cooking Time: 20 Minutes
Ingredients:
3 tsp vegetable oil

1 leek, chopped
1 rutabaga, sliced
3 cups zucchinis, chopped
1 avocado, chopped
Salt and black pepper to taste
4 cups vegetable broth
2 tbsp fresh mint, chopped
Directions:
In a pot, sauté leek, zucchini, and rutabaga in warm oil for about 7-10 minutes. Season with black pepper and salt. Pour in broth and bring to a boil. Lower the heat and simmer for 20 minutes.
Lift from the heat. In batches, add the soup and avocado to a blender. Blend until creamy and smooth. Serve in bowls topped with fresh mint.
Nutrition Info: Calories 378 Fat: 24.5g, Net Carbs: 9.3g, Protein: 8.2g

Kebab Stew

Servings: 2
Cooking Time: 35 Minutes
Ingredients:
1lb cubed, seasoned kebab meat
1lb cooked chickpeas
1 cup low sodium vegetable broth
1tbsp black pepper
Directions:
Mix all the ingredients in your Instant Pot.
Cook on Stew for 35 minutes.
Release the pressure naturally.
Nutrition Info: Calories: 290; Carbs: 22; Sugar: 4; Fat: 10; Protein: 34; GL: 6

Meatless Ball Soup

Servings: 2
Cooking Time: 15 Minutes
Ingredients:
1lb minced tofu
0.5lb chopped vegetables
2 cups low sodium vegetable broth
1tbsp almond flour
salt and pepper
Directions:
Mix the tofu, flour, salt and pepper.
Form the meatballs. Place all the ingredients in your Instant Pot. Cook on Stew for 15 minutes.
Release the pressure naturally.
Nutrition Info: Calories: 240; Carbs: 9; Sugar: 3; Fat: 10; Protein: 35; GL: 5

Tofu Soup

Servings: 8Cooking Time: 10 Minutes
Ingredients:
1 lb. cubed extra-firm tofu
3 diced medium carrots
8 c. low-sodium vegetable broth
½ tsp. freshly ground white pepper
8 minced garlic cloves
6 sliced and divided scallions
4 oz. sliced mushrooms
1-inch minced fresh ginger piece
Directions:
Pour the broth into a stockpot. Add all of the ingredients except for the tofu and last 2 scallions. Bring to a boil over high heat.
Once boiling, add the tofu. Reduce heat to low, cover, and simmer for 5 minutes.
Remove from heat, ladle soup into bowls, and garnish with the remaining sliced scallions. Serve immediately.
Nutrition Info: Calories: 91, Fat:3 g, Carbs:8 g, Protein:6 g, Sugars:4 g, Sodium:900 mg

Chicken Zoodle Soup

Servings: 2
Cooking Time: 35 Minutes
Ingredients:
1lb chopped cooked chicken
1lb spiralized zucchini
1 cup low sodium chicken soup
1 cup diced vegetables
Directions:
Mix all the ingredients except the zucchini in your Instant Pot.
Cook on Stew for 35 minutes.
Release the pressure naturally.
Stir in the zucchini and allow to heat thoroughly.
Nutrition Info: Calories: 250; Carbs: 5; Sugar: 0; Fat: 10; Protein: 40; GL: 1

Cheese Cream Soup With Chicken & Cilantro

Servings: 4
Cooking Time: 10 Minutes
Ingredients:
1 carrot, chopped
1 onion, chopped
2 cups cooked and shredded chicken

3 tbsp butter
4 cups chicken broth
2 tbsp cilantro, chopped
1/3 cup buffalo sauce
½ cup cream cheese
Salt and black pepper, to taste
Directions:
In a skillet over medium heat, warm butter and sauté carrot and onion until tender, about 5 minutes.
Add to a food processor and blend with buffalo sauce and cream cheese, until smooth. Transfer to a pot, add chicken broth and heat until hot but do not bring to a boil. Stir in chicken, salt, pepper and cook until heated through. When ready, remove to soup bowls and serve garnished with cilantro.
Nutrition Info: Calories 487, Fat: 41g, Net Carbs: 7.2g, Protein: 16.3g

Spicy Pepper Soup

Servings: 2
Cooking Time: 15 Minutes
Ingredients:
1lb chopped mixed sweet peppers
1 cup low sodium vegetable broth
3tbsp chopped chili peppers
1tbsp black pepper
Directions:
Mix all the ingredients in your Instant Pot.
Cook on Stew for 15 minutes.
Release the pressure naturally. Blend.
Nutrition Info: Calories: 100; Carbs: 11; Sugar: 4; Fat: 2; Protein: 3; GL: 6

Awesome Chicken Enchilada Soup

Servings: 4
Cooking Time: 30 Minutes
Ingredients:
2 tbsp coconut oil
1 lb boneless, skinless chicken thighs
¾ cup red enchilada sauce, sugar-free
¼ cup water
¼ cup onion, chopped
3 oz canned diced green chilis
1 avocado, sliced
1 cup cheddar cheese, shredded
¼ cup pickled jalapeños, chopped
½ cup sour cream
1 tomato, diced

Directions:
Put a large pan over medium heat. Add coconut oil and warm. Place in the chicken and cook until browned on the outside. Stir in onion, chillis, water, and enchilada sauce, then close with a lid. Allow simmering for 20 minutes until the chicken is cooked through.
Spoon the soup on a serving bowl and top with the sauce, cheese, sour cream, tomato, and avocado.
Nutrition Info: Calories: 643, Fat: 44.2g, Net Carbs: 9.7g, Protein: 45.8g

Zucchini-basil Soup

Servings: 5Cooking Time: 10 Minutes
Ingredients:
1/3 c. packed basil leaves
¾ c. chopped onion
¼ c. olive oil
2 lbs. trimmed and sliced zucchini
2 chopped garlic cloves
4 c. divided water
Directions:
Peel and julienne the skin from half of zucchini; toss with 1/2 teaspoon salt and drain in a sieve until wilted, at least 20 minutes. Coarsely chop remaining zucchini.
Cook onion and garlic in oil in a saucepan over medium-low heat, stirring occasionally, until onions are translucent. Add chopped zucchini and 1 teaspoon salt and cook, stirring occasionally.
Add 3 cups water and simmer with the lid ajar until tender. Pour the soup in a blender and purée soup with basil.
Bring remaining cup water to a boil in a small saucepan and blanch julienned zucchini. Drain.
Top soup with julienned zucchini. Season soup with salt and pepper and serve.
Nutrition Info: Calories: 169.3, Fat:13.7 g, Carbs:12 g, Protein:2 g,Sugars:3.8 g, Sodium:8 mg

Sweet And Sour Soup

Servings: 2
Cooking Time: 35 Minutes
Ingredients:
1lb cubed chicken breast
1lb chopped vegetables
1 cup low carb sweet and sour sauce
0.5 cup diabetic marmalade

Directions:
Mix all the ingredients in your Instant Pot.
Cook on Stew for 35 minutes.
Release the pressure naturally.
Nutrition Info:Calories: 305; Carbs: 4; Sugar: 1.2; Fat: 12; Protein: 40; GL: 2

Curried Shrimp & Green Bean Soup

Servings: 4
Cooking Time: 10 Minutes
Ingredients:
1 onion, chopped
2 tbsp red curry paste
2 tbsp butter
1-pound jumbo shrimp, peeled and deveined
2 tsp ginger-garlic puree
1 cup coconut milk
Salt and chili pepper to taste
1 bunch green beans, halved
1 tbsp cilantro, chopped
Directions:
Add the shrimp to melted butter in a saucepan over medium heat, season with salt and pepper, and cook until they are opaque, 2 to 3 minutes. Remove to a plate. Add in the ginger-garlic puree, onion, and red curry paste and sauté for 2 minutes until fragrant.
Stir in the coconut milk; add the shrimp, salt, chili pepper, and green beans. Cook for 4 minutes. Reduce the heat to a simmer and cook an additional 3 minutes, occasionally stirring. Adjust taste with salt, fetch soup into serving bowls, and serve sprinkled with cilantro.
Nutrition Info: Calories 351, Fat 32.4g, Net Carbs 3.2g, Protein 7.7g

Beef Borscht Soup

Servings: 8
Cooking Time: 30 Minutes
Ingredients:
2 lbs ground beef
3 beets, peeled and diced
2 large carrots, diced
3 stalks of celery, diced
1 onion, diced
2 cloves garlic, diced
3 cups shredded cabbage
6 cups beef stock
½ tbsp thyme

1 bay leaf
Salt and ground black pepper to taste
Directions:
Preheat the Instant Pot by selecting SAUTÉ.
Add the ground beef and cook, stirring, for 5 minutes, until browned.
Combine all the rest ingredients in the Instant Pot and stir to mix. Close and lock the lid.
Press the CANCEL button to stop the SAUTE function, then select the MANUAL setting and set the cooking time for 15 minutes at HIGH pressure.Once timer goes off, allow to Naturally Release for 10 minutes, then release any remaining pressure manually. Uncover the pot.
Let the dish sit for 5-10 minutes and serve.
Nutrition Info: Calories 301 Fat 27.2 g Carbohydrates 13.6 g Sugar 6 g Protein 3 g Cholesterol 33 mg

Broccoli & Spinach Soup

Servings: 4
Cooking Time: 20 Minutes
Ingredients:
2 tbsp butter
1 onion, chopped
1 garlic clove, minced
2 heads broccoli, cut in florets
2 stalks celery, chopped
4 cups vegetable broth
1 cup baby spinach
Salt and black pepper to taste
1 tbsp basil, chopped
Parmesan cheese, shaved to serve
Directions:
Melt the butter in a saucepan over medium heat. Sauté the garlicand onion for 3 minutes until softened. Mix in the broccoli and celery, and cook for 4 minutes until slightly tender. Pour in the broth, bring to a boil, then reduce the heat to medium-low and simmer covered for about 5 minutes.
Drop in the spinach to wilt, adjust the seasonings, and cook for 4 minutes. Ladle soup into serving bowls. Serve with a sprinkle of grated Parmesan cheese and chopped basil.
Nutrition Info: Calories 123 Fat 11g Net Carbs 3.2g Protein 1.8g

Vegetable Chicken Soup

Servings: 6
Cooking Time: 6 Hours
Ingredients:
4 cups chicken, boneless, skinless, cooked and diced
4 tsp garlic, minced
2/3 cups onion, diced
1 1/2 cups carrot, diced
6 cups chicken stock
2 Tbsp lime juice
1/4 cup jalapeño pepper, diced
1/2 cup tomatoes, diced
1/2 cup fresh cilantro, chopped
1 tsp chili powder
1 Tbsp cumin
1 3/4 cups tomato juice
2 tsp sea salt
Directions:
Add all ingredients to a crock pot and stir well.
Cover and cook on low for 6 hours.
Stir well and serve.
Nutrition Info: Calories 192 Fat 3.8 g Carbohydrates 9.8 g Sugar 5.7 g Protein 29.2 g Cholesterol 72 mg

Beef Barley Soup

Servings: 8
Cooking Time: 30 Minutes
Ingredients:
2 tbsp olive oil
2 lbs beef chuck roast, cut into 1½ inch steaks
Salt and ground black pepper to taste
2 onions, chopped
4 cloves of garlic, sliced
4 large carrots, chopped
1 stalk of celery, chopped
1 cup pearl barley, rinsed
1 bay leaf
8 cups chicken stock
1 tbsp fish sauce
Directions:
Select the SAUTÉ setting on the Instant Pot and heat the oil.
Sprinkle the beef with salt and pepper. Put in the pot and brown for about 5 minutes. Turn and brown the other side.
Remove the meat from the pot.

Add the onion, garlic, carrots, and celery. Stir and sauté for 6 minutes.
Return the beef to the pot. Add the pearl barley, bay leaf, chicken stock and fish sauce. Stir well.
Close and lock the lid. Press the CANCEL button to reset the cooking program, then press the MANUAL button and set the cooking time for 30 minutes at HIGH pressure.
Once cooking is complete, let the pressure Release Naturally for 15 minutes. Release any remaining steam manually. Uncover the pot.
Remove cloves garlic, large vegetable chunks and bay leaf.
Taste for seasoning and add more salt if needed.
Nutrition Info: Calories 200 Fat 27.2 g Carbohydrates 13.6 g Sugar 2 g Protein 4.4 g Cholesterol 32 mg

Sirloin Carrot Soup

Servings: 6
Cooking Time: 10 Minutes
Ingredients:
1 lb. chopped carrots and celery mix
32 oz. low-sodium beef stock
1/3 c. whole-wheat flour
1 lb. ground beef sirloin
1 tbsp. olive oil
1 chopped yellow onion
Directions:
Heat up the olive oil in a saucepan over medium-high flame; add the beef and the flour.
Stir well and cook to brown for 4-5 minutes.
Add the celery, onion, carrots, and stock; stir and bring to a simmer.
Turn down the heat to low and cook for 12-15 minutes.
Serve warm.
Nutrition Info: Calories: 140, Fat: 4.5 g,Carbs: 16 g, Protein: 9 g, Sugars: 3 g, Sodium:670 mg

Mexican Chicken Soup

Servings: 6
Cooking Time: 4 Hours
Ingredients:
1 1/2 lb chicken thighs, skinless and boneless
14 oz chicken stock
14 oz salsa
8 oz Monterey Jack cheese, shredded

Directions:
Place chicken into a crock pot.
Pour remaining ingredients over the chicken.
Cover and cook on high for 4 hours.
Remove chicken from crock pot and shred using forks.
Return shredded chicken to the crock pot and stir well.
Serve and enjoy.
Nutrition Info: Calories 371 Fat 19.5 g Carbohydrates 5.7 g Sugar 2.2 g Protein 42.1 g Cholesterol 135 mg

Mushroom Cream Soup With Herbs

Servings: 4
Cooking Time: 15 Minutes
Ingredients:
1 onion, chopped
½ cup crème fraiche
¼ cup butter
12 oz white mushrooms, chopped
1 tsp thyme leaves, chopped
1 tsp parsley leaves, chopped
1 tsp cilantro leaves, chopped
2 garlic cloves, minced
4 cups vegetable broth
Salt and black pepper, to taste
Directions:
Add butter, onion and garlic to a large pot over high heat and cook for 3 minutes until tender. Add mushrooms, salt and pepper, and cook for 10 minutes. Pour in the broth and bring to a boil.
Reduce the heat and simmer for 10 minutes. Puree the soup with a hand blender until smooth. Stir in crème fraiche. Garnish with herbs before serving.
Nutrition Info: Calories 213 Fat: 18g Net Carbs: 4.1g Protein: 3.1g

Beef & Mushroom Barley Soup

Servings: 6
Cooking Time: 1 Hour And 20 Minutes
Ingredients:
½ cup of pearl barley
1 cup of water
4 cups of low-sodium beef broth
½ teaspoon thyme, dried
6 garlic cloves, minced
3 celery stalks, chopped
1 onion, chopped

2 carrots, chopped
8-ounces of mushrooms, sliced
1 tablespoon extra-virgin olive oil
¼ teaspoon freshly ground black pepper
1 lb. Of beef stew meat, cubed
Directions:
Season your meat with salt and pepper.
Heat the oil in an Instant Pot over high heat. Add the beef and brown, then remove meat and set aside.
Add your mushrooms to the pot and cook for about 1 to 2 minutes or until they begin to soften. Remove the mushrooms from pot and set them aside along with the meat.
Add your carrots, celery, and onions into the pot. Sauté vegetables for about 4 minutes or until they begin to soften. Add your garlic into pot and cook until fragrant.
Place the meat and mushrooms back into the pot, then add the beef broth, thyme, and water. Set your pot pressure to high and cook for 15 minutes. Allow the pressure to release naturally.
Open your Instant Pot and add the barley. Use the slow cooker function on the pot, with the lid having vent open, then continue cooking for an additional hour or until your barley is cooked and tender. Serve and enjoy!
Nutrition Info: Carbs per serving: 19g

Spicy Chicken Pepper Stew

Servings: 6
Cooking Time: 6 Hours
Ingredients:
3 chicken breasts, skinless and boneless, cut into small pieces
1 tsp garlic, minced
1 tsp ground ginger
2 tsp olive oil
2 tsp soy sauce
1 Tbsp fresh lemon juice
1/2 cup green onions, sliced
1 Tbsp crushed red pepper
8 oz chicken stock
1 bell pepper, chopped
1 green chili pepper, sliced
2 jalapeño peppers, sliced
1/2 tsp black pepper
1/4 tsp sea salt

Directions:

Add all ingredients to a large mixing bowl and mix well. Place inthe refrigerator overnight.

Pour marinated chicken mixture into a crock pot.

Cover and cook on low for 6 hours.

Stir well and serve.

Nutrition Info: Calories 171 Fat 7.4 g Carbohydrates 3.7 g Sugar 1.7 g Protein 22 g Cholesterol 65 mg

Cream Pepper Stew

Servings: 4

Cooking Time: 10 Min.

Ingredients:

1 (preferably medium size) celery stalk, chopped

1 (preferably medium size) yellow bell pepper, chopped

1 (preferably medium size) green bell pepper, chopped

2 large red bell peppers, chopped

1 small red onion, chopped

2 tablespoons butter

1/2 cup cream cheese, full-fat

1/4 teaspoon dried thyme, (finely ground)

1/2 teaspoon black pepper, (finely ground)

1 teaspoon dried parsley, (finely ground)

1 teaspoon salt

2 cups vegetable stock

1 cup heavy cream

Directions:

Arrange Instant Pot over a dry platform in your kitchen. Open its top lid and switch it on.

Find and press "SAUTE" cooking function; add the butter in it and allow it to heat.

In the pot, add the onions, bell pepper, and celery; cook (while stirring) until turns translucent and softened for around 3-4 minutes.

Pour in the vegetable stock and heavy cream — season with salt, pepper, parsley, and thyme.

Close the lid to create a locked chamber; make sure that safety valve is in locking position.

Find and press "MANUAL" cooking function; timer to 6 minuteswith default "HIGH" pressure mode.

Allow the pressure to build to cook the ingredients. After cooking time is over press "CANCEL" setting. Find and press "QPR" cooking function. This setting is for quick release of inside pressure.

Slowly open the lid, mix in the cream; take out the cooked in serving plates or serving bowls, and enjoy the keto .

Nutrition Info: Calories - 286 Fat: 27g Saturated Fat: 6g Trans Fat: 0g Carbohydrates: 9g Fiber: 3g Sodium: 523mg Protein: 5g

Easy Beef Mushroom Stew

Servings: 8

Cooking Time: 8 Hours

Ingredients:

2 lb stewing beef, cubed

1 packet dry onion soup mix

4 oz can mushrooms, sliced

14 oz can cream of mushroom soup

1/2 cup water

1/4 tsp black pepper

1/2 tsp salt

Directions:

Spray a crock pot inside with cooking spray.

Add all ingredients into the crock pot and stir well.

Cover and cook on low for 8 hours.

Stir well and serve.

Nutrition Info: Calories 237 Fat 8.5 g Carbohydrates 2.7 g Sugar 0.4 g Protein 35.1 g Cholesterol 101 mg

Summer Squash Soup With Crispy Chickpeas

Servings: 4

Cooking Time: 20 Minutes

Ingredients:

¼ teaspoon smoked paprika

1 teaspoon extra-virgin olive oil, plus one tablespoon

1 (15-ounce) can low-sodium chickpeas, drained and rinsed

2 tablespoons plain low-fat Greek yogurt

freshly ground black pepper

3 garlic cloves, minced

½ onion, diced

3 cups of low-sodium vegetable broth

3 medium zucchinis, coarsely chopped

pinch of sea salt, plus ½ teaspoon

Directions:

Preheat your oven to 425° Fahrenheit. Line a baking sheet with some parchment paper.

In a mixing bowl, toss your chickpeas with one teaspoon of olive oil, the smoked paprika, and a pinch of sea salt. Transfer your mixture to the baking sheet, then roast until crispy for about 20 minutes, stirring once. Set aside.

In a pot, heat the remaining 1 tablespoon of oil over medium heat.

Add your zucchini, onion, broth, and garlic to the pot and bring to a boil. Lower the heat to simmer, then cook until the onion and zucchini are tender, for about 20 minutes.

In a blender jar, puree your soup, then return it to the pot.

Add the yogurt, and the remaining ½ teaspoon of sea salt, and pepper, then stir well. Serve topped with roasted chickpeas and enjoy!

Nutrition Info: Carbs per serving: 24g

Healthy Chicken Kale Soup

Servings: 6
Cooking Time: 6 Hours 15 Minutes
Ingredients:
2 lb chicken breasts, skinless and boneless
1/4 cup fresh lemon juice
5 oz baby kale
32 oz chicken stock
1/2 cup olive oil
1 large onion, sliced
14 oz chicken broth
1 Tbsp extra-virgin olive oil
Salt
Directions:
Heat the extra-virgin olive oil in a pan over medium heat.
Season chicken with salt and place in the hot pan.
Cover pan and cook chicken for 15 minutes.
Remove chicken from the pan and shred it using forks.
Add shredded chicken to a crock pot.
Add sliced onion, olive oil, and broth to a blender and blend until combined.
Pour blended mixture into the crock pot.
Add remaining ingredients to the crock pot and stir well.
Cover and cook on low for 6 hours.
Stir well and serve.
Nutrition Info: Calories 493 Fat 31.3 g Carbohydrates 5.8 g Sugar 1.9 g Protein 46.7 g Cholesterol 135 mg

Easy Beef Stew

Servings: 6
Cooking Time: 5 Minutes
Ingredients:
1 shredded green cabbage head
4 chopped carrots
2 ½ lbs. non-fat beef brisket
3 chopped garlic cloves
Black pepper
2 bay leaves
4 c. low-sodium beef stock
Directions:
Put the beef brisket in a pot, add stock, pepper, garlic and bay leaves, provide your simmer over medium heat and cook for an hour.
Add carrots and cabbage, stir, cook for a half-hour more, divide into bowls and serve for lunch. Enjoy!
Nutrition Info: Calories: 271, Fat:8 g,Carbs:16 g, Protein:9 g, Sugars:3.4 g, Sodium:760 mg

Chicken Bacon Soup

Servings: 4
Cooking Time: 40 Minutes
Ingredients:
6 boneless, skinless chicken thighs, make cubes
½ cup chopped celery
4 minced garlic cloves
6-ounce mushrooms, sliced
½ cup chopped onion
8-ounce softened cream cheese
¼ cup softened butter
1 teaspoon dried thyme
Salt and (finely ground) black pepper, as per taste preference
2 cups chopped spinach
8 ounces cooked bacon slices, chopped
3 cups (preferably homemade) chicken broth
1 cup heavy cream
Directions:
Arrange Instant Pot over a dry platform in your kitchen. Open its top lid and switch it on.
Add the ingredients except for the cream, spinach, and bacon; gently stir to mix well. Close the lid to create a locked chamber; make sure that safety valve is in locking position. Find and press "SOUP" cooking function; timer to 30 minutes with default "HIGH" pressure mode. Allow the

pressure to build to cook the ingredients. After cooking time is over press "CANCEL" setting. Find and press "NPR" cooking function. This setting is for the natural release of inside pressure and it takes around 10 minutes to slowly release pressure.

Slowly open the lid, stir in cream and spinach.

Take out the cooked in serving plates or serving bowls and enjoy the keto. Top with the bacon.

Nutrition Info: Calories - 456 Fat: 38g Saturated Fat: 13g Trans Fat: 0g Carbohydrates: 7g Fiber: 1g Sodium: 742mg Protein: 23g

Rhubarb Stew

Servings: 3
Cooking Time: 10 Minutes
Ingredients:
1 tsp. grated lemon zest
1 ½ c. coconut sugar
Juice of 1 lemon - 1 ½ c. water
4 ½ c. roughly chopped rhubarbs
Directions:
In a pan, combine the rhubarb while using water, fresh lemon juice, lemon zest and coconut sugar, toss, bring using a simmer over medium heat, cook for 5 minutes, and divide into bowls and serve cold. Enjoy!

Nutrition Info: Calories: 108, Fat:1 g, Carbs:8 g, Protein:5 g, Sugars:2 g, Sodium:0 mg

Buffalo Chicken Soup

Servings: 8
Cooking Time: 30 Minutes
Ingredients:
2 chicken breasts, boneless, skinless, frozen or fresh
1 clove garlic, chopped
¼ cup onion, diced
½ cup celery, diced
2 tbsp butter
1 tbsp ranch dressing mix
3 cups chicken broth
1/3 cup hot sauce
2 cups cheddar cheese, shredded
1 cup heavy cream
Directions:
In the Instant Pot, combine the chicken breasts, garlic, onion, celery, butter, ranch dressing mix, broth, and hot sauce.

Close and lock the lid. Select MANUAL and cook at HIGH pressure for 10 minutes.

Once cooking is complete, let the pressure Release Naturally for10 minutes. Release any remaining steam manually. Uncover the pot.

Transfer the chicken to a plate and shred the meat. Return to the pot.

Add the cheese and heavy cream. Stir well. Let sit for 5 minutes and serve.

Nutrition Info: Calories 303 Fat 27.5 g Carbohydrates 13.8 g Sugar 5 g Protein 4.g Cholesterol 33 mg

Chinese Tofu Soup

Servings: 2
Cooking Time: 10 Minutes
Ingredients:
2 cups chicken stock
1 tbsp soy sauce, sugar-free
2 spring onions, sliced
1 tsp sesame oil, softened
2 eggs, beaten
1-inch piece ginger, grated
Salt and black ground, to taste
½ pound extra-firm tofu, cubed
A handful of fresh cilantro, chopped
Directions:
Boil in a pan over medium heat, soy sauce, chicken stock and sesame oil. Place in eggs as you whisk to incorporate completely. Change heat to low and add salt, spring onions, black pepper and ginger; cook for 5 minutes. Place in tofu and simmer for 1 to 2 minutes.

Divide into soup bowls and serve sprinkled with fresh cilantro.

Nutrition Info: Calories 163; Fat: 10g, Net Carbs: 2.4g, Protein: 14.5g

Healthy Spinach Soup

Servings: 8
Cooking Time: 3 Hours
Ingredients:
3 cups frozen spinach, chopped, thawed and drained
8 oz cheddar cheese, shredded
1 egg, lightly beaten
10 oz can cream of chicken soup
8 oz cream cheese, softened

Directions:
Add spinach to a large bowl. Purée the spinach.
Add egg, chicken soup, cream cheese, and pepper to the spinach purée and mix well.
Transfer spinach mixture to a crock pot.
Cover and cook on low for 3 hours.
Stir in cheddar cheese and serve.
Nutrition Info: Calories 256 Fat 21.9 g Carbohydrates 4.1 g Sugar 0.5 g Protein 11.1 g Cholesterol 84 mg

Cream Of Tomato Soup

Servings: 2
Cooking Time: 15 Minutes
Ingredients:
1lb fresh tomatoes, chopped
1.5 cups low sodium tomato puree
1tbsp black pepper
Directions:
Mix all the ingredients in your Instant Pot.
Cook on Stew for 15 minutes.
Release the pressure naturally.
Blend.
Nutrition Info: Calories: 20; Carbs: 2; Sugar: 1; Fat: 0; Protein: 3; GL: 1

Tasty Basil Tomato Soup

Servings: 6
Cooking Time: 6 Hours
Ingredients:
28 oz can whole peeled tomatoes
1/2 cup fresh basil leaves
4 cups chicken stock
1 tsp red pepper flakes
3 garlic cloves, peeled
2 onions, diced
3 carrots, peeled and diced
3 Tbsp olive oil
1 tsp salt
Directions:
Add all ingredients to a crock pot and stir well.
Cover and cook on low for 6 hours.
Purée the soup until smooth using an immersion blender.
Season soup with pepper and salt.
Serve and enjoy.
Nutrition Info: Calories 126 Fat 7.5 g Carbohydrates 13.3 g Sugar 7 g Protein 2.5 g Cholesterol 0 mg

Fake-on Stew

Servings: 2
Cooking Time: 25 Minutes
Ingredients:
0.5lb soy bacon
1lb chopped vegetables
1 cup low sodium vegetable broth
1tbsp nutritional yeast
Directions:
Mix all the ingredients in your Instant Pot.
Cook on Stew for 25 minutes.
Release the pressure naturally.
Nutrition Info: Calories: 200; Carbs: 12; Sugar: 3; Fat: 7; Protein: 41; GL: 5

Coconut Chicken Soup

Servings: 4
Cooking Time: 18 Minutes
Ingredients:
4 cloves of garlic, minced
1-pound chicken breasts, skin-on
4 cups of water
2 tablespoons olive oil
1 onion, diced
1 cup of coconut milk
(finely ground) black pepper and salt as per taste preference
2 tablespoons sesame oil

Directions:
Arrange Instant Pot over a dry platform in your kitchen. Open its top lid and switch it on.
Find and press "SAUTE" cooking function; add the oil in it and allow it to heat.
In the pot, add the onions, garlic; cook (while stirring) until turns translucent and softened for around 1-2 minutes.
Stir in the chicken breasts; stir, and cook for 2 more minutes.
Pour in water and coconut milk — season to taste.
Close the lid to create a locked chamber; make sure that safety valve is in locking position.
Find and press "MANUAL" cooking function; timer to 15 minutes with default "HIGH" pressure mode.
Allow the pressure to build to cook the ingredients. After cooking time is over press "CANCEL" setting. Find and press "NPR" cooking function.

This setting is for the natural release of inside pressure and it takes around 10 minutes to slowly release pressure.

Slowly open the lid, Drizzle with sesame oil on top. Take out the cooked in serving plates or serving bowls and enjoy the keto.

Nutrition Info: Calories - 328 Fat: 31g Saturated Fat: 6g Trans Fat: 0g Carbohydrates: 6g Fiber: 4g Sodium: 76mg Protein: 21g

Herb Tomato Soup

Servings: 8
Cooking Time: 6 Hours
Ingredients:
55 oz can tomatoes, diced
1/2 onion, minced
2 cups chicken stock
1 cup half and half
4 Tbsp butter
1 bay leaf
1/2 tsp black pepper
1/2 tsp garlic powder
1 tsp oregano
1 tsp dried thyme
1 cup carrots, diced
1/4 tsp black pepper
1/2 tsp salt
Directions:
Add all ingredients to a crock pot and stir well.
Cover and cook on low for 6 hours.
Discard bay leaf and purée the soup using an immersion blender until smooth.
Serve and enjoy.
Nutrition Info: Calories 145 Fat 9.4 g Carbohydrates 13.9 g Sugar 7.9 g Protein 3.2 g Cholesterol 26 mg

Flavorful Broccoli Soup

Servings: 6
Cooking Time: 4 Hours 15 Minutes
Ingredients:
20 oz broccoli florets
4 oz cream cheese
8 oz cheddar cheese, shredded
1/2 tsp paprika
1/2 tsp ground mustard
3 cups chicken stock
2 garlic cloves, chopped
1 onion, diced
1 cup carrots, shredded
1/4 tsp baking soda
1/4 tsp salt
Directions:
Add all ingredients except cream cheese and cheddar cheese to a crock pot and stir well.
Cover and cook on low for 4 hours.
Purée the soup using an immersion blender until smooth.
Stir in the cream cheese and cheddar cheese.
Cover and cook on low for 15 minutes longer.
Season with pepper and salt.
Serve and enjoy.
Nutrition Info: Calories 275 Fat 19.9 g Carbohydrates 11.9 g Sugar 4 g Protein 14.4 g Cholesterol 60 mg

Beef And Cabbage Soup

Servings: 6Cooking Time: 35 Minutes
Ingredients:
2 tbsp coconut oil
1 onion, diced
1 clove garlic, minced
1 lb ground beef
14 oz can diced tomatoes, undrained
4 cups water
Salt and ground black pepper to taste
1 head cabbage, chopped
Directions:
Preheat the Instant Pot by selecting SAUTÉ. Add and heat the oil.
Add the onion and garlic and sauté for 2 minutes.
Add the beef and cook, stirring, for 2-3 minutes until lightly brown.
Pour in the water and tomatoes. Season with salt and pepper, stir well.
Press the CANCEL key to stop the SAUTÉ function.
Close and lock the lid. Select MANUAL and cook at HIGH pressure for 12 minutes.
When the timer goes off, use a Quick Release. Carefully open the lid.
Add the cabbage, select SAUTÉ and simmer for 5 minutes.
Serve.
Nutrition Info: Calories 335 Fat 10 g Carbohydrates 13.6 g Sugar 6 g Protein 4.9 g Cholesterol 33 mg

Shiitake Soup

Servings: 2Cooking Time: 35 Minutes
Ingredients:
1 cup shiitake mushrooms
1 cup diced vegetables
1 cup low sodium vegetable broth
2tbsp 5 spice seasoning
Directions:
Mix all the ingredients in your Instant Pot.
Cook on Stew for 35 minutes.
Release the pressure naturally.
Nutrition Info: Calories: 70; Carbs: 5; Sugar: 1; Fat: 2; Protein: 2; GL: 1

Sausage & Turnip Soup

Servings: 4
Cooking Time: 20 Minutes
Ingredients:
3 turnips, chopped
2 celery sticks, chopped
2 tbsp butter
1 tbsp olive oil
1 pork sausage, sliced
2 cups vegetable broth
½ cup sour cream - 3 green onions, chopped
2 cups water
Salt and black pepper, to taste
Directions:
Sauté the green onions in melted butter over medium heat until soft and golden, about 3-4 minutes. Add celery and turnip, and cook for another 5 minutes. Pour over the vegetable broth and water over.
Bring to a boil, simmer covered, and cook for about 20 minutes until the vegetables are tender. Remove from heat. Puree the soup with a hand blender until smooth. Add sour cream and adjust the seasoning. Warm the olive oil in a skillet. Add the pork sausage andcook for 5 minutes. Serve the soup in deep bowls topped with pork sausage.
Nutrition Info: Calories 275, Fat: 23.1g, Net Carbs: 6.4g, Protein: 7.4g

Simple Chicken Soup

Servings: 4
Cooking Time: 25 Minutes
Ingredients:
2 frozen, boneless chicken breasts

4 medium-sized potatoes, cut into chunks
3 carrots, peeled and cut into chunks
½ big onion, diced
2 cups chicken stock
2 cups water
Salt and ground black pepper to taste
Directions:
In the Instant Pot, combine the chicken breasts, potatoes, carrots, onion, stock, water, salt and pepper to taste.
Close and lock the lid. Select MANUAL and cook at HIGH pressure for 25 minutes.
Once timer goes off, allow to Naturally Release for 10 minutes, and then release any remaining pressure manually. Uncover the pot.
Serve.
Nutrition Info: Calories 301 Fat 27.2 g Carbohydrates 13.6 g Sugar 6 g Protein 4.9 g Cholesterol 33 mg

Black Bean Soup

Servings: 4
Cooking Time: 10 Minutes
Ingredients:
1 tsp. cinnamon powder
32 oz. low-sodium chicken stock
1 chopped yellow onion
1 chopped sweet potato
38 oz. no-salt-added, drained and rinsed canned black beans
2 tsps. organic olive oil
Directions:
Heat up a pot using the oil over medium heat, add onion and cinnamon, stir and cook for 6 minutes. Add black beans, stock and sweet potato, stir, cook for 14 minutes, puree utilizing an immersion blender, divide into bowls and serve for lunch.
Enjoy!
Nutrition Info: Calories: 221, Fat:3 g,Carbs:15 g, Protein:7 g, Sugars:4 g, Sodium:511 mg

Thick Creamy Broccoli Cheese Soup

Servings: 4
Cooking Time: 10 Minutes
Ingredients:
1 tbsp olive oil
2 tbsp peanut butter
¾ cup heavy cream
1 onion, diced

1 garlic, minced
4 cups chopped broccoli
4 cups veggie broth
2 ¾ cups cheddar cheese, grated
¼ cup cheddar cheese to garnish
Salt and black pepper, to taste
½ bunch fresh mint, chopped
Directions:
Warm olive oil and peanut butter in a pot over medium heat. Sauté onion and garlic for 3 minutes or until tender, stirring occasionally. Season with salt and black pepper. Add the broth and broccoli and bring to a boil.
Reduce the heat and simmer for 10 minutes. Puree the soup with a hand blender until smooth. Add in the cheese and cook about 1 minute. Stir in the heavy cream. Serve in bowls with the reserved grated cheddar cheese and sprinkled with fresh mint.
Nutrition Info: Calories 552, Fat: 49.5g, Net Carbs: 6.9g, Protein: 25g

Delicious Chicken Soup

Servings: 4
Cooking Time: 4 Hours 30 Minutes
Ingredients:
1 lb chicken breasts, boneless and skinless
2 Tbsp fresh basil, chopped
1 1/2 cups mozzarella cheese, shredded
2 garlic cloves, minced
1 Tbsp Parmesan cheese, grated
2 Tbsp dried basil
2 cups chicken stock
28 oz tomatoes, diced
1/4 tsp pepper
1/2 tsp salt
Directions:
Add chicken, Parmesan cheese, dried basil, tomatoes, garlic, pepper, and salt to a crock pot and stir well to combine. Cover and cook on low for 4 hours. Add fresh basil and mozzarella cheese and stir well. Cover again and cook for 30 more minutes or until cheese is melted. Remove chicken from the crock pot and shred using forks. Return shredded chicken to the crock pot and stir to mix. Serve and enjoy.
Nutrition Info: Calories 299 Fat 11.6 g Carbohydrates 9.3 g Sugar 5.6 g Protein 38.8 g Cholesterol 108 mg

Chicken And Dill Soup

Servings: 6
Cooking Time: 10 Minutes
Ingredients:
1 c. chopped yellow onion
1 whole chicken
1 lb. sliced carrots
6 c. low-sodium veggie stock
¼ tsp. black pepper and salt
½ c. chopped red onion
2 tsps. chopped dill
Directions:
Put chicken in a pot, add water to pay for, give your boil over medium heat, cook first hour, transfer to a cutting board, discard bones, shred the meat, strain the soup, get it back on the pot, heat it over medium heat and add the chicken.
Also add the carrots, yellow onion, red onion, a pinch of salt, black pepper and also the dill, cook for fifteen minutes, ladle into bowls and serve. Enjoy!
Nutrition Info: Calories: 202, Fat:6 g, Carbs:8 g, Protein:12 g, Sugars:6 g, Sodium:514 mg

Broccoli Stilton Soup

Servings: 2
Cooking Time: 35 Minutes
Ingredients:
1lb chopped broccoli
0.5lb chopped vegetables
1 cup low sodium vegetable broth
1 cup Stilton
Directions:
Mix all the ingredients in your Instant Pot.
Cook on Stew for 35 minutes.
Release the pressure naturally.
Blend the soup.
Nutrition Info: Calories: 280; Carbs: 9; Sugar: 2; Fat: 22; Protein: 13; GL: 4

Creamy Broccoli Cauliflower Soup

Servings: 6
Cooking Time: 6 Hours
Ingredients:
2 cups cauliflower florets, chopped
3 cups broccoli florets, chopped
3 1/2 cups chicken stock
1 large carrot, diced

1/2 cup shallots, diced
2 garlic cloves, minced
1 cup plain yogurt
6 oz cheddar cheese, shredded
1 cup coconut milk - Pepper
Salt
Directions:
Add all ingredients except milk, cheese, and yogurt to a crock pot and stir well.
Cover and cook on low for 6 hours.
Purée the soup using an immersion blender until smooth.
Add cheese, milk, and yogurt and blend until smooth and creamy.
Season with pepper and salt.
Serve and enjoy.
Nutrition Info: Calories 281 Fat 20 g Carbohydrates 14.4 g Sugar 6.9 g Protein 13.1 g Cholesterol 32 mg

Zoodle Won-ton Soup

Servings: 2
Cooking Time: 5 Minutes
Ingredients:
1lb spiralized zucchini
1 pack unfried won-tons
1 cup low sodium beef broth
2tbsp soy sauce
Directions:
Mix all the ingredients in your Instant Pot.
Cook on Stew for 5 minutes.
Release the pressure naturally.
Nutrition Info: Calories: 300; Carbs: 6; Sugar: 1; Fat: 9; Protein: 43; GL: 2

Pumpkin Spice Soup

Servings: 2
Cooking Time: 35 Minutes
Ingredients:
1lb cubed pumpkin
1 cup low sodium vegetable broth
2tbsp mixed spice
Directions:
Mix all the ingredients in your Instant Pot.
Cook on Stew for 35 minutes.
Release the pressure naturally.
Blend the soup.
Nutrition Info: Calories: 100; Carbs: 7; Sugar: 1; Fat: 2; Protein: 3; GL: 1

Kidney Bean Stew

Servings: 2
Cooking Time: 15 Minutes
Ingredients:
1lb cooked kidney beans
1 cup tomato passata
1 cup low sodium beef broth
3tbsp Italian herbs
Directions:
Mix all the ingredients in your Instant Pot.
Cook on Stew for 15 minutes.
Release the pressure naturally.
Nutrition Info: Calories: 270; Carbs: 16; Sugar: 3; Fat: 10; Protein: 23; GL: 8

Cream Zucchini Soup

Servings: 4
Cooking Time: 8 Minutes
Ingredients:
2 cups vegetable stock
2 garlic cloves, crushed
1 tablespoon butter
4 (preferably medium size) zucchinis, peeled and chopped
1 small onion, chopped
2 cups heavy cream
1/2 teaspoon dried oregano, (finely ground)
1/2 teaspoon black pepper, (finely ground)
1 teaspoon dried parsley, (finely ground)
1 teaspoon of sea salt
Lemon juice (optional)
Directions:
Arrange Instant Pot over a dry platform in your kitchen. Open its top lid and switch it on.
Find and press "SAUTE" cooking function; add the butter in it and allow it to melt.
In the pot, add the onions, zucchini, garlic; cook (while stirring) until turns translucent and softened for around 2-3 minutes.
Add the vegetable broth and sprinkle with salt, oregano, pepper, and parsley; gently stir to mix well.
Close the lid to create a locked chamber; make sure that safety valve is in locking position.
Find and press "MANUAL" cooking function; timer to 5 minutes with default "HIGH" pressure mode.
Allow the pressure to build to cook the ingredients.

After cooking time is over press "CANCEL" setting. Find and press "QPR" cooking function. This setting is for quick release of inside pressure. Slowly open the lid, take out the cooked in serving plates or serving bowls, and enjoy the keto . Top with some lemon juice.

Nutrition Info: Calories - 264 Fat: 26g Saturated Fat: 7g Trans Fat: 0g Carbohydrates: 11g Fiber: 3g Sodium: 564mg Protein: 4g

Spinach & Basil Chicken Soup

Servings: 4
Cooking Time: 10 Minutes
Ingredients:
1 cup spinach
2 cups cooked and shredded chicken
4 cups chicken broth
1 cup cheddar cheese, shredded
4 ounces' cream cheese
½ tsp chili powder
½ tsp ground cumin
½ tsp fresh parsley, chopped
Salt and black pepper, to taste
Directions:
In a pot, add the chicken broth and spinach, bring to a boil and cook for 5-8 minutes. Transfer to a food processor, add in the cream cheese and pulse until smooth. Return the mixture to a pot and place over medium heat. Cook until hot, but do not bring to a boil.
Add chicken, chili powder, and cumin and cook for about 3-5 minutes, or until it is heated through.

Stir in cheddar cheese and season with salt and pepper. Serve hot in bowls sprinkled with parsley.
Nutrition Info: Calories 351, Fat: 22.4g, Net Carbs: 4.3g, Protein: 21.6g

Easy Wonton Soup

Servings: 6
Cooking Time: 20 Minutes
Ingredients:
4 sliced scallions
¼ tsp. ground white pepper
2 c. sliced fresh mushrooms
4 minced garlic cloves
6 oz. dry whole-grain yolk-free egg noodles
½ lb. lean ground pork
1 tbsp. minced fresh ginger
8 c. low-sodium chicken broth
Directions:
Place a stockpot over medium heat. Add the ground pork, ginger, and garlic and sauté for 5 minutes. Drain any excess fat, then return to stovetop.
Add the broth and bring to a boil. Once boiling, stir in the mushrooms, noodles, and white pepper. Cover and simmer for 10 minutes.
Remove pot from heat. Stir in the scallions and serve immediately.
Nutrition Info: Calories: 143, Fat:4 g, Carbs:14 g, Protein:12 g, Sugars:0.8 g, Sodium:901 mg

Chapter 7
Meatless Recipes

Harvest Salad

Servings: 6Cooking Time: 25 Minutes
Ingredients:
- 10 oz. kale, deboned and chopped
- 1 ½ cup blackberries
- ½ butternut squash, cubed
- ¼ cup goat cheese, crumbled
- What you'll need from store cupboard:
- Maple Mustard Salad Dressing (chapter 16)
- 1 cup raw pecans
- 1/3 cup raw pumpkin seeds
- ¼ cup dried cranberries
- 3 1/2 tbsp. olive oil
- 1 ½ tbsp. sugar free maple syrup
- 3/8 tsp salt, divided
- Pepper, to taste
- Nonstick cooking spray

Directions:
1. Heat oven to 400 degrees. Spray a baking sheet with cooking spray.
2. Spread squash on the prepared pan, add 1 ½ tablespoons oil, 1/8 teaspoon salt, and pepper to squash and stir to coat the squash evenly. Bake 20-25 minutes.
3. Place kale in a large bowl. Add 2 tablespoons oil and ½ teaspoon salt and massage it into the kale with your hands for 3-4 minutes.
4. Spray a clean baking sheet with cooking spray. In a medium bowl, stir together pecans, pumpkin seeds, and maple syrup until nuts are coated. Pour onto prepared pan and bake 8-10 minutes, these can be baked at the same time as the squash.
5. To assemble the salad: place all of the Ingredients in a large bowl. Pour dressing over and toss to coat. Serve.

Nutrition Info: Calories 436 Total Carbs 24g Net Carbs 17g Protein 9g Fat 37g Sugar 5g Fiber 7g

Spicy Potatoes

Servings: 4
Cooking Time: 30 Minutes
Ingredients:
- 400g potatoes
- 2 tbsp. spicy paprika
- 1 tbsp. olive oil
- cottage cheese
- Salt to taste

Directions:
1. Wash the potatoes with a brush. Unpeeled, cut vertically in a crescent shape, about 1 finger thick Place the potatoes in a bowl and cover with water. Let stand for about half an hour.
2. Preheat the air fryer. Set the timer of 5 minutes and the temperature to 2000C.
3. Drain the water from the potatoes and dry with paper towels or a clean cloth. Put them back in the bowl and pour the oil, salt and paprika over them. Mix well with your hands so that all of them are covered evenly with the spice mixture. Pour the spiced potatoes in the basket of the air fryer. Set the timer for 30 minutes and press the power button. Stir the potatoes in half the time.
4. Remove the potatoes from the air fryer, place on a plate.

Nutrition Info: Calories: 153 Cal Carbs: 2 g Fat: 11 g Protein: 4 g Fiber: 0 g

Buffalo Cauliflower Wings

Servings: 6
Cooking Time: 30 Minutes
Ingredients:
- 1-tablespoon almond flour
- 1 medium head of cauliflower
- 1 ½-teaspoon salt
- 4 tablespoons hot sauce
- 1-tablespoon olive oil

Directions:
1. Switch on the air fryer, insert fryer basket, grease it with olive oil, then shut with its lid, set the fryer at 400 degrees F and preheat for 5minutes.
2. Meanwhile, cut cauliflower into bite-size florets and set aside.
3. Place flour in a large bowl, whisk in salt, oil and hot sauce until combined, add cauliflower florets and toss until combined.
4. Open the fryer, add cauliflower florets in it in a single layer, close with its lid and cook for 15 minutes until nicely golden and crispy, shaking halfway through the frying.
5. When air fryer beeps, open its lid, transfer cauliflower florets onto a serving plate and keep warm.
6. Cook the remaining cauliflower florets in the same manner and serve.

Nutrition Info: Calories: 48 Cal Carbs: 2 g Fat: 11 g Protein: 4 g Fiber: 0.3 g

Asian Noodle Salad

Servings: 4
Ingredients:
- 2 carrots, sliced thin
- 2 radish, sliced thin
- 1 English cucumber, sliced thin
- 1 mango, julienned
- 1 bell pepper, julienned
- 1 small serrano pepper, seeded and sliced thin
- 1 bag tofu Shirataki Fettuccini noodles
- ¼ cup lime juice
- ¼ cup fresh basil, chopped
- ¼ cup fresh cilantro, chopped
- 2 tbsp. fresh mint, chopped
- What you'll need from the store cupboard
- 2 tbsp. rice vinegar

- 2 tbsp. sweet chili sauce
- 2 tbsp. roasted peanuts finely chopped
- 1 tbsp. Splenda
- ½ tsp sesame oil

Directions:
1. Pickle the vegetables: In a large bowl, place radish, cucumbers, and carrots. Add vinegar, coconut sugar, and lime juice and stir tocoat the vegetables. Cover and chill 15 – 20 minutes.
2. Prep the noodles: remove the noodles from the package and rinse under cold water. Cut into smaller pieces. Pat dry with paper towels.
3. To assemble the salad. Remove the vegetables from the marinade, reserving marinade, and place in a large mixing bowl. Add noodles, mango, bell pepper, chili, and herbs.
4. In a small bowl, combine 2 tablespoons marinade with the chili sauce and sesame oil. Pour over salad and toss to coat. Top with peanuts and serve.

Nutrition Info: Calories 158 Total Carbs 30g Net Carbs 24g Protein 4g Fat 4g Sugar 19g Fiber 6g

Cheesy Mushroom And Pesto Flatbreads

Servings: 2
Cooking Time: 13 To 17 Minutes
Ingredients:
- 1 teaspoon extra-virgin olive oil
- ½ red onion, sliced
- ½ cup sliced mushrooms
- Salt and freshly ground black pepper, to taste
- ¼ cup store-bought pesto sauce
- 2 whole-wheat flatbreads
- ¼ cup shredded Mozzarella cheese

Directions:
1. Preheat the oven to 350°F (180°C).
2. Heat the olive oil in a small skillet over medium heat. Add the onion slices and mushrooms to the skillet, and sauté for 3 to 5 minutes, stirring occasionally, or until they start to soften. Season with salt and pepper.
3. Meanwhile, spoon 2 tablespoons of pesto sauce onto each flatbread and spread it all over. Evenly divide the mushroom mixture between two flatbreads, then scatter each top with 2 tablespoons of shredded cheese.

4. Transfer the flatbreads to a baking sheet and bake until the cheese melts and bubbles, about 10 to 12 minutes.

5. Let the flatbreads cool for 5 minutes and serve warm.

Nutrition Info: calories: 346 fat: 22.8g protein: 14.2g carbs:27.6g fiber: 7.3g sugar: 4.0g sodium: 790mg

Honey Roasted Carrots

Servings: 2-4
Cooking Time: 12 Minutes
Ingredients:
- 454g of rainbow carrots, peeled and washed
- 15 ml of olive oil
- 30 ml honey
- 2 sprigs of fresh thyme
- Salt and pepper to taste

Directions:
1. Wash the carrots and dry them with a paper towel. Leave aside.
2. Preheat the air fryer for a few minutes an 1800C.
3. Place the carrots in a bowl with olive oil, honey, thyme, salt, and pepper. Place the carrots in the air fryer at 1800C for 12 minutes. Be sure to shake the baskets in the middle of cooking.

Nutrition Info: Calories: 123Fat: 42g Carbohydrate: 9g Protein: 1g

Mushrooms Stuffed With Tomato

Servings: 4
Cooking Time: 50 Minutes
Ingredients:
- 8 large mushrooms
- 250g of minced meat
- 4 cloves of garlic
- Extra virgin olive oil
- Salt
- Ground pepper
- Flour, beaten egg and breadcrumbs
- Frying oil
- Fried Tomato Sauce

Directions:
1. Remove the stem from the mushrooms and chop it. Peel the garlic and chop. Put some extra virgin olive oil in a pan and add the garlic and mushroom stems.
2. Sauté and add the minced meat. Sauté well until the meat is wellcooked and season.
3. Fill the mushrooms with the minced meat.
4. Press well and take the freezer for 30 minutes.
5. Pass the mushrooms with flour, beaten egg and breadcrumbs. Beaten egg and breadcrumbs.
6. Place the mushrooms in the basket of the air fryer.
7. Select 20 minutes, 1800C.
8. Distribute the mushrooms once cooked in the dishes.
9. Heat the tomato sauce and cover the stuffed mushrooms.

Nutrition Info: Calories: 160 Cal Carbs: 2 g Fat: 11 g Protein: 4 g Fiber: 0 g

Cheesy Summer Squash And Quinoa Casserole

Servings: 8
Cooking Time: 27 To 30 Minutes
Ingredients:
- 1 tablespoon extra-virgin olive oil
- 1 Vidalia onion, thinly sliced
- 1 large portobello mushroom, thinly sliced
- 6 yellow summer squash, thinly sliced
- 1 cup shredded Parmesan cheese, divided
- 1 cup shredded Cheddar cheese
- ½ cup tri-color quinoa
- ½ cup whole-wheat bread crumbs
- 1 tablespoon Creole seasoning

Directions:
1. Preheat the oven to 350°F (180°C).
2. Heat the olive oil in a large cast iron pan over medium heat.
3. Sauté the onion, mushroom, and squash in the oil for 7 to 10 minutes, stirring occasionally, or until the vegetables are softened.
4. Remove from the heat and add ½ cup of Parmesan cheese and the Cheddar cheese to the vegetables. Stir well.
5. Mix together the quinoa, bread crumbs, the remaining Parmesan cheese, Creole seasoning in a small bowl, then scatter the mixture over the vegetables.

6. Place the cast iron pan in the preheated oven and bake until browned and cooked through, about 20 minutes.Cool for 10 minutes and serve on plates while warm.

Nutrition Info: calories: 184 fat: 8.9g protein: 11.7g carbs: 17.6g fiber: 3.2g sugar: 3.8g sodium: 140mg

Eggplant Parmesan

Servings: 4Cooking Time: 15 Minutes
Ingredients:

- 1/2 cup and 3 tablespoons almond flour, divided
- 1.25-pound eggplant, ½-inch sliced
- One tablespoon chopped parsley
- 1 teaspoon Italian seasoning
- 2 teaspoons salt
- 1-cup marinara sauce
- 1 egg, pastured
- 1-tablespoon water
- 3 tablespoons grated parmesan cheese, reduced-fat
- 1/4 cup grated mozzarella cheese, reduced-fat

Directions:

1. Slice the eggplant into ½-inch pieces, place them in a colander, sprinkle with 1 ½-teaspoon salt on both sides and let it rest for 15 minutes.
2. Meanwhile, place ½-cup flour in a bowl, add egg and water and whisk until blended.
3. Place remaining flour in a shallow dish, add remaining salt, Italian seasoning, and parmesan cheese and stir until mixed.
4. Switch on the air fryer, insert fryer basket, grease it with olive oil, then shut with its lid, set the fryer at 360 degrees F and preheat for 5 minutes.
5. Meanwhile, drain the eggplant pieces, pat them dry, and then dip each slice into the egg mixture and coat with flour mixture.
6. Open the fryer; add coated eggplant slices in it in a single layer, close with its lid and cook for 8 minutes until nicely golden and cooked, flipping the eggplant slices halfway through the frying.
7. Then top each eggplant slice with a tablespoon of marinara sauce and some of the mozzarella cheese and continue air frying for 1 to 2 minutes or until cheese has melted.
8. When air fryer beeps, open its lid, transfer eggplants onto a serving plate and keep them

warm.Cook remaining eggplant slices in the same manner and serve.

Nutrition Info: Calories: 123 Cal Carbs: 2 g Fat: 11 g Protein: 4 g Fiber: 6 g

Sweet Potato Salt And Pepper

Servings: 4Cooking Time: 20 Minutes
Ingredients:

- 1 large sweet potato
- Extra virgin olive oil
- Salt
- Ground pepper

Directions:

1. Peel the sweet potato and cut into thin strips, if you have a mandolin it will be easier for you.
2. Wash well and put salt.
3. Add a little oil to impregnate the sweet potato in strips and place in the air fryer basket.
4. Select 1800C, 30 minutes or so. From time to time, shake the basket so that the sweet potato moves.Pass to a tray or plate and sprinkle with fine salt and ground pepper.

Nutrition Info: Calories: 107 Fat: 0.6g Carbohydrates: 24.19g Protein: 1.61g Sugar: 5.95g Cholesterol: 0mg

Simple Sautéed Greens

Servings: 4
Cooking Time: 10 Minutes
Ingredients:

- 2 tablespoons extra-virgin olive oil
- 1 pound (454 g) Swiss chard, coarse stems removed and leaves chopped
- 1 pound (454 g) kale, coarse stems removed and leaves chopped
- ½ teaspoon ground cardamom
- 1 tablespoon freshly squeezed lemon juice
- Sea salt and freshly ground black pepper, to taste

Directions:

1. Heat the olive oil in a large skillet over medium-high heat.
2. Add the Swiss chard, kale, cardamon, and lemon juice to the skillet, and stir to combine. Cook for about 10 minutes, stirring continuously, or until the greens are wilted.

3.	Sprinkle with the salt and pepper and stir well.
4.	Serve the greens on a plate while warm.
Nutrition Info: calories: 139 fat: 6.8g protein: 5.9g carbs: 15.8g fiber: 3.9g sugar: 1.0g sodium: 350mg

Sweet Potato Chips

Servings: 4
Cooking Time: 10 Minutes
Ingredients:
- 2 large sweet potatoes, cut into strips 25 mm thick
- 15 ml of oil
- 10g of salt
- 2g black pepper
- 2g of paprika
- 2g garlic powder
- 2g onion powder

Directions:
1.	Cut the sweet potatoes into strips 25 mm thick.
2.	Preheat the air fryer for a few minutes.
3.	Add the cut sweet potatoes in a large bowl and mix with the oil until the potatoes are all evenly coated.
4.	Sprinkle salt, black pepper, paprika, garlic powder and onion powder. Mix well.
5.	Place the French fries in the preheated baskets and cook for 10 minutes at 205°C. Be sure to shake the baskets halfway through cooking.
Nutrition Info: Calories: 123 Cal Carbs: 2 g Fat: 11 g Protein: 4 g Fiber: 0 g

Chili Relleno Casserole

Servings: 8
Cooking Time: 35 Minutes
Ingredients:
- 3 eggs
- 1 cup Monterey jack pepper cheese, grated
- 3⁄4 cup half-n-half
- ½ cup cheddar cheese, grated
- What you'll need from store cupboard:
- 2 (7 oz.) cans whole green chilies, drain well
- ½ tsp salt
- Nonstick cooking spray

Directions:
1.	Heat oven to 350 degrees. Spray an 8-inch baking pan with cooking spray.

2.	Slice each chili down one long side and lay flat. Arrange half the chilies in the prepared baking pan, skin side down, in single layer.
3.	Sprinkle with the pepper cheese and top with remaining chilies, skin side up.
4.	In a small bowl, beat eggs, salt, and half-n-half. Pour over chilies. Top with cheddar cheese.
5.	Bake 35 minutes, or until top is golden brown. Let rest 10 minutes before serving.
Nutrition Info: Calories 295 Total Carbs 36g Net Carbs 22g Protein 13g Fat 13g Sugar 21g Fiber 14g

Cauliflower Rice

Servings: 3 Cooking Time: 27 Minutes
Ingredients:
- 1 cup diced carrot
- 6 ounces tofu, extra-firm, drained
- 1/2 cup diced white onion
- 2 tablespoons soy sauce
- 1-teaspoon turmeric - For the Cauliflower:
- 1/2 cup chopped broccoli
- 3 cups cauliflower rice
- 1 tablespoon minced garlic
- 1/2 cup frozen peas
- 1 tablespoon minced ginger
- 2 tablespoons soy sauce
- 1-tablespoon apple cider vinegar
- 1 1/2 teaspoons toasted sesame oil

Directions:
1.	Switch on the air fryer, insert fryer pan, grease it with olive oil, then shut with its lid, set the fryer at 370 degrees F and preheat for 5 minutes.
2.	Meanwhile, place tofu in a bowl, crumble it, then add remaining ingredients and stir until mixed.
3.	Open the fryer, add tofu mixture in it, and spray with oil, close with its lid and cook for 10 minutes until nicely golden and crispy, stirring halfway through the frying.
4.	Meanwhile, place all the ingredients for cauliflower in a bowl and toss until mixed.
5.	When air fryer beeps, open its lid, add cauliflower mixture, shake the pan gently to mix and continue cooking for 12 minutes, shaking halfway through the frying.
Nutrition Info: Calories: 258 Cal Carbs: 2 g Fat: 11 g Protein: 4 g Fiber: 7 g

Autumn Slaw

Servings: 8
Cooking Time: 2 Hours
Ingredients:

- 10 cup cabbage, shredded
- ½ red onion, diced fine
- ¾ cup fresh Italian parsley, chopped
- What you'll need from store cupboard:
- ¾ cup almonds, slice & toasted
- ¾ cup dried cranberries
- 1/3 cup vegetable oil
- ¼ cup apple cider vinegar
- 2 tbsp. sugar free maple syrup
- 4 tsp Dijon mustard
- ½ teaspoon salt
- Salt & pepper, to taste

Directions:

1. In a large bowl, whisk together vinegar, oil, syrup, Dijon, and ½ teaspoon salt. Add the onion and stir to combine. Let rest 10 minutes, or cover and refrigerate until ready to use.
2. After 10 minutes, add remaining Ingredients to the dressing mixture and toss to coat. Taste and season with salt and pepper if needed. Cover and chill 2 hours before serving.

Nutrition Info: Calories 133 Total Carbs 12g net Carbs 8g Protein 2g Fat 9g Sugar 5g Fiber 4g

Pizza Stuffed Portobello's

Servings: 4
Cooking Time: 10 Minutes
Ingredients:

- 8 Portobello mushrooms, stems removed
- 1 cup mozzarella cheese, grated
- 1 cup cherry tomatoes, sliced
- ½ cup crushed tomatoes
- ½ cup fresh basil, chopped
- What you'll need from store cupboard:
- 2 tbsp. balsamic vinegar
- 1 tbsp. olive oil
- 1 tbsp. oregano
- 1 tbsp. red pepper flakes
- ½ tbsp. garlic powder
- ¼ tsp pepper
- Pinch salt

Directions:

1. Heat oven to broil. Line a baking sheet with foil.
2. Place mushrooms, stem side down, on foil and drizzle with oil. Sprinkle with garlic powder, salt and pepper. Broil for 5 minutes.
3. Flip mushrooms over and top with crushed tomatoes, oregano, parsley, pepper flakes, cheese and sliced tomatoes. Broil another 5 minutes.
4. Top with basil and drizzle with balsamic. Serve.

Nutrition Info:Calories 113 Total Carbs 11g Net Carbs 7g Protein 9g Fat 5g Sugar 3g Fiber 4g

Cajun Style French Fries

Servings: 4
Cooking Time: 28 Minutes
Ingredients:

- 2 reddish potatoes, peeled and cut into strips of 76 x 25 mm
- 1 liter of cold water
- 15 ml of oil
- 7g of Cajun seasoning
- 1g cayenne pepper
- Tomato sauce or ranch sauce, to serve

Directions:

1. Cut the potatoes into 76 x 25 mm strips and soak them in water for 15 minutes.
2. Drain the potatoes, rinse with cold, dry water with paper towels.
3. Preheat the air fryer, set it to 195°C.
4. Add oil and spices to the potatoes, until they are completely covered.
5. Add the potatoes to the preheated air fryer and set the timer to 28 minutes.
6. Be sure to shake the baskets in the middle of cooking. Remove the baskets from the air fryer when you have finished cooking and season the fries with salt and pepper.

Nutrition Info: Calories: 158 Cal Carbs: 2 g Fat: 11 g Protein: 4 g Fiber: 0 g

Avocado & Citrus Shrimp Salad

Servings: 4
Cooking Time: 5 Minutes
Ingredients:

- 1 lb. medium shrimp, peeled and deveined, remove tails

- 8 cup salad greens
- 1 lemon
- 1 avocado, diced
- 1 shallot, diced fine
- What you'll need from store cupboard:
- ½ cup almonds, sliced and toasted
- 1 tbsp. olive oil
- Salt and freshly ground black pepper

Directions:
1. Cut the lemon in half and squeeze the juice, from both halves, into a small bowl, set aside. Slice the lemon into thin wedges.
2. Heat the oil in a skillet over medium heat. Add lemon wedges and let cook, about 1 minute, to infuse the oil with the lemons.
3. Add the shrimp and cook, stirring frequently, until shrimp turn pink. Discard the lemon wedges and let cool.
4. Place the salad greens in a large bowl. Add the shrimp, with the juices from the pan, and toss to coat. Add remaining Ingredients and toss to combine. Serve.

Nutrition Info: Calories 425 Total Carbs 17 Net Carbs 8g Protein 35 Fat 26 Sugar 2 Fiber 9

Florentine Pizza

Servings: 2
Cooking Time: 20 Minutes
Ingredients:
- 1 3/4 cup grated mozzarella cheese
- ½ cup frozen spinach, thaw
- 1 egg
- 2 tbsp. reduced fat parmesan cheese, grated
- 2 tbsp. cream cheese, soft
- What you'll need from the store cupboard
- ¾ cup almond flour
- ¼ cup light Alfredo sauce
- ½ tsp Italian seasoning
- ¼ tsp red pepper flakes
- Pinch of salt

Directions:
1. Heat oven to 400 degrees.
2. Squeeze all the excess water out of the spinach.
3. In a glass bowl, combine mozzarella and almond flour. Stir in cream cheese. Microwave 1 minute on high, then stir. If the mixture is not melted, microwave another 30 seconds.
4. Stir in the egg, seasoning, and salt. Mix well. Place dough on a piece of parchment paper and press into a 10-inch circle.
5. Place directly on the oven rack and bake 8-10 minutes or until lightly browned.
6. Remove the crust and spread with the Alfredo sauce, then add spinach, parmesan and red pepper flakes evenly over top. Bake another 8-10 minutes. Slice and serve.

Nutrition Info: Calories 441 Total Carbs 14g Net Carbs 9g Protein 24g Fat 35g Sugar 4g Fiber 5g

Vegetables In Air Fryer

Servings: 2
Cooking Time: 30 Minutes
Ingredients:
- 2 potatoes
- 1 zucchini
- 1 onion
- 1 red pepper
- 1 green pepper

Directions:
1. Cut the potatoes into slices.
2. Cut the onion into rings.
3. Cut the zucchini slices
4. Cut the peppers into strips.
5. Put all the ingredients in the bowl and add a little salt, ground pepper and some extra virgin olive oil.
6. Mix well.
7. Pass to the basket of the air fryer.
8. Select 1600C, 30 minutes.
9. Check that the vegetables are to your liking.

Nutrition Info: Calories: 135Cal Carbs: 2 g Fat: 11 g Protein: 4 g Fiber: 05g

Tofu Bento

Servings: 4
Cooking Time: 10 Minutes
Ingredients:
- 1 pkg. extra firm tofu
- 1 red bell pepper, sliced
- 1 orange bell pepper, sliced
- 2 cup cauliflower rice, cooked
- 2 cups broccoli, chopped

- ¼ cup green onion, sliced
- What you'll need from store cupboard:
- 2 tbsp. low-sodium soy sauce
- 1 tbsp. olive oil
- 1 tsp ginger, 1 tsp garlic powder
- 1 tsp onion powder
- 1 tsp chili paste

Directions:
1. Remove tofu from package and press with paper towels to absorb all excess moisture, let set for 15 minutes.
2. Chop tofu into cubes. Add tofu and seasonings to a large Ziploc bag and shake to coat.
3. Heat oil in a large skillet over medium heat. Add tofu and vegetables and cook, stirring frequently, 5-8 minutes, until tofu is browned on all sides and vegetables are tender.
4. To serve, place ½ cup cauliflower rice on 4 plates and top evenly with tofu mixture.

Nutrition Info: Calories 93 Total Carbs 12g Net Carbs 8g Protein 7g Fat 3g Sugar 5g Fiber 4g

Tofu In Peanut Sauce

Servings: 4 Cooking Time: 1 Hour 25 Minutes
Ingredients:
- 1 pkg. extra firm tofu, pressed 15 minutes and cut into cubes
- 1 pkg. fresh baby spinach
- 2 limes
- 1 tbsp. margarine
- What you'll need from store cupboard:
- ½ cup raw peanut butter
- 2 tbsp. lite soy sauce
- 3 cloves garlic, chopped fine
- ½ tsp ginger
- ¼ tsp red pepper flakes

Directions:
1. Melt margarine in a large saucepan. Add tofu and garlic and cook, stirring occasionally, 5-10 minutes, or until tofu starts to brown.
2. Add remaining Ingredients, except spinach and bring to simmer. Reduce heat, cover and cook, stirring occasionally 30-35 minutes.
3. Stir in the spinach and cook 15 minutes more. Serve.

Nutrition Info: Calories 325 Total Carbs 15g Net Carbs 10g Protein 18g Fat 24g Sugar 5g Fiber 5g

Mexican Scrambled Eggs & Greens

Servings: 4
Cooking Time: 5 Minutes
Ingredients:
- 8 egg whites
- 4 egg yolks
- 3 tomatoes, cut in ½-inch pieces
- 1 jalapeno pepper, slice thin
- ½ avocado, cut in ½-inch pieces
- ½ red onion, diced fine
- ½ head Romaine lettuce, torn
- ½ cup cilantro, chopped
- 2 tbsp. fresh lime juice
- What you'll need from store cupboard:
- 12 tortilla chips, (chapter 5), broken into small pieces
- 2 tbsp. water
- 1 tbsp. olive oil
- ¾ tsp pepper, divided
- ½ tsp salt, divided

Directions:
1. In a medium bowl, combine tomatoes, avocado, onion, jalapeno, cilantro, lime juice, ¼ teaspoon salt, and ¼ teaspoon pepper.
2. In a large bowl, whisk egg whites, egg yolks, water, and remaining salt and pepper. Stir in tortilla chips.
3. Heat oil in a large skillet over medium heat. Add egg mixture and cook, stirring frequently, 3-5 minutes, or desired doneness.
4. To serve, divide lettuce leaves among 4 plates. Add scrambled egg mixture and top with salsa.

Nutrition Info: Calories 280 Total Carbs 10g Net Carbs 6g Protein 15g Fat 21g Sugar 4g Fiber 4g

Sweet Potato Cauliflower Patties

Servings: 7
Cooking Time: 40 Minutes
Ingredients:
- 1 green onion, chopped
- 1 large sweet potato, peeled
- 1 teaspoon minced garlic
- 1-cup cilantro leaves
- 2-cup cauliflower florets
- ¼-teaspoon ground black pepper

- 1/4 teaspoon salt
- 1/4 cup sunflower seeds
- 1/4 teaspoon cumin
- 1/4 cup ground flaxseed
- 1/2 teaspoon red chili powder
- 2 tablespoons ranch seasoning mix
- 2 tablespoons arrowroot starch

Directions:

1. Cut peeled sweet potato into small pieces, and then place them in a food processor and pulse until pieces are broken up.

2. Then add onion, cauliflower florets, and garlic, pulse until combined, add remaining ingredients and pulse more until incorporated.

3. Tip the mixture in a bowl, shape the mixture into seven 1 ½ inch thick patties, each about ¼ cup, then place them on a baking sheet and freeze for 10 minutes.

4. Switch on the air fryer, insert fryer basket, grease it with olive oil, then shut with its lid, set the fryer at 400 degrees F and preheat for 10 minutes.

5. Open the fryer, add patties in it in a single layer, close with its lidand cook for 20 minutes until nicely golden and cooked, flipping the patties halfway through the frying.

6. When air fryer beeps, open its lid, transfer patties onto a serving plate and keep them warm.

7. Cook the remaining patties in the same manner and serve.

Nutrition Info: Calories: 85Cal Carbs: 2 g Fat: 11 g Protein: 4 g Fiber: 5 g

Healthy Taco Salad

Servings: 4
Cooking Time: 10 Minutes
Ingredients:

- 2 whole Romaine hearts, chopped
- 1 lb. lean ground beef
- 1 whole avocado, cubed
- 3 oz. grape tomatoes, halved
- ½ cup cheddar cheese, cubed
- 2 tbsp. sliced red onion
- What you'll need from the store cupboard
- 1/2 batch Tangy Mexican Salad Dressing (chapter 16)
- 1 tsp ground cumin
- Salt and pepper to taste

Directions:

1. Cook ground beef in a skillet over medium heat. Break the beef up into little pieces as it cooks. Add seasonings and stir to combine. Drain grease and let cool for about 5 minutes.

2. To assemble the salad, place all Ingredients into a large bowl. Toss to mix then add dressing and toss. Top with reduced-fat sour cream and/or salsa if desired.

Nutrition Info: Calories 449 Total Carbs 9g Net Carbs 4g Protein 40g Fat 22g Sugar 3g Fiber 5g

Wilted Dandelion Greens With Sweet Onion

Servings: 4
Cooking Time: 12 Minutes
Ingredients:

- 1 tablespoon extra-virgin olive oil
- 1 Vidalia onion, thinly sliced
- 2 garlic cloves, minced
- 2 bunches dandelion greens, roughly chopped
- ½ cup low-sodium vegetable broth
- Freshly ground black pepper, to taste

Directions:

1. Heat the olive oil in a large skillet over low heat.

2. Cook the onion and garlic for 2 to 3 minutes until tender, stirring occasionally.

3. Add the dandelion greens and broth and cook for 5 to 7 minutes, stirring frequently, or until the greens are wilted.

4. Transfer to a plate and season with black pepper. Serve warm.

Nutrition Info: calories: 81 fat: 3.8g protein: 3.1g carbs: 10.7g fiber: 3.8g sugar: 2.0g sodium: 72mg

Asian Fried Eggplant

Servings: 4
Cooking Time: 40 Minutes
Ingredients:

- 1 large eggplant, sliced into fourths
- 3 green onions, diced, green tips only
- 1 tsp fresh ginger, peeled & diced fine
- What you'll need from store cupboard:
- ¼ cup + 1 tsp cornstarch
- 1 ½ tbsp. soy sauce
- 1 ½ tbsp. sesame oil

- 1 tbsp. vegetable oil
- 1 tbsp. fish sauce
- 2 tsp Splenda
- ¼ tsp salt

Directions:

1. Place eggplant on paper towels and sprinkle both sides with salt. Let for 1 hour to remove excess moisture. Pat dry with more paper towels.
2. In a small bowl, whisk together soy sauce, sesame oil, fish sauce, Splenda, and 1 teaspoon cornstarch.
3. Coat both sides of the eggplant with the ¼ cup cornstarch, usemore if needed.
4. Heat oil in a large skillet, over med-high heat. Add ½ the ginger and 1 green onion, then lay 2 slices of eggplant on top. Use ½ the sauce mixture to lightly coat both sides of the eggplant. Cook 8-10 minutes per side. Repeat.
5. Serve garnished with remaining green onions.

Nutrition Info: Calories 155 Total Carbs 18g Net Carbs 13g Protein 2g Fat 9g Sugar 6g Fiber 5g

Chicken Guacamole Salad

Servings: 6
Cooking Time: 20 Minutes
Ingredients:

- 1 lb. chicken breast, boneless & skinless
- 2 avocados
- 1-2 jalapeno peppers, seeded & diced
- 1/3 cup onion, diced
- 3 tbsp. cilantro, diced
- 2 tbsp. fresh lime juice
- What you'll need from store cupboard:
- 2 cloves garlic, diced
- 1 tbsp. olive oil
- Salt & pepper, to taste

Directions:

1. Heat oven to 400 degrees. Line a baking sheet with foil.
2. Season chicken with salt and pepper and place on prepared pan. Bake 20 minutes, or until chicken is cooked through. Let cool completely.
3. Once chicken has cooled, shred or dice and add to a large bowl. Add remaining Ingredients and mix well, mashing the avocado as you mix it in.

Taste and season with salt and pepper as desired. Serve immediately.

Nutrition Info: Calories 324 Total Carbs 12g Net Carbs 5g Protein 23g Fat 22g Sugar 1g Fiber 7g

Warm Portobello Salad

Servings: 4
Cooking Time: 10 Minutes
Ingredients:

- 6 cup mixed salad greens
- 1 cup Portobello mushrooms, sliced
- 1 green onion, sliced
- What you'll need from store cupboard:
- Walnut or Warm Bacon Vinaigrette (chapter 16)
- 1 tbsp. olive oil
- 1/8 tsp ground black pepper

Directions:

1. Heat oil in a nonstick skillet over med-high heat. Add mushrooms and cook, stirring occasionally, 10 minutes, or until they are tender. Stir in onions and reduce heat to low.
2. Place salad greens on serving plates, top with mushrooms and sprinkle with pepper. Drizzle lightly with your choice of vinaigrette.

Nutrition Info: Calories 81 Total Carbs 9g Protein 4g Fat 4g Sugar 0g Fiber 0g

Layered Salad

Servings: 10
Cooking Time:
Ingredients:

- 6 slices bacon, chopped and cooked crisp
- 2 tomatoes, diced - 2 stalks celery, sliced
- 1 head romaine lettuce, diced
- 1 red bell pepper, diced
- 1 cup frozen peas, thawed
- 1 cup sharp cheddar cheese, grated
- 1/4 cup red onion, diced fine
- What you'll need from the store cupboard
- 1 cup fat-free ranch dressing

Directions:

1. Use a 9x13- inch glass baking dish and layer half the lettuce, pepper, celery, tomatoes, peas, onion, cheese, bacon, and dressing. Repeat. Serve or cover and chill until ready to serve.

Nutrition Info: Calories 130 Total Carbs 14g Net Carbs 12g Protein6g Fat 6g Sugar 5g Fiber 2g

Hassel Back Potatoes

Servings: 2
Cooking Time: 40 Minutes
Ingredients:
- 4 medium reddish potatoes washed and drained
- 30 ml of olive oil
- 12g of salt
- 1g black pepper
- 1g garlic powder
- 28g melted butter
- 8g parsley, freshly chopped, to decorate

Directions:
1.   Wash and scrub potatoes. Let them dry with a paper towel.
2.   Cut the slits, 6 mm away, on the potatoes, stopping before you cut them completely, so that all the slices are connected approximately 13 mm at the bottom of the potato.
3.   Preheat the air fryer for 6 minutes, set it to 175°C.
4.   Cover the potatoes with olive oil and season evenly with salt, black pepper, and garlic powder.
5.   Add the potatoes in the air fryer and cook for 30 minutes at 175°C.
6.   Brush the melted butter over the potatoes and cook for another 10 minutes at 175 ° C.
7.   Garnish with freshly chopped parsley.
Nutrition Info: Calories: 415 Fat: 42g Carbohydrate: 9g Protein: 1g

Baked "potato" Salad

Servings: 8
Cooking Time: 15 Minutes
Ingredients:
- 2 lb. cauliflower, separated into small florets
- 6-8 slices bacon, chopped and fried crisp
- 6 boiled eggs, cooled, peeled, and chopped
- 1 cup sharp cheddar cheese, grated
- ½ cup green onion, sliced
- What you'll need from the store cupboard
- 1 cup reduced-fat mayonnaise
- 2 tsp yellow mustard
- 1 ½ tsp onion powder, divided
- Salt and fresh-ground black pepper to taste

Directions:
1.   Place cauliflower in a vegetable steamer, or a pot with a steamer insert, and steam 5-6 minutes.
2.   Drain the cauliflower and set aside.
3.   In a small bowl, whisk together mayonnaise, mustard, 1 teaspoon onion powder, salt, and pepper.
4.   Pat cauliflower dry with paper towels and place in a large mixing bowl. Add eggs, salt, pepper, remaining ½ teaspoon onion powder, then dressing. Mix gently to combine Ingredients together.
5.   Fold in the bacon, cheese, and green onion. Serve warm or cover and chill before serving.
Nutrition Info: Calories 247 Total Carbs 8g Net Carbs 5g Protein 17g Fat 17g Sugar 3g Fiber 3g

Butternut Noodles With Mushroom Sauce

Servings: 4
Cooking Time: 15 Minutes
Ingredients:
- ¼ cup extra-virgin olive oil
- ½ red onion, finely chopped
- 1 pound (454 g) cremini mushrooms, sliced
- 1 teaspoon dried thyme
- ½ teaspoon sea salt
- 3 garlic cloves, minced
- ½ cup dry white wine
- Pinch red pepper flakes
- 4 cups butternut noodles
- 4 ounces (113 g) Parmesan cheese, grated (optional)

Directions:
1.   Heat the olive oil in a large skillet over medium-high heat until shimmering.
2.   Add the onion, mushrooms, thyme, and salt to the skillet. Sauté for 6 minutes, stirring occasionally, or until the mushrooms begin to brown.
3.   Stir in the garlic and cook for 30 seconds until fragrant.
4.   Fold in the wine and red pepper flakes and whisk to combine.
5.   Add the butternut noodles to the skillet and continue cooking for 5 minutes, stirring occasionally, or until the noodles are softened.

6. Divide the mixture among four bowls. Sprinkle the grated Parmesan cheese on top, if desired.

Nutrition Info: calories: 243 fat: 14.2g protein: 3.7g carbs: 21.9g fiber: 4.1g sugar: 2.1g sodium: 157mg

Caprese Salad

Servings: 4
Cooking Time: 10 Minutes
Ingredients:

- 3 medium tomatoes, cut into 8 slices
- 2 (1-oz.) slices mozzarella cheese, cut into strips
- ¼ cup fresh basil, sliced thin
- What you'll need from store cupboard:
- 2 tsp extra-virgin olive oil
- 1/8 tsp salt
- Pinch black pepper

Directions:

1. Place tomatoes and cheese on serving plates. Sprinkle with salt and pepper. Drizzle oil over and top with basil. Serve.

Nutrition Info: Calories 77 Total Carbs 4g Protein 5g Fat 5g Sugar 2g Fiber 1g

Asparagus Avocado Soup

Servings: 4
Cooking Time: 20 Minutes
Ingredients:

- 1 avocado, peeled, pitted, cubed
- 12 ounces asparagus
- ½-teaspoon ground black pepper
- 1-teaspoon garlic powder
- 1-teaspoon sea salt
- 2 tablespoons olive oil, divided
- 1/2 of a lemon, juiced
- 2 cups vegetable stock

Directions:

1. Switch on the air fryer, insert fryer basket, grease it with olive oil, then shut with its lid, set the fryer at 425 degrees F and preheat for 5 minutes.
2. Meanwhile, place asparagus in a shallow dish, drizzle with 1-tablespoon oil, sprinkle with garlic powder, salt, and black pepper and toss until well mixed. Open the fryer, add asparagus in it, close with its lid and cook for 10 minutes until nicely golden and roasted, shaking halfway through the frying. When air fryer beeps, open its lid and

transfer asparagus to a food processor. Add remaining ingredients into a food processor and pulse until well combined and smooth. Tip the soup in a saucepan, pour in water if the soup is too thick and heat it over medium-low heat for 5 minutes until thoroughly heated. Ladle soup into bowls and serve.

Nutrition Info: Calories: 208 Cal Carbs: 2 g Fat: 11 g Protein: 4 g Fiber: 5 g

Roasted Broccoli With Garlic

Servings: 3
Cooking Time: 10 Minutes
Ingredients:

- 1 large broccoli cut 5
- 15 ml of olive oil - 3g garlic powder
- 3g of salt - 1g black pepper

Directions:

1. Preheat the air fryer for 5 minutes. Set it to 150°C.
2. Sprinkle the broccoli pieces with olive oil and mix them untilthey are well covered.
3. Mix broccoli with seasonings.
4. Add the broccoli to the preheated air fryer at 1500C for 5 minutes.

Nutrition Info: Calories: 278Fat: 4.2g Carbohydrate: 9g Protein: 1g

Roasted Asparagus And Red Peppers

Servings: 4
Cooking Time: 15 Minutes
Ingredients:

- 1 pound (454 g) asparagus, woody ends trimmed, cut into 2-inch segments
- 2 red bell peppers, seeded, cut into 1-inch pieces
- 1 small onion, quartered
- 2 tablespoons Italian dressing

Directions:

1. Preheat the oven to 400°F (205°C). Line a baking sheet with parchment paper and set aside.
2. Combine the asparagus with the peppers, onion, and dressing in a large bowl, and toss well.
3. Arrange the vegetables on the baking sheet and roast for about 15 minutes until softened. Flip the vegetables with a spatula once during cooking.
4. Transfer to a large platter and serve.

Nutrition Info: calories: 92 fat: 4.8g protein: 2.9g carbs: 10.7g fiber: 4.0g sugar: 5.7g sodium: 31mg

Chopped Veggie Salad

Servings: 4
Cooking Time: 15 Minutes
Ingredients:
- 1 cucumber, chopped
- 1 pint cherry tomatoes, cut in half
- 3 radishes, chopped
- 1 yellow bell pepper chopped
- ½ cup fresh parsley, chopped
- What you'll need from store cupboard:
- 3 tbsp. lemon juice
- 1 tbsp. olive oil
- Salt to taste

Directions:
1. Place all Ingredients in a large bowl and toss to combine. Serve immediately, or cover and chill until ready to serve.

Nutrition Info: Calories 70 Total Carbs 9g Net Carbs 7g Protein 2g Fat 4g Sugar 5g Fiber 2g

Zucchini Fritters

Servings: 4
Cooking Time: 10 Minutes
Ingredients:
- 3 zucchini, grated
- 2 eggs
- 1 onion, diced
- ¾ cups feta cheese, crumbled
- ¼ cup fresh dill, chopped
- 1 tbsp. margarine
- What you'll need from store cupboard:
- ½ cup flour
- 1 tsp salt
- Pepper to taste
- Oil for frying

Directions:
1. Place zucchini in a large colander and sprinkle with the salt. Toss with fingers and let sit 30 minutes. Squeeze with back of spoon to remove the excess water. Place the zucchini between paper towels and squeeze again. Place in large bowl and let dry.
2. Melt margarine in a large skillet over med-high heat. Add onion and cook until soft, about 5 minutes. Add to zucchini along with the feta and dill and mix well.

3. In a small bowl, whisk together the flour and eggs. Pour over zucchini and mix well.
4. Add oil to the skillet to equal ½-inch and heat over med-high heat until very hot. Drop golf ball sized scoops of zucchini mixtureinto oil and flatten into a patty. Cook until golden brown on both sides. Transfer to paper towel line plate.
5. Serve with Garlic Dipping Sauce, (chapter 16), or sauce of your choice.

Nutrition Info: Calories 253 Total Carbs 21g Net Carbs 18g Protein 10g Fat 15g Sugar 5g Fiber 3g

Egg Stuffed Zucchini Balls

Servings: 4Cooking Time: 45-60 Minutes
Ingredients:
- 2 zucchinis
- 1 onion
- 1 egg
- 120g of grated cheese
- 4 eggs
- Salt
- Ground pepper
- Flour

Directions:
1. Chop the zucchini and onion in the Thermo mix, 10 seconds speed 8, in the Cuisine with the kneader chopper at speed 10 about 15 seconds or we can chop the onion by hand and the zucchini grate. No matter how you do it, the important thing is that the zucchini and onion are as small as possible.
2. Put in a bowl and add the cheese and the egg. Pepper and bind well.
3. Incorporate the flour, until you have a very brown dough with which you can wrap the eggs without problems.
4. Cook the eggs and peel.
5. Cover the eggs with the zucchini dough and pass through the flour.
6. Place the four balls in the basket of the air fryer and paint with oil.
7. Select 1800C and leave for 45 to 60 minutes or until you see that the balls are crispy on the outside.

Nutrition Info: Calories: 23 Cal Carbs: 2 g Fat: 11 g Protein: 4 gFiber: 15 g

Cauliflower "mac" And Cheese

Servings: 6
Cooking Time: 50 Minutes
Ingredients:
- 1 small head cauliflower, separated into small florets
- 1 ½ cup reduced-fat sharp cheddar cheese, grated
- 1 cup low-fat milk
- 1/2 cup chopped onion
- 2 tablespoons margarine, divided
- What you'll need:
- 2 tbsp. whole wheat flour
- 2 tbsp. whole wheat bread crumbs
- 1 tsp olive oil
- 1 tsp yellow mustard
- ½ tsp garlic powder
- ¼ tsp salt
- ¼ tsp black pepper
- Nonstick cooking spray

Directions:
1. Heat oven to 400 degrees. Coat a baking sheet with cooking spray.
2. In a medium bowl, combine oil, salt, pepper, onion, and cauliflower. Toss until cauliflower is coated evenly. Spread on baking sheet and cook 25-30 minutes until lightly browned.
3. In a medium saucepan, over medium heat, melt 1 ½ tablespoons margarine. Whisk in flour until no lumps remain.
4. Add milk and continue whisking until sauce thicken. Stir in mustard, garlic powder, and cheese until melted and smooth. Add cauliflower and mix well.
5. Pour into a 1 ½-quart baking dish.
6. In a small glass bowl, melt remaining margarine in microwave. Stir in bread crumbs until moistened. Sprinkle evenly over cauliflower.
7. Bake 20 minutes until bubbling and golden brown on top.

Nutrition Info: Calories 154 Total Carbs 15g Net Carbs 12g Protein8g Fat 8g Sugar 4g Fiber 3g

Roasted Potatoes

Servings: 4
Cooking Time: 20 Minutes
Ingredients:
- 227g of small fresh potatoes, cleaned and halved
- 30 ml of olive oil
- 3g of salt
- 1g black pepper
- 2g garlic powder
- 1g dried thyme
- 1g dried rosemary

Directions:
1. Preheat the air fryer for a few minutes. Set it to 195°C.
2. Cover the potatoes in half with olive oil and mix the seasonings.
3. Place the potatoes in the preheated air fryer. Set the time to 20 minutes. Be sure to shake the baskets in the middle of cooking.

Nutrition Info: Calories: 93 Fat: 0.2g Carbohydrate: 9g Protein: 1g

Roasted Brussels Sprouts With Wild Rice Bowl

Servings: 4
Cooking Time: 12 Minutes
Ingredients:
- 2 cups sliced Brussels sprouts
- 2 teaspoons plus 2 tablespoons extra-virgin olive oil
- 1 teaspoon Dijon mustard
- Juice of 1 lemon
- 1 garlic clove, minced
- ½ teaspoon salt
- ¼ teaspoon freshly ground black pepper
- 1 cup sliced radishes
- 1 cup cooked wild rice
- 1 avocado, sliced

Directions:
1. Preheat the oven to 400°F (205°C). Line a baking sheet with parchment paper and set aside.
2. Add 2 teaspoons of olive oil and Brussels sprouts to a medium bowl and toss to coat well.
3. Spread out the oiled Brussels sprouts on the prepared baking sheet. Roast in the preheated oven for 12 minutes, or until the Brussels sprouts

are browned and crisp. Stir the Brussels sprouts once during cooking to ensure even cooking.

4.   Meanwhile, make the dressing by whisking together the remaining olive oil, mustard, lemon juice, garlic, salt, and pepper in a small bowl.

5.   Remove the Brussels sprouts from the oven to a large bowl. Add the radishes and cooked wild rice to the bowl. Drizzle with the prepared dressing and gently toss to coat everything evenly.

6.   Divide the mixture into four bowls and scatter each bowl evenly with avocado slices. Serve immediately.

Nutrition Info: calories: 177 fat: 10.7g protein: 2.3g carbs: 17.6g fiber: 5.1g sugar: 2.0g sodium: 297mg

Garlicky Mushrooms

Servings: 4
Cooking Time: 12 Minutes
Ingredients:

- 1 tablespoon butter
- 2 teaspoons extra-virgin olive oil
- 2 pounds (907 g) button mushrooms, halved
- 2 teaspoons minced fresh garlic
- 1 teaspoon chopped fresh thyme
- Sea salt and freshly ground black pepper, to taste

Directions:

1.   Heat the butter and olive oil in a large skillet over medium-high heat.

2.   Add the mushrooms and sauté for 10 minutes, stirring occasionally, or until the mushrooms are lightly browned and cooked through.

3.   Stir in the garlic and thyme and cook for an additional 2 minutes.

4.   Season with salt and pepper and serve on a plate.

Nutrition Info: calories: 96 fat: 6.1g protein: 6.9g carbs: 8.2g fiber: 1.7g sugar: 3.9g sodium: 91mg

Tofu Salad Sandwiches

Servings: 4
Cooking Time: 20 Minutes
Ingredients:

- 1 pkg. silken firm tofu, pressed
- 4 lettuce leaves
- 2 green onions, diced
- ¼ cup celery, diced
- What you'll need from store cupboard:
- 8 slices bread, (chapter 14)
- ¼ cup lite mayonnaise
- 2 tbsp. sweet pickle relish
- 1 tbsp. Dijon mustard
- ¼ tsp turmeric
- ¼ tsp salt
- 1/8 tsp cayenne pepper

Directions:

1.   Press tofu between layers of paper towels for 15 minutes to remove excess moisture. Cut into small cubes.

2.   In a medium bowl, stir together remaining Ingredients. Fold in tofu. Spread over 4 slices of bread. Top with a lettuce leaf and another slice of bread. Serve.

Nutrition Info: Calories 378 Total Carbs 15g Net Carbs 13g Protein 24g Fat 20g Sugar 2g Fiber 2g

Roasted Tomato Brussels Sprouts

Servings: 4
Cooking Time: 20 Minutes
Ingredients:

- 1 pound (454 g) Brussels sprouts, trimmed and halved
- 1 tablespoon extra-virgin olive oil
- Sea salt and freshly ground black pepper, to taste
- ½ cup sun-dried tomatoes, chopped
- 2 tablespoons freshly squeezed lemon juice
- 1 teaspoon lemon zest

Directions:

1.   Preheat the oven to 400°F (205°C). Line a large baking sheetwith aluminum foil.

2.   Toss the Brussels sprouts in the olive oil in a large bowl until well coated. Sprinkle with salt and pepper.

3.   Spread out the seasoned Brussels sprouts on the prepared baking sheet in a single layer.

4.   Roast in the preheated oven for 20 minutes, shaking the pan halfway through, or until the Brussels sprouts are crispy and browned on the outside.

5.   Remove from the oven to a serving bowl. Add the tomatoes, lemon juice, and lemon zest, and stir to incorporate. Serve immediately.

Nutrition Info: calories: 111 fat: 5.8g protein: 5.0g carbs: 13.7g fiber: 4.9g sugar: 2.7g sodium: 103mg

Butternut Fritters

Servings: 6Cooking Time: 15 Minutes
Ingredients:

- 5 cup butternut squash, grated
- 2 large eggs
- 1 tbsp. fresh sage, diced fine
- What you'll need from store cupboard:
- 2/3 cup flour
- 2 tbsp. olive oil
- Salt and pepper, to taste

Directions:

1. Heat oil in a large skillet over med-high heat.
2. In a large bowl, combine squash, eggs, sage and salt and pepper to taste. Fold in flour.
3. Drop ¼ cup mixture into skillet, keeping fritters at least 1 inch apart. Cook till golden brown on both sides, about 2 minutes per side.
4. Transfer to paper towel lined plate. Repeat. Serve immediately with your favorite dipping sauce.

Nutrition Info: Calories 164 Total Carbs 24g Net Carbs 21g Protein 4g Fat 6g Sugar 3g Fiber 3g

Crock Pot Stroganoff

Servings: 2Cooking Time: 2 Hours
Ingredients:

- 8 cups mushrooms, cut into quarters
- 1 onion, halved and sliced thin
- 4 tbsp. fresh parsley, chopped
- 1 ½ tbsp. low fat sour cream
- What you'll need from store cupboard:
- 1 cup low sodium vegetable broth
- 3 cloves garlic, diced fine
- 2 tsp smoked paprika
- Salt and pepper to taste

Directions:

1. Add all Ingredients, except sour cream and parsley to crock pot.cover and cook on high 2 hours.
2. Stir in sour cream and serve garnished with parsley.

Nutrition Info: Calories 111 Total Carbs 18g Net Carbs 14g Protein 10g Fat 2g Sugar 8g Fiber 4g

Lobster Roll Salad With Bacon Vinaigrette

Servings: 6
Cooking Time: 35 Minutes
Ingredients:

- 6 slices bacon
- 2 whole grain ciabatta rolls, halved horizontally
- 3 medium tomatoes, cut into wedges
- 2 (8 oz.) spiny lobster tails, fresh or frozen (thawed) - 2 cups fresh baby spinach
- 2 cups romaine lettuce, torn
- 1 cup seeded cucumber, diced
- 1 cup red sweet peppers, diced
- 2 tablespoons shallot, diced fine
- 2 tablespoons fresh chives, diced fine
- What you'll need from the store cupboard
- 2 cloves garlic, diced fine
- 3 tbsp. white wine vinegar
- 3 tbsp. olive oil, divided

Directions:

1. Heat a grill to medium heat, or medium heat charcoals.
2. Rinse lobster and pat dry. Butterfly lobster tails. Place on the grill, cover and cook 25 – 30 minutes, or until meat is opaque.
3. Remove lobster and let cool.
4. In a small bowl, whisk together 2 tablespoons olive oil and garlic. Brush the cut sides of the rolls with oil mixture. Place on grill, cut side down, and cook until crisp, about 2 minutes. Transfer to cutting board.
5. While lobster is cooking, chop bacon and cook in a medium skillet until crisp. Transfer to paper towels. Reserve 1 tablespoon bacon grease.
6. To make the vinaigrette: combine reserved bacon grease, vinegar, shallot, remaining 1 tablespoons oil and chives in a glass jar with an air-tight lid. Screw on the lid and shake to combine.
7. Remove the lobster from the shells and cut into 1 ½-inch pieces. Cut rolls into 1-inch cubes.
8. To assemble salad: in a large bowl, combine spinach, romaine, tomatoes, cucumber, peppers, lobster, and bread cubes. Toss to combine. Transfer to serving platter and drizzle with vinaigrette. Sprinkle bacon over top and serve.

Nutrition Info: Calories 255 Total Carbs 18g Net Carbs 16g Protein 20g Fat 11g Sugar 3g Fiber 2g

Orange Tofu

Servings: 4
Cooking Time: 2 Hours
Ingredients:

- 1 package extra firm tofu, pressed for at least 15 minutes, cut into cubes
- 2 cups broccoli florets, fresh
- 1 tbsp. margarine
- What you'll need from store cupboard:
- ¼ cup orange juice
- ¼ cup reduced sodium soy sauce
- ¼ cup honey
- 2 cloves garlic, diced fine

Directions:

1. Melt butter in a medium skillet, over medium high heat. Add tofu and garlic and cook, stirring occasionally until tofu starts to brown, about 5-10 minutes. Transfer to crock pot.
2. Whisk the wet Ingredients together in a small bowl. Pour over tofu and add the broccoli.
3. Cover and cook on high 90 minutes, or on low 2 hours.
4. Serve over cauliflower rice (chapter13).

Nutrition Info: Calories 137 Total Carbs 24g Net Carbs 22g Protein 4g Fat 4g Sugar 20g Fiber 2g

Pomegranate & Brussels Sprouts Salad

Servings: 6Cooking Time: 10 Minutes
Ingredients:

- 3 slices bacon, cooked crisp & crumbled
- 3 cup Brussels sprouts, shredded
- 3 cup kale, shredded
- 1 ½ cup pomegranate seeds
- What you'll need from store cupboard:
- ½ cup almonds, toasted & chopped
- ¼ cup reduced fat parmesan cheese, grated
- Citrus Vinaigrette, (chapter 16)

Directions:

1. Combine all Ingredients in a large bowl.
2. Drizzle vinaigrette over salad, and toss to coat well. Serve garnished with more cheese if desired.

Nutrition Info: Calories 256 Total Carbs 15g Net Carbs 10g Protein 9g Fat 18g Sugar 5g Fiber 5g

Strawberry & Avocado Salad

Servings: 6Cooking Time: 10 Minutes
Ingredients:

- 6 oz. baby spinach
- 2 avocados, chopped
- 1 cup strawberries, sliced
- ¼ cup feta cheese, crumbled
- What you'll need from store cupboard:
- Creamy Poppy Seed Dressing (chapter 16)
- ¼ cup almonds, sliced

Directions:

1. Add spinach, berries, avocado, nuts and cheese to a large bowl and toss to combine.
2. Pour ½ recipe of Creamy Poppy Seed Dressing over salad and toss to coat. Add more dressing if desired. Serve.

Nutrition Info: Calories 253 Total Carbs 19g Net Carbs 13g Protein 4g Fat 19g Sugar 9g Fiber 6g

Vegetables With Provolone

Servings: 4Cooking Time: 30 Minutes
Ingredients:

- 1 bag of 400g of frozen tempura vegetables
- Extra virgin olive oil
- Salt
- 1 slice of provolone cheese

Directions:

1. Put the vegetables in the basket of the air fryer. Add some strands of extra virgin olive oil and close.
2. Select 20 minutes, 2000C.
3. Pass the vegetables to a clay pot and place the provolone cheese on top.
4. Take to the oven, 1800C, about 10 minutes or so or until you see that, the cheese has melted to your liking.

Nutrition Info: Calories: 104Cal Carbs: 2 g Fat: 11 g Protein: 4 g Fiber: 0 g

Potato Wedges

Servings: 4
Cooking Time: 20 Minutes
Ingredients:

- 2 large thick potatoes, rinsed and cut into wedges 102 mm long
- 23 ml of olive oil
- 3g garlic powder

- 1g onion powder
- 3g of salt
- 1g black pepper
- 5g grated Parmesan cheese
- Tomato sauce or ranch sauce, for server

Directions:
1. Cut the potatoes into 102 mm long pieces.
2. Preheat the air fryer for 5 minutes. Set it to 195°C.
3. Cover the potatoes with olive oil and mix the condiments and Parmesan cheese until they are well covered.
4. Add the potatoes to the preheated fryer. Set the time to 20 minutes.
5. Be sure to shake the baskets in the middle of cooking.

Nutrition Info: Calories: 156 Fat: 8.01g Carbohydrate: 20.33g Protein: 1.98gSugar: 0.33g Cholesterol: 0mg

Crispy Tofu With Chili Garlic Noodles

Servings: 8
Cooking Time: 15 Minutes
Ingredients:

- 1 lb. extra firm tofu, cut in 1-inch slices & press 30 minutes
- 3 green onions, slice & separate white part from green
- 1 bell pepper, sliced thin
- 1 medium carrot, sliced thin
- 4 tbsp. cilantro, diced
- What you'll need from store cupboard:
- 1 recipe Homemade Pasta, cook & drain (chapter 15)
- 12 cloves garlic, diced fine
- 3 tbsp. lite soy sauce
- 3 tbsp. oyster sauce
- 2 tbsp. red chili paste
- 2 tbsp. cornstarch, plus more as needed
- 2 tbsp. sunflower oil
- 1 tbsp. fish sauce
- 1 tsp Splenda
- Red chili flakes, to taste
- Sesame seeds, to top

Directions:
1. In a small bowl, stir together soy sauce, oyster sauce, chili paste, fish sauce, and Splenda.
2. Crumble tofu into a medium bowl. Add cornstarch and toss to coat well.
3. Heat oil in a large skillet over med-high heat. Add tofu and cook until brown and crispy, break tofu up as it cooks. Transfer to a plate.
4. Add more oil, if needed, to the skillet and sauté carrot and bell pepper until they start to soften, about 3 minutes. Add to tofu.
5. Add the garlic and white parts of the onions and cook 30 seconds, stirring. Stir in sauce mixture and cook 2 minutes or until sauce coats the back of a spoon.
6. Add the pasta along with the tofu and vegetables. Stir to coat. Sprinkle with chili flakes. Serve garnished with green parts of onions, sesame seeds, and cilantro.

Nutrition Info: Calories 266 Total Carbs 26g Net Carbs 24g Protein 23g Fat 12g Sugar 12g Fiber 4g

Asian Style Slaw

Servings: 8Cooking Time: 2 Hours
Ingredients:

- 1 lb. bag coleslaw mix
- 5 scallions, sliced
- What you'll need from store cupboard:
- 1 cup sunflower seeds
- 1 cup almonds, sliced
- 3 oz. ramen noodles, broken into small pieces
- ¾ cup vegetable oil
- ½ cup Splenda - 1/3 cup vinegar

Directions:
1. In a large bowl, combine coleslaw, sunflower seeds, almonds, and scallions.
2. Whisk together the oil, vinegar and Splenda in a large measuring cup. Pour over salad, and stir to combine.
3. Stir in ramen noodles, cover and chill 2 hours.

Nutrition Info: Calories 354 Total Carbs 24g Net Carbs 21g Protein 5g Fat 26g Sugar 10g Fiber 3g

Shrimp & Avocado Salad

Servings: 4
Cooking Time: 5 Minutes
Ingredients:

- ½ lb. raw shrimp, peeled and deveined
- 3 cups romaine lettuce, chopped
- 1 cup napa cabbage, chopped
- 1 avocado, pit removed and sliced
- ¼ cup red cabbage, chopped
- 1/4 cucumber, julienned
- 2 tbsp. green onions, diced fine
- 2 tbsp. fresh cilantro, diced
- 1 tsp fresh ginger, diced fine
- What you'll need from the store cupboard
- 2 tbsp. coconut oil
- 1 tbsp. sesame seeds
- 1 tsp Chinese five spice
- Fat-free Ranch dressing

Directions:

1. Toast sesame seeds in a medium skillet over medium heat. Shake the skillet to prevent them from burning. Cook until they start to brown, about 2 minutes. Set aside.
2. Add the coconut oil to the skillet. Pat the shrimp dry and sprinkle with the five spice. Add to hot oil. Cook 2 minutes per side, or until they turn pink. Set aside.
3. Arrange lettuce and cabbage on a serving platter. Top with green onions, cucumber, and cilantro. Add shrimp and avocado.
4. Drizzle with desired amount of dressing and sprinkle sesame seeds over top. Serve.

Nutrition Info: Calories 306 Total Carbs 20g Net Carbs 15g Protein 15g Fat 19g Sugar 4g Fiber 5g

Garden Vegetable Pasta

Servings: 6
Cooking Time: 30 Minutes
Ingredients:

- 2 lbs. fresh cherry tomatoes, halved
- 2 zucchini, chopped
- 2 ears corn, cut kernels off the cob
- 1 yellow squash, chopped
- ½ cup mozzarella cheese, grated
- ½ cup fresh basil, sliced thin
- What you'll need from store cupboard:

- Homemade Pasta, cook & drain, (chapter 15)
- 5 tbsp. olive oil, divided
- 2 cloves garlic crushed
- Crushed red pepper flakes, to taste
- Salt, to taste

Directions:

1. Heat 3 tablespoons oil in a large skillet over medium heat. Add garlic and tomatoes. Cover, reduce heat to low, and cook 15 minutes, stirring frequently.
2. In a separate skillet, heat remaining oil over med-high heat. Add zucchini, squash, and corn. Reduce heat to medium, and cook until vegetables are tender. Sprinkle with salt.
3. Heat oven to 400 degrees.
4. In a large bowl combine tomato mixture, vegetables, and pasta, toss to mix. Pour into a 9x13-inch baking dish and top with cheese. Bake 10 minutes, or until cheese melts and begins to brown. Serve.

Nutrition Info: Calories 347 Total Carbs 31g Net Carbs 24g Protein 21g Fat 18g Sugar 13g Fiber 7g

Teriyaki Tofu Burger

Servings: 2
Cooking Time: 15 Minutes
Ingredients:

- 2 3 oz. tofu portions, extra firm, pressed between paper towels 15 minutes
- ¼ red onion, sliced
- 2 tbsp. carrot, grated
- 1 tsp margarine
- Butter leaf lettuce
- What you'll need from store cupboard:
- 2 100% whole wheat sandwich thins
- 1 tbsp. teriyaki marinade
- 1 tbsp. Sriracha
- 1 tsp red chili flakes

Directions:

1. Heat grill, or charcoal, to a medium heat.
2. Marinate tofu in teriyaki marinade, red chili flakes and Sriracha.
3. Melt margarine in a small skillet over med-high heat. Add onions and cook until caramelized, about 5 minutes.
4. Grill tofu for 3-4 minutes per side.

5. To assemble, place tofu on bottom roll. Top with lettuce, carrot, and onion. Add top of the roll and serve.

Nutrition Info: Calories 178 Total Carbs 27g Net Carbs 20g Protein 12g Fat 5g Sugar 5g Fiber 7g

Tofu Curry

Servings: 4
Cooking Time: 2 Hours
Ingredients:

- 2 cup green bell pepper, diced
- 1 cup firm tofu, cut into cubes
- 1 onion, peeled and diced
- What you'll need from store cupboard:
- 1 ½ cups canned coconut milk
- 1 cup tomato paste
- 2 cloves garlic, diced fine
- 2 tbsp. raw peanut butter
- 1 tbsp. garam masala
- 1 tbsp. curry powder
- 1 ½ tsp salt

Directions:

1. Add all Ingredients, except the tofu to a blender or food processor. Process until thoroughly combined.
2. Pour into a crock pot and add the tofu. Cover and cook on high 2hours.
3. Stir well and serve over cauliflower rice.

Nutrition Info: Calories 389 Total Carbs 28g Net Carbs 20g Protein 13g Fat 28g Sugar 16g Fiber 8g

Faux Chow Mein

Servings: 4
Cooking Time: 20 Minutes
Ingredients:

- 1 large spaghetti squash, halved and seeds removed
- 3 stalks celery, sliced diagonally
- 1 onion, diced fine
- 2 cup Cole slaw mix
- 2 tsp fresh ginger, grated
- What you'll need from store cupboard:
- ¼ cup Tamari
- 3 cloves garlic, diced fine
- 3-4 tbsp. water
- 2 tbsp. olive oil
- 1 tbsp. Splenda
- ¼ tsp pepper

Directions:

1. Place squash, cut side down, in shallow glass dish and add water. Microwave on high 8-10 minutes, or until squash is soft. Use a fork to scoop out the squash into a bowl.
2. In a small bowl, whisk together Tamari, garlic, sugar, ginger and pepper.
3. Heat oil in large skillet over med-high heat. Add onion and celery and cook, stirring frequently, 3-4 minutes. Add Cole slaw and cook until heated through, about 1 minute.
4. Add the squash and sauce mixture and stir well. Cook 2 minutes, stirring frequently. Serve.

Nutrition Info: Calories 129 Total Carbs 13g Net Carbs 11g Protein 3g Fat 7g Sugar 6g Fiber 2g

Roasted Tomato And Bell Pepper Soup

Servings: 6
Cooking Time: 35 Minutes
Ingredients:

- 2 tablespoons extra-virgin olive oil, plus more for coating the baking dish
- 16 plum tomatoes, cored and halved
- 4 celery stalks, coarsely chopped
- 4 red bell peppers, seeded, halved
- 4 garlic cloves, lightly crushed
- 1 sweet onion, cut into eighths
- Sea salt and freshly ground black pepper, to taste
- 6 cups low-sodium chicken broth
- 2 tablespoons chopped fresh basil
- 2 ounces (57 g) goat cheese, grated

Directions:

1. Preheat the oven to 400°F (205°C). Coat a large baking dish lightly with olive oil.
2. Put the tomatoes in the oiled dish, cut-side down. Scatter the celery, bell peppers, garlic, and onion on top of the tomatoes. Drizzle with 2 tablespoons of olive oil and season with salt and pepper.
3. Roast in the preheated oven for about 30 minutes, or until the vegetables are fork-tender and slightly charred.
4. Remove the vegetables from the oven. Let them rest for a few minutes until cooled slightly.

5. Transfer to a food processor, along with the chicken broth, and purée until fully mixed and smooth.

6. Pour the purée soup into a medium saucepan and bring it to a simmer over medium-high heat. Sprinkle the basil and grated cheese on top before serving.

Nutrition Info: calories: 187 fat: 9.7g protein: 7.8g carbs: 21.3g fiber: 6.1g sugar: 14.0g sodium: 825mg

Festive Holiday Salad

Servings: 8
Cooking Time: 1 Hour
Ingredients:
- 1 head broccoli, separated into florets
- 1 head cauliflower, separated into florets
- 1 red onion, sliced thin
- 2 cup cherry tomatoes, halved
- ½ cup fat free sour cream
- What you'll need from store cupboard:
- 1 cup lite mayonnaise
- 1 tbsp. Splenda

Directions:
1. In a large bowl combine vegetables.
2. In a small bowl, whisk together mayonnaise, sour cream and Splenda. Pour over vegetables and toss to mix.
3. Cover and refrigerate at least 1 hour before serving.

Nutrition Info: Calories 152 Total Carbs 12g Net Carbs 10g Protein 2g Fat 10g Sugar 5g Fiber 2g

Grilled Vegetable & Noodle Salad

Servings: 4
Cooking Time: 10 Minutes
Ingredients:
- 2 ears corn-on-the-cob, husked
- 1 red onion, cut in ½-inch thick slices
- 1 tomato, diced fine
- 1/3 cup fresh basil, diced
- 1/3 cup feta cheese, crumbled
- What you'll need from store cupboard:
- 1 recipe Homemade Noodles, (chapter 15) cook & drain
- 4 tbsp. Herb Vinaigrette, (chapter 16)
- Nonstick cooking spray
-

Directions:
1. Heat grill to medium heat. Spray rack with cooking spray.
2. Place corn and onions on the grill and cook, turning when needed, until lightly charred and tender, about 10 minutes.
3. Cut corn off the cob and place in a medium bowl. Chop the onion and add to the corn.
4. Stir in noodles, tomatoes, basil, and vinaigrette, toss to mix. Sprinkle cheese over top and serve.

Nutrition Info: Calories 330 Total Carbs 19g Net Carbs 16g Protein 10g Fat 9g Sugar 5g Fiber 3g

Creamy Macaroni And Cheese

Servings: 6
Cooking Time: 25 Minutes
Ingredients:
- 1 cup fat-free evaporated milk
- ½ cup skim milk
- ½ cup low-fat Cheddar cheese
- ½ cup low-fat cottage cheese
- 1 teaspoon nutmeg
- Pinch cayenne pepper
- Sea salt and freshly ground black pepper, to taste
- 6 cups cooked whole-wheat elbow macaroni
- 2 tablespoons grated Parmesan cheese

Directions:
1. Preheat the oven to 350°F (180°C).
2. Heat the milk in a large saucepan over low heat until it steams.
3. Add the Cheddar cheese and cottage cheese to the milk, and keep whisking, or until the cheese is melted.
4. Add the nutmeg and cayenne pepper and stir well. Sprinkle the salt and pepper to season.
5. Remove from the heat. Add the cooked macaroni to the cheese mixture and stir until well combined. Transfer the macaroni and cheese to a large casserole dish and top with the grated Parmesan cheese. Bake in the preheated oven for about 20 minutes, or until bubbly and lightly browned. Divide the macaroni and cheese among six bowls and serve.

Nutrition Info: calories: 245 fat: 2.1g protein: 15.7g carbs: 43.8g fiber: 3.8g sugar: 6.8g sodium: 186mg

Creamy Pasta With Peas

Servings: 4
Cooking Time: 10 Minutes
Ingredients:

- 4 tomatoes, deseeded & diced
- 4 oz. fat free cream cheese, cut in cubes
- 1 cup peas, thawed
- ½ cup skim milk
- 4 tbsp. fresh parsley, diced
- What you'll need from store cupboard:
- ½ recipe Homemade Pasta, cook & drain, (chapter 15)
- 4 cloves garlic, diced fine
- 3 tbsp. olive oil
- 1 tsp oregano
- 1 tsp basil
- ½ tsp garlic salt

Directions:
1.   Heat oil in a large skillet over medium heat. Add garlic and tomatoes, cook 3-4 minutes, stirring frequently.
2.   Add peas, milk, cream cheese, and seasonings. Cook, stirring, 5 minutes, or until cream cheese has melted.
3.   Add pasta and toss to coat. Serve garnished with parsley.

Nutrition Info: Calories 332 Total Carbs 19g Net Carbs 14g Protein 14g Fat 23g Sugar 10g Fiber 5g

Sesame Bok Choy With Almonds

Servings: 4
Cooking Time: 7 Minutes
Ingredients:

- 2 teaspoons sesame oil
- 2 pounds (907 g) bok choy, cleaned and quartered
- 2 teaspoons low-sodium soy sauce
- Pinch red pepper flakes
- ½ cup toasted sliced almonds

Directions:
1.   Heat the sesame oil in a large skillet over medium heat until hot.
2.   Sauté the bok choy in the hot oil for about 5 minutes, stirring occasionally, or until tender but still crisp.

3.   Add the soy sauce and red pepper flakes and stir to combine. Continue sautéing for 2 minutes.Transfer to a plate and serve topped with sliced almonds.

Nutrition Info: calories: 118 fat: 7.8g protein: 6.2g carbs: 7.9g fiber: 4.1g sugar: 3.0g sodium: 293mg

Roasted Cauliflower With Tomatoes

Servings: 4Cooking Time: 45 Minutes
Ingredients:

- 1 large head cauliflower, separated in florets
- 3 scallions, sliced
- 1 onion, diced fine
- What you'll need from store cupboard:
- 15 oz. can petite tomatoes, diced
- 4 cloves garlic, diced fine
- 4 tbsp. olive oil, divided
- 1 tbsp. red wine vinegar
- 1 tbsp. balsamic vinegar
- 3 tsp Splenda
- 1 tsp salt
- 1 tsp pepper
- ½ tsp chili powder

Directions:
1.   Heat oven to 400 degrees.
2.   Place cauliflower on a large baking sheet and drizzle with 2 tablespoons of oil. Sprinkle with salt and pepper, to taste. Use hands to rub oil and seasoning into florets then lay in single layer. Roast until fork tender.
3.   Heat 1 tablespoon oil in a large skillet over med-low heat. Add onion and cook until soft.
4.   Stir in tomatoes, with juice, Splenda, both vinegars, and the teaspoon of salt. Bring to a boil, reduce heat and simmer 20-25 minutes. For a smooth sauce, use an immersion blender to process until smooth, or leave it chunky.
5.   In a separate skillet, heat remaining oil over med-low heat and saute garlic 1-2 minutes. Stir in tomato sauce, and increase heat to medium. Cook, stirring frequently, 5 minutes. Add chili powder and cauliflower and toss to coat. Serve garnished with scallions.

Nutrition Info: Calories 107 Total Carbs 23g Net Carbs 16g Protein 6g Fat 0g Sugar 12g Fiber 7g

Fried Avocado

Servings: 2Cooking Time: 10 Minutes
Ingredients:
- 2 avocados cut into wedges 25 mm thick
- 50g Pan crumbs bread
- 2g garlic powder
- 2g onion powder
- 1g smoked paprika
- 1g cayenne pepper
- Salt and pepper to taste
- 60g all-purpose flour
- 2 eggs, beaten
- Nonstick Spray Oil
- Tomato sauce or ranch sauce, to serve

Directions:
1. Cut the avocados into 25 mm thick pieces.
2. Combine the crumbs, garlic powder, onion powder, smoked paprika, cayenne pepper and salt in a bowl.
3. Separate each wedge of avocado in the flour, then dip the beaten eggs and stir in the breadcrumb mixture.
4. Preheat the air fryer.
5. Place the avocados in the preheated air fryer baskets, spray with oil spray and cook at 205°C for 10 minutes. Turn the fried avocado halfway through cooking and sprinkle with cooking oil.

Nutrition Info: Calories: 123 Cal Carbs: 2 g Fat: 11 g Protein: 4 g Fiber: 0 g

French Toast

Servings: 8
Cooking Time: 15 Minutes
Ingredients:
- For the bread:
- 500g of flour
- 25g of oil
- 300 g of water
- 25g of fresh bread yeast
- 12g of salt
- For French toast:
- Milk and cinnamon or milk and sweet wine
- Eggs
- Honey

Directions:
1. The first thing is to make bread a day before. Put in the Master Chef Gourmet the ingredients of the bread and knead 1 minute at speed Let the dough rise 1 hour and knead 1 minute at speed 1 again. Remove the dough and divide into 4 portions. Make a ball and spread like a pizza. Roll up to make a small loaf of bread and let rise 1 hour or so.
2. Take to the oven and bake 40 minutes, 2000C. Let the bread cool on a rack and reserve for the next day. Cut the bread into slices and reserve.
3. Prepare the milk to wet the slices of bread.
4. To do so, put the milk to heat, like 500 ml or so with a cinnamon stick or the same milk with a glass of sweet wine, as you like.
5. When the milk has started to boil, remove from heat, and let cool.
6. Beat the eggs.
7. Place a rack on a plate and we dip the slices of bread in the cold milk, then in the beaten egg and pass to the rack with the plate underneath to release the excess liquid.
8. Put the slices of bread in the bucket of the air fryer, in batches, not piled up, and we take the air fryer, 180 degrees, 10 minutes each batch.
9. When you have all the slices passed through the air fryer, put the honey in a casserole, like 500g, next to 1 small glass of water and 4 tablespoons of sugar. When the honey starts to boil, lower the heat, and pass the bread slices through the honey.
10. Place in a fountain and the rest of the honey we put it on top, bathing again the French toast. Ready our French toast, when they cool, they can already be eaten.

Nutrition Info: Calories: 224 Fat: 15.2g Carbohydrates: 17.39g Protein: 4.81g Sugar: 5.76g Cholesterol: 84mg

Butter-orange Yams

Servings: 8
Cooking Time: 45 Minutes
Ingredients:
- 2 medium jewel yams, cut into 2-inch dices
- 2 tablespoons unsalted butter
- Juice of 1 large orange
- 1½ teaspoons ground cinnamon

- ¼ teaspoon ground ginger
- ¾ teaspoon ground nutmeg
- ⅛ teaspoon ground cloves

Directions:

1. Preheat the oven to 350°F (180°C).
2. Arrange the yam dices on a rimmed baking sheet in a single layer. Set aside.
3. Add the butter, orange juice, cinnamon, ginger, nutmeg, and garlic cloves to a medium saucepan over medium-low heat. Cook for 3 to 5 minutes, stirring continuously, or until the sauce begins to thicken and bubble.
4. Spoon the sauce over the yams and toss to coat well.
5. Bake in the preheated oven for 40 minutes until tender.
6. Let the yams cool for 8 minutes on the baking sheet before removing and serving.

Nutrition Info: calories: 129 fat: 2.8g protein: 2.1g carbs: 24.7g fiber: 5.0g sugar: 2.9g sodium: 28mg

Grilled Portobello & Zucchini Burger

Servings: 2
Cooking Time: 10 Minutes
Ingredients:

- 2 large portabella mushroom caps
- ½ small zucchini, sliced
- 2 slices low fat cheese - Spinach
- What you'll need from store cupboard:
- 2 100% whole wheat sandwich thins
- 2 tsp roasted red bell peppers
- 2 tsp olive oil

Directions:

1. Heat grill, or charcoal, to med-high heat.
2. Lightly brush mushroom caps with olive oil. Grill mushroom caps and zucchini slices until tender, about 3-4 minutes per side.
3. Place on sandwich thin. Top with sliced cheese, roasted red bell pepper, and spinach. Serve.

Nutrition Info: Calories 177 Total Carbs 26g Protein 15g Fat 3g Sugar 3g Fiber 8g

Tarragon Spring Peas

Servings: 6
Cooking Time: 12 Minutes
Ingredients:

- 1 tablespoon unsalted butter

- ½ Vidalia onion, thinly sliced
- 1 cup low-sodium vegetable broth
- 3 cups fresh shelled peas
- 1 tablespoon minced fresh tarragon

Directions:

1. Melt the butter in a skillet over medium heat.
2. Sauté the onion in the melted butter for about 3 minutes until translucent, stirring occasionally.
3. Pour in the vegetable broth and whisk well. Add the peas and tarragon to the skillet and stir to combine.
4. Reduce the heat to low, cover, and cook for about 8 minutes more, or until the peas are tender.
5. Let the peas cool for 5 minutes and serve warm.

Nutrition Info: calories: 82 fat: 2.1g protein: 4.2g carbs: 12.0g fiber: 3.8g sugar: 4.9g sodium: 48mg

Potatoes With Provencal Herbs With Cheese

Servings: 4 Cooking Time: 20 Minutes
Ingredients:

- 1kg of potatoes
- Provencal herbs
- Extra virgin olive oil
- Salt - Grated cheese

Directions:

1. Peel the potatoes and cut the cane salt and sprinkle with Provencal herbs.
2. Put in the basket and add some strands of extra virgin olive oil.
3. Take the air fryer and select 1800C, 20 minutes. Take out and move on to a large plate.
4. Cover cheese.
5. Gratin in the microwave or in the oven, a few minutes until the cheese is melted.

Nutrition Info: Calories: 437 Fat: 0.6g Carbohydrates: 24.19g Protein: 1g Sugar: 5.g Cholesterol: 0mg

Spiced Potato Wedges

Servings: 4
Cooking Time: 40 Minutes
Ingredients:

- 8 medium potatoes

- Salt
- Ground pepper
- Garlic powder
- Aromatic herbs, the one we like the most
- 2 tbsp. extra virgin olive oil
- 4 tbsp. breadcrumbs or chickpea flour.

Directions:

1.   Put the unpeeled potatoes in a pot with boiling water and a little salt.
2.   Let cook 5 minutes. Drain and let cool. Cut into thick segments, without peeling.
3.   Put the potatoes in a bowl and add salt, pepper, garlic powder, the aromatic herb that we have chosen oil and breadcrumbs or chickpea flour.
4.   Stir well and leave 15 minutes. Pass to the basket of the air fryer and select 20 minutes, 1800C.
5.   From time to time shake the basket so that the potatoes mix and change position. Check that they are tender.

Nutrition Info: Calories: 123 Cal Carbs: 2 g Fat: 11 g Protein: 4 g Fiber: 0 g

Roasted Delicata Squash With Thyme

Servings: 4Cooking Time: 20 Minutes
Ingredients:

- 1 (1- to 1½-pound / 454- to 680-g) delicata squash, halved, seeded, and cut into ½-inch-thick strips
- 1 tablespoon extra-virgin olive oil
- ½ teaspoon dried thyme
- ¼ teaspoon salt
- ¼ teaspoon freshly ground black pepper

Directions:

1.   Preheat the oven to 400°F (205°C). Line a baking sheet with parchment paper and set aside.
2.   Add the squash strips, olive oil, thyme, salt, and pepper in a large bowl, and toss until the squash strips are fully coated.
3.   Place the squash strips on the prepared baking sheet in a single layer. Roast for about 20 minutes until lightly browned, flipping the strips halfway through.
4.   Remove from the oven and serve on plates.

Nutrition Info: calories: 78 fat: 4.2g protein: 1.1g carbs: 11.8g fiber: 2.1g sugar: 2.9g sodium: 122mg

Scrambled Eggs With Beans, Zucchini, Potatoes And Onions

Servings: 4
Cooking Time: 35 Minutes
Ingredients:

- 300g of beans
- 2 onions
- 1 zucchini
- 4 potatoes
- 8 eggs
- Extra virgin olive oil
- Salt
- Ground pepper
- A splash of soy sauce

Directions:

1.   Put the beans taken from their pod to cook in abundant saltwater. Drain when they are tender and reserve.
2.   Peel the potatoes and cut into dice. Season and put some threads of oil. Mix and take to the air fryer. Select 1800C, 15 minutes.
3.   After that time, add together with the potatoes, diced zucchini, and onion in julienne, mix and select 1800C, 20 minutes.
4.   From time to time, mix and stir.
5.   Pass the contents of the air fryer together with the beans to a pan.
6.   Add a little soy sauce and salt to taste.
7.   Sauté and peel the eggs.
8.   Do the scrambled.

Nutrition Info: Calories: 65 Cal Carbs: 2 g Fat: 11 g Protein: 4 g Fiber: 0 g

Cantaloupe & Prosciutto Salad

Servings: 4Cooking Time: 15 Minutes
Ingredients:

- 6 mozzarella balls, quartered
- 1 medium cantaloupe, peeled and cut into small cubes
- 4 oz. prosciutto, chopped
- 1 tbsp. fresh lime juice
- 1 tbsp. fresh mint, chopped
- What you'll need from store cupboard
- 2 tbsp. extra virgin olive oil
- 1 tsp honey

Directions:

1. In a large bowl, whisk together oil, lime juice, honey, and mint. Season with salt and pepper to taste.
2. Add the cantaloupe and mozzarella and toss to combine. Arrange the mixture on a serving plate and add prosciutto. Serve.
Nutrition Info: Calories 240 Total Carbs 6g Protein 18g Fat 16g Sugar 4g Fiber 0g

Green Beans

Servings: 4
Cooking Time: 13 Minutes
Ingredients:
- 1-pound green beans
- ¾-teaspoon garlic powder
- ¾-teaspoon ground black pepper
- 1 ¼-teaspoon salt
- ½-teaspoon paprika
Directions:
1. Switch on the air fryer, insert fryer basket, grease it with olive oil, then shut with its lid, set the fryer at 400 degrees F and preheat for 5 minutes.
2. Meanwhile, place beans in a bowl, spray generously with olive oil, sprinkle with garlic powder, black pepper, salt, and paprika and toss until well coated.
3. Open the fryer, add green beans in it, close with its lid and cook for 8 minutes until nicely golden and crispy, shaking halfway through the frying.
4. When air fryer beeps, open its lid, transfer green beans onto a serving plate and serve.
Nutrition Info: Calories: 45Cal Carbs: 2 g Fat: 11 g Protein: 4 g Fiber: 3 g

Holiday Apple & Cranberry Salad

Servings: 10Cooking Time: 15 Minutes
Ingredients:
- 12 oz. salad greens
- 3 Honeycrisp apples, sliced thin
- 1/2 lemon
- ½ cup blue cheese, crumbled
- What you'll need from store cupboard:
- Apple Cider Vinaigrette (chapter 16)
- 1 cup pecan halves, toasted
- ¾ cup dried cranberries
Directions:

1. Put the apple slices in a large plastic bag and squeeze the half lemon over them. Close the bag and shake to coat.
2. In a large bowl, layer greens, apples, pecans, cranberries, andblue cheese. Just before serving, drizzle with enough vinaigrette to dress the salad. Toss to coat all Ingredients evenly.
Nutrition Info: Calories 291 Total Carbs 19g Net Carbs 15g Protein 5g Fat 23g Sugar 13g Fiber 4g

Asparagus & Bacon Salad

Servings: 1
Cooking Time: 5 Minutes
Ingredients:
- 1 hard-boiled egg, peeled and sliced
- 1 2/3 cups asparagus, chopped
- 2 slices bacon, cooked crisp and crumbled
- What you'll need from store cupboard:
- 1 tsp extra virgin olive oil
- 1 tsp red wine vinegar
- ½ tsp Dijon mustard
- Pinch salt and pepper, to taste
Directions:
1. Bring a pot of water to a boil. Add the asparagus and cook 2-3 minutes or until tender-crisp. Drain and add cold water to stop the cooking process.
2. In a small bowl, whisk together, mustard, oil, vinegar, and salt and pepper to taste.
3. Place the asparagus on a plate, top with egg and bacon. Drizzle with vinaigrette and serve.
Nutrition Info: Calories 356 Total Carbs 10g Net Carbs 5g Protein 25g Fat 25g Sugar 5g Fiber 5g

Eggplant-zucchini Parmesan

Servings: 6Cooking Time: 2 Hours
Ingredients:
- 1 medium eggplant, peeled and cut into 1-inch cubes
- 1 medium zucchini, cut into 1-inch pieces
- 1 medium onion, cut into thin wedges
- What you'll need from store cupboard:
- 1½ cups purchased light spaghetti sauce
- 2/3 cup reduced fat parmesan cheese, grated
Directions:
1. Place the vegetables, spaghetti sauce and 1/3 cup parmesan in the crock pot. Stir to

combine. Cover and cook on high 2 – 2 1/2 hours, or on low 4-5 hours.

2.	Sprinkle remaining parmesan on top before serving.

Nutrition Info: Calories 81 Total Carbs 12g Net Carbs 7g Protein 5g Fat 2g Sugar 7g Fiber 5g

Southwest Chicken Salad

Servings: 6
Ingredients:

- 2 cups chicken, cooked and shredded
- 1 small red bell pepper, diced fine
- ¼ cup red onion, diced fine
- What you'll need from the store cupboard
- 1/4 cup reduced-fat mayonnaise
- 1 ½ tsp ground cumin
- 1 tsp garlic powder
- 1/2 tsp coriander
- Salt and pepper to taste

Directions:

1.	Combine all Ingredients in a large bowl and mix to thoroughly combine. Taste and adjust seasonings as desired. Cover and chill until ready to serve.

Nutrition Info: Calories 117 Total Carbs 4g Net Carbs 0g Protein 14g Fat 5g Sugar 2g Fiber 0g

Tempeh Lettuce Wraps

Servings: 2Cooking Time: 5 Minutes
Ingredients:

- 1 pkg. tempeh, crumbled
- 1 head butter-leaf lettuce
- ½ red bell pepper, diced
- ½ onion, diced
- What you'll need from store cupboard:
- 1 tbsp. garlic, diced fine
- 1 tbsp. olive oil
- 1 tbsp. low-sodium soy sauce
- 1 tsp ginger,- 1 tsp onion powder
- 1 tsp garlic powder

Directions:

1.	Heat oil and garlic in a large skillet over medium heat.

2.	Add onion, tempeh, and bell pepper and sauté for 3 minutes.

3.	Add soy sauce and spices and cook for another 2 minutes.

4.	Spoon mixture into lettuce leaves.

Nutrition Info: Calories 130 Total Carbs 14g Net Carbs 10g Protein 8g Fat 5g Sugar 2g Fiber 4g

Crispy Rye Bread Snacks With Guacamole And Anchovies

Servings: 4Cooking Time: 10 Minutes
Ingredients:

- 4 slices of rye bread
- Guacamole
- Anchovies in oil

Directions:

1.	Cut each slice of bread into 3 strips of bread.

2.	Place in the basket of the air fryer, without piling up, and we go in batches giving it the touch you want to give it. You can select 1800C, 10 minutes.

3.	When you have all the crusty rye bread strips, put a layer of guacamole on top, whether homemade or commercial.

4.	In each bread, place 2 anchovies on the guacamole.

Nutrition Info: Calories: 180Cal Carbs: 4 g Fat: 11 g Protein: 4 g Fiber: 09 g

Lime Asparagus With Cashews

Servings: 4Cooking Time: 15 To 20 Minutes
Ingredients:

- 2 pounds (907 g) asparagus, woody ends trimmed
- 1 tablespoon extra-virgin olive oil
- Sea salt and freshly ground black pepper, to taste
- ½ cup chopped cashews
- Zest and juice of 1 lime

Directions:

1.	Preheat the oven to 400°F (205°C). Line a baking sheet with aluminum foil.

2.	Toss the asparagus with the olive oil in a medium bowl. Sprinkle the salt and pepper to season.

3.	Arrange the asparagus on the baking sheet and bake for 15 to 20 minutes, or until lightly browned and tender.

4. Remove the asparagus from the oven to a serving bowl. Add the cashews, lime zest and juice, and toss to coat well. Serve immediately.
Nutrition Info: calories: 173 fat: 11.8g protein: 8.0g carbs: 43.7g fiber: 4.9g sugar: 5.0g sodium: 65mg

Cabbage Wedges

Servings: 6Cooking Time: 29 Minutes
Ingredients:
- 1 small head of green cabbage
- 6 strips of bacon, thick-cut, pastured
- 1-teaspoon onion powder
- ½-teaspoon ground black pepper
- 1-teaspoon garlic powder
- ¾-teaspoon salt
- 1/4 teaspoon red chili flakes
- 1/2 teaspoon fennel seeds
- 3 tablespoons olive oil

Directions:
1. Switch on the air fryer, insert fryer basket, grease it with olive oil, then shut with its lid, set the fryer at 350 degrees F and preheat for 5 minutes.
2. Open the fryer, add bacon strips in it, close with its lid and cook for 10 minutes until nicely golden and crispy, turning the baconhalfway through the frying.
3. Meanwhile, prepare the cabbage, for this, remove the outer leaves of the cabbage, and then cut it into eight wedges, keeping the core intact. Prepare the spice mix and for this, place onion powder in a bowl, add black pepper, garlic powder, salt, red chili, and fennel and stir until mixed. Drizzle cabbage wedges with oil and then sprinkle with spice mix until well coated.
4. When air fryer beeps, open its lid, transfer bacon strips to a cutting board and let it rest.
5. Add seasoned cabbage wedges into the fryer basket, close with its lid, then cook for 8 minutes at 400 degrees F, flip the cabbage, spray with oil and continue air frying for 6 minutes until nicely golden and cooked.
6. When done, transfer cabbage wedges to a plate. Chop the bacon, sprinkle it over cabbage and serve.
Nutrition Info: Calories: 123 Cal Carbs: 2 g Fat: 11 g Protein: 4 g Fiber: 0 g

Broccoli & Bacon Salad

Servings: 4
Ingredients:
- 2 cups broccoli, separated into florets
- 4 slices bacon, chopped and cooked crisp
- ½ cup cheddar cheese, cubed
- ¼ cup low-fat Greek yogurt
- 1/8 cup red onion, diced fine
- 1/8 cup almonds, sliced
- What you'll need from the store cupboard
- ¼ cup reduced-fat mayonnaise
- 1 tbsp. lemon juice
- 1 tbsp. apple cider vinegar
- 1 tbsp. granulated sugar substitute
- ¼ tsp salt
- ¼ tsp pepper

Directions:
1. In a large bowl, combine broccoli, onion, cheese, bacon, and almonds.
2. In a small bowl, whisk remaining Ingredients together till combined.
3. Pour dressing over broccoli mixture and stir. Cover and chill at least 1 hour before serving.
Nutrition Info: Calories 217 Total Carbs 12g Net Carbs 10g Protein 11g Fat 14g Sugar 6g Fiber 2g

Black Pepper & Garlic Tofu

Servings: 4
Cooking Time: 40 Minutes
Ingredients:
- 14 oz. pkg. extra firm tofu
- 1 lb. asparagus, trim & cut in 1-inch pieces
- 8 oz. kale, remove stems & slice leaves
- 3 oz. Shiitake mushrooms, sliced
- 1 onion, halved & slice in thin wedges
- 1 green bell pepper, sliced
- What you'll need from store cupboard:
- ½ cup low sodium vegetable broth
- 8 cloves garlic, pressed, divided
- 2 ½ tbsp. light soy sauce, divided
- 2 -4 tbsp. water
- 2 tsp cornstarch
- 2 tsp black pepper, freshly ground, divided
- 1 tsp rice vinegar
- 1 tsp sriracha

Directions:
1. Heat oven to 400 degrees. Line a baking sheet with parchment paper.
2. Cut tofu in ½-inch slices and press between paper towels to remove excess moisture. Cut each slice into smaller rectangles.
3. In a Ziploc bag combine, 1 tablespoon soy sauce, water, 2 tablespoons garlic, rice vinegar, and 1 teaspoon pepper. Add tofu and turn to coat. Let marinate 15 minutes.
4. Place the tofu on the prepared pan and bake 15 minutes. Flipover and bake 15 minutes more. Remove from oven.
5. Place a large nonstick skillet over med-high heat. Add onion and cook until translucent, stirring frequently. Add bell pepper and cook 1 minute more.
6. Add garlic and mushrooms and cook 2 minutes, add a little water if the vegetables start to stick.
7. Stir in the kale and 2 tablespoons water and cover. Let cook 1 minutes, then stir and add more water if needed. Cover and cook another minute before adding asparagus and cook, stirring, until asparagus is tender crisp.
8. In a small bowl, stir together remaining soy sauce, broth, Sriracha, cornstarch, and pepper. Pour over vegetables and cook until heated through.
9. To serve plate the vegetables and place tofu on top.
Nutrition Info: Calories 176 Total Carbs 33g Net Carbs 27g Protein 16g Fat 4g Sugar 12g Fiber 6g

Watermelon & Arugula Salad

Servings: 6
Cooking Time: 1 Hour
Ingredients:
- 4 cups watermelon, cut in 1-inch cubes
- 3 cup arugula
- 1 lemon, zested
- ½ cup feta cheese, crumbled
- ¼ cup fresh mint, chopped
- 1 tbsp. fresh lemon juice
- What you'll need from store cupboard:
- 3 tbsp. olive oil
- Fresh ground black pepper
- Salt to taste

Directions:
1. Combine oil, zest, juice and mint in a large bowl. Stir together.
2. Add watermelon and gently toss to coat. Add remaining Ingredients and toss to combine. Taste and adjust seasoning as desired.
3. Cover and chill at least 1 hour before serving.
Nutrition Info:Calories 148 Total Carbs 10g Net Carbs 9g Protein 4g Fat 11g Sugar 7g Fiber 1g

Broccoli & Mushroom Salad

Servings: 4
Cooking Time: 10 Minutes
Ingredients:
- 4 sun-dried tomatoes, cut in half
- 3 cup torn leaf lettuce
- 1 ½ cup broccoli florets
- 1 cup mushrooms, sliced
- 1/3 cup radishes, sliced
- What you'll need from store cupboard:
- 2 tbsp. water
- 1 tbsp. balsamic vinegar
- 1 tsp vegetable oil
- ¼ tsp chicken bouillon granules
- ¼ tsp parsley
- ¼ tsp dry mustard
- 1/8 tsp cayenne pepper

Directions:
1. Place tomatoes in a small bowl and pour boiling water over, just enough to cover. Let stand 5 minutes, drain.
2. Chop tomatoes and place in a large bowl. Add lettuce, broccoli, mushrooms, and radishes.
3. In a jar with a tight fitting lid, add remaining Ingredients and shake well. Pour over salad and toss to coat. Serve.
Nutrition Info: Calories 54, Total Carbs 9g Net Carbs 7g Protein 3g Fat 2g Sugar 2g Fiber 2g

Crust Less Broccoli Quiche

Servings: 6
Cooking Time: 1 Hour
Ingredients:
- 3 large eggs
- 2 cups broccoli florets, chopped

- 1 small onion, diced
- 1 cup cheddar cheese, grated
- 2/3 cup unsweetened almond milk
- ½ cup feta cheese, crumbled
- What you'll need from store cupboard:
- 1 tbsp. extra virgin olive oil
- ½ tsp sea salt
- ¼ tsp black pepper
- Nonstick cooking spray

Directions:

1. Heat oven to 350 degrees. Spray a 9-inch baking dish with cooking spray.
2. Heat the oil in a large skillet over medium heat. Add onion and cook 4-5 minutes, until onions are translucent.
3. Add broccoli and stir to combine. Cook until broccoli turns a bright green, about 2 minutes. Transfer to a bowl.
4. In a small bowl, whisk together almond milk, egg, salt, and pepper. Pour over the broccoli. Add the cheddar cheese and stir the Ingredients together. Pour into the prepared baking dish.
5. Sprinkle the feta cheese over the top and bake 45 minutes to 1 hour, or until eggs are set in the middle and top is lightly browned. Serve.

Nutrition Info: Calories 182 Total Carbs 5g Net Carbs 4g Protein 10g Fat 14g Sugar 2g Fiber 1g

Zucchini "pasta" Salad

Servings: 5
Cooking Time: 1 Hour
Ingredients:

- 5 oz. zucchini, spiralized
- 1 avocado, peeled and sliced
- 1/3 cup feta cheese, crumbled
- ¼ cup tomatoes, diced
- ¼ cup black olives, diced
- What you'll need from the store cupboard
- 1/3 cup Green Goddess Salad Dressing
- 1 tsp olive oil
- 1 tsp basil
- Salt and pepper to taste

Directions:

1. Place zucchini on paper towel lined cutting board. Sprinkle with a little bit of salt and let sit for 30 minutes to remove excess water. Squeeze gently.

2. Add oil to medium skillet and heat over med-high heat. Add zucchini and cook, stirring frequently, until soft, about 3 – 4 minutes.
3. Transfer zucchini to a large bowl and add remaining Ingredients, except for the avocado. Cover and chill for 1 hour.
4. Serve topped with avocado.

Nutrition Info: Calories 200 Total Carbs 7g Net Carbs 4g Protein 3g Fat 18g Sugar 2g Fiber 3g

Homemade Vegetable Chili

Servings: 4
Cooking Time: 15 Minutes
Ingredients:

- 2 tablespoons extra-virgin olive oil
- 1 onion, finely chopped
- 1 green bell pepper, deseeded and chopped
- 1 (14-ounce / 397-g) can kidney beans, drained and rinsed
- 2 (14-ounce / 397-g) cans crushed tomatoes
- 2 cups veggie crumbles
- 1 teaspoon garlic powder
- 1 tablespoon chili powder
- ½ teaspoon sea salt

Directions:

1. Heat the olive oil in a large skillet over medium-high heat until shimmering.
2. Add the onion and bell pepper and sauté for 5 minutes, stirring occasionally.
3. Fold in the beans, tomatoes, veggie crumbles, garlic powder, chili powder, and salt. Stir to incorporate and bring them to a simmer.
4. Reduce the heat and cook for an additional 5 minutes, stirring occasionally, or until the mixture is heated through. Allow the mixture to cool for 5 minutes and serve warm.

Nutrition Info: calories: 282 fat: 10.1g protein: 16.7g carbs: 38.2g fiber: 12.9g sugar: 7.2g sodium: 1128mg

Collard Greens With Tomato

Servings: 4
Cooking Time: 20 Minutes
Ingredients:

- 1 cup low-sodium vegetable broth, divided
- ½ onion, thinly sliced
- 2 garlic cloves, thinly sliced

- 1 medium tomato, chopped
- 1 large bunch collard greens including stems, roughly chopped
- 1 teaspoon ground cumin
- ½ teaspoon freshly ground black pepper

Directions:
1. Add ½ cup of vegetable broth to a Dutch oven over medium heat and bring to a simmer.
2. Stir in the onion and garlic and cook for about 4 minutes until tender.
3. Add the remaining broth, tomato, greens, cumin, and pepper, and gently stir to combine.
4. Reduce the heat to low and simmer uncovered for 15 minutes. Serve warm.

Nutrition Info: calories: 68 fat: 2.1g protein: 4.8g carbs: 13.8g fiber: 7.1g sugar: 2.0g sodium: 67mg

Okra

Servings: 4
Cooking Time: 10 Minutes
Ingredients:
- 1-cup almond flour
- 8 ounces fresh okra
- 1/2 teaspoon sea salt
- 1-cup milk, reduced-fat
- 1 egg, pastured

Directions:
1. Crack the egg in a bowl, pour in the milk and whisk until blended.
2. Cut the stem from each okra, then cut it into ½-inch pieces, add them into egg and stir until well coated.
3. Mix flour and salt and add it into a large plastic bag.
4. Working on one okra piece at a time, drain the okra well by letting excess egg drip off, add it to the flour mixture, then seal the bag and shake well until okra is well coated.
5. Place the coated okra on a grease air fryer basket, coat remaining okra pieces in the same manner and place them into the basket.
6. Switch on the air fryer, insert fryer basket, spray okra with oil, then shut with its lid, set the fryer at 390 degrees F and cook for 10 minutes until nicely golden and cooked, stirring okra halfway through the frying.

Nutrition Info: Calories: 250Cal Carbs: 2 g Fat: 11 g Protein: 4 g Fiber: 2 g

Grilled Tofu & Veggie Skewers

Servings: 6
Cooking Time: 15 Minutes
Ingredients:
- 1 block tofu
- 2 small zucchini, sliced
- 1 red bell pepper, cut into 1-inch cubes
- 1 yellow bell pepper, cut into 1-inch cubes
- 1 red onion, cut into 1-inch cubes
- 2 cups cherry tomatoes
- What you'll need from store cupboard:
- 2 tbsp. lite soy sauce
- 3 tsp barbecue sauce (chapter 15)
- 2 tsp sesame seeds
- Salt & pepper, to taste
- Nonstick cooking spray

Directions:
1. Press tofu to extract liquid, for about half an hour. Then, cut tofu into cubes and marinate in soy sauce for at least 15 minutes.
2. Heat the grill to med-high heat. Spray the grill rack with cooking spray.
3. Assemble skewers with tofu alternating with vegetables.
4. Grill 2-3 minutes per side until vegetables start to soften, and tofu is golden brown. At the very end of cooking time, season with salt and pepper and brush with barbecue sauce. Serve garnished with sesame seeds.

Nutrition Info: Calories 64 Total Carbs 10g Net Carbs 7g Protein 5g Fat 2g Sugar 6g Fiber 3g

Tex Mex Veggie Bake

Servings: 8
Cooking Time: 35 Minutes
Ingredients:
- 2 cup cauliflower, grated
- 1 cup fat free sour cream
- 1 cup reduced fat cheddar cheese, grated
- 1 cup reduced fat Mexican cheese blend, grated
- ½ cup red onion, diced
- What you'll need from store cupboard:
- 11 oz. can Mexicorn, drain
- 10 oz. tomatoes & green chilies
- 2 ¼ oz. black olives, drain
- 1 cup black beans, rinsed

- 1 cup salsa
- ¼ tsp pepper
- Nonstick cooking spray

Directions:

1.	Heat oven to 350 degrees. Spray a 2 ½-quart baking dish with cooking spray.

2.	In a large bowl, combine beans, corn, tomatoes, salsa, sour cream, cheddar cheese, pepper, and cauliflower. Transfer to baking dish. Sprinkle with onion and olives.

3.	Bake 30 minutes. Sprinkle with Mexican blend cheese and bake another 5-10 minutes, or until cheese is melted and casserole is heated through. Let rest 10 minutes before serving.

Nutrition Info: Calories 266 Total Carbs 33g Net Carbs 27g Protein 16g Fat 8g Sugar 8g Fiber 6g

Pad Thai

Servings: 6
Cooking Time: 30 Minutes
Ingredients:

- 12 oz. extra firm tofu organic, cut into 1-inch cubes
- 2 zucchini, shredded into long zoodles
- 1 carrot, grated
- 3 cups bean sprouts
- 2 Green onions sliced
- 1 cup red cabbage, shredded
- ¼ cup cilantro, chopped
- What you'll need from store cupboard:
- ¼ cup lime juice
- 2 cloves garlic, diced fine
- 2 tbsp. reduced fat peanut butter
- 2 tbsp. tamari
- 1 tbsp. sesame seeds
- ½ tbsp. sesame oil
- 2 tsp red chili flakes

Directions:

1.	Heat half the oil in a saucepan over medium heat. Add tofu and cook until it starts to brown, about 5 minutes. Add garlic and stir until light brown.

2.	Add zucchini, carrot, cabbage, lime juice, peanut butter, tamari, and chili flakes. Stir to combine all Ingredients. Cook, stirring frequently, until vegetables are tender, about 5 minutes. Add bean sprouts and remove from heat.

3.	Serve topped with green onions, sesame seeds and cilantro.

Nutrition Info: Calories 134 Total Carbs 13g Net Carbs 11g Protein 12g Fat 6g Sugar 3g Fiber 2g

Pecan Pear Salad

Servings: 8
Cooking Time: 15 Minutes
Ingredients:

- 10 oz. mixed greens
- 3 pears, chopped
- ½ cup blue cheese, crumbled
- What you'll need from store cupboard:
- 2 cup pecan halves
- 1 cup dried cranberries
- ½ cup olive oil
- 6 tbsp. champagne vinegar
- 2 tbsp. Dijon mustard
- ¼ tsp salt

Directions:

1.	In a large bowl combine greens, pears, cranberries and pecans.

2.	Whisk remaining Ingredients, except blue cheese, together in a small bowl Pour over salad and toss to coat. Serve topped with blue cheese crumbles.

Nutrition Info: Calories 325 Total Carbs 20g Net Carbs 14g Protein 5g Fat 26g Sugar 10g Fiber 6g

Chapter 8
Salads Recipe

Asian Noodle Salad

Prep time: 30 minutes, Serves: 4
Ingredients:
2 carrots, sliced thin
2 radish, sliced thin
1 English cucumber, sliced thin
1 mango, julienned
1 bell pepper, julienned
1 small serrano pepper, seeded and sliced thin
1 bag tofu Shirataki Fettuccini noodles
¼ cup lime juice
¼ cup fresh basil, chopped
¼ cup fresh cilantro, chopped
2 tbsp. fresh mint, chopped
What you'll need from the store cupboard
2 tbsp. rice vinegar
2 tbsp. sweet chili sauce
2 tbsp. roasted peanuts finely chopped
1 tbsp. Splenda
½ tsp sesame oil
Instructions:
Pickle the vegetables: In a large bowl, place radish, cucumbers, and carrots. Add vinegar, coconut sugar, and lime juice and stir to coat the vegetables. Cover and chill 15 – 20 minutes.
Prep the noodles: remove the noodles from the package and rinse under cold water. Cut into smaller pieces. Pat dry with paper towels.
To assemble the salad. Remove the vegetables from the marinade, reserving marinade, and place in a large mixing bowl. Add noodles, mango, bell pepper, chili, and herbs.
In a small bowl, combine 2 tablespoons marinade with the chilisauce and sesame oil. Pour over salad and toss to coat. Top with peanuts and serve.
Nutrition Facts Per Serving
Calories 158 Total Carbs 30g Net Carbs 24g Protein 4g Fat 4g Sugar 19g Fiber 6g

Asian Style Slaw

Prep time: 5 minutes, chill time: 2 hours, Serves: 8
Ingredients:
1 lb. bag coleslaw mix
5 scallions, sliced
What you'll need from store cupboard:
1 cup sunflower seeds
1 cup almonds, sliced
3 oz. ramen noodles, broken into small pieces
¾ cup vegetable oil
½ cup Splenda
1/3 cup vinegar
Instructions:
In a large bowl, combine coleslaw, sunflower seeds, almonds, and scallions.
Whisk together the oil, vinegar and Splenda in a large measuring cup. Pour over salad, and stir to combine.
Stir in ramen noodles, cover and chill 2 hours.
Nutrition Facts Per Serving
Calories 354 Total Carbs 24g Net Carbs 21g Protein 5g Fat 26g Sugar 10g Fiber 3g

Asparagus & Bacon Salad

Prep time: 5 minutes, Cook time: 5 minutes, Serves: 1
Ingredients:
1 hard-boiled egg, peeled and sliced
1 2/3 cups asparagus, chopped
2 slices bacon, cooked crisp and crumbled

What you'll need from store cupboard:
1 tsp extra virgin olive oil
1 tsp red wine vinegar
½ tsp Dijon mustard
Pinch salt and pepper, to taste
Instructions:
Bring a pot of water to a boil. Add the asparagus and cook 2-3 minutes or until tender-crisp. Drain and add cold water to stop the cooking process.
In a small bowl, whisk together, mustard, oil, vinegar, and salt and pepper to taste.
Place the asparagus on a plate, top with egg and bacon. Drizzle with vinaigrette and serve.
Nutrition Facts Per Serving
Calories 356 Total Carbs 10g Net Carbs 5g Protein 25g Fat 25g Sugar 5g Fiber 5g

Autumn Slaw

Prep time: 15 minutes, chill time: 2 hours, Serves: 8
Ingredients:
10 cup cabbage, shredded
½ red onion, diced fine
¾ cup fresh Italian parsley, chopped
What you'll need from store cupboard:
¾ cup almonds, slice & toasted
¾ cup dried cranberries
1/3 cup vegetable oil
¼ cup apple cider vinegar
2 tbsp. sugar free maple syrup
4 tsp Dijon mustard
½ teaspoon salt
Salt & pepper, to taste
Instructions:
In a large bowl, whisk together vinegar, oil, syrup, Dijon, and ½ teaspoon salt. Add the onion and stir to combine. Let rest 10 minutes, or cover and refrigerate until ready to use.
After 10 minutes, add remaining Ingredients to the dressing mixture and toss to coat. Taste and season with salt and pepper if needed. Cover and chill 2 hours before serving.
Nutrition Facts Per Serving
Calories 133 Total Carbs 12g net Carbs 8g Protein 2g Fat 9g Sugar 5g Fiber 4g

Avocado & Citrus Shrimp Salad

Prep time: 10 minutes, Cook time: 5 minutes, Serves: 4
Ingredients:
1 lb. medium shrimp, peeled and deveined, remove tails
8 cup salad greens
1 lemon
1 avocado, diced
1 shallot, diced fine
What you'll need from store cupboard:
½ cup almonds, sliced and toasted
1 tbsp. olive oil
Salt and freshly ground black pepper
Instructions:
Cut the lemon in half and squeeze the juice, from both halves, into a small bowl, set aside. Slice the lemon into thin wedges.
Heat the oil in a skillet over medium heat. Add lemon wedges and let cook, about 1 minute, to infuse the oil with the lemons.
Add the shrimp and cook, stirring frequently, until shrimp turn pink. Discard the lemon wedges and let cool.
Place the salad greens in a large bowl. Add the shrimp, with the juices from the pan, and toss to coat. Add remaining Ingredients and toss to combine. Serve.
Nutrition Facts Per Serving
Calories 425 Total Carbs 17 Net Carbs 8g Protein 35 Fat 26 Sugar 2 Fiber 9

Baked "Potato" Salad

Prep time: 15 minutes, Cook time: 15 minutes, Serves: 8
Ingredients:
2 lb. cauliflower, separated into small florets
6-8 slices bacon, chopped and fried crisp
6 boiled eggs, cooled, peeled, and chopped
1 cup sharp cheddar cheese, grated
½ cup green onion, sliced
What you'll need from the store cupboard
1 cup reduced-fat mayonnaise
2 tsp yellow mustard
1 ½ tsp onion powder, divided
Salt and fresh-ground black pepper to taste

Instructions:

Place cauliflower in a vegetable steamer, or a pot with a steamer insert, and steam 5-6 minutes.

Drain the cauliflower and set aside.

In a small bowl, whisk together mayonnaise, mustard, 1 teaspoon onion powder, salt, and pepper.Pat cauliflower dry with paper towels and place in a large mixing bowl. Add eggs, salt, pepper, remaining ½ teaspoon onion powder, then dressing. Mix gently to combine Ingredients together.

Fold in the bacon, cheese, and green onion. Serve warm or cover and chill before serving.

Nutrition Facts Per Serving

Calories 247 Total Carbs 8g Net Carbs 5g Protein 17g Fat 17g Sugar 3g Fiber 3g

Broccoli & Bacon Salad

Prep time: 10 minutes, Serves: 4

Ingredients:

2 cups broccoli, separated into florets

4 slices bacon, chopped and cooked crisp

½ cup cheddar cheese, cubed

¼ cup low-fat Greek yogurt

1/8 cup red onion, diced fine

1/8 cup almonds, sliced

What you'll need from the store cupboard

¼ cup reduced-fat mayonnaise

1 tbsp. lemon juice

1 tbsp. apple cider vinegar

1 tbsp. granulated sugar substitute

¼ tsp salt

¼ tsp pepper

Instructions:

In a large bowl, combine broccoli, onion, cheese, bacon, and almonds.In a small bowl, whisk remaining Ingredients together till combined.

Pour dressing over broccoli mixture and stir. Cover and chill at least 1 hour before serving.

Nutrition Facts Per Serving

Calories 217 Total Carbs 12g Net Carbs 10g Protein 11g Fat 14g Sugar 6g Fiber 2g

Broccoli & Mushroom Salad

Total time: 10 minutes, Serves: 4

Ingredients:

4 sun-dried tomatoes, cut in half

3 cup torn leaf lettuce

1 ½ cup broccoli florets

1 cup mushrooms, sliced

1/3 cup radishes, sliced

What you'll need from store cupboard:

2 tbsp. water

1 tbsp. balsamic vinegar

1 tsp vegetable oil

¼ tsp chicken bouillon granules

¼ tsp parsley

¼ tsp dry mustard

1/8 tsp cayenne pepper

Instructions:

Place tomatoes in a small bowl and pour boiling water over, just enough to cover. Let stand 5 minutes, drain.

Chop tomatoes and place in a large bowl. Add lettuce, broccoli, mushrooms, and radishes.

In a jar with a tight fitting lid, add remaining Ingredients and shake well. Pour over salad and toss to coat. Serve.

Nutrition Facts Per Serving

Calories 54, Total Carbs 9g Net Carbs 7g Protein 3g Fat 2g Sugar 2g Fiber 2g

Cantaloupe & Prosciutto Salad

Total time: 15 minutes, Serves: 4

Ingredients:

6 mozzarella balls, quartered

1 medium cantaloupe, peeled and cut into small cubes

4 oz. prosciutto, chopped

1 tbsp. fresh lime juice

1 tbsp. fresh mint, chopped

What you'll need from store cupboard

2 tbsp. extra virgin olive oil

1 tsp honey

Instructions:

In a large bowl, whisk together oil, lime juice, honey, and mint. Season with salt and pepper to taste.

Add the cantaloupe and mozzarella and toss to combine. Arrange the mixture on a serving plate and add prosciutto. Serve.

Nutrition Facts Per Serving

Calories 240 Total Carbs 6g Protein 18g Fat 16g Sugar 4g Fiber 0g

Caprese Salad

Total time: 10 minutes, Serves: 4
Ingredients:
3 medium tomatoes, cut into 8 slices
2 (1-oz.) slices mozzarella cheese, cut into strips
¼ cup fresh basil, sliced thin
What you'll need from store cupboard:
2 tsp extra-virgin olive oil
1/8 tsp salt
Pinch black pepper
Instructions:
Place tomatoes and cheese on serving plates. Sprinkle with salt and pepper. Drizzle oil over and top with basil. Serve.Nutrition Facts Per Serving
Calories 77 Total Carbs 4g Protein 5g Fat 5g Sugar 2g Fiber 1g

Celery Apple Salad

Prep time: 5 minutes, Total time: 15 minutes, Serves: 4
Ingredients:
2 green onions, diced
2 Medjool dates, pitted & diced fine
1 honey crisp apple, sliced thin
2 cup celery, sliced
½ cup celery leaves, diced
What you'll need from store cupboard:
1/4 cup walnuts, chopped
Maple Shallot Vinaigrette, (chapter 16)
Instructions:
Heat oven to 375 degrees. Place walnuts on a cookie sheet and bake 10 minutes, stirring every few minutes, to toast.In a large bowl, combine all Ingredients and toss to mix.
Drizzle vinaigrette over and toss to coat. Serve immediately.
Nutrition Facts Per Serving
Calories 171 Total Carbs 25g Net Carbs 21g Protein 3g Fat 8g Sugar 15g Fiber 4g

Chicken Guacamole Salad

Prep time: 10 minutes, Cook time: 20 minutes, Serves: 6
Ingredients:
1 lb. chicken breast, boneless & skinless
2 avocados
1-2 jalapeno peppers, seeded & diced
1/3 cup onion, diced

3 tbsp. cilantro, diced
2 tbsp. fresh lime juice
What you'll need from store cupboard:
2 cloves garlic, diced
1 tbsp. olive oil
Salt & pepper, to taste
Instructions:
Heat oven to 400 degrees. Line a baking sheet with foil.
Season chicken with salt and pepper and place on prepared pan. Bake 20 minutes, or until chicken is cooked through. Let cool completely.
Once chicken has cooled, shred or dice and add to a large bowl. Add remaining Ingredients and mix well, mashing the avocado as you mix it in. Taste and season with salt and pepper as desired. Serve immediately.
Nutrition Facts Per Serving
Calories 324 Total Carbs 12g Net Carbs 5g Protein 23g Fat 22g Sugar 1g Fiber 7g

Chopped Veggie Salad

Total time: 15 minutes, Serves: 4
Ingredients:
1 cucumber, chopped
1 pint cherry tomatoes, cut in half
3 radishes, chopped
1 yellow bell pepper chopped
½ cup fresh parsley, chopped
What you'll need from store cupboard:
3 tbsp. lemon juice
1 tbsp. olive oil - Salt to taste
Instructions:
Place all Ingredients in a large bowl and toss to combine. Serve immediately, or cover and chill until ready to serve.
Nutrition Facts Per Serving
Calories 70 Total Carbs 9g Net Carbs 7g Protein 2g Fat 4g Sugar 5g Fiber 2g

Creamy Crab Slaw

Prep time: 10 minutes, chill time: 1 hour, Serves: 4
Ingredients:
½ lb. cabbage, shredded
½ lb. red cabbage, shredded
2 hard-boiled eggs, chopped
Juice of 1/2 lemon
What you'll need from store cupboard:
2 6 oz. cans crabmeat, drained

½ cup lite mayonnaise
1 tsp celery seeds
Salt & pepper, to taste
Instructions:
In a large bowl, combine both kinds of cabbage.
In a small bowl, combine mayonnaise, lemon juice, and celery seeds. Add to cabbage and toss to coat. Add crab and eggs and toss to mix, season with salt and pepper. Cover and refrigerate 1 hour before serving.
Nutrition Facts Per Serving
Calories 380 Total Carbs 25g Net Carbs 17g Protein 18g Fat 24g Sugar 13g Fiber 8g

Festive Holiday Salad

Prep time: 10 minutes, chill time: 1 hour, Serves: 8
Ingredients:
1 head broccoli, separated into florets
1 head cauliflower, separated into florets
1 red onion, sliced thin
2 cup cherry tomatoes, halved
½ cup fat free sour cream
What you'll need from store cupboard:
1 cup lite mayonnaise
1 tbsp. Splenda
Instructions:
In a large bowl combine vegetables.
In a small bowl, whisk together mayonnaise, sour cream and Splenda. Pour over vegetables and toss to mix.Cover and refrigerate at least 1 hour before serving.
Nutrition Facts Per Serving
Calories 152 Total Carbs 12g Net Carbs 10g Protein 2g Fat 10g Sugar 5g Fiber 2g

Grilled Vegetable & Noodle Salad

Prep time: 15 minutes, Cook time: 10 minutes, Serves: 4
Ingredients:
2 ears corn-on-the-cob, husked
1 red onion, cut in ½-inch thick slices
1 tomato, diced fine
1/3 cup fresh basil, diced
1/3 cup feta cheese, crumbled
What you'll need from store cupboard:
1 recipe Homemade Noodles, (chapter 15) cook & drain
4 tbsp. Herb Vinaigrette, (chapter 16)
Nonstick cooking spray

Instructions:
Heat grill to medium heat. Spray rack with cooking spray.
Place corn and onions on the grill and cook, turning when needed, until lightly charred and tender, about 10 minutes.
Cut corn off the cob and place in a medium bowl. Chop the onion and add to the corn.
Stir in noodles, tomatoes, basil, and vinaigrette, toss to mix. Sprinkle cheese over top and serve.
Nutrition Facts Per Serving
Calories 330 Total Carbs 19g Net Carbs 16g Protein 10g Fat 9g Sugar 5g Fiber 3g

Harvest Salad

Prep time: 15 minutes, Cook time: 25 minutes, Serves: 6
Ingredients:
10 oz. kale, deboned and chopped
1 ½ cup blackberries
½ butternut squash, cubed
¼ cup goat cheese, crumbled
What you'll need from store cupboard:
Maple Mustard Salad Dressing (chapter 16)
1 cup raw pecans
1/3 cup raw pumpkin seeds
¼ cup dried cranberries
3 1/2 tbsp. olive oil
1 ½ tbsp. sugar free maple syrup
3/8 tsp salt, divided
Pepper, to taste
Nonstick cooking spray
Instructions:
Heat oven to 400 degrees. Spray a baking sheet with cooking spray.
Spread squash on the prepared pan, add 1 ½ tablespoons oil, 1/8 teaspoon salt, and pepper to squash and stir to coat the squash evenly. Bake 20-25 minutes.
Place kale in a large bowl. Add 2 tablespoons oil and ½ teaspoon salt and massage it into the kale with your hands for 3-4 minutes.
Spray a clean baking sheet with cooking spray. In a medium bowl, stir together pecans, pumpkin seeds, and maple syrup until nuts are coated. Pour onto prepared pan and bake 8-10 minutes, these can be baked at the same time as the squash.

To assemble the salad: place all of the Ingredients in a large bowl. Pour dressing over and toss to coat. Serve.

Nutrition Facts Per Serving

Calories 436 Total Carbs 24g Net Carbs 17g Protein 9g Fat 37g Sugar 5g Fiber 7g

Healthy Taco Salad

Prep time: 15 minutes, Cook time: 10 minutes, Serves: 4

Ingredients:

2 whole Romaine hearts, chopped

1 lb. lean ground beef

1 whole avocado, cubed

3 oz. grape tomatoes, halved

½ cup cheddar cheese, cubed

2 tbsp. sliced red onion

What you'll need from the store cupboard

1/2 batch Tangy Mexican Salad Dressing (chapter 16)

1 tsp ground cumin

Salt and pepper to taste

Instructions:

Cook ground beef in a skillet over medium heat. Break the beef up into little pieces as it cooks. Add seasonings and stir to combine. Drain grease and let cool for about 5 minutes.

To assemble the salad, place all Ingredients into a large bowl. Toss to mix then add dressing and toss. Top with reduced-fat sour cream and/or salsa if desired.

Nutrition Facts Per Serving

Calories 449 Total Carbs 9g Net Carbs 4g Protein 40g Fat 22g Sugar 3g Fiber 5g

Holiday Apple & Cranberry Salad

Total time: 15 minutes, Serves: 10

Ingredients:

12 oz. salad greens

3 Honeycrisp apples, sliced thin

1/2 lemon

½ cup blue cheese, crumbled

What you'll need from store cupboard:

Apple Cider Vinaigrette (chapter 16)

1 cup pecan halves, toasted

¾ cup dried cranberries

Instructions:

Put the apple slices in a large plastic bag and squeeze the half lemon over them. Close the bag and shake to coat.

In a large bowl, layer greens, apples, pecans, cranberries, and blue cheese. Just before serving, drizzle with enough vinaigrette to dress the salad. Toss to coat all Ingredients evenly.

Nutrition Facts Per Serving

Calories 291 Total Carbs 19g Net Carbs 15g Protein 5g Fat 23g Sugar 13g Fiber 4g

Layered Salad

Prep time: 10 minutes, Serves: 10

Ingredients:

6 slices bacon, chopped and cooked crisp

2 tomatoes, diced

2 stalks celery, sliced

1 head romaine lettuce, diced

1 red bell pepper, diced

1 cup frozen peas, thawed

1 cup sharp cheddar cheese, grated

1/4 cup red onion, diced fine

What you'll need from the store cupboard

1 cup fat-free ranch dressing

Instructions:

Use a 9x13- inch glass baking dish and layer half the lettuce, pepper, celery, tomatoes, peas, onion, cheese, bacon, and dressing. Repeat. Serve or cover and chill until ready to serve.

Nutrition Facts Per Serving

Calories 130 Total Carbs 14g Net Carbs 12g Protein 6g Fat 6g Sugar 5g Fiber 2g

Lobster Roll Salad with Bacon Vinaigrette

Prep time: 10 minutes, Cook time: 35 minutes, Serves: 6

Ingredients:

6 slices bacon

2 whole grain ciabatta rolls, halved horizontally

3 medium tomatoes, cut into wedges

2 (8 oz.) spiny lobster tails, fresh or frozen (thawed)

2 cups fresh baby spinach

2 cups romaine lettuce, torn

1 cup seeded cucumber, diced

1 cup red sweet peppers, diced

2 tablespoons shallot, diced fine

2 tablespoons fresh chives, diced fine

What you'll need from the store cupboard

2 cloves garlic, diced fine

3 tbsp. white wine vinegar

3 tbsp. olive oil, divided

Instructions:

Heat a grill to medium heat, or medium heat charcoals.

Rinse lobster and pat dry. Butterfly lobster tails. Place on the grill, cover and cook 25 – 30 minutes, or until meat is opaque.Remove lobster and let cool.In a small bowl, whisk together 2 tablespoons olive oil and garlic. Brush the cut sides of the rolls with oil mixture. Place on grill, cut side down, and cook until crisp, about 2 minutes. Transfer to cutting board.

While lobster is cooking, chop bacon and cook in a medium skillet until crisp. Transfer to paper towels. Reserve 1 tablespoon bacon grease.

To make the vinaigrette: combine reserved bacon grease, vinegar, shallot, remaining 1 tablespoons oil and chives in a glass jar with an air-tight lid. Screw on the lid and shake to combine.Remove the lobster from the shells and cut into 1 ½-inch pieces. Cut rolls into 1-inch cubes.To assemble salad: in a large bowl, combine spinach, romaine, tomatoes, cucumber, peppers, lobster, and bread cubes. Toss to combine. Transfer to serving platter and drizzle with vinaigrette.

Sprinkle bacon over top and serve.

Nutrition Facts Per Serving

Calories 255 Total Carbs 18g Net Carbs 16g Protein 20g Fat 11g Sugar 3g Fiber 2g

Mustard "Potato" Salad

Prep time: 15 minutes, Cook time: 5 minutes, Serves: 8

Ingredients:

2 pounds cauliflower, separated into small florets

1 boiled egg, peeled and diced

½ cup celery, diced

¼ cup red onion, diced

What you'll need from the store cupboard

¼ cup light mayonnaise

1 tbsp. pickle relish

1 tbsp. Dijon mustard

¼ tsp celery seed

¼ tsp black pepper

Instructions:

Place cauliflower in a vegetable steamer and cook 5 minutes, or until almost tender. Drain and let cool.

In a small bowl, whisk together mayonnaise, relish, mustard, celery seed and pepper.

Once cauliflower is cooled off pat dry and place in a large bowl. Add egg, celery and onion.

Pour dressing over vegetables and mix, gently, to combine. Cover and chill at least 2 hours before serving.

Nutrition Facts Per Serving

Calories 71 Total Carbs 9g Net Carbs 6g Protein 3g Fat 3g Sugar 4g Fiber 3g

Pecan Pear Salad

Total time: 15 minutes, Serves: 8

Ingredients:

10 oz. mixed greens

3 pears, chopped

½ cup blue cheese, crumbled

What you'll need from store cupboard:

2 cup pecan halves

1 cup dried cranberries

½ cup olive oil

6 tbsp. champagne vinegar

2 tbsp. Dijon mustard

¼ tsp salt

Instructions:

In a large bowl combine greens, pears, cranberries and pecans.

Whisk remaining Ingredients , except blue cheese, together in a small bowl Pour over salad and toss to coat. Serve topped with blue cheese crumbles.

Nutrition Facts Per Serving

Calories 325 Total Carbs 20g Net Carbs 14g Protein 5g Fat 26g Sugar 10g Fiber 6g

Pickled Cucumber & Onion Salad

Total time: 10 minutes, Serves: 2

Ingredients:

½ cucumber, peeled and sliced

¼ cup red onion, sliced thin

What you'll need from store cupboard:

1 tbsp. olive oil

1 tbsp. white vinegar

1 tsp dill

Instructions:

Place all Ingredients in a medium bowl and toss to combine. Serve.

Nutrition Facts Per Serving

Calories 79 Total Carbs 4g Net Carbs 3g Protein 1g Fat 7g Sugar 2g Fiber 1g

Pomegranate & Brussels Sprouts Salad

Prep time: 10 minutes, Total time: 10 minutes, serves; 6

Ingredients:

3 slices bacon, cooked crisp & crumbled

3 cup Brussels sprouts, shredded

3 cup kale, shredded

1 ½ cup pomegranate seeds

What you'll need from store cupboard:

½ cup almonds, toasted & chopped

¼ cup reduced fat parmesan cheese, grated

Citrus Vinaigrette, (chapter 16)

Instructions:

Combine all Ingredients in a large bowl.

Drizzle vinaigrette over salad, and toss to coat well. Serve garnished with more cheese if desired.Nutrition Facts Per Serving

Calories 256 Total Carbs 15g Net Carbs 10g Protein 9g Fat 18g Sugar 5g Fiber 5g

Shrimp & Avocado Salad

Prep time: 20 minutes, Cook time: 5 minutes, Serves: 4

Ingredients:

½ lb. raw shrimp, peeled and deveined

3 cups romaine lettuce, chopped

1 cup napa cabbage, chopped

1 avocado, pit removed and sliced

¼ cup red cabbage, chopped

1/4 cucumber, julienned

2 tbsp. green onions, diced fine

2 tbsp. fresh cilantro, diced

1 tsp fresh ginger, diced fine

What you'll need from the store cupboard

2 tbsp. coconut oil

1 tbsp. sesame seeds

1 tsp Chinese five spice

Fat-free Ranch dressing

Instructions:

Toast sesame seeds in a medium skillet over medium heat. Shake the skillet to prevent them from burning. Cook until they start to brown, about 2 minutes. Set aside.

Add the coconut oil to the skillet. Pat the shrimp dry and sprinkle with the five spice. Add to hot oil. Cook 2 minutes per side, or until they turn pink. Set aside.

Arrange lettuce and cabbage on a serving platter. Top with green onions, cucumber, and cilantro. Add shrimp and avocado.

Drizzle with desired amount of dressing and sprinkle sesame seeds over top. Serve.

Nutrition Facts Per Serving

Calories 306 Total Carbs 20g Net Carbs 15g Protein 15g Fat 19g Sugar 4g Fiber 5g

Southwest Chicken Salad

Prep time: 10 minutes, Serves: 6

Ingredients:

2 cups chicken, cooked and shredded

1 small red bell pepper, diced fine

¼ cup red onion, diced fine

What you'll need from the store cupboard

1/4 cup reduced-fat mayonnaise

1 ½ tsp ground cumin

1 tsp garlic powder

1/2 tsp coriander

Salt and pepper to taste

Instructions:

Combine all Ingredients in a large bowl and mix to thoroughly combine. Taste and adjust seasonings as desired. Cover and chill until ready to serve.

Nutrition Facts Per Serving

Calories 117 Total Carbs 4g Net Carbs 0g Protein 14g Fat 5g Sugar 2g Fiber 0g

Strawberry & Avocado Salad

Total time: 10 minutes, Serves: 6

Ingredients:

6 oz. baby spinach

2 avocados, chopped

1 cup strawberries, sliced

¼ cup feta cheese, crumbled

What you'll need from store cupboard:

Creamy Poppy Seed Dressing (chapter 16)

¼ cup almonds, sliced

Instructions:

Add spinach, berries, avocado, nuts and cheese to a large bowl and toss to combine.

Pour ½ recipe of Creamy Poppy Seed Dressing over salad and toss to coat. Add more dressing if desired. Serve.
Nutrition Facts Per Serving
Calories 253 Total Carbs 19g Net Carbs 13g Protein 4g Fat 19g Sugar 9g Fiber 6g

Summer Corn Salad

Prep time: 10 minutes, chill time: 2 hours, Serves: 8
Ingredients:
2 avocados, cut into 1/2-inch cubes
1 pint cherry tomatoes, cut in half
2 cups fresh corn kernels, cooked
½ cup red onion, diced fine
¼ cup cilantro, chopped
1 tbsp. fresh lime juice
½ tsp lime zest
What you'll need from store cupboard:
2 tbsp. olive oil
¼ tsp salt
¼ tsp pepper
Instructions:
In a large bowl, combine corn, avocado, tomatoes, and onion.
In a small bowl, whisk together remaining Ingredients until combined. Pour over salad and toss to coat.
Cover and chill 2 hours. Serve.
Nutrition Facts Per Serving
Calories 239 Total Carbs 20g Net Carbs 13g Protein 4g Fat 18g Sugar 4g Fiber 7g

Warm Portobello Salad

Prep time: 5 minutes, Cook time: 10 minutes, Serves: 4
Ingredients:
6 cup mixed salad greens
1 cup Portobello mushrooms, sliced
1 green onion, sliced
What you'll need from store cupboard:
Walnut or Warm Bacon Vinaigrette (chapter 16)
1 tbsp. olive oil
1/8 tsp ground black pepper
Instructions:
Heat oil in a nonstick skillet over med-high heat. Add mushrooms and cook, stirring occasionally, 10 minutes, or until they are tender. Stir in onions and reduce heat to low.

Place salad greens on serving plates, top with mushrooms and sprinkle with pepper. Drizzle lightly with your choice of vinaigrette.
Nutrition Facts Per Serving
Calories 81 Total Carbs 9g Protein 4g Fat 4g Sugar 0g Fiber 0g

Watermelon & Arugula Salad

Prep time: 10 minutes, chill time: 1 hour Serves: 6
Ingredients:
4 cups watermelon, cut in 1-inch cubes
3 cup arugula
1 lemon, zested
½ cup feta cheese, crumbled
¼ cup fresh mint, chopped
1 tbsp. fresh lemon juice
What you'll need from store cupboard:
3 tbsp. olive oil
Fresh ground black pepper
Salt to taste
Instructions:
Combine oil, zest, juice and mint in a large bowl. Stir together.
Add watermelon and gently toss to coat. Add remaining Ingredients and toss to combine. Taste and adjust seasoning as desired.
Cover and chill at least 1 hour before serving.
Nutrition Facts Per Serving
Calories 148 Total Carbs 10g Net Carbs 9g Protein 4g Fat 11g Sugar 7g Fiber 1g

Zucchini "Pasta" Salad

Prep time: 45 minutes, chill time: 1 hour, Serves: 5
Ingredients:
5 oz. zucchini, spiralized
1 avocado, peeled and sliced
1/3 cup feta cheese, crumbled
¼ cup tomatoes, diced
¼ cup black olives, diced
What you'll need from the store cupboard
1/3 cup Green Goddess Salad Dressing
1 tsp olive oil
1 tsp basil
Salt and pepper to taste
Instructions:
Place zucchini on paper towel lined cutting board. Sprinkle with a little bit of salt and let sit for 30 minutes to remove excess water. Squeeze gently.

Add oil to medium skillet and heat over med-high heat. Add zucchini and cook, stirring frequently, until soft, about 3 – 4 minutes.

Transfer zucchini to a large bowl and add remaining Ingredients, except for the avocado. Cover and chill for 1 hour.

Serve topped with avocado.

Nutrition Facts Per Serving

Calories 200 Total Carbs 7g Net Carbs 4g Protein 3g Fat 18g Sugar 2g Fiber 3g

Chapter 9
Sauces, Dips & Dressings Recipe

Alfredo Sauce

Prep time: 5 minutes, Cook time: 10 minutes, Serves: 6
Ingredients:
1 ½ cup heavy cream
1 tbsp. margarine
What you'll need from store cupboard:
½ cup reduced fat parmesan cheese
4 cloves garlic, diced fine
Black pepper
Salt
Nutmeg
Instructions:
Melt butter in a medium saucepan over medium heat. Add garlic and sauté for about 30 seconds, until fragrant.
Add the heavy cream. Bring to a gentle simmer, then continue to simmer for about 5 minutes, until it begins to thicken and sauce is reduced by about 1/3.
Reduce heat to low. Gradually whisk in the Parmesan cheese. Keep whisking over low heat, until smooth. Add salt, pepper, and nutmeg to taste. (If sauce is thicker than you like, thin it out with more cream.)
Nutrition Facts Per Serving
Calories 147 Total Carbs 2g Protein 2g Fat 14g Sugar 0g Fiber 0g

All Purpose Beef Marinade

Prep time: 10 minutes, Total time: 10 minutes, Serves: 8
Ingredients:
6 limes zested
1 bunch cilantro, diced
What you'll need from store cupboard:
¼ c olive oil
6 cloves garlic, diced fine
Instructions:
Mix all Ingredients in an airtight container.
Keep refrigerated for up to 3 months or frozen up to 6 months. Serving size is 1 tablespoon.
Nutrition Facts Per Serving
Calories 78 Total Carbs 1g Protein 0g Fat 8g Sugar 0g Fiber 0g

All Purpose Chicken Marinade

Prep time: 5 minutes, total time, 5 minutes, Serves: 24
Ingredients:
1 onion, quartered
½ lemon, with skin
½ orange, with skin
3 tbsp. rosemary, diced
2 tbsp. thyme, diced
What you'll need from store cupboard
½ cup olive oil
6 cloves garlic, diced fine
Instructions:
Place all Ingredients in a food processor and pulse until combined.
Store in an air tight container in the refrigerator up to 3 months. Serving size is 1 tablespoon.
Nutrition Facts Per Serving
Calories 41 Total Carbs 1g Protein 0g Fat 4g Sugar 1g Fiber 0g

Almond Vanilla Fruit Dip

Prep time: 5 minutes, Total time: 10 minutes, Serves: 10
Ingredients:
2 ½ cup fat free half-n-half
What you'll need from store cupboard:
4-serving size fat-free sugar-free vanilla instant pudding mix
1 tbsp. Splenda
1 tsp vanilla
1 tsp almond extract
Instructions:
Place all Ingredients in a medium bowl, and beat on medium speed 2 minutes. Cover and chill until ready to serve. Serve with fruit for dipping. Serving size is ¼ cup.
Nutrition Facts Per Serving
Calories 87 Total Carbs 4g Protein 2g Fat 7g Sugar 1g Fiber 0g

Apple Cider Vinaigrette

Total time: 5 minutes, Serves: 8
What you'll need from store cupboard:
½ cup sunflower oil
¼ cup apple cider vinegar
¼ cup apple juice, unsweetened
2 tbsp. honey
1 tbsp. lemon juice
½ tsp salt
Freshly ground black pepper, to taste
Instructions:
Place all Ingredients in a mason jar. Screw on lid and shake until everything is thoroughly combined. Store in refrigerator until ready to use. Shake well before using.
Nutrition Facts Per Serving
Calories 138 Total Carbs 4g Protein 0g Fat 13g Sugar 4g Fiber 0g

Bacon Cheeseburger Dip

Prep time: 5 minutes, Cook time: 30 minutes, Serves: 8
Ingredients:
1 lb. lean ground beef
1 pkg. cream cheese, soft
2 cups low fat cheddar cheese, grated
1 cup fat free sour cream
2/3 cup bacon, cooked crisp and crumbled

What you'll need from store cupboard:
10 oz. can tomatoes with green chilies
Instructions:
Heat oven to 350 degrees.
Place a large skillet over med-high heat and cook beef, breaking it up with a wooden spoon, until no longer pink. Drain off the fat.
In a large bowl, combine remaining Ingredients until mixed well. Stir in beef.
Pour into a small baking dish. Bake 20-25 minutes or until mixture is hot and bubbly. Serve warm.
Nutrition Facts Per Serving
Calories 268 Total Carbs 9g Protein 33g Fat 10g Sugar 2g Fiber 0g

Basic Salsa

Prep time: 15 minutes, chill time: 1 hour: Serves: 8
Ingredients:
8 tomatoes
2-3 jalapeno peppers, depending on how spicy you like it
2 limes, juiced
What you'll need from store cupboard:
4 cloves garlic
1 tbsp. salt
Nonstick cooking spray
Instructions:
Heat oven to broil. Spray a baking sheet with cooking spray.
Place tomatoes, peppers, and garlic on prepared pan and broil 8-10 minutes, turning occasionally, until skin on the vegetables begins to char and peel way.
Let cool. Remove skins.
Place vegetables in a food processor and pulse. Add salt and lime juise and pulse until salsa reaches desired consistency.
Store in a jar with an airtight lid in the refrigerator up to 7 days. Serving size is ¼ cup.
Nutrition Facts Per Serving
Calories 31 Total Carbs 7g Net Carbs 5g Protein 1g Fat 0g Sugar 4g Fiber 2g

BBQ Sauce

Prep time: 5 minutes, Cook time: 20 minutes, Serves: 20
What you'll need from store cupboard:
2 1/2 6 oz. cans tomato paste
1 ½ cup water

½ cup apple cider vinegar

1/3 cup swerve confectioners

2 tbsp. Worcestershire sauce

1 tbsp. liquid hickory smoke

2 tsp smoked paprika

1 tsp garlic powder

½ tsp onion powder

½ tsp salt

¼ tsp chili powder

¼ tsp cayenne pepper

Instructions:

Whisk all Ingredients, but water, together in a saucepan. Add water, starting with 1 cup, whisking it in, until mixture resembles a thin barbecue sauce. Bring to a low boil over med-high heat. Reduce heat to med-low and simmer, stirring frequently, 20 minutes, or sauce has thickened slightly.

Taste and adjust seasoning until you like it. Cool completely. Store in a jar with an airtight lid in the refrigerator. Serving size is 2 tablespoons of sauce.

Nutrition Facts Per Serving

Calories 24 Total Carbs 9g Net Carbs 8g Protein 1g Fat 0g Sugar 7g Fiber 1g

Berry Dessert Sauce

Prep time: 5 minutes, Cook time: 3 hours, Serves: 12

Ingredients

8 oz. strawberries, hulled and halved

6 oz. blackberries

4 oz. blueberries

What you'll need from store cupboard:

¼ cup Splenda

Instructions:

Add the berries and Splenda to the crock pot. Stir to mix. Cover and cook for 3 hours on a low heat.

Ladle the sauce into a jar with an air tight lid, and let cool completely before screwing on the lid and storing in the refrigerator. Serving size is 1 tablespoon.

Nutrition Facts Per Serving

Calories 48 Total Carbs 10g Net Carbs 8g Protein 1g Fat 0g Sugar 8g Fiber 2g

Blackberry Spread

Prep time: 5 minutes, Cook time: 30 minutes, Serves: 16

Ingredients:

1 lb. blackberries

1 lemon, juiced

What you'll need from store cupboard:

¼ cup Splenda

Instructions:

Place blackberries, Splenda and lemon juice in a medium sauce pan over med-high heat. Cook berries down, stirring occasionally, about 30 minutes, or mixture resembles a thick syrup.

Scoop 1/2 cup of the mixture out and place it in a bowl.

Place a fine mesh sieve over the bowl and strain the rest of the mixture through, pressing and scraping to get as much of the moisture out that you can. Discard solids. Stir jam in bowl and place in a jar with an air-tight lid.

Nutrition Facts Per Serving

Calories 28 Total Carbs 6g Net Carbs 4g Protein 0g Fat 0g Sugar 4g Fiber 2g

Blueberry Orange Dessert Sauce

Prep time: 5 minutes, Cook time: 10 minutes, Serves: 16

Ingredients:

1 ½ cup orange segments

1 cup blueberries

¼ cup orange juice

What you'll need from store cupboard:

¼ cup water

1/3 cup almonds, sliced

3 tbsp. Splenda

1 tbsp. cornstarch

1/8 tsp salt

Instructions:

In a small saucepan, combine Splenda, cornstarch, and salt. Whisk in orange juice and water until smooth.

Bring to a boil over med-high heat, cook, stirring frequently, 1-2 minutes or until thickened.

Reduce heat and stir in fruit. Cook 5 minutes. Remove from heat and let cool completely.

Store in an airtight jar in the refrigerator until ready to use. Serving size is 1 tablespoon.

Nutrition Facts Per Serving

Calories 46 Total Carbs 8g Protein 1g Fat 1g Sugar 6g Fiber 0g

Caramel Sauce

Prep time: 5 minutes, Cook time: 10 minutes, Serves: 12
Ingredients:
2/3 cup heavy cream
1/3 cup margarine
What you'll need from store cupboard:
3 tbsp. Splenda
1 tsp vanilla
Instructions:
Add the margarine and Splenda to a medium saucepan and place over low heat. Once the margarine melts, cook 3-4 minutes, stirring occasionally, until golden brown.
Stir in the cream and bring to a low boil. Reduce heat and simmer 7-10 minutes, stirring occasionally, until mixture is a caramel color and coats the back of a spoon.
Remove from heat and whisk in the vanilla. Cool completely and pour into a jar with an air tight lid. Store in the refrigerator. Serving size is 1 tablespoon.
Nutrition Facts Per Serving
Calories 84 Total Carbs 3g Protein 0g Fat 7g Sugar 3g Fiber 0g

Cheesy Jalapeno Dip

Prep time: 5 minutes, cook time; 3 hours, Serves: 10
Ingredients:
4 pkgs. cream cheese, soft
1 ½ cups low fat cheddar cheese, grated
1 cup bacon, cooked and crumbled
1 cup fat free sour cream
1 fresh jalapeño, sliced
What you'll need from store cupboard
2 cans jalapenos, diced
1 packet ranch dressing mix
Instructions:
In a large bowl, mix cream cheese, 2/3 cup bacon, diced jalapenos, 1 cup cheddar cheese, sour cream and dressing.
Spread in crock pot. Top with remaining bacon and cheese. Arrange sliced jalapeno across the top. Cover and cook on low 3 hours. Serve warm.
Nutrition Facts Per Serving
Calories 233 Total Carbs 12g Protein 24g Fat 9g Sugar 2g Fiber 0g

Chinese Hot Mustard

Prep time: 15 mins, Total time: 15 minutes, Serves: 4
What you'll need from store cupboard:
1 tbsp. mustard powder
1½ tsp hot water
½ tsp vegetable oil
½ tsp rice vinegar
⅛ tsp salt
⅛ tsp white pepper
Instructions:
In a small bowl, mix together the dry Ingredients. Add water and stir until mixture resembles liquid paste and dry Ingredients are absorbed.
Stir in oil and vinegar until thoroughly combined. Cover and let rest 10 minutes.
Stir again. Taste and adjust any seasonings if desired. Cover and refrigerate until ready to use.
Nutrition Facts Per Serving
Calories 19 Total Carbs 1g Protein 1g Fat 1g Sugar 0g Fiber 0g

Cinnamon Blueberry Sauce

Prep time: 5 minutes, Cook time: 10 minutes, Serves: 16
Ingredients:
2 cup blueberries
2 tbsp. fresh lemon juice
What you'll need from store cupboard:
¼ cup Splenda
¼ cup water
2 tsp corn starch
½ tsp cinnamon
Instructions:
In a small saucepan, over medium heat, Splenda and cornstarch. Stir in remaining Ingredients and bring to a boil, stirring frequently.
Reduce heat and simmer 5 minutes, until thickened. Let cool completely.
Pour into a jar with an airtight lid and refrigerate until ready to use. Serving size is 1 tablespoon.
Nutrition Facts Per Serving
Calories 27 Total Carbs 6g Protein 0g Fat 0g Sugar 5g Fiber 0g

Citrus Vinaigrette

Prep time: 5 minutes, Total time: 10 minutes, Serves: 6

Ingredients:

1 orange, zested and juiced

1 lemon, zested and juiced

What you'll need from store cupboard:

¼ cup extra virgin olive oil

1 tsp Dijon mustard

1 tsp honey

1 clove garlic, crushed

Salt & pepper, to taste

Instructions:

Place the zest and juices, mustard, honey, garlic, salt and pepper in a food processor. Pulse to combine.

With the machine running, slowly pour in the olive oil and process until combined.

Use right away, or store in a jar with an airtight lid in the refrigerator.

Nutrition Facts Per Serving

Calories 94 Total Carbs 6g Net Carbs 5g Protein 0g Fat 8g Sugar 4g Fiber 1g

Cranberry Orange Compote

Prep time: 5 minutes, Cook time: 10 minutes, Serves: 8

Ingredients:

1 lb. fresh cranberries, rinsed and drained

1 large orange, halved

What you'll need from store cupboard:

1 tsp vanilla

1 tsp cinnamon

Instructions:

Add cranberries to a medium saucepan and place over medium heat. Squeeze both halves of the orange, with pulp, into the berries. Stir in vanilla and cinnamon.

Cook, stirring frequently, until berries start to open. Reduce heat and continue cooking for 10 minutes, or until mixture starts to thicken.

Let cool 15 minutes, then spoon into a jar with an airtight lid. Refrigerate until ready to use.

Nutrition Facts Per Serving

Calories 43 Total Carbs 8g Net Carbs 5g Protein 0g Fat 0g Sugar 4g Fiber 3g

Creamy Poppy Seed Dressing

Total time: 5 minutes, Serves: 6

Ingredients:

⅓ cup light mayonnaise

¼ cup skim milk

What you'll need from store cupboard:

3 tbsp. Splenda

4 tsp cider vinegar

2 tsp poppy seeds

Instructions:

In a small bowl, whisk all Ingredients together until thoroughly combined. Store in an airtight jar in the refrigerator.

Nutrition Facts Per Serving

Calories 90 Total Carbs 10g Protein 1g Fat 5g Sugar 7g Fiber 0g

Dry Rub for Pork

Prep time: 5 minutes, Total time: 5 minutes, Serves: 16

What you'll need from store cupboard:

2 tbsp. ground coffee, extra fine ground

2 tbsp. chipotle powder

1 tbsp. smoked paprika

1 tbsp. Splenda brown sugar

1 tbsp. salt

1 tsp ginger

1 tsp mustard powder

1 tsp coriander

Instructions:

Mix all Ingredients together.

Store in airtight container in cool, dry place for up to 1 month.

Nutrition Facts Per Serving

Calories 5 Total Carbs 1g Protein 0g Fat 0g Sugar 1g Fiber 0g

Easy Cheesy Dipping Sauce

Prep time: 2 minutes, Cook time: 5 minutes, Serves: 2

Ingredients:

¾ cup skim milk

¾ cup reduced-fat cheddar cheese

1 tbsp. margarine

What you'll need from store cupboard:

1 tbsp. flour

Pinch of cayenne

Salt and pepper

Instructions:

Melt margarine in a small saucepan over medium heat. Whisk in flour and cook, whisking constantly, until golden brown, about 1 minutes.

Slowly add milk and continue whisking until no lumps remain. Cook, whisking constantly, until mixture thickens and starts to bubble, 3-4 minutes. Stir in cheese until smooth. Season with cayenne, salt and pepper to taste.

Nutrition Facts Per Serving

Calories 219 Total Carbs 8g Protein 16g Fat 15g Sugar 5g Fiber 0g

Garlic Dipping Sauce

Prep time: 5 minutes, Total time: 5 minutes, Serves: 4

Instructions:

1 cup Greek yogurt

1 tbsp. fresh dill, diced fine

What you'll need from store cupboard:

2 cloves garlic, diced fine

Instructions:

In a small bowl, whisk all Ingredients together. Serve warm or cover and chill until ready to use.

Nutrition Facts Per Serving

Calories 40 Total Carbs 2g Protein 5g Fat 1g Sugar 2g Fiber 0g

Herb Vinaigrette

Prep time: 5 minutes, mix time: 5 minutes, Serves: 12

Ingredients:

2 tbsp. shallot, diced fine

1 tbsp. fresh basil, diced

1 tbsp. fresh oregano, diced

1 tbsp. fresh tarragon, diced

What you'll need from store cupboard:

¼ cup extra virgin olive oil

¼ cup low sodium chicken broth

¼ cup red-wine vinegar - ¼ teaspoon salt

¼ teaspoon freshly ground pepper

Instructions:

Place all Ingredients in a jar with an air tight lid. Secure lid and shake vigorously to combine.

Refrigerate until ready to use. Will keep up to 2 days. Serving size is 1 tablespoon.

Nutrition Facts Per Serving

Calories 39 Total Carbs 0 Protein 0g Fat 4g Sugar 0g Fiber 0g

Horseradish Mustard Sauce

Prep time: 5 minutes, Total time: 5 minutes, Serves: 8

Ingredients:

¼ cup fat free sour cream

What you'll need from store cupboard:

¼ cup lite mayonnaise

1 ½ tsp lemon juice

1 tsp Splenda

½ tsp ground mustard

½ tsp Dijon mustard

½ tsp horseradish

Instructions:

In a small bowl, combine all Ingredients until thoroughly combined.

Store in an air tight jar in the refrigerator until ready to use. Serving size is 1 tablespoon.

Nutrition Facts Per Serving

Calories 36 Total Carbs 2g Protein 0g Fat 2g Sugar 1g Fiber 0g

Italian Salad Dressing

Prep time: 5 minutes, Total time: 5 minutes, Serves: 8

Ingredients:

2 tbsp. lemon juice

What you'll need from store cupboard:

¾ cup olive oil

¼ cup red wine vinegar

2 cloves of garlic, diced

2 tsp Italian seasoning

1 tsp oregano

½ tsp honey

½ tsp salt

¼ tsp black pepper

¼ tsp red pepper flakes

Instructions:

Combine all Ingredients in a measuring cup or jar. Whisk well.

Store in jar or bottle with an air tight lid for up to 1 week. Serving size is 1 tablespoon.

Nutrition Facts Per Serving

Calories 167 Total Carbs 1g Protein 0g Fat 18g Sugar 0g Fiber 0g

Italian Salsa

Prep time: 10 minutes, chill time: 1 hour, Serves: 16

Ingredients:

4 plum tomatoes, diced

½ red onion, diced fine

2 tbsp. fresh parsley, diced

What you'll need from store cupboard:

12 Kalamata olives, pitted and chopped

2 cloves garlic, diced fine

1 tbsp. balsamic vinegar

1 tbsp. olive oil

2 tsp capers, drained

¼ tsp salt

¼ tsp pepper

Instructions:

In a medium bowl, combine all Ingredients and stir to mix. Cover and chill 1 hour before using.

Store in a jar with an airtight lid in the refrigerator up to 7 days. Stir before using.

Nutrition Facts Per Serving

Calories 21 Total Carbs 2g Protein 0g Fat 1g Sugar 1g Fiber 0g

Maple Mustard Salad Dressing

Total time: 5 minutes, Serves: 6

What you'll need from store cupboard:

2 tbsp. balsamic vinegar

2 tbsp. olive oil

1 tbsp. sugar free maple syrup

1 tsp Dijon mustard

1/8 tsp sea salt

Instructions:

Place all the Ingredients in a jar with a tight fitting lid. Screw on lid and shake to combine. Store in refrigerator until ready to use.

Nutrition Facts Per Serving

Calories 48 Total Carbs 2g Protein 0g Fat 5g Sugar 0g Fiber 0g

Maple Shallot Vinaigrette

Prep time: 3 minutes, Total time: 5 minutes, Serves: 4

Ingredients:

1 tbsp. shallot, diced fine

What you'll need from store cupboard:

2 tbsp. apple cider vinegar

1 tbsp. spicy brown mustard

1 tbsp. olive oil

2 tsp sugar free maple syrup

Instructions:

Place all Ingredients in a small jar with an airtight lid. Shake well to mix. Refrigerate until ready to use. Serving size is 1 tablespoon.

Nutrition Facts Per Serving

Calories 45 Total Carbs 5g Protein 0g Fat 2g Sugar 0g Fiber 0g

Marinara Sauce

Prep time: 10 minutes, Cook time: 30 minutes, Serves: 6

What you'll need from store cupboard:

28 oz. can diced tomatoes, undrained

4–6 cloves garlic, diced fine

4 tbsp. extra virgin olive oil

2 tbsp. tomato paste

1 tbsp. basil,

1 tsp Splenda

1 tsp salt

Instructions:

Heat oil in saucepan over medium heat. Add the garlic and cook 1 minute.

Stir in the tomato paste and cook 1 minute more. Add the tomatoes and basil and simmer 10-15 minutes, breaking up the tomatoes as they cook.

Stir in Splenda and salt. Use an immersion blender and process to desired consistency.

Let cool and store in a jar with an airtight lid in the refrigerator up to 7 days. Or use right away.

Nutrition Facts Per Serving

Calories 179 Total Carbs 13g Net Carbs 10g Protein 2g Fat 14g Sugar 8g Fiber 3g

Orange Marmalade

Prep time: 30 minutes, Cook time: 30 minutes, Serves: 48

Ingredients:

4 navel oranges

1 lemon

What you'll need from store cupboard:

2 ½ cup water

¼ cup warm water

4 tbsp. Splenda

1 oz. gelatin

Instructions:

Quarter the oranges and remove all the pulp. Scrap the white part off the rind and cut it into thin 2-

inch strips. Remove as much of the membrane between orange segments as you can and place the seeds in a small piece of cheesecloth, pull up the sides to make a "bag" and tie closed.

Repeat with the lemon but discard the seeds. Cut the lemon rind into smaller strips than the orange rind.

Chop the orange and lemon pulp and add it to a medium saucepan along with 2 ½ cups water. Bring to a rapid boil over med-high heat.

Reduce heat to med-low and add the bag of seeds. Boil gently for 30 minutes, or until the citrus fruit is soft. Remove and discard the seed bag.

Dissolve the gelatin in the warm water. Add it to the orange mixture with ½ the Splenda. Being careful not to burn yourself, taste the marmalade and adjust sweetener as desired.

Spoon the marmalade into 3 ½-pint jars with air-tight lids. Seal and chill.

Nutrition Facts Per Serving

Calories 15 Total Carbs 3g Protein 1g Fat 0g Sugar 3g Fiber 0g

Peach Pepper Relish

Prep time: 10 minutes, chill time: 2 hours, Serves: 16

Ingredients:

2 peaches, peeled and diced

1 green onion, diced fine

1/3 cup bell pepper, diced

1/3 cup red pepper, diced

2 tbsp. fresh mint, diced

What you'll need from store cupboard:

1 tbsp. lemon juice

1 tbsp. sugar free peach preserves

Instructions:

In a medium bowl, stir together peaches, onion, peppers, and mint.

In a small bowl, combine lemon juice and preserves. Pour over peach mixture and toss to coat.

Place in an airtight container and refrigerate up to 2 hours or overnight. Serving size is 2 tablespoons.

Nutrition Facts Per Serving

Calories 10 Total Carbs 3g Protein 0g Fat 0g Sugar 2g Fiber 0g

Pear & Poppy Jam

Prep time: 2 hours, Cook time: 30 minutes, Serves: 32

Ingredients:

3 pears, peeled, seeded and chopped

½ lemon

What you'll need from store cupboard:

¾ cup Splenda

1 tbsp. poppy seeds

Instructions:

Place pears in a large bowl. Sprinkle with Splenda and toss to coat. Squeeze the lemon over the pears and toss again. Let sit for 2 hours so the fruit will release its juice.

Place poppy seeds in a medium saucepan over medium heat. Cook, stirring, 1-2 minutes to lightly toast the. Transfer them to a bowl.

Add the pears, with the juice, to the saucepan and bring to a boil, stirring frequently. Reduce the heat and let boil 10 minutes or until thickened.

Spoon ½ the pears into a blender and process until smooth. Add the puree back to the saucepan along with the poppy seeds. Continue cooking 5-10 minutes or the jam is thick.

Spoon into 2 pint sized jars with air tight lids. Let cool completely, screw on the lids and store in the refrigerator. Serving size is 1 tablespoon.

Nutrition Facts Per Serving

Calories 36 Total Carbs 8g Net Carbs 7g Protein 0g Fat 0g Sugar 6g Fiber 1g

Pineapple Mango Hot Sauce

Prep time: 10 minutes, Cook time: 20 minutes, Serves: 16

Ingredients:

2 cherry peppers, diced

1 ghost pepper, diced

1 cup pineapple, diced

½ cup mango, diced

2 tbsp. cilantro, diced

What you'll need from store cupboard:

1 cup water

½ cup vinegar

1 tsp olive oil

1 tsp Splenda

1 tsp paprika

Salt, to taste

Instructions:

Heat oil in a large saucepan over medium heat. Add peppers and fruit and cook 8 minutes to soften.

Add remaining Ingredients and bring to a boil. Reduce heat and simmer 20 minutes. Remove from heat and let cool.

Add mixture to a food processor and pulse until smooth. Pour into sterilized bottles, secure lids and refrigerate until ready to use.

Nutrition Facts Per Serving

Calories 16 Total Carbs 3g Protein 0g Fat 0g Sugar 2g Fiber 0g

Pizza Sauce

Prep time: 5 minutes, Cook time: 5 minutes, Serves: 8

Ingredients:

½ cup yellow onion, diced

What you'll need from store cupboard:

15 oz. tomatoes, crushed, no sugar added

1/3 cup + 1 tbsp. olive oil

3 cloves garlic, diced

2 tsp parsley

1 tsp rosemary

1 tsp thyme

1 tsp smoked paprika

Salt, to taste

Instructions:

Heat 1 tablespoon oil in a small skillet over medium heat. Add onion and garlic and cook until onions are translucent.

In a medium saucepan, over medium heat, stir all Ingredients together, along with onions. Bring to a simmer and cook 2-3 minutes, stirring constantly.

Remove from heat and let cool completely. Store in a jar with an air tight lid in the refrigerator up to 2 weeks. Or in the freezer up to 6 months.

Nutrition Facts Per Serving

Calories 179 Total Carbs 8g Net carbs 6g Protein 2g Fat 17g Sugar 5g Fiber 2g

Queso Verde

Prep time: 10 minutes, Cook time: 30 minutes, Serves: 10

Ingredients:

½ package cream cheese, soft

½ cup white American cheese, cubed

½ cup white cheddar cheese, cubed

½ cup pepper Jack cheese, cubed

¼ cup skim milk

What you'll need from store cupboard

½ cup salsa verde

½ cup green chilies, diced

Nonstick cooking spray

Instructions:

Heat oven to 325. Spray a small baking dish with cooking spray.

In a medium mixing bowl, combine all Ingredients. Add to prepared baking dish.

Bake 30 minutes, stirring every 8-10 minutes, until cheese is melted and dip is hot and bubbly. Serve warm.

Nutrition Facts Per Serving

Calories 105 Total Carbs 3g Net Carbs 2g Protein 7g Fat 7g Sugar 1g Fiber 1g

Raspberry & Basil Jam

Prep time: 5 minutes, Cook time: 20 minutes, Serves: 24

Ingredients:

2 lbs. fresh raspberries

1/3 cup fresh basil, diced fine

2 tbsp. lemon juice

What you'll need from store cupboard

½ cup Splenda

Instructions:

Add berries and lemon juice to a large saucepan and place over medium heat. Use a wooden spoon to break up the berries. Bring to a low boil and simmer 5-6 minutes, or until mixture starts to bubble.

Stir in Splenda and cook, stirring frequently, until Splenda is dissolved and mixture resembles syrup, about 15 minutes.

Remove from heat and stir in the basil. Spoon into glass jars with air tight lids. Let cool completely then add lids and refrigerate. Serving size is 1 tablespoon.

Nutrition Facts Per Serving

Calories 40 Total Carbs 8g Net Carbs 6g Protein 0g Fat 0g Sugar 6g Fiber 2g

Roasted Tomato Salsa

Prep time: 10 minutes, Cook time: 30 minutes, Serves: 8

Ingredients:

6 plum tomatoes

1 ¼ cup cilantro

What you'll need from store cupboard:
2 tsp olive oil
1 tsp adobo sauce
½ tsp salt, divided
Nonstick cooking spray
Instructions:
Heat oven to 425 degrees. Spray a broiler pan with cooking spray.
Cut tomatoes in half and remove seeds. Place, cut side up, on broiler pan. Brush with oil and sprinkle with ¼ teaspoon salt. Turn tomatoes cut side down and bake 30-40 minutes or until edges are browned.
Place cilantro in food processor and pulse until coarsely chopped. Add tomatoes, adobo, and remaining salt. Process until chunky. Store in jar with air tight lid and refrigerate until ready to use. Serving size is 2 tablespoons.
Nutrition Facts Per Serving
Calories 33 Total Carbs 5g Net Carbs 4g Protein 1g Fat 1g Sugar 4g Fiber 1g

Spaghetti Sauce

Prep time: 20 minutes, Cook time: 30 minutes, Serves: 6
Ingredients:
1 onion, diced
1 carrot, grated
1 stalk celery, diced
1 zucchini, grated
What you'll need from store cupboard:
1 (28 oz.) Italian-style tomatoes, in puree
1 (14 ½ oz.) diced tomatoes, with juice
½ cup water
2 cloves garlic, diced fine
½ tbsp. oregano
1 tsp olive oil
1 tsp basil
1 tsp thyme
1 tsp salt
¼ tsp red pepper flakes
Instructions:
Heat oil in a large saucepan over medium heat. Add vegetables and garlic. Cook, stirring frequently, until vegetables get soft, about 5 minutes.
Add remaining Ingredients, use the back of a spoon to break up tomatoes. Bring to a simmer and cook, partially covered, over med-low heat 30 minutes, stirring frequently.Store sauce in an air-

tight container in the refrigerator up to 3 days, or in the freezer up to 3 months.
Nutrition Facts Per Serving
Calories 47 Total Carbs 8g Net Carbs 6g Protein 2g Fat 1g Sugar 3g Fiber 2g

Spicy Asian Vinaigrette

Prep time: 5 minutes, Total time: 10 minutes, Serves: 4
Ingredients:
1-inch piece fresh ginger, peel & quarter
1 tbsp. fresh lemon juice
What you'll need from store cupboard:
¼ cup sesame oil
2 cloves garlic, peeled
2 tbsp. rice vinegar
1 tbsp. Chinese hot mustard, (chapter 16)
1 tsp light soy sauce
1/8 tsp red pepper flakes
Instructions:
Place all Ingredients in a food processor or blender and process until smooth.
Store in a jar with an airtight lid. Serving size is 2 tablespoons
Nutrition Facts Per Serving
Calories 172 Total Carbs 7g Protein 2g Fat 17g Sugar 2g Fiber 0g

Spicy Peanut Sauce

Prep time: 5 minutes, Cook time: 5 minutes, Serves: 20
Ingredients:
¼ cup fresh lime juice
2 tbsp. fresh ginger, peeled and grated
What you'll need from store cupboard:
1 ½ cups reduced-sodium, low-fat chicken broth
1 cup reduced-fat peanut butter
3 tbsp. Splenda brown sugar
2 tbsp. low-sodium soy sauce
½ tsp crushed red pepper flakes
Instructions:
In a small saucepan, over medium heat, heat peanut butter until melted. Add broth and stir until combined.
Add remaining Ingredients, and cook over med-low heat 5 minutes, stirring frequently, until thickened.Use over shrimp, scallops, chicken, turkey or beef. Serving size is 2 tablespoons.

Store in air-tight container in the refrigerator up to 3 days.
Nutrition Facts Per Serving
Calories 90 Total Carbs 9g Net Carbs 8g Protein 3g Fat 5g Sugar 4g Fiber 1g

Spicy Sweet Dipping Sauce

Prep time: 5 minutes, total time 5 minutes, Serves: 16
Ingredients:
¼ tsp habanero pepper, diced fine
1 tbsp. lime juice
What you'll need from store cupboard:
1 cup sugar free orange marmalade
1 tbsp. fish sauce
½ tsp red pepper flakes
¼ tsp sesame oil
Pinch of salt
Instructions:
Mix all Ingredients together in a small bowl. Spoon into a jar with an air tight lid and store in the refrigerator.
Serving size is 1 tablespoon. Will last up to one week in the refrigerator.
Nutrition Facts Per Serving
Calories 12 Total Carbs 5g Protein 0g Fat 0g Sugar 0g Fiber 0g

Sriracha Dipping Sauce

Prep time: 1 minute, Total time: 2 minutes, Serves: 6
Ingredients:
2 tsp fresh lime juice
What you'll need from store cupboard:
½ cup lite mayonnaise
2 tbsp. Sriracha sauce
1 tbsp. Splenda
1 tsp Worcestershire sauce
Instructions:
In a small bowl, stir all the Ingredients together until smooth.
Use right away, or cover and refrigerate until ready to use. Serving size is 1 ½ tablespoons.
Nutrition Facts Per Serving
Calories 83 Total Carbs 5g Protein 0g Fat 7g Sugar 2g Fiber 0g

Strawberry Rhubarb Jelly

Prep time: 15 minutes, Cook time: 15 minutes, serves; 64
Ingredients:
5 cups rhubarb, cut in ½-inch slices
2 cups strawberries, hulled and halved
1 tbsp. fresh lemon juice
What you'll need from store cupboard:
2 ¼ cup Splenda
Instructions:
Add all Ingredients to a large sauce pan and place over medium heat. Bring to a boil, stirring frequently.
Reduce heat, cover, and simmer 15-20 minutes, until rhubarb is soft and mixture has thickened, stirring occasionally.
Spoon into 2 pint sized jars and let cool completely. Add the lids and store in refrigerator. Serving size is 1 tablespoon.
Nutrition Facts Per Serving
Calories 37 Total Carbs 7g Protein 0g Fat 0g Sugar 7g Fiber 0g

Sugar Free Ketchup

Prep time: 5 minutes, Total time: 5 minutes, Serves: 28
What you'll need from store cupboard
12 oz. tomato paste
1 ½ cup water
1/3 cup white vinegar
1 tbsp. salt
3 tsp Splenda
1 tsp onion powder
Instructions:
In a large bowl, combine water, vinegar, Splenda, onion powder, and salt. Whisk in tomato paste until smooth.
Pour into a glass jar with an air tight lid and store in refrigerator until ready to use. Serving size is 2 tablespoons.
Nutrition Facts Per Serving
Calories 15 Total Carbs 3g Protein 0g Fat 0g Sugar 2g Fiber 0g

Tangy Mexican salad dressing

Total time: 5 minutes, Serves: 8
Ingredients:
½ cup cilantro, diced fine

3 tbsp. fresh lime juice

What you'll need from store cupboard:

½ cup sunflower oil

2 tbsp. water

1 tbsp. apple cider vinegar

2 tsp honey

1 tsp garlic salt

½ teaspoon Mexican oregano

Freshly ground black pepper, to taste

Instructions:

Add all Ingredients to a food processor or blender. Pulse until well blended and emulsified. Taste and adjust seasonings as desired.

Store in an air-tight container in the refrigerator. To serve, bring to room temperature and shake well.

Nutrition Facts Per Serving

Calories 127 Total Carbs 2g Protein 0 Fat 14g Sugar 2g Fiber 0g

Teriyaki Sauce

Prep time: 5 minutes, Cook time: 10 minutes, Serves: 16

What you'll need from store cupboard:

1 ¼ cup water, divided

¼ cup lite soy sauce

2 tbsp. + ½ tsp liquid stevia

1 ½ tbsp. corn starch

½ tsp ginger

¼ tsp garlic powder

Instructions:

Combine soy sauce, 1 cup water, ginger, garlic powder, and stevia in a small saucepan. Place over med-low heat and bring to a simmer.

Whisk the corn starch with the ¼ cup water until smooth. Add it to the sauce in the pan and mix thoroughly. Let sauce simmer until it starts to thicken, about 1 minute.

Remove from heat and cool completely. Sauce will continue to thicken as it cools. Use as a marinade or dipping sauce. Serving size is 1 tablespoon.

Nutrition Facts Per Serving

Calories 5 Total Carbs 1g Protein 0g Fat 0g Sugar 0g Fiber 0g

Walnut Vinaigrette

Total time: 5 minutes, Serves: 4

What you'll need from store cupboard:

½ cup water

¼ cup balsamic vinegar

¼ cup walnuts

¼ cup raisins

1 clove garlic

1 tsp Dijon mustard

¼ tsp thyme

Instructions:

Place all Ingredients in a blender or food processor and pulse until smooth. Store in a jar with an air tight lid in the refrigerator.

Nutrition Facts Per Serving

Calories 53 Total Carbs 2g Net Carbs 1g Protein 2g Fat 5g Sugar 0g Fiber 1g

Warm Bacon Vinaigrette Dressing

Prep time: 5 minutes, Cook time: 10 minutes, Serves: 4

Ingredients:

6 pieces thick sliced bacon, cooked crisp and crumbled

1 shallot, diced fine

What you'll need from store cupboard:

½ cup red wine vinegar

2 cloves garlic, diced fine

1 ½ tsp Splenda brown sugar

¾ tsp Dijon mustard

Salt

Fresh ground black pepper

Instructions:

After cooking the bacon, pour out all but 3 tablespoons grease into a jar, save for later.

Add the garlic and shallot to remaining hot grease and cook 2-3 minutes, or until soft.

Add Splenda and stir until it dissolves. Whisk in remaining Ingredients and season with salt and pepper to taste. Use immediately with your favorite salad.

Nutrition Facts Per Serving

Calories 115 Total Carbs 2g Protein 7g Fat 8g Sugar 1g Fiber 0g

Chapter 10
Grains, Legumes & Pasta Recipe

Cauliflower Puree

Prep time: 10 minutes, Cook time: 15 minutes, Serves: 6

Ingredients:

2 ½ lbs. cauliflower florets

½ leek, white and pale green part, halved

4 tbsp. butter

2 tsp fresh parsley, diced

What you'll need from store cupboard:

2 tbsp. low sodium chicken broth

2 tsp extra virgin olive oil

4 cloves garlic, diced fine

¼ tsp salt

¼ tsp pepper

Instructions:

Place the cauliflower in a steamer basket over boiling water. Cover and steam 10-15 minutes or until fork tender.

Rinse the leek under water and pat dry. Chop into thin slices.

Heat oil in a large skillet over med-low heat. Add the leek and cook 2-3 minutes, or until soft. Add the garlic and cook 1 minute more.

Add all Ingredients to a food processor and pulse until almost smooth. Serve warm, or refrigerate for a later use.

Nutrition Facts Per Serving

Calories 146 Total Carbs 14g Net Carbs 8g Protein 5g Fat 9g Sugar 6g Fiber 6g

Cauliflower "Rice"

Prep time: 5 minutes, Cook time: 10 minutes, Serves: 4

Ingredients:

1 small head cauliflower, separated into small florets

What you'll need from store cupboard:

1 tablespoon olive oil

1 clove of garlic, diced fine

½ tsp salt

Instructions:

Use a cheese grater to rice the cauliflower, using the big holes. Or, use a food processor and short pulses until it resembles rice.

In a nonstick skillet, over med-high heat, heat oil until hot. Add garlic and cook 1 minutes, stirring frequently. Add cauliflower and cook, stirring, 7-9 minutes, or until it is tender and starts to brown.

Serve as is or use in your favorite recipes.

Nutrition Facts Per Serving

Calories 48, Total Carbs 4g Net Carbs 2g Protein 1g Fat 4g Sugar 2g Fiber 2g

Cauliflower Pizza Crust

Prep time: 15 minutes, Cook time: 30 minutes, Serves: 8

Ingredients:

1 ½ lb. cauliflower, separated in florets

1 egg

What you'll need from store cupboard:

1 ½ cup reduced fat parmesan cheese

½ tbsp. Italian seasoning

½ tsp garlic powder

Instructions:

Heat oven to 400 degrees. Line a pizza pan, or stone, with parchment paper.

Place the cauliflower in a food processor and pulse until it resembles rice.

Cook the cauliflower in a skillet over medium heat, stirring frequently, until soft, about 10 minutes.

In a large bowl, whisk the egg, cheese and seasonings.

Place the cauliflower in a clean kitchen towel and squeeze out any excess moisture. Stir into cheese mixture to form a soft dough, press with a spatula if needed.

Spread the dough on the prepared pan about ¼-inch thick. Bake 20 minutes, or until top is dry and firm and edges are golden brown.

Let cool 5-10 minutes, the crust will firm up as it cools. Add desired toppings and bake 5-10 minutes more. Slice and serve.

Nutrition Facts Per Serving

Calories 158 Total Carbs 10g net Carbs 6g Protein 12g Fat 9g Sugar 4g Fiber 4g

Cheese Biscuits

Prep time: 20 minutes, Cook time: 20 minutes, Serves: 16

Ingredients:

8 oz. low fat cream cheese

3 cup mozzarella cheese, grated

4 eggs

2 tbsp. margarine, melted

What you'll need from store cupboard:

1-1/3 cup almond flour

4 tbsp. baking powder

Nonstick cooking spray

Instructions:

Heat oven to 400° degrees. Spray a 12-inch cast iron skillet with cooking spray

In a saucepan over low heat, melt the cream cheese and mozzarella together. Stir until smooth. Remove from heat.

In a large bowl, combine the melted cheese, eggs, baking powder, and flour. Mix until smooth. Let rest for 10 to 20 minutes.

Use a large cookie scoop, to scoop dough and place in prepared skillet. Refrigerate 10 minutes.

Bake for 20 to 25 minutes, until golden brown. Brush biscuits with melted margarine.

Nutrition Facts Per Serving

Calories 106 Total Carbs 5g Net Carbs 4g Protein 7g Fat 8g Sugar 0g Fiber 1g

Cheesy Cauliflower Puree

Prep time: 5 minutes, Cook time: 15 minutes, Serves: 6

Ingredients:

2 ½ lbs. cauliflower florets, steamed

4 oz. reduced fat sharp cheddar cheese, grated

2 tbsp. half-n-half

1 tbsp. butter

What you'll need from store cupboard:

½ tsp salt

½ tsp pepper

Instructions:

Steam the cauliflower until it is fork tender, drain. Add the cauliflower and remaining Ingredients to a food processor. Pulse until almost smooth. Serve warm.

You can make it ahead of time and just reheat it as needed also.

Nutrition Facts Per Serving

Calories 145 Total Carbs 10g Net Carbs 5g Protein 9g Fat 9g Sugar 5g Fiber 5g

Chickpea Tortillas

Prep time: 5 minutes, Cook time: 10 minutes, Serves: 4

Ingredients:

1 cup chickpea flour

1 cup water

¼ tsp salt

Nonstick cooking spray

Instructions:

In a large bowl, whisk all Ingredients together until no lumps remain.

Spray a skillet with cooking spray and place over med-high heat.

Pour batter in, ¼ cup at a time, and tilt pan to spread thinly.

Cook until golden brown on each side, about 2 minutes per side.

Use for taco shells, enchiladas, quesadillas or whatever you desire.

Nutrition Facts Per Serving

Calories 89 Total Carbs 13g Net Carbs 10g Protein 5g Fat 2g Sugar 3g Fiber 3g

"Cornbread" Stuffing

Prep time: 15 minutes, Cook time: 40 minutes, Serves: 6
Ingredients:
1 strip bacon, diced
1 egg
1 cup onion, diced
1 cup celery, diced
2 tbsp. margarine, divided
What you'll need from store cupboard:
1 cup almond flour
¼ cup low sodium chicken broth
3 cloves garlic, diced fine
2 tbsp. stone-ground cornmeal
1 tsp thyme
1 tsp sage
¾ tsp salt
Fresh ground black pepper, to taste
Instructions:
Heat the oven to 375 degrees.
Melt 1 tablespoon margarine in a skillet over low heat. Add onions and celery and cook, stirring, until soft, about 10 minutes. Add garlic and seasonings and cook 1-2 minutes more. Remove from heat and let cool.
Place the almond flour, cornmeal and bacon in a food processor and pulse until combined. Add the broth and egg and pulse just to combine. Add the onion mixture and pulse just until mixed.
Place remaining tablespoon of margarine in a cast iron skillet, or baking dish, and melt in the oven until hot. Swirl the pan to coat with melted margarine.
Spread the dressing in the pan and bake 30 minutes or until top is nicely browned and center is cooked through. Serve.
Nutrition Facts Per Serving
Calories 177 Total Carbs 9g Net Carbs 6g Protein 6g Fat 14g Sugar 2g Fiber 3g

"Flour" Tortillas

Prep time: 10 minutes, cook time 15 minutes, Serves: 4
Ingredients:
¾ cup egg whites
What you'll need from store cupboard:
1/3 cup water
¼ cup coconut flour
1 tsp sunflower oil
½ tsp salt
½ tsp cumin
½ tsp chili powder
Instructions:
Add all Ingredients, except oil, to a food processor and pulse until combined. Let rest 7-8 minutes.
Heat oil in a large skillet over med-low heat. Pour ¼ cup batter into center and tilt to spread to 7-8-inch circle.
When the top is no longer shiny, flip tortilla and cook another 1-2 minutes. Repeat with remaining batter.Place each tortilla on parchment paper and slightly wipe off any access oil.Nutrition Facts Per Serving
Calories 27 Total Carbs 1g Protein 5g Fat 0g Sugar 0g Fiber 0g

Flourless "Burger Buns"

Prep time: 10 minutes, Cook time: 35 minutes, Serves: 4
Ingredients:
4 egg yolks, room temp
4 egg whites, room temp
¼ cup low fat ricotta cheese
What you'll need from store cupboard:
¼ cup reduced fat parmesan cheese
1/4 tsp cream of tartar
Instructions:
Heat oven to 300 degrees. Line a baking sheet with parchment paper.In a large bowl, whisk egg yolks, ricotta and parmesan cheese until smooth.In a separate bowl, beat egg whites until foamy, then add in cream of tartar and beat until stiff peaks form.Add some beaten egg white to the egg yolk mixture and mix lightly. Slowly and lightly fold in the remaining egg white to the egg yolk mixture until just blended.Spoon the batter onto prepared pan to make 8 buns. Bake 35 minutes. Use as bread for sandwiches or eat on its own.
Nutrition Facts Per Serving
Calories 50 Total Carbs 1g Protein 4g Fat 3g Sugar 1g Fiber 0g

Fried Rice

Prep time: 5 minutes, Cook time: 15 minutes, Serves: 8
Ingredients:
2 cups sugar snap peas

2 egg whites

1 egg

What you'll need from store cupboard:

1 cup instant brown rice, cooked according to directions

2 tbsp. lite soy sauce

Instructions:

Add the peas to the cooked rice and mix to combine.

In a small skillet, scramble the egg and egg whites. Add the rice and peas to the skillet and stir in soy sauce. Cook, stirring frequently, about 2-3 minutes, or until heated through. Serve.

Nutrition Facts Per Serving

Calories 107 Total Carbs 20g Net Carbs 19g Protein 4g Fat 1g Sugar 1g Fiber 1g

Garlic Basil Breadsticks

Prep time: 10 minutes, Cook time: 10 minutes, Serves: 4

Ingredients:

2 eggs, beaten

2 cup mozzarella cheese, grated

2 tbsp. cream cheese

2 tbsp. fresh basil, diced

What you'll need from store cupboard:

4 tbsp. coconut flour

4 cloves garlic, crushed

Nonstick cooking spray

Instructions:

Heat oven to 400 degrees. Spray a baking sheet with cooking spray.

Add mozzarella, cream cheese, crushed garlic and basil to a microwaveable bowl. Mix and then cook for 1 minute. Stir well to make sure the cheeses are melted and then add in the flour and egg.

Mix well, use your hands if needed to form into a dough.

Break off pieces of the dough and roll into a long finger shapes. Place on prepared pan.

Bake 8-10 minutes or until the dough begins to brown. Remove from heat and let cool slightly before serving.

Nutrition Facts Per Serving

Calories 153 Total Carbs 10g Net Carbs 5g Protein 9g Fat 8g Sugar 1g Fiber 5g

Healthy Loaf of Bread

Prep time: 10 minutes, Cook time: 30 minutes, Serves: 20

Ingredients:

6 eggs, separated

4 tbsp. butter, melted

What you'll need from store cupboard:

1 ½ cup almond flour, sifted

3 tsp baking powder

¼ tsp cream of tartar

1/8 tsp salt

Butter flavored cooking spray

Instructions:

Heat oven to 375 degrees. Spray an 8-inch loaf pan with cooking spray.

In a large bowl, beat egg whites and cream of tartar until soft peaks form

Add the yolks, 1/3 of egg whites, butter, flour, baking powder, and salt to a food processor and pulse until combined.

Add remaining egg whites and pulse until thoroughly combined, being careful not to over mix the dough.

Pour into prepared pan and bake 30 minutes, or until bread passes the toothpick test. Cool 10 minutes in the pan then invert and cool completely before slicing.

Nutrition Facts Per Serving

Calories 81 Total Carbs 2g Net Carbs 1g Protein 3g Fat 7g Sugar 0g Fiber 1g

Homemade Noodles

Prep time: 5 minutes, chill time; 4 hours, Serves: 2

Ingredients:

1 cup mozzarella cheese, grated

1 egg yolk

Instructions:

Add the mozzarella to a bowl and microwave for 1-2 minutes, until melted. Let cool for 30 seconds. With a rubber spatula, gently fold the egg yolk into the cheese.

Turn the mixture out onto a parchment paper-lined baking sheet. Place another piece of parchment paper on top of the dough and press down with your hand until thin.

Remove the top piece of parchment and cut the dough into thin strips. Place the "pasta" on a rack and refrigerate for four hours or overnight.

To cook, place in boiling water for 1 minute. Drain and run cool water over to prevent sticking. Serve with your favorite sauce.

Nutrition Facts Per Serving

Calories 67 Total Carbs 1g Protein 5g Fat 5g Sugar 0g Fiber 0g

Homemade Pasta

Prep time: 20 minutes, Cook time: 5 minutes, Serves: 8

Ingredients:

1 egg + 2 egg yolks

What you'll need from store cupboard:

1 ¾ cup soy flour

¼ cup ground wheat germ

3-4 tbsp. cold water

1 tsp light olive oil

½ tsp salt

Instructions:

In a large bowl, whisk egg, egg yolks, oil and 3 tablespoons water until smooth.

In a separate bowl, combine flour, wheat germ, and salt. Stir into egg mixture until smooth. Use the last tablespoon of water if needed to make a smooth dough.

Turn out onto a lightly floured surface and knead 5-8 minutes or until smooth. Cover and let rest 10 minutes.

Divide dough into 4 equal pieces and roll out, one at a time, as thin as possible, or run it through a pasta machine until it reaches the thinnest setting. Let dough dry out for 30 minutes. Cut into desired size with pasta machine or pizza cutter. It not using right away, let it dry overnight on a pasta or cooling rack. Fresh pasta should be used within 3 days.It will store in the freezer, after drying for just an hour, in an airtight bag, 6-8 months. Pasta dried overnight can be stored in an airtight container for up to 1 week.

To cook it when fresh, add to a pot of boiling water for 4-5 minutes or until tender. Dried pasta will take a couple minutes longer.

Nutrition Facts Per Serving

Calories 152 Total Carbs 12g Net Carbs 9g Protein 16g Fat 5g Sugar 6g Fiber 3g

Light Beer Bread

Prep time: 5 minutes, Cook time: 55 minutes, Serves: 14

Ingredients:

¼ cup butter, soft

What you'll need from store cupboard:

12 oz. light beer

3 cup low carb baking mix

1/3 cup Splenda

Instructions:

Heat oven to 375 degrees. Use 1 tablespoon butter to grease the bottom of a 9x5-inch loaf pan.

In a large bowl, whisk together beer, baking mix, and Splenda. Pour into prepared pan.

Bake 45-55 minutes or until golden brown. Cool in pan 10 minutes, remove from pan and cool on wire rack.

In a small glass bowl, melt remaining butter in a microwave and brush over warm loaf. Cool 15 minutes before slicing.

Nutrition Facts Per Serving

Calories 162 Total Carbs 16g Net Carbs 12g Protein 9g Fat 5g Sugar 5g Fiber 4g

Mexican "Rice"

Prep time: 5 minutes, Cook time: 10 minutes, Serves: 6

Ingredients:

2 cups cauliflower rice, cooked

1 small jalapeño, seeded and diced fine

½ white onion, diced

What you'll need from store cupboard:

½ cup water

½ cup tomato paste

3 cloves garlic, diced fine

2 tsp salt

2 tsp olive oil

Instructions:

Heat oil in skillet over medium heat. Add onion, garlic, jalapeno, and salt and cook 3-4 min, stirring frequently.

In a small bowl, whisk water and tomato paste together. Add to skillet. Cook, stirring frequently, 3-5 minutes.

Stir in cauliflower, and cook just until heated through and most of the liquid is absorbed. Serve.
Nutrition Facts Per Serving
Calories 46 Total Carbs 7g Net Carbs 5g Protein 2g Fat 2g Sugar 4g Fiber 2g

No Corn "Cornbread"

Prep time: 10 minutes, Cook time: 25 minutes, Serves: 16
Ingredients:
4 eggs, room temperature
1/3 cup butter, melted
What you'll need from store cupboard:
1 ½ cup almond flour, sifted
1/3 cup Splenda
1 tsp baking powder
Instructions:
Heat oven to 350 degrees. Line an 8-inch baking dish with parchment paper.
In a large bowl, whisk together eggs, butter, and Splenda. Stir in the flour and baking powder until no lumps remain.
Pour batter into prepared dish and smooth the top. Bake 25-30 minutes or until edges are golden brown and it passes the toothpick test.
Let cool 5 minutes before slicing and serving.
Nutrition Facts Per Serving
Calories 121 Total Carbs 6g Net Carbs 5g Protein 3g Fat 9g Sugar 4g Fiber 1g

Quick Coconut Flour Buns

Prep time: 5 minutes, Cook time: 20 minutes, Serves: 4
Ingredients:
3 eggs, room temperature
2 tbsp. coconut milk, room temperature
What you'll need from store cupboard:
¼ cup coconut flour
2 tablespoons coconut oil, soft
1 tbsp. honey
½ tsp baking powder
½ tsp salt
Instructions:
Heat oven to 375 degrees. Line a cookie sheet with parchment paper.
In a small bowl, sift together flour, baking powder and salt.

In a medium bowl, combine eggs, coconut oil, milk, and honey, mix well. Slowly add dry Ingredients to the egg mixture. Batter will be thick but make sure there is no lumps.
Form into 4 balls and place on prepared pan. Press down into rounds ½-inch thick. Bake 15-20 minutes or until buns pass the toothpick test.
Nutrition Facts Per Serving
Calories 143 Total Carbs 6g Protein 4g Fat 12g Sugar 5g Fiber 0g

Pizza Crust

Prep time: 20 minutes, Cook time: 40 minutes, Serves: 4
Ingredients:
1 ½ cup mozzarella cheese, grated
2 oz. cream cheese
1 egg, beaten
What you'll need from store cupboard:
¾ cup almond flour
½ tsp Italian seasoning
½ tsp salt
½ tsp garlic powder
½ tsp onion powder
Instructions:
Heat oven to 400 degrees. Line a large baking sheet with parchment paper.
In large bowl, microwave cream cheese and mozzarella for 60 seconds. Remove from microwave and stir. Return to microwave and cook another 30 seconds. Stir until well combined.
Add flour, salt, onion powder, garlic powder, and egg. Stir until almond flour is well incorporated into cheese. If mixture becomes too sticky, microwave another 10-15 seconds to warm up.
Place dough on parchment paper and roll out thin. Poke holes in crust with fork. Bake 10 minutes.
Remove from oven and turn over. Bake another 10 minutes.
Remove from oven and top with desired pizza toppings.
Return to oven and bake another 10 minutes, until toppings are hot and cheese is melted.
Nutrition Facts Per Serving
Calories 198 Total Carbs 5g Net Carbs 3g Protein 9g Fat 17g Sugar 1g Fiber 2g

Chapter 11
Poultry Recipes

Crunchy Chicken Fingers

Servings: 2
Cooking Time: 4 Minutes
Ingredients:
2 medium-sized chicken breasts, cut in stripes
3 tbsp parmesan cheese
¼ tbsp fresh chives, chopped
⅓ cup breadcrumbs
1 egg white
2 tbsp plum sauce, optional
½ tbsp fresh thyme, chopped
½ tbsp black pepper
1 tbsp water
Directions:
Preheat the Air Fryer to 360 F. Mix the chives, parmesan, thyme, pepper and breadcrumbs. In another bowl, whisk the egg white and mix with the water. Dip the chicken strips into the egg mixture and the breadcrumb mixture. Place the strips in the air fryer basket and cook for 10 minutes. Serve with plum sauce.
Nutrition Info: Calories: 253; Carbs: 31g; Fat: 18g; Protein: 28g

Polynesian Chicken

Servings: 6 Cups
Cooking Time: 4 Hours
Ingredients:
3 garlic cloves, minced
2 bell peppers, cut into 1/2-inch strips
1 (20-ounce) can pineapple chunks in juice, drained, with juice reserved
1 1/2-pound boneless chicken breasts, cut into 2-inch cubes
1/3 cup honey
2 tablespoons tapioca flour
3 tablespoons low-sodium soy sauce
1 teaspoon ground ginger
Directions:
Add reserved pineapple juice, 3 tablespoons of soy sauce, 1/3 cup honey, 1 teaspoon ground ginger and 3 minced cloves of garlic into a bowl; whisk well. Then add 2 tablespoons tapioca flour and whisk again until combined.
Add chicken along with chunks of pineapple into a slow cooker.
Pour mixture of pineapple juice over chicken and cover the cooker.
Cook for about 4-5 hours on low, until chicken is completely cooked through.
Then add strips of bell pepper in the last hour of cooking. Serve and enjoy!
Nutrition Info: 273 calories; 26 g fat; 37 g total carbs; 26 g protein

Buffalo Chicken

Servings: 8
Cooking Time: 30 Minutes
Ingredients:
2 celery stalks, diced
1 medium-sized onion, chopped
100 ml buffalo wing sauce
100 ml chicken broth
21 kg chicken breasts, frozen
Directions:
Add the celery, onions, wing sauce, chicken broth and chicken to the Instant Pot. Cook frozen chicken on high pressure for 20 minutes. Turn the pressure valve to "Vent" to release all of the pressure.
Remove the chicken breasts from the pot, and shred.
You can remove most of the liquid from the pot, or not.
Nutrition Info: Calories: 197 Fat: 8g Carbohydrates: 16g Protein: 14g

Chicken & Peanut Stir-fry

Servings: 4
Cooking Time: 15 Minutes
Ingredients:
3 tablespoons lime juice
½ teaspoon lime zest

4 cloves garlic, minced
2 teaspoons chili bean sauce
1 tablespoon fish sauce
1 tablespoon water
2 tablespoons peanut butter
3 teaspoons oil, divided
1 lb. chicken breast, sliced into strips
1 red sweet pepper, sliced into strips
3 green onions, sliced thinly
2 cups broccoli, shredded
2 tablespoons peanuts, chopped
Directions:
In a bowl, mix the lime juice, lime zest, garlic, chili bean sauce, fish sauce, water and peanut butter. Mix well.
In a pan over medium high heat, add 2 teaspoons of oil.
Cook the chicken until golden on both sides.
Pour in the remaining oil.
Add the pepper and green onions.
Add the chicken, broccoli and sauce.
Cook for 2 minutes.
Top with peanuts before serving.
Nutrition Info: Calories 368 Total Fat 11 g Saturated Fat 2 g Cholesterol 66 mg Sodium 556 mg Total Carbohydrate 34 g Dietary Fiber 3 g Total Sugars 4 g Protein 32 g Potassium 482 mg

Meatballs Curry

Servings: 6
Cooking Time: 25 Minutes
Ingredients:
For Meatballs:
1 pound lean ground chicken
1 tablespoon onion paste
1 teaspoons fresh ginger paste
1 teaspoons garlic paste
1 green chili, chopped finely
1 tablespoon fresh cilantro leaves, chopped
1 teaspoon ground coriander
½ teaspoon cumin seeds
½ teaspoon red chili powder
½ teaspoon ground turmeric
1/8 teaspoon salt
For Curry:
3 tablespoons olive oil
½ teaspoon cumin seeds
1 (1-inch) cinnamon stick
2 onions, chopped

1 teaspoons fresh ginger, minced
1 teaspoons garlic, minced
4 tomatoes, chopped finely
2 teaspoons ground coriander
1 teaspoon garam masala powder
½ teaspoon ground nutmeg
½ teaspoon red chili powder
½ teaspoon ground turmeric
Salt, as required
1 cup filtered water
3 tablespoons fresh cilantro, chopped
Directions:
For meatballs: in a large bowl, add all ingredients and mix until well combined.
Make small equal-sized meatballs from mixture.
In a large deep skillet, heat the oil over medium heat and cook the meatballs for about 3-5 minutes or until browned from all sides.
Transfer the meatballs into a bowl.
In the same skillet, add the cumin seeds and cinnamon stick and sauté for about 1 minute.
Add the onions and sauté for about 4-5 minutes.
Add the ginger and garlic paste and sauté for about 1 minute.
Add the tomato and spices and cook, crushing with the back of spoon for about 2-3 minutes.
Add the water and meatballs and bring to a boil.
Now, reduce the heat to low and simmer for about 10 minutes.
Serve hot with the garnishing of cilantro.
Meal Prep Tip: Transfer the curry into a large bowl and set aside to cool. Divide the curry into 5 containers evenly. Cover the containers and refrigerate for 1-2 days. Reheat in the microwave before serving.
Nutrition Info: Calories 196 Total Fat 11.4 g Saturated Fat 2.4 g Cholesterol 53 mg Total Carbs 7.9 g Sugar 3.9 g Fiber 2.1 g Sodium 143 mg Potassium 279 mg Protein 16.7 g

Jerk Style Chicken Wings

Servings: 2-3
Cooking Time: 25 Minutes.
Ingredients:
1g ground thyme
1g dried rosemary
2g allspice
4g ground ginger
3 g garlic powder

2g onion powder
1g of cinnamon
2g of paprika
2g chili powder
1g nutmeg
Salt to taste
30 ml of vegetable oil
0.5 - 1 kg of chicken wings
1 lime, juice
Directions:
Select Preheat, set the temperature to 200°C and press Start/Pause.
Combine all spices and oil in a bowl to create a marinade.
Mix the chicken wings in the marinade until they are well covered.
Place the chicken wings in the preheated air fryer.
Select Chicken and press Start/Pause. Be sure to shake the baskets in the middle of cooking.
Remove the wings and place them on a serving plate.
Squeeze fresh lemon juice over the wings and serve.
Nutrition Info: Calories: 240 Fat: 15g Carbohydrate: 5g Protein: 19g Sugars: 4g Cholesterol: 60mg

Italian Chicken

Servings: 4
Cooking Time: 16 Minutes
Ingredients:
5 chicken thighs
1 tbsp. olive oil
1/4 cup parmesan; grated
1/2 cup sun dried tomatoes
2 garlic cloves; minced
1 tbsp. thyme; chopped.
1/2 cup heavy cream
3/4 cup chicken stock
1 tsp. red pepper flakes; crushed
2 tbsp. basil; chopped
Salt and black pepper to the taste
Directions:
Season chicken with salt and pepper, rub with half of the oil, place in your preheated air fryer at 350 °F and cook for 4 minutes.
Meanwhile; heat up a pan with the rest of the oil over medium high heat, add thyme garlic, pepper flakes, sun dried tomatoes, heavy cream, stock,
parmesan, salt and pepper; stir, bring to a simmer, take off heat and transfer to a dish that fits your air fryer.
Add chicken thighs on top, introduce in your air fryer and cook at 320 °F, for 12 minutes. Divide among plates and serve with basil sprinkled on top.
Nutrition Info: Calories: 272; Fat: 9; Fiber: 12; Carbs: 37; Protein: 23

Coconut Chicken

Servings: 6 Cooking Time: 4 Hours
Ingredients:
2 garlic cloves, minced
Fresh cilantro, minced
1/2 cup light coconut milk
6 tablespoons sweetened coconut, shredded and toasted
2 tablespoons brown sugar
6 (about 1-1/2 pounds) boneless skinless chicken thighs
2 tablespoons reduced-sodium soy sauce
1/8 teaspoon ground cloves
Directions:
Mix brown sugar, 1/2 cup light coconut milk, 2 tablespoons soy sauce, 1/8 teaspoon ground cloves and 2 minced cloves of garlic in a bowl.
Add 6 chicken boneless thighs into a Crockpot.
Now pour the mixture of coconut milk over chicken thighs. Cover the cooker and cook for about 4-5 hours on low.
Serve coconut chicken with cilantro and coconut; enjoy!
Nutrition Info: 201 calories; 10 g fat; 6 g total carbs; 21 g protein

Spicy Lime Chicken

Servings: 6
Cooking Time: 3 Hours
Ingredients:
3 tablespoons lime juice
Fresh cilantro leaves
1-1/2 pounds (about 4) boneless skinless chicken breast halves
1 teaspoon lime zest, grated
2 cups chicken broth
1 tablespoon chili powder
Directions:
Add chicken breast halves into a slow cooker.

Add 1 tablespoon chili powder, 3 tablespoons lime juice and 2 cups chicken broth in a small bowl; mix well and pour over chicken.

Cover the cooker and cook for about 3 hours on low. Once done, take chicken out from the cooker and let it cool.

Once cooled, shred chicken by using forks and transfer back to the Crockpot.

Stir in 1 teaspoon grated lime zest. Serve spicy lime chicken with cilantro and enjoy!

Nutrition Info:132 calories; 3 g fat; 2 g total carbs; 23 g protein

Crock-pot Slow Cooker Ranch Chicken

Servings: 4
Cooking Time: 4 Hours
Ingredients:
1 cup chive and onion cream cheese spread
½ teaspoon freshly ground black pepper
4 boneless chicken breasts
1 1-oz package ranch dressing and seasoning mix
½ cup low sodium chicken stock
Directions:
Spray the Crock-Pot slow cooker with cooking spray and preheat it.

Dry chicken with paper towel and transfer it to the Crock-Pot slow cooker.

Cook each side, until chicken is browned, for about 4-5 minutes.

Add ½ cup low sodium chicken stock, 1 1-oz. package ranch dressing and seasoning mix, 1 cup chive and onion cream cheese spread and ½ teaspoon freshly ground black pepper. Cover the Crock-Pot slow cooker and cook for about 4 hours on Low or until the internal temperature reaches 165 F. Once cooked, take it out from the Crock-Pot slow cooker. Whisk the sauce present in the Crock-Pot slow cooker until smooth. If you need thick sauce, then cook for about 5-10 minutes, with frequent stirring. Garnish chicken with sliced onions and bacon and serve.

Nutrition Info: 362 calories; 18.5 g fat; 9.7 g total carbs; 37.3 g protein

Mustard Chicken With Basil

Servings: 4
Cooking Time: 30 Minutes
Ingredients:
1 tsp Chicken stock

2 Chicken breasts; skinless and boneless chicken breasts: halved
1 tbsp Chopped basil
What you'll need from the store cupboard:
Salt and black pepper
1 tbsp Olive oil
½ tsp Garlic powder
½ tsp Onion powder
1 tsp Dijon mustard
Directions:
Press 'Sauté' on the instant pot and add the oil. When it is hot, brown the chicken in it for 2-3 minutes.

Mix in the remaining ingredients and seal the lid to cook for 12 minutes at high pressure.

Natural release the pressure for 10 minutes, share into plates and serve.

Nutrition Info: Calories 34, fat 3.6, carbs 0.7, protein 0.3, fiber 0.1

Chicken Chili

Servings: 6
Cooking Time: 40 Minutes
Ingredients:
4 cups low-sodium chicken broth, divided
3 cups boiled black beans, divided
1 tablespoon extra-virgin olive oil
1 large onion, chopped
1 jalapeño pepper, seeded and chopped
4 garlic cloves, minced
1 teaspoon dried thyme, crushed
1½ tablespoons ground coriander
1 tablespoon ground cumin
½ tablespoon red chili powder
4 cups cooked chicken, shredded
1 tablespoon fresh lime juice
¼ cup fresh cilantro, chopped
Directions:
In a food processor, add 1 cup of broth and 1 can of black beans and pulse until smooth.

Transfer the beans puree into a bowl and set aside.

In a large pan, heat the oil over medium heat and sauté the onion and jalapeño for about 4-5 minutes.

Add the garlic, spices and sea salt and sauté for about 1 minute.

Add the beans puree and remaining broth and bring to a boil.

Now, reduce the heat to low and simmer for about 20 minutes.

Stir in the remaining can of beans, chicken and lime juice and bring to a boil.

Now, reduce the heat to low and simmer for about 5-10 minutes.

Serve hot with the garnishing of cilantro.

Meal Prep Tip: Transfer the chili into a large bowl and set aside to cool. Divide the chili into 6 containers evenly. Cover the containers and refrigerate for 1-2 days. Reheat in the microwave before serving.

Nutrition Info: Calories 356 Total Fat 7.1 g Saturated Fat 1.2 g Cholesterol 72 mg Total Carbs 33 g Sugar 2.7 g Fiber 11.6 g Sodium 130 mg Potassium 662 mg Protein 39.6 g

Chicken With Cashew Nuts

Servings: 4
Cooking Time: 30 Minutes
Ingredients:
1 lb chicken cubes
2 tbsp soy sauce
1 tbsp corn flour
2 ½ onion cubes
1 carrot, chopped
⅓ cup cashew nuts, fried
1 capsicum, cut
2 tbsp garlic, crushed
Salt and white pepper
Directions:
Marinate the chicken cubes with ½ tbsp of white pepper, ½ tsp salt, 2 tbsp soya sauce, and add 1 tbsp corn flour.

Set aside for 25 minutes. Preheat the Air Fryer to 380 F and transfer the marinated chicken. Add the garlic, the onion, the capsicum, and the carrot; fry for 5-6 minutes. Roll it in the cashew nuts before serving.

Nutrition Info: Calories: 425; Carbs: 25g; Fat: 35g; Protein: 53g

Chuck And Veggies

Servings: 2
Cooking Time: 9 Hours
Ingredients:
¼ cup dry red wine
¼ teaspoon salt
8 oz. boneless lean chuck roast

¼ teaspoon black pepper
8 oz. frozen pepper stir-fry
1 teaspoon Worcestershire sauce
8 oz. whole mushrooms
1 teaspoon instant coffee granules
1 1/4 cups fresh green beans, trimmed
1 dried bay leaf
Directions:
Mix all the ingredients except salt in a bowl; combine well and then transfer to a slow cooker.

Cover the cooker and cook for about 9 hours on low and 4 1/2 hours on high, until beef is completely cooked through and tender.

Stir in ¼ teaspoon salt gently. Take out the vegetables and beef and transfer to 2 shallow bowls.

Pour liquid into the skillet; boil it lightly and cook until liquid reduces to ¼ cup, for about 1 1/2 minutes.

Pour over veggies and beef. Discard bay leaf and serve.

Nutrition Info: 215 calories; 5 g fat; 17 g total carbs; 26 g protein

Chicken & Broccoli Bake

Servings: 6
Cooking Time: 45 Minutes
Ingredients:
6 (6-ounce) boneless, skinless chicken breasts
3 broccoli heads, cut into florets
4 garlic cloves, minced
¼ cup olive oil
1 teaspoon dried oregano, crushed
1 teaspoon dried rosemary, crushed
Sea Salt and ground black pepper, as required
Directions:
Preheat the oven to 375 degrees F. Grease a large baking dish.

In a large bowl, add all the ingredients and toss to coat well.

In the bottom of prepared baking dish, arrange the broccoli florets and top with chicken breasts in a single layer.

Bake for about 45 minutes.

Remove from the oven and set aside for about 5 minutes before serving.

Meal Prep Tip: Remove the baking dish from the oven and set aside to cool completely. In 6 containers, divide the chicken breasts and broccoli evenly and refrigerate for about 2 days. Reheat in microwave before serving.

Nutrition Info: Calories 443 Total Fat 21.5 g Saturated Fat 4.7 g Cholesterol 151 mg Total Carbs 9.4 g Sugar 2.2g Fiber 3.6 g Sodium 189 mg Potassium 831 mg Protein 53 g

Rosemary Lemon Chicken

Servings: 4
Cooking Time: 14 Minutes
Ingredients:
1 kg chicken breast halves
1 lemon, peeled and sliced into rounds
1/2 orange, peeled and sliced into rounds, or to taste
3 cloves roasted garlic, or to taste
salt and ground black pepper to taste
1 1/2 tablespoons olive oil, or to taste
1 1/2 teaspoons agave syrup, or to taste (optional)
1/4 cup water
2 sprigs fresh rosemary, stemmed, or to taste
Directions:
Place chicken in the Instant Pot. Add lemon, orange, and garlic; season with salt and pepper. Drizzle olive oil and agave syrup (if using) on top. Add water and rosemary. Put the lid on the cooker and Lock in place.
Select the "Meat" and "Stew" settings for High pressure, and cook for 14 minutes. Allow pressure to release naturally, about 20 minutes.
Nutrition Info:Calories 325 Fat 5 g Carbohydrates 20 g Sugar 2 g Protein 10 g Cholesterol 33 mg

Ginger Flavored Chicken

Servings: 6
Cooking Time: 15 Minutes
Ingredients:
1 kg boneless, skinless chicken breasts (frozen OR thawed)
6 tablespoons soy sauce
3 tablespoons rice vinegar
1/2 tablespoon honey
3 tablespoons water, broth, or orange juice
2 tablespoons chopped fresh ginger
6 cloves garlic, minced
3 teaspoons corn starch
Directions:
Place chicken breasts in Instant Pot.

In a small mixing bowl, whisk together: vinegar, soy sauce, honey, water, ginger and garlic. Pour mixture over chicken and coat evenly.

Secure lid on Instant Pot and cook at High pressure for 15 minutes. When the meat is cooked, release steam.

Remove chicken breasts and place on a cutting board. Bring remaining sauce in pan up to a simmer (use the Saute feature on an electric cooker). Combine cornstarch with 3 teaspoons cold water and then pour mixture into pan. Simmer until sauce is thickened and the turn off heat.

Shred chicken and return to pot with sauce.

Nutrition Info: Calories 313 Fat 25.6 g Carbohydrates 15.6 g Sugar 7 g Protein 8 g Cholesterol 36 mg

Crock-pot Slow Cooker Tex-mex Chicken

Servings: 6
Cooking Time: 4 Hours 40 Minutes
Ingredients:
4 tablespoons cup water
1 teaspoon ground cumin
1 lb boneless chicken thighs, visible fat removed, rinsed, and patted dry
1 (10 oz) can diced tomatoes and green chilies
1 (16 oz) package frozen onion and pepper strips, thawed
Directions:
Spray a skillet with cooking spray and turn heat flame on.

Place chicken thighs into the skillet and cook each side until browned over medium heat. Once browned, take out from the skillet.

To the same skillet, add peppers and onions and cook until tender.

Transfer cooked peppers and onions into 4- to 5-quart Crock-Pot slow cooker followed by chicken thighs on top.

Place tomatoes along with 4 tablespoons of water over chicken. Cook for about 4 hours on Low.

Add 1 teaspoon ground cumin and cook further for half an hour.

Once done, take it out and serve right away!

Nutrition Info: 121 calories; 3.2 g fat; 6.4 g total carbs; 16 g protein

Slow-cooker Chicken Fajita Burritos

Servings: 8
Cooking Time: 6 Hrs
Ingredients:
1 teaspoon cumin
1 cup cheddar cheese + 2 tablespoons reduced-fat, shredded
1 lb. chicken strips, skinless and boneless
8 large low-carb tortillas
1 green pepper, sliced
1 can (15 oz) black beans, rinsed and drained
1 red pepper, sliced
1/3 cup water
1 medium onion, sliced
½ cup salsa
1 tablespoon chili powder
1 teaspoon garlic powder
Directions:
Place strips of chicken breast in a slow-cooker.
Top chicken with all ingredients mentioned above except for cheese and tortillas. Cover the cooker and cook for approximately 6 hours, until done.
Shred chicken with a fork.
Serve half cup of chicken on each tortilla along with the bean mixture.
Finish with 2 tablespoons of shredded cheese, then fold tortilla into a burrito.
Nutrition Info: 250 calories; 7 g fat; 31 g total carbs; 28 g protein

Chicken With Chickpeas

Servings: 4
Cooking Time: 36 Minutes
Ingredients:
2 tablespoons olive oil
1 pound skinless, boneless chicken breast, cubed
2 carrots, peeled and sliced
1 onion, chopped
2 celery stalks, chopped
2 garlic cloves, chopped
1 tablespoon fresh ginger root, minced
½ teaspoon dried oregano, crushed
¾ teaspoon ground cumin
½ teaspoon paprika
¼-13 teaspoon cayenne pepper
¼ teaspoon ground turmeric
1 cup tomatoes, crushed
1½ cups low-sodium chicken broth
1 zucchini, sliced
1 cup boiled chickpeas, drained
1 tablespoon fresh lemon juice
Directions:
In a large nonstick pan, heat the oil over medium heat and cook the chicken cubes for about 4-5 minutes.
With a slotted spoon, transfer the chicken cubes onto a plate.
In the same pan, add the carrot, onion, celery and garlic and sauté for about 4-5 minutes.
Add the ginger, oregano and spices and sauté for about 1 minute.
Add the chicken, tomato and broth and bring to a boil.
Now, reduce the heat to low and simmer for about 10 minutes.
Add the zucchini and chickpeas and simmer, covered for about 15 minutes.
Stir in the lemon juice and serve hot.
Meal Prep Tip: Transfer the chicken mixture into a large bowl and set aside to cool. Divide the mixture into 4 containers evenly. Cover the containers and refrigerate for 1-2 days. Reheat in the microwave before serving.
Nutrition Info: Calories 308 Total Fat 12.3 g Saturated Fat 2.7 g Cholesterol 66 mg Total Carbs 19 g Sugar 5.3g Fiber 4.7 g Sodium 202 mg Potassium 331 mg Protein 30.7 g

Garlic Soy-glazed Chicken

Servings: 6
Cooking Time: 25 Minutes
Ingredients:
2 pounds' boneless chicken thighs
What you'll need from the store cupboard:
Salt and pepper
1 tablespoon minced garlic
¼ cup soy sauce
¾ cup apple cider vinegar
Directions:
Season the chicken with salt and pepper, then add it to the Instant Pot, skin-side down.
Whisk together the apple cider vinegar, soy sauce, and garlic then add to the pot.
Close and lock the lid, then press the Manual button and adjust the timer to 15 minutes.
When the timer goes off, let the pressure vent naturally.

When the pot has depressurized, open the lid. Remove the chicken to a baking sheet and place under the broiler for 3 to 5 minutes until the skin is crisp.

Meanwhile, turn the Instant Pot on to Sauté and cook until the sauce thickens, stirring as needed.

Serve the chicken with the sauce spooned over it.

Nutrition Info: calories 335 fat 23g protein 27.5g carbs 1.5g fiber 0g net carbs 1.5g

Chicken Tikka Masala

Servings: 4
Cooking Time: 10 Minutes
Ingredients:
2 tablespoons olive oil
1 small onion, diced
3 cloves garlic, minced
1 (2-inch) piece fresh ginger, peeled and grated
1/2 cup chicken broth,
1 1/2 tablespoons garam masala
1 teaspoon paprika
1/2 teaspoon ground turmeric
1/2 teaspoon salt
1/4 teaspoon cayenne pepper
750 gr boneless, skinless chicken meat, cut into small pieces
450 g can tomatoes, juices included
1/2 cup coconut milk
Fresh cilantro, chopped
Directions:
Set the cooker to the Sauté. Add the oil, and when it's hot, add the onion and sauté until softened, about 3 minutes. Add the garlic and ginger and cook until soft.

Add half of the chicken broth. Cook for couple of minutes, stirring all the time, add the garam masala, paprika, turmeric, salt, and cayenne pepper, and stir to combine.

Add the chicken and the remaining chicken broth and the tomatoes.

Close and lock the lid. Pressure-cook for 10 minutes at High pressure. When it's cooked, do a quick release of the pressure.

Stir the coconut milk into the sauce.

Serving suggestion: Serve on a bed of cauliflower "rice", or boiled potatoes.

Nutrition Info: Calories 245 Fat 25 g Carbohydrates 12.6 g Sugar 4g Protein 5 g Cholesterol 35 mg

Lemon Garlic Turkey

Servings: 4
Cooking Time: 5 Minutes
Ingredients:
4 turkey breasts fillet
2 cloves garlic, minced
1 tablespoon olive oil
3 tablespoons lemon juice
1 oz. Parmesan cheese, shredded
Pepper to taste
1 tablespoon fresh sage, snipped
1 teaspoon lemon zest
Directions:
Pound the turkey breast until flat.
In a bowl, mix the olive oil, garlic and lemon juice. Add the turkey to the bowl.
Marinate for 1 hour.
Broil for 5 minutes until turkey is fully cooked.
Sprinkle cheese on top on the last minute of cooking.
In a bowl, mix the pepper, sage and lemon zest. Sprinkle this mixture on top of the turkey before serving.
Nutrition Info: Calories 188 Total Fat 7 g Saturated Fat 2 g Cholesterol 71 mg Sodium 173 mg Total Carbohydrate 2 g Dietary Fiber 0 g Total Sugars 0 g Protein 29 g Potassium 264 mg

Whole Roasted Chicken

Servings: 6
Cooking Time: 10 Minutes
Ingredients:
1 whole chicken (about 2 kg)
1 tablespoon chopped fresh rosemary
1 1/2-2 tablespoons olive oil, plus a bit more for drizzling in pan
4-6 cloves garlic
1/2 teaspoon paprika
Salt and pepper to taste
Zest from 1 lemon
1 cup chicken broth
1 large onion, quartered
Directions:
Rinse the chicken with cold water and pat dry with paper towels. Place in baking pan and set aside.
Preheat Instant Pot and go to Saute mode.
In a small bowl combine rosemary, olive oil, garlic, paprika, salt, pepper, and lemon zest. After

removing the zest, cut lemon in half and stuff in cavity of chicken. Spread spice mixture all over the chicken, spreading evenly. Drizzle some olive oil in your hot pan and place chicken breast-side down into pot. Leave for 3-4 minutes, until golden brown. Flip chicken over and bake the other side. Remove chicken from pan and set onto the baking dish where it was before. Add broth to pan. Place onion on bottom of pan, place chicken on top (breast-side up) and secure lid.

Cook on High pressure for 6 minutes per pound. When it's cooked, wait for 10 minutes before releasing steam. Remove chicken and wait for at least 5 minutes before slicing.

Nutrition Info: Calories 301 Fat 27.2 g Carbohydrates 13.6 g Sugar 6 g Protein 4.9 g Cholesterol 33 mg

Fried Chicken Tamari And Mustard

Servings: 4
Cooking Time: 1h 20 Minutes
Ingredients:
1kg of very small chopped chicken
Tamari Sauce
Original mustard
Ground pepper
1 lemon
Flour
Extra virgin olive oil
Directions:
Put the chicken in a bowl, you can put the chicken with or without the skin, to everyone's taste.

Add a generous stream of tamari, one or two tablespoons ofmustard, a little ground pepper and a splash of lemon juice.

Link everything very well and let macerate an hour. Pass the chicken pieces for flour and place in the air fryer basket. Put 20 minutes at 200 degrees. At half time, move the chicken from the basket.

Do not crush the chicken, it is preferable to make two or three batches of chicken to pile up and do not fry the pieces well.

Nutrition Info: Calories: 100 Fat: 6g Carbohydrates 0g Protein: 18g Sugar: 0g

Herbed Chicken

Servings: 4Cooking Time: 50 Minutes
Ingredients:
1 whole chicken

1 tsp. garlic powder
1 tsp. onion powder
1/2 tsp. thyme; dried
1 tsp. rosemary; dried
1 tbsp. lemon juice
2 tbsp. olive oil
Salt and black pepper to the taste
Directions:
Season chicken with salt and pepper, rub with thyme, rosemary, garlic powder and onion powder, rub with lemon juice and olive oil and leave aside for 30 minutes.Put chicken in your air fryer and cook at 360 °F, for 20 minutes on each side. Leave chicken aside to cool down, carve and serve.

Nutrition Info: Calories: 390; Fat: 10; Fiber: 5; Carbs: 22; Protein: 20

Juicy Whole Chicken

Servings: 6
Cooking Time: 30 Minutes
Ingredients:
2 tbsp olive oil
300 ml chicken broth
3 red potatoes
1 chicken, whole
Spices of your choice, eg thyme, oregano, salt, garlic salt
Directions:
Put your Instant Pot on Saute, Low Setting.

Add olive oil and when it's hot, add chicken to the pot and lightly cook for about 2 minutes. Repeat with the other side. Turn off by pressing Cancel.Remove browned meat from Instant Pot and add chicken broth, potatoes, and the chicken (whole or in pieces). Chicken should be on top of the potatoes.Close lid, make sure steam valve is secure, and set to Poultry, normal setting, for 25 minutes. When it's cooked, do a quick release

Nutrition Info: Calories 301 Fat 27.2 g Carbohydrates 13.6 g Sugar 6 g Protein 4.9 g Cholesterol 33 mg

Tasty Chicken Tenders

Servings: 4
Cooking Time: 25 Minutes.
Ingredients:
1 ½ lbs chicken tenders
1 tbsp. extra virgin olive oil
1 tsp. rotisserie chicken seasoning

2 tbsp. BBQ sauce
Directions:
Add all ingredients except oil in a zip-lock bag.
Seal bag and place in the refrigerator for 2-3 hours.
Heat oil in a large pan over medium heat.
Cook marinated chicken tenders in a pan until lightly brown and cooked.
Nutrition Info: Calories 365 Fat 16.1 g, Carbohydrates 2.8 g, Sugar 2 g, Protein 49.2 g, Cholesterol 151 mg

Salted Biscuit Pie Turkey Chops

Servings: 4
Cooking Time: 20 Minutes
Ingredients:
8 large turkey chops
300 gr of crackers
2 eggs
Extra virgin olive oil
Salt - Ground pepper
Directions:
Put the turkey chops on the worktable, and salt and pepper.
Beat the eggs in a bowl.
Crush the cookies in the Thermo mix with a few turbo strokes until they are made grit, or you can crush them with the blender.Put the cookies in a bowl.Pass the chops through the beaten egg and then passed them through the crushed cookies. Press well so that the empanada is perfect.
Paint the empanada with a silicone brush and extra virgin olive oil.
Put the chops in the basket of the air fryer, not all will enter. They will be done in batches.
Select 200 degrees, 15 minutes.
When you have all the chops made, serve.
Nutrition Info: Calories: 126 Fat: 6g Carbohydrates 0g Protein: 18g Sugar: 0g

Creamy Chicken, Peas And Rice

Servings: 4
Cooking Time: 20 Minutes
Ingredients:
1 lb. chicken breasts; skinless, boneless and cut into quarters
1 cup white rice; already cooked
1 cup chicken stock
1/4 cup parsley; chopped.
2 cups peas; frozen
1 ½ cups parmesan; grated
1 tbsp. olive oil
3 garlic cloves; minced
1 yellow onion; chopped
1/2 cup white wine
1/4 cup heavy cream
Salt and black pepper to the taste
Directions:
Season chicken breasts with salt and pepper, drizzle half of the oil over them, rub well, put in your air fryer's basket and cook them at 360 °F, for 6 minutes.
Heat up a pan with the rest of the oil over medium high heat, add garlic, onion, wine, stock, salt, pepper and heavy cream; stir, bring to a simmer and cook for 9 minutes.
Transfer chicken breasts to a heat proof dish that fits your air fryer, add peas, rice and cream mix over them, toss, sprinkle parmesan and parsley all over, place in your air fryer and cook at 420 °F, for 10 minutes. Divide among plates and serve hot.
Nutrition Info: Calories: 313; Fat: 12; Fiber: 14; Carbs: 27; Protein: 44

Oregano Flavored Chicken Olives

Servings: 4
Cooking Time: 15 Minutes
Ingredients:
2 pieces (without skin and bones) Chicken breasts
2 pieces Eggplants
1 tbsp Oregano
1 cup Tomato passata
What you'll need from the store cupboard:
Salt and Black pepper to taste
2 tbsp Olive oil
Directions:
In the instant pot mix all the ingredients, then cover them and cook for 20 minutes on high temperature.
Release the pressure gradually for 10 minutes then split them among your plates before eating.
Nutrition Info: Calories: 362, Fat: 16.1, Fiber: 4.4g, Carbs: 5.4g, Protein: 36.4g

Chinese Stuffed Chicken

Servings: 8
Cooking Time: 30 Minutes
Ingredients:
1 whole chicken

10 wolfberries
2 red chilies; chopped
4 ginger slices
1 yam; cubed
1 tsp. soy sauce
3 tsp. sesame oil
Salt and white pepper to the taste
Directions:
Season chicken with salt, pepper, rub with soy sauce and sesame oil and stuff with wolfberries, yam cubes, chilies and ginger.
Place in your air fryer, cook at 400 °F, for 20 minutes and then at 360 °F, for 15 minutes. Carve chicken, divide among plates and serve.
Nutrition Info: Calories: 320; Fat: 12; Fiber: 17; Carbs: 22; Protein: 12

Chicken & Spinach

Servings: 4
Cooking Time: 13 Minutes
Ingredients:
2 tablespoons olive oil
1 lb. chicken breast fillet, sliced into small pieces
Salt and pepper to taste
4 cloves garlic, minced
1 tablespoon lemon juice
½ cup dry white wine
1 teaspoon lemon zest
10 cups fresh spinach, chopped
4 tablespoons Parmesan cheese, grated
Directions:
Pour oil in a pan over medium heat.
Season chicken with salt and pepper.
Cook in the pan for 7 minutes until golden on both sides.
Add the garlic and cook for 1 minute.
Stir in the lemon juice and wine.
Sprinkle lemon zest on top.
Simmer for 5 minutes.
Add the spinach and cook until wilted.
Serve with Parmesan cheese.
Nutrition Info: Calories 334 Total Fat 12 g Saturated Fat 3 g Cholesterol 67 mg Sodium 499 mg Total Carbohydrate 25 g Dietary Fiber 2 g Total Sugars 1 g Protein 29 g Potassium 685 mg

Air Fried Chicken With Honey And Lemon

Servings: 4
Cooking Time: 50 Minutes
Ingredients:
The Stuffing:
1 whole chicken, 3 lb
2 red and peeled onions
2 tbsp olive oil
2 apricots
1 zucchini
1 apple
2 cloves finely chopped garlic
Fresh chopped thyme
Salt and pepper
The Marinade:
5 oz honey
juice from 1 lemon
2 tbsp olive oil
Salt and pepper
Directions:
For the stuffing, chop all ingredients into tiny pieces. Transfer to a large bowl and add the olive oil. Season with salt and black pepper. Fill the cavity of the chicken with the stuffing, without packing it tightly.
Place the chicken in the Air Fryer and cook for 35 minutes at 340 F. Warm the honey and the lemon juice in a large pan; season with salt and pepper. Reduce the temperature of the Air Fryer to 320 F. Brush the chicken with some of the honey-lemon marinade and return it to the fryer.
Cook for another 70 minutes; brush the chicken every 20-25 minutes with the marinade. Garnish with parsley, and serve with potatoes.
Nutrition Info: Calories: 342; Carbs: 68g; Fat: 28g; Protein: 33g

Honey Mustard Chicken

Servings: 4
Cooking Time: 12 Minutes
Ingredients:
2 tablespoons honey mustard
2 teaspoons olive oil
Salt to taste
1 lb. chicken tenders
1 lb. baby carrots, steamed
Chopped parsley

Directions:

Preheat your oven to 450 degrees F.

Mix honey mustard, olive oil and salt.

Coat the chicken tenders with the mixture.

Place the chicken on a single layer on the baking pan.

Bake for 10 to 12 minutes.

Serve with steamed carrots and garnish with parsley.

Nutrition Info: Calories 366 Total Fat 8 g Saturated Fat 2 g Cholesterol 63 mg Sodium 543 mg Total Carbohydrate 46 g Dietary Fiber 8 g Total Sugars 13 g Protein 33 g Potassium 377 mg

Greek Chicken Lettuce Wraps

Servings: 4

Cooking Time: 8 Minutes

Ingredients:

2 tablespoons freshly squeezed lemon juice

1 teaspoon lemon zest

5 teaspoons olive oil, divided

3 teaspoons garlic, minced and divided

1 teaspoon dried oregano

¼ teaspoon red pepper, crushed

1 lb. chicken tenders

1 cucumber, sliced in half and grated

Salt and pepper to taste

¾ cup non-fat Greek yogurt

2 teaspoons fresh mint, chopped

2 teaspoons fresh dill, chopped

4 lettuce leaves

½ cup red onion, sliced

1 cup tomatoes, chopped

Directions:

In a bowl, mix the lemon juice, lemon zest, half of oil, half of garlic, and red pepper.

Coat the chicken with the marinade.

Marinate it for 1 hour.

Toss grated cucumber in salt.

Squeeze to release liquid.

Add the yogurt, dill, salt, pepper, remaining garlic and remaining oil.

Grill the chicken for 4 minutes per side.

Shred the chicken and put on top of the lettuce leaves.

Top with the yogurt mixture, onion and tomatoes.

Wrap the lettuce leaves and secure with a toothpick.

Nutrition Info: Calories 353 Total Fat 9 g Saturated Fat 1 g Cholesterol 58 mg Sodium 559 mg Total Carbohydrate 33 g Dietary Fiber 6 g Total Sugars 6 g Protein 37 g Potassium 459 mg

Spicy Honey Orange Chicken

Servings: 4

Cooking Time: 10 Minutes

Ingredients:

1 ½ pounds chicken breast, washed and sliced

Parsley to taste

1 cup coconut, shredded

¾ cup breadcrumbs

2 whole eggs, beaten

½ cup flour

½ tsp pepper

Salt to taste

½ cup orange marmalade

1 tbsp red pepper flakes

¼ cup honey

3 tbsp dijon mustard

Directions:

Preheat your Air Fryer to 400 F. In a mixing bowl, combine coconut, flour, salt, parsley and pepper. In another bowl, add the beaten eggs. Place breadcrumbs in a third bowl. Dredge chicken in egg mix, flour and finally in the breadcrumbs. Place the chicken in the Air Fryer cooking basket and bake for 15 minutes.

In a separate bowl, mix honey, orange marmalade, mustard and pepper flakes. Cover chicken with marmalade mixture and fry for 5 more minutes. Enjoy!

Nutrition Info: Calories: 246; Carbs: 21g; Fat: 6g; Protein: 25g

Chicken Soup

Servings: 6

Cooking Time: 30 Minutes

Ingredients:

4 lbs Chicken, cut into pieces

5 carrots, sliced thick

8 cups of water

2 celery stalks, sliced 1 inch thick

2 large onions, sliced

Directions:

In a large pot add chicken, water, and salt. Bring to boil.

Add celery and onion in the pot and stir well.

Turn heat to medium-low and simmer for 30 minutes.

Add carrots and cover pot with a lid and simmer for 40 minutes.

Remove Chicken from the pot and remove bones and cut Chicken into bite-size pieces.

Return chicken into the pot and stir well.

Serve and enjoy.

Nutrition Info: Calories: 89 Fat: 6.33g Carbohydrates: 0g Protein: 7.56g Sugar: 0g Cholesterol: 0mg

Ginger Chili Broccoli

Servings: 5

Cooking Time: 15 Minutes

Ingredients:

8 cups broccoli florets

1/2 cup olive oil

2 fresh lime juice

2 tbsp fresh ginger, grated

2 tsp chili pepper, chopped

Directions:

Add broccoli florets into the steamer and steam for 8 minutes.

Meanwhile, for dressing in a small bowl, combine limejuice, oil, ginger, and chili pepper.

Add steamed broccoli in a large bowl then pour dressing over broccoli. Toss well.

Nutrition Info: Calories 239 Fat 20.8 g Carbohydrates 13.7 g Sugar 3 g Protein 4.5 g Cholesterol 0 mg

Italian Style Chicken Breast

Servings: 3

Cooking Time: 15 Minutes

Ingredients:

1 tablespoon olive oil

3 boneless, skinless chicken breasts

1/4 teaspoon garlic powder and regular salt per breast

dash black pepper

1/8 teaspoon dried oregano

1/8 teaspoon dried basil

250 ml water

Directions:

Set the Instant Pot to Saute, and add oil to the pot.

Season one side of the chicken breasts and once the oil is hot, carefully add the chicken breasts, seasoned side down, to the pot.

In the meantime, season the second side.

Cook about 3 to 4 minutes on each side, and remove from pot with the tongs.

Add 250 ml water to the pot, plus the trivet.

Place the chicken on the trivet.

Lock the lid, and cook on manual High for 5 minutes.

Allow the chicken to naturally release for a few minutes, and then quick release the rest.

Remove from the pot and wait for at least 5 minutes before slicing.

Nutrition Info: Calories 202 Fat 29 g Carbohydrates 13.6 g Sugar 6 g Protein 4.9 g Cholesterol 33 mg

Garlic Chives Chicken

Servings: 4

Cooking Time: 10 Minutes

Ingredients:

1 lb. (no skin and bones) Chicken breast

1 tbsp Chives

1 cup Chicken stock

1 cup Coconut cream

3 tbsp Garlic cloves (sliced)

What you'll need from the store cupboard:

1 and a half tbsp Balsamic vinegar

Salt and Black pepper to taste

Directions:

In the instant pot, mix the chicken with all the remaining ingredients, then cover them and cook for 20 minutes on high temperature.

Release the pressure gradually for 10 minutes then split them among your plates before eating.

Nutrition Info: Calories: 360, Fat: 22.1, Fiber: 1.4g, Carbs: 4.1g, Protein: 34.5g

Breaded Chicken Fillets

Servings: 4

Cooking Time: 25 Minutes

Ingredients:

3 small chicken breasts or 2 large chicken breasts

Salt

Ground pepper

3 garlic cloves

1 lemon

Beaten eggs

Breadcrumbs

Extra virgin olive oil

Directions:

Cut the breasts into fillets.

Put in a bowl and add the lemon juice, chopped garlic cloves and pepper.

Flirt well and leave 10 minutes.

Beat the eggs and put breadcrumbs on another plate.

Pass the chicken breast fillets through the beaten egg and the breadcrumbs.

When you have them all breaded, start to fry.

Paint the breaded breasts with a silicone brush and extra virgin olive oil.

Place a batch of fillets in the basket of the air fryer and select 10 minutes 180 degrees.

Turn around and leave another 5 minutes at 180 degrees.

Nutrition Info: Calories: 120 Fat: 6g Carbohydrates 0g Protein: 18g Sugar: 0g

Chicken Wings With Garlic Parmesan

Servings: 3

Cooking Time: 25 Minutes

Ingredients:

25g cornstarch

20g grated Parmesan cheese

9g garlic powder

Salt and pepper to taste

680g chicken wings

Nonstick Spray Oil

Directions:

Select Preheat, set the temperature to 200 °C and press Start / Pause.

Combine corn starch, Parmesan, garlic powder, salt, and pepper in a bowl.

Mix the chicken wings in the seasoning and dip until well coated.

Spray the baskets and the air fryer with oil spray and add the wings, sprinkling the tops of the wings as well.

Select Chicken and press Start/Pause. Be sure to shake the baskets in the middle of cooking.

Sprinkle with what's left of the Parmesan mix and serve.

Nutrition Info: Calories: 204 Fat: 15g Carbohydrates: 1g Proteins: 12g Sugar: 0g Cholesterol: 63mg

Chicken Salad

Servings: 6

Cooking Time: 30 Minutes

Ingredients:

1 kg chicken breast

125 ml chicken broth

1 teaspoon salt

½ teaspoon black pepper

Directions:

Add all of the ingredients to the Instant Pot.

Secure the lid, close the pressure valve and cook for 20 minutes at High pressure.

Quick release pressure.

Shred the chicken. Store in an air-tight container with the liquid to help keep the meat moist.

Nutrition Info: Calories 356 Fat 27.2 g Carbohydrates 13.6 g Sugar 3 g Protein 4.9 g Cholesterol 5 mg

Duck With Garlic And Onion Sauce

Servings: 4

Cooking Time: 20 Minutes

Ingredients:

2 tbsp Coriander

2 pieces Spring onions

1 lb. (no skin and bones) Duck legs

2 pieces Garlic cloves

2 tbsp Tomato passata

What you'll need from the store cupboard:

2 tbsp Melted ghee

Directions:

Put the instant pot on Sauté option, then put the ghee and cook it. After that, put the spring onions and the other ingredients excluding the tomato passata and the meat then heat it for 5 minutes.

Put the meat and cook for 5 minutes.

Put the sauce then cover it and heat it for 25 minutes on high temperature.

Release the pressure gradually for 10 minutes then split them among your plates before eating.

Nutrition Info: Calories: 263, Fat: 13.2g, Fiber: 0.2g, Carbs: 1.1g, Protein: 33.5g

Crock-pot Slow Cooker Mulligatawny Soup

Servings: 8
Cooking Time: 6 Hours
Ingredients:
2 whole cloves
1/4 cup green pepper, chopped
1 carton (32 oz.) low-sodium chicken broth
1/4 teaspoon pepper
1 can (14 1/2 oz.) diced tomatoes
1/2 teaspoon sugar
2 cups cubed cooked chicken
1 teaspoon curry powder
1 large tart green apple, peeled and chopped
1 teaspoon salt - 1/4 cup onion, finely chopped
2 teaspoon lemon juice
1/4 cup carrot, chopped
1 tablespoon fresh parsley, minced
Directions:
Add all ingredients in a 3- or 4-qt. Crock-Pot slow cooker and combine well. Cover the cooker and cook for about 6-8 hours on Low.
Once done, remove cloves and serve.
Nutrition Info: 107 calories; 2 g fat; 10 g total carbs; 12 g protein

Lemon Chicken With Basil

Servings: 4
Cooking Time: 1h
Ingredients:
1kg chopped chicken
1 or 2 lemons
Basil, salt, and ground pepper
Extra virgin olive oil
Directions:
Put the chicken in a bowl with a jet of extra virgin olive oil.
Put salt, pepper, and basil.
Bind well and let stand for at least 30 minutes stirring occasionally.
Put the pieces of chicken in the air fryer basket and take the air fryer
Select 30 minutes.
Occasionally remove.
Take out and put another batch.
Do the same operation.
Nutrition Info: Calories: 126 Fat: 6g Carbohydrates 0g Protein: 18g Sugar: 0g

Chicken, Oats & Chickpeas Meatloaf

Servings: 4
Cooking Time: 1¼ Hours
Ingredients:
½ cup cooked chickpeas
2 egg whites
2½ teaspoons poultry seasoning
Ground black pepper, as required
10 ounce lean ground chicken
1 cup red bell pepper, seeded and minced
1 cup celery stalk, minced
1/3 cup steel-cut oats
1 cup tomato puree, divided
2 tablespoons dried onion flakes, crushed
1 tablespoon prepared mustard

Directions:
Preheat the oven to 350 degrees F. Grease a 9x5-inch loaf pan.
In a food processor, add chickpeas, egg whites, poultry seasoning and black pepper and pulse until smooth.
Transfer the mixture into a large bowl.
Add the chicken, veggies oats, ½ cup of tomato puree and onion flakes and mix until well combined.
Transfer the mixture into prepared loaf pan evenly.
With your hands, press, down the mixture slightly.
In another bowl mix together mustard and remaining tomato puree.
Place the mustard mixture over loaf pan evenly.
Bake for about 1-1¼ hours or until desired doneness.
Remove from the oven and set aside for about 5 minutes before slicing.g.
Cut into desired sized slices and serve.
Meal Prep Tip: In a resealable plastic bag, place the cooled meatloaf slices and seal the bag. Refrigerate for about 2-4 days. Reheat in the microwave on High for about 1 minute before serving.
Nutrition Info: Calories 229 Total Fat 5.6 g Saturated Fat 1.4 g Cholesterol 50 mg Total Carbs 23.7 g Sugar 5.2 g Fiber 4.7 g Sodium 227 mg Potassium 509 mg Protein 21.4 g

Turkey And Spring Onions Mix

Servings: 4
Cooking Time: 10 Minutes
Ingredients:
Cilantro
4 pieces Spring onions (sliced)
1 piece (no skin and bones) Turkey breast
1 cup Tomato passata
What you'll need from the store cupboard:
2 tbsp Avocado oil
Salt and Black pepper to taste
Directions:
Put the instant pot on Sauté option, then put the oil and cook it. After that, put the meat then heat it for 5 minutes.
Put the other ingredients, then cover it and heat it for 20 minuteson high temperature.
Release the pressure gradually for 10 minutes then split them among your plates before eating.
Nutrition Info: Calories: 222, Fat: 6.7g, Fiber: 1.6g, Carbs: 4.8g, Protein: 34.4g

Chinese Chicken Wings

Servings: 6
Cooking Time: 10 Minutes
Ingredients:
16 chicken wings
2 tbsp. honey
2 tbsp. soy sauce
Salt and black pepper to the taste
1/4 tsp. white pepper
3 tbsp. lime juice
Directions:
In a bowl, mix honey with soy sauce, salt, black and white pepper and lime juice, whisk well, add chicken pieces, toss to coat and keep in the fridge for 2 hours.
Transfer chicken to your air fryer, cook at 370 °F, for 6 minutes on each side, increase heat to 400 °F and cook for 3 minutes more. Serve hot.
Nutrition Info: Calories: 372; Fat: 9; Fiber: 10; Carbs: 37; Protein: 24

Basil Chili Chicken

Servings: 4
Cooking Time: 20 Minutes
Ingredients:
half cup Chicken stock

1 lb. Chicken breast
2 tsp Sweet paprika
1 cup Coconut cream
2 tbsp Basil (sliced)
What you'll need from the store cupboard:
Salt and Black pepper to taste
1 tbsp Chili powder
Directions:
In your instant pot, mix the chicken with the other ingredients, then stir them a little, then cover them then heat for 20 minutes on high temperature. Release the pressure gradually for 10 minutes then split them among plates before you eat them.
Nutrition Info: Calories: 364, Fat: 23.2, Fiber: 2.3g, Carbs: 5.1g, Protein: 35.4g

Turkey With Lentils

Servings: 7
Cooking Time: 51 Minutes
Ingredients:
3 tablespoons olive oil, divided
1 onion, chopped
1 tablespoon fresh ginger, minced
4 garlic cloves, minced
3 plum tomatoes, chopped finely
2 cups dried red lentils, soaked for 30 minutes and drained
2 cups filtered water
2 teaspoons cumin seeds
½ teaspoon cayenne pepper
1 pound lean ground turkey.
1 jalapeño pepper, seeded and chopped
2 scallions, chopped
¼ cup fresh cilantro, chopped
Directions:
In a Dutch oven, heat 1 tablespoon of oil over medium heat and sauté the onion, ginger and garlic for about 5 minutes.
Stir in tomatoes, lentils and water and bring to a boil
Now, reduce the heat to medium-low and simmer, covered for about 30 minutes.
Meanwhile, in a skillet, heat remaining oil over medium heat and sauté the cumin seeds and cayenne pepper for about 1 minute.
Transfer the mixture into a small bowl and set aside.
In the same skillet, add turkey and cook for about 4-5 minutes.

Add the jalapeño and scallion and cook for about 4-5 minutes.

Add the spiced oil mixture and stir to combine well.

Transfer the turkey mixture in simmering lentils and simmer for about 10-15 minutes or until desired doneness.

Serve hot.

Meal Prep Tip: Transfer the turkey mixture into a large bowl and set aside to cool. Divide the mixture into 4 containers evenly. Cover the containers and refrigerate for 1-2 days. Reheat in the microwave before serving.

Nutrition Info: Calories 361 Total Fat 11.5.4 g Saturated Fat 2.4 g Cholesterol 46 mg Total Carbs 37 g Sugar 3.4 g Fiber 18 g Sodium 937mg Potassium 331 mg Protein 27.9 g

Chicken Cacciatore

Servings: 4
Cooking Time: 10 Minutes
Ingredients:
8 chicken drumsticks; bone-in
1/2 cup black olives; pitted and sliced
1 bay leaf
1 tsp. garlic powder
1 yellow onion; chopped
28 oz. canned tomatoes and juice; crushed
1 tsp. oregano; dried
Salt and black pepper to the taste
Directions:
In a heat proof dish that fits your air fryer, mix chicken with salt, pepper, garlic powder, bay leaf, onion, tomatoes and juice, oregano and olives; toss, introduce in your preheated air fryer and cook at 365 °F, for 20 minutes. Divide among plates and serve.
Nutrition Info: Calories: 300; Fat: 12; Fiber: 8; Carbs: 20; Protein: 24

Crock-pot Buffalo Chicken Dip

Servings: 10
Cooking Time: 3 Hours
Ingredients:
2 cups cooked chicken, chopped into small pieces
1 cup ranch dressing
16 oz cream cheese, cubed and softened
5 ounces' hot sauce

Directions:
add 5 oz hot sauce, 16 ounces cubed cream cheese, and 1 cup ranch dressing to a 3-quart Crock-Pot slow cooker. Cover it and cook for about 2 hours on Low, with occasional stirring.
Once cheese is melted, add 2 cups of cooked chicken. Cover the Crock-Pot slow cooker again and cook again for 1 hour on Low.
Serve buffalo chicken along with veggies or any of your favorite chips.
Nutrition Info: 344 calories; 29 g fat; 5 g total carbs; 15 g protein

Chicken & Tofu

Servings: 6
Cooking Time: 25 Minutes
Ingredients:
2 tablespoons olive oil, divided
2 tablespoons orange juice
1 tablespoon Worcestershire sauce
1 tablespoon low-sodium soy sauce
1 teaspoon ground turmeric
1 teaspoon dry mustard
8 oz. chicken breast, cooked and sliced into cubes
8 oz. extra-firm tofu, drained and sliced into cubed
2 carrots, sliced into thin strips
1 cup mushroom, sliced
2 cups fresh bean sprouts
3 green onions, sliced
1 red sweet pepper, sliced into strips
Directions:
In a bowl, mix half of the oil with the orange juice, Worcestershire sauce, soy sauce, turmeric and mustard.
Coat all sides of chicken and tofu with the sauce.
Marinate for 1 hour.
In a pan over medium heat, add 1 tablespoon oil.
Add carrot and cook for 2 minutes.
Add mushroom and cook for another 2 minutes.
Add bean sprouts, green onion and sweet pepper. Cook for two to three minutes.
Stir in the chicken and heat through.
Nutrition Info: Calories 285 Total Fat 9 g Saturated Fat 1 g Cholesterol 32 mg Sodium 331 mg Total Carbohydrate 30 g Dietary Fiber 4 g Total Sugars 4 g Protein 20 g Potassium 559 mg

Peppered Broccoli Chicken

Servings: 4
Cooking Time: 30 Minutes
Ingredients:
1 tbsp Sage (sliced)
1 cup Broccoli florets
1 lb. (no bones and skin) Chicken breast
3 pieces Garlic cloves
1 cup Tomato passata
What you'll need from the store cupboard:
Salt and Black pepper to taste
2 tbsp. Olive oil
Directions:
Put the instant pot on Sauté option, then put the oil and cook it. After that, put the chicken and garlic then heats it for 5 minutes.
Put the other ingredients, then cover it and heat it for 25 minutes on high temperature.
Release the pressure gradually for 10 minutes then split them among your plates before eating.
Nutrition Info: Calories: 217, Fat: 10.1g, Fiber: 1.8g, Carbs: 5.9g, Protein: 25.4g

Peppered Chicken Breast With Basil

Servings: 4Cooking Time: 20 Minutes
Ingredients:
¼ cup Red bell peppers
1 cup Chicken stock
2 pieces (no skin and bones) Chicken breasts
4 pieces Garlic cloves (crushed)
1 and a half tbsp Basil (crushed)
What you'll need from the store cupboard:
1 tbsp Chili powder
Directions:
In the instant pot, combine the ingredients then cover them and cook for 25 minutes on high temperature.
Release the pressure quickly for 5 minutes then split them among your plates before eating.
Nutrition Info: Calories: 230, Fat: 12.4g, Fiber: 0.8g, Carbs: 2.7g, Protein: 33.2g

Spicy Chicken Drumsticks

Servings: 6
Cooking Time: 10 Minutes
Ingredients:
1/2 cup ketchup
1/4 cup dark brown sugar

1/4 cup red wine vinegar
3 tablespoon soy sauce
1 tablespoon chicken seasoning
Salt to taste
6 chicken drumsticks
Directions:
Combine ketchup, brown sugar, red wine vinegar, soy sauce, seasoning, and salt in the Instant Pot. Add chicken pieces and stir to coat.
Close Instant Pot Lid, and make sure steam release handle is in the 'Sealing' position.
Cook on 'Manual' (or 'Pressure Cook') for 12 minutes.
Do a quick release of pressure and carefully open the Instant Pot.
Remove chicken pieces and set aside.
Press 'Saute' and cook the sauce thickened, about 5 to 7 minutes.
Nutrition Info: Calories 145 Fat 28 g Carbohydrates 13.6 g Sugar 2 g Protein 4.9 g Cholesterol 45 mg

Crock Pot Chicken Cacciatore

Servings: 6
Cooking Time: 4 Hours
Ingredients:
1 can (14.5 oz) tomatoes, diced
6 medium chicken thighs, skins removed
1 onion, sliced
1 tablespoon Italian seasoning
1 green bell pepper, seeded and sliced
3 clove garlic, minced
2 can (6-oz, no salt added) tomato paste
Directions:
To a Crock-Pot slow cooker, add all ingredients and cook for 4 hours on High.
Once done, serve chicken cacciatore with whole wheat rotini pasta, if desired.
Nutrition Info: 170 calories; 5 g fat; 18 g total carbs; 16 g protein

Chicken Cabbage Curry

Servings: 4
Cooking Time: 30 Minutes
Ingredients:
1 kg of boneless chicken, cut into small pieces
2 cans of coconut milk
3 tablespoons of curry paste
1 small onion, diced

1 medium red bell pepper
1 medium green bell pepper
1/2 head of a big cabbage
Directions:
Dissolve the curry paste into the coconut milk and stir well. Pour into the Instant Pot.
Add the chicken to the coconut curry mixture.
Chop both peppers into cubes and add to the pot.
Add the onion.
Cut the cabbage into slices and add to the pot. Make sure all the ingredients are coated with coconut milk.
Put the lid on, seal and cook on Low for 30 minutes.
When it's cooked, open carefully and serve immediately.
Nutrition Info: Calories 301 Fat 27.2 g Carbohydrates 13.6 g Sugar6 g Protein 4.9 g Cholesterol 33 mg

Crock-pot Slow Cooker Chicken & Sweet Potatoes

Servings: 4
Cooking Time: 5-7 Hours
Ingredients:
1 1/2 cup low-sodium and low-fat chicken broth
1 bay leave
4 (4 oz) chicken thighs, skinless and boneless
2 tablespoons Dijon mustard
1 onion, chopped
¼ teaspoon dried thyme
2 large sweet potatoes, peeled and sliced into large rounds
3 tablespoons Splenda Brown Sugar blend
Directions:
Place 4 (4 oz) chicken thighs into the Crock-Pot slow cooker.
Top chicken thighs with sliced potatoes and chopped onions.
Now add all leftover ingredients to the Crock-Pot slow cooker. Cook for about 5-7 hours on low until chicken is completely cooked through.
Once done, remove bay leaf from the Crock-Pot slow cooker.
Serve right away.
Nutrition Info: 75 calories; 7 g fat; 32 g total carbs; 21 g protein

Chicken And Asparagus

Servings: 4
Cooking Time: 10 Minutes
Ingredients:
8 chicken wings; halved
8 asparagus spears
1 tbsp. rosemary; chopped
1 tsp. cumin; ground
Salt and black pepper to the taste
Directions:
Pat dry chicken wings, season with salt, pepper, cumin and rosemary, put them in your air fryer's basket and cook at 360 °F, for 20 minutes.
Meanwhile; heat up a pan over medium heat, add asparagus, add water to cover, steam for a few minutes; transfer to a bowl filled with ice water, drain and arrange on plates.

Add chicken wings on the sideand serve.
Nutrition Info: Calories: 270; Fat: 8; Fiber: 12; Carbs: 24; Protein: 22

Fried Lemon Chicken

Servings: 6
Cooking Time: 20 Minutes.
Ingredients:
6 chicken thighs
2 tbsp. olive oil
2 tbsp. lemon juice
1 tbsp. Italian herbal seasoning mix
1 tsp. Celtic sea salt
1 tsp. ground fresh pepper
1 lemon, thinly slice
Directions:
Add all ingredients, except sliced lemon, to bowl or bag, stir to cover chicken.
Let marinate for 30 minutes overnight.
Remove the chicken and let the excess oil drip (it does not need to dry out, just do not drip with tons of excess oil).
Arrange the chicken thighs and the lemon slices in the fryer basket, being careful not to push the chicken thighs too close to each other.
Set the fryer to 200 degrees and cook for 10 minutes.

Remove the basket from the fryer and turn the chicken thighs to the other side.

Cook again at 200 for another 10 minutes.

Nutrition Info: Calories: 215 Fat: 13g Carbohydrates: 1g Protein: 2 Sugar: 1g Cholesterol: 130mg

Mustard And Maple Turkey Breast

Servings: 6
Cooking Time: 1 Hr
Ingredients:
5 lb of whole turkey breast
¼ cup maple syrup
2 tbsp dijon mustard
½ tbsp smoked paprika
1 tbsp thyme
2 tbsp olive oil
½ tbsp sage
½ tbsp salt and black pepper
1 tbsp butter, melted
Directions:
Preheat the Air fryer to 350 F and brush the turkey with the olive oil. Combine all herbs and seasoning, in a small bowl, and rub the turkey with the mixture. Air fry the turkey for 25 minutes. Flip the turkey on its side and continue to cook for 12 more minutes.

Now, turn on the opposite side, and again, cook for an additional 12 minutes. Whisk the butter, maple and mustard together in a small bowl. When done, brush the glaze all over the turkey. Return to the air fryer and cook for 5 more minutes, until nice and crispy.

Nutrition Info: Calories: 529; Carbs: 77g; Fat: 20g; Protein: 13g

Dry Rub Chicken Wings

Servings: 4
Cooking Time: 30 Minutes
Ingredients:
9g garlic powder
1 cube of chicken broth, reduced sodium
5g of salt
3g black pepper
1g smoked paprika
1g cayenne pepper
3g Old Bay seasoning, sodium free
3g onion powder
1g dried oregano
453g chicken wings
Nonstick Spray Oil
Ranch sauce, to serve
Directions:
Preheat the air fryer. Set the temperature to 180 °C.
Put ingredients in a bowl and mix well.
Season the chicken wings with half the seasoning mixture and sprinkle abundantly with oil spray.
Place the chicken wings in the preheated air fryer.
Select Chicken, set the timer to 30 minutes.
Shake the baskets halfway through cooking.
Nutrition Info:Calories: 120 Fat: 6g Carbohydrates 0g Protein: 18g Sugar: 0g

Chapter 12
Fish And Seafood Recipes

Grilled Tuna Steaks

Servings: 6
Cooking Time: 10 Minutes,
Ingredients:
6 6 oz. tuna steaks
3 tbsp. fresh basil, diced
What you'll need from store cupboard:
4 ½ tsp olive oil
¾ tsp salt
¼ tsp pepper
Nonstick cooking spray
Directions:
Heat grill to medium heat. Spray rack with cooking spray. Drizzle both sides of the tuna with oil. Sprinkle with basil, salt and pepper.
Place on grill and cook 5 minutes per side, tuna should be slightly pink in the center. Serve.
Nutrition Info: Calories 343 Total Carbs 0g Protein 51g Fat 14g Sugar 0g Fiber 0g

Delicious Fish Tacos

Servings: 8
Cooking Time: 8 Minutes
Ingredients:
4 tilapia fillets
1/4 cup fresh cilantro, chopped
1/4 cup fresh lime juice
2 tbsp paprika
1 tbsp olive oil

Pepper
Salt
Directions:
Pour 2 cups of water into the instant pot then place steamer rack in the pot.
Place fish fillets on parchment paper.
Season fish fillets with paprika, pepper, and salt and drizzle with oil and lime juice.
Fold parchment paper around the fish fillets and place them on a steamer rack in the pot.
Seal pot with lid and cook on high for 8 minutes.
Once done, release pressure using quick release. Remove lid.
Remove fish packet from pot and open it.
Shred the fish with a fork and serve.
Nutrition Info: Calories 67 Fat 2.5 g Carbohydrates 1.1 g Sugar 0.2 g Protein 10.8 g Cholesterol 28 mg

Shrimp Coconut Curry

Servings: 2
Cooking Time: 20 Minutes
Ingredients:
0.5lb cooked shrimp
1 thinly sliced onion
1 cup coconut yogurt
3tbsp curry paste
1tbsp oil or ghee
Directions:
Set the Instant Pot to sauté and add the onion, oil, and curry paste.
When the onion is soft, add the remaining ingredients and seal.
Cook on Stew for 20 minutes.
Release the pressure naturally.
Nutrition Info: Calories: 380 Carbs 13; Sugar 4; Fat 22; Protein 40; GL 14

Salmon & Shrimp Stew

Servings: 6Cooking Time: 21 Minutes
Ingredients:
2 tablespoons olive oil
½ cup onion, chopped finely

2 garlic cloves, minced

1 Serrano pepper, chopped

1 teaspoon smoked paprika

4 cups fresh tomatoes, chopped

4 cups low-sodium chicken broth

1 pound salmon fillets, cubed

1 pound shrimp, peeled and deveined

2 tablespoons fresh lime juice

¼ cup fresh basil, chopped

¼ cup fresh parsley, chopped

Ground black pepper, as required

2 scallions, chopped

Directions:

In a large soup pan, melt coconut oil over medium-high heat and sauté the onion for about 5-6 minutes.Add the garlic, Serrano pepper and smoked paprika and sauté for about 1 minute.

Add the tomatoes and broth and bring to a gentle simmer over medium heat.

Simmer for about 5 minutes.Add the salmon and simmer for about 3-4 minutes.

Stir in the remaining seafood and cook for about 4-5 minutes.

Stir in the lemon juice, basil, parsley, sea salt and black pepper and remove from heat.

Serve hot with the garnishing of scallion.

Meal Prep Tip: Transfer the stew into a large bowl and set aside to cool. Divide the stew into 4 containers evenly. Cover the containers and refrigerate for 1-2 days. Reheat in the microwave before serving.

Nutrition Info: Calories 271 Total Fat 11 g Saturated Fat 1.8 g Cholesterol 193 mg Total Carbs 8.6 g Sugar 3.8 g Fiber 2.1 g Sodium 273 mg Potassium 763 mg Protein 34.7 g

Swordfish With Tomato Salsa

Servings: 4

Cooking Time: 12 Minutes

Ingredients:

1 cup tomato, chopped

¼ cup tomatillo, chopped

2 tablespoons fresh cilantro, chopped

¼ cup avocado, chopped

1 clove garlic, minced

1 jalapeño pepper, chopped

1 tablespoon lime juice

Salt and pepper to taste

4 swordfish steaks

1 clove garlic, sliced in half

2 tablespoons lemon juice

½ teaspoon groundcumin

Directions:

Preheat your grill.

In a bowl, mix the tomato, tomatillo, cilantro, avocado, garlic, jalapeño, lime juice, salt and pepper.

Cover the bowl with foil and put in the refrigerator.

Rub each swordfish steak with sliced garlic.

Drizzle lemon juice on both sides.

Season with salt, pepper andcumin.

Grill for 12 minutes or until the fish is fully cooked.

Serve with salsa.

Nutrition Info: Calories 125 g Fat 27.2 g Carbohydrates 13.6 g Protein 7 g Cholesterol 31 mg

Shrimp Boil

Servings: 4

Cooking Time: 15 Minutes

Ingredients:

8 oz. raw shrimp, unpeeled

8 0oz. chicken sausage, small 1 inch pieces

8 oz. baby potatoes

1 sliced leek

2 corns, cut into half

What you will need from the store cupboard:

3 tablespoons lemon juice

10 cups of water

¼ cup Old Bay seasoning

Melted butter

Lemon wedges

Directions:

Bring together the lemon juice, Old Bay, and water in your pot. Boil.

Include potatoes and cook for 5-7 minutes.

Add the sausage, shrimp, leek, and corn. Cook while stirring for another 5 minutes. The vegetables should be tender and the shrimp must be pink. Now divide the vegetables, sausage, and shrimp with spoon and tongs among the serving bowls. Drizzle the cooking liquid equally.

Serve with butter (optional).

Nutrition Info: Calories 202, Carbohydrates 22g, Fiber 2g, Sugar 0g, Cholesterol 109mg, Total Fat 5g, Protein 19g

Shrimp & Artichoke Skillet

Servings: 4
Cooking Time: 10 Minutes
Ingredients:
1 ½ cups shrimp, peel & devein
2 shallots, diced
1 tbsp. margarine
What you'll need from store cupboard
2 12 oz. jars artichoke hearts, drain & rinse
2 cups white wine
2 cloves garlic, diced fine
Directions:
Melt margarine in a large skillet over med-high heat. Add shallot and garlic and cook until they start to brown, stirring frequently.
Add artichokes and cook 5 minutes. Reduce heat and add wine. Cook 3 minutes, stirring occasionally.
Add the shrimp and cook just until they turn pink. Serve.
Nutrition Info: Calories 487 Total Carbs 26g Net Carbs 17g Protein 64g Fat 5g Sugar 3g Fiber 9g

Red Clam Sauce & Pasta

Servings: 4
Cooking Time: 3 Hours,
Ingredients:
1 onion, diced
¼ cup fresh parsley, diced
What you'll need from store cupboard:
2 6 ½ oz. cans clams, chopped, undrained
14 ½ oz. tomatoes, diced, undrained
6 oz. tomato paste
2 cloves garlic, diced
1 bay leaf - 1 tbsp. sunflower oil
1 tsp Splenda
1 tsp basil
½ tsp thyme
½ Homemade Pasta, cook & drain (chapter 15)
Directions:
Heat oil in a small skillet over med-high heat. Add onion and cook until tender, Add garlic and cook 1 minute more. Transfer to crock pot.
Add remaining Ingredients, except pasta, cover and cook on low 3-4 hours.
Discard bay leaf and serve over cooked pasta.
Nutrition Info: Calories 223 Total Carbs 32g Net Carbs 27g Protein 12g Fat 6g Sugar 15g Fiber 5g

Grilled Herbed Salmon With Raspberry Sauce & Cucumber Dill Dip

Servings: 4Cooking Time: 30 Minutes
Ingredients:
3 salmon fillets
1 tablespoon olive oil
Salt and pepper to taste
1 teaspoon fresh sage, chopped
1 tablespoon fresh parsley, chopped
2 tablespoons apple juice
1 cup raspberries
1 teaspoon Worcestershire sauce
1 cup cucumber, chopped
2 tablespoons light mayonnaise
½ teaspoon dried dill
Directions:
Coat the salmon fillets with oil.
Season with salt, pepper, sage and parsley.
Cover the salmon with foil.
Grill for 20 minutes or until fish is flaky.
While waiting, mix the apple juice, raspberries and Worcestershire sauce.
Pour the mixture into a saucepan over medium heat.Bring to a boil and then simmer for 8 minutes.In another bowl, mix the rest of the ingredients.Serve salmon with raspberry sauce and cucumber dip.
Nutrition Info: Calories 256 Total Fat 15 g Saturated Fat 3 g Cholesterol 68 mg Sodium 176 mg Total Carbohydrate 6 g Dietary Fiber 1 g Total Sugars 5 g Protein 23 g Potassium 359 mg

Shrimp With Green Beans

Servings: 4
Cooking Time: 2 Minutes
Ingredients:
¾ pound fresh green beans, trimmed
1 pound medium frozen shrimp, peeled and deveined
2 tablespoons fresh lemon juice
2 tablespoons olive oil
Salt and ground black pepper, as required
Directions:
Arrange a steamer trivet in the Instant Pot and pour cup of water.
Arrange the green beans on top of trivet in a single layer and top with shrimp.
Drizzle with oil and lemon juice.

Sprinkle with salt and black pepper.

Close the lid and place the pressure valve to "Seal" position.

Press "Steam" and just use the default time of 2 minutes.

Press "Cancel" and allow a "Natural" release.

Open the lid and serve.

Nutrition Info:Calories: 223, Fats: 1g, Carbs: 7.9g, Sugar: 1.4g, Proteins: 27.4g, Sodium: 322mg

Crab Curry

Servings: 2

Cooking Time: 20 Minutes

Ingredients:

0.5lb chopped crab

1 thinly sliced red onion

0.5 cup chopped tomato

3tbsp curry paste

1tbsp oil or ghee

Directions:

Set the Instant Pot to sauté and add the onion, oil, and curry paste.

When the onion is soft, add the remaining ingredients and seal.

Cook on Stew for 20 minutes.

Release the pressure naturally.

Nutrition Info: Calories 2; Carbs 11; Sugar 4; Fat 10; Protein 24; GL 9

Mussels In Tomato Sauce

Servings: 4

Cooking Time: 3 Minutes

Ingredients:

2 tomatoes, seeded and chopped finely

2 pounds mussels, scrubbed and de-bearded

1 cup low-sodium chicken broth

1 tablespoon fresh lemon juice

2 garlic cloves, minced

Directions:

In the pot of Instant Pot, place tomatoes, garlic, wine and bay leaf and stir to combine.

Arrange the mussels on top.

Close the lid and place the pressure valve to "Seal" position. Press "Manual" and cook under "High Pressure" for about 3 minutes.

Press "Cancel" and carefully allow a "Quick" release. Open the lid and serve hot.

Nutrition Info: Calories 213, Fats 25.2g, Carbs 11g, Sugar 1. Proteins 28.2g, Sodium 670mg

Shrimp Salad

Servings: 6

Cooking Time: 4 Minutes

Ingredients:

For Salad:

1 pound shrimp, peeled and deveined

Salt and ground black pepper, as required

1 teaspoon olive oil

1½ cups carrots, peeled and julienned

1½ cups red cabbage, shredded

1½ cup cucumber, julienned

5 cups fresh baby arugula

¼ cup fresh basil, chopped

¼ cup fresh cilantro, chopped

4 cups lettuce, torn

¼ cup almonds, chopped

For Dressing:

2 tablespoons natural almond butter

1 garlic clove, crushed

1 tablespoon fresh cilantro, chopped

1 tablespoon fresh lime juice

1 tablespoon unsweetened applesauce

2 teaspoons balsamic vinegar

½ teaspoon cayenne pepper

Salt, as required

1 tablespoon water

1/3 cup olive oil

Directions:

Slowly, add the oil, beating continuously until smooth.

For salad: in a bowl, add shrimp, salt, black pepper and oil and toss to coat well.

Heat a skillet over medium-high heat and cook the shrimp forabout 2 minutes per side.

Remove from the heat and set aside to cool.

In a large bowl, add the shrimp, vegetables and mix well.

For dressing: in a bowl, add all ingredients except oil and beat until well combined.

Place the dressing over shrimp mixture and gently, toss to coat well.

Serve immediately.

Meal Prep Tip: Divide dressing in 6 large mason jars evenly. Place the remaining ingredients in the layers of carrots, followed by cabbage, cucumber, arugula, basil, cilantro, shrimp, lettuce and almonds.

Cover each jar with the lid tightly and refrigerate for about 1 day. Shake the jars well just before serving.

Nutrition Info: Calories 274 Total Fat 17.7 g Saturated Fat 2.4 g Cholesterol 159 mg Total Carbs 10 g Sugar 3.8 g Fiber 2.9 g Sodium 242 mg Potassium 481 mg Protein 20.5 g

Grilled Herbed Salmon With Raspberry Sauce & Cucumber Dill Dip

Servings: 4
Cooking Time: 30 Minutes
Ingredients:
3 salmon fillets
1 tablespoon olive oil
Salt and pepper to taste
1 teaspoon fresh sage, chopped
1 tablespoon fresh parsley, chopped
2 tablespoons apple juice
1 cup raspberries
1 teaspoon Worcestershire sauce
1 cup cucumber, chopped
2 tablespoons light mayonnaise
½ teaspoon dried dill
Directions:
Coat the salmon fillets with oil.
Season with salt, pepper, sage and parsley.
Cover the salmon with foil.
Grill for 20 minutes or until fish is flaky.
While waiting, mix the apple juice, raspberries and Worcestershire sauce.
Pour the mixture into a saucepan over medium heat.
Bring to a boil and then simmer for 8 minutes.
In another bowl, mix the rest of the ingredients.
Serve salmon with raspberry sauce and cucumber dip.
Nutrition Info: Calories 301 Fat 27.2 g Carbohydrates 13.6 g Protein 4.9 g Cholesterol 33 mg

Cajun Shrimp & Roasted Vegetables

Servings: 4
Cooking Time: 15 Minutes
Ingredients:
1 lb. large shrimp, peeled and deveined
2 zucchinis, sliced
2 yellow squash, sliced
½ bunch asparagus, cut into thirds
2 red bell pepper, cut into chunks
What you'll need from store cupboard:
2 tbsp. olive oil
2 tbsp. Cajun Seasoning
Salt & pepper, to taste
Directions:
Heat oven to 400 degrees.
Combine shrimp and vegetables in a large bowl. Add oil and seasoning and toss to coat.
Spread evenly in a large baking sheet and bake 15-20 minutes, or until vegetables are tender. Serve.
Nutrition Info: Calories 251 Total Carbs 13g Net Carbs 9g Protein 30g Fat 9g Sugar 6g Fiber 4g

Parmesan Herb Fish

Servings: 4
Cooking Time: 15 Minutes
Ingredients:
16 oz. tilapia fillets
1/3 cup almonds, sliced and chopped
½ teaspoon parsley, chopped
¼ cup dry bread crumbs
What you will need from the store cupboard:
½ teaspoon garlic powder
¼ teaspoon black pepper, ground
½ teaspoon paprika
3 tablespoons Parmesan cheese, grated
Olive oil
Directions:
Preheat your oven to 350 °F.
Mix the bread crumbs, almonds, seasonings and Parmesan cheese in a dish.
Brush oil lightly on the fish.
Coat the almond mix evenly.
Now keep the fish on a greased foil-lined baking pan.
Bake for 10-12 minutes. The fish should flake easily with your fork.
Nutrition Info: Calories 225, Carbohydrates 7g, Fiber 1g, Cholesterol 57mg, Total Fat 9g, Protein 29g, Sodium 202mg

Lemony Salmon

Servings: 3
Cooking Time: 3 Minutes
Ingredients:
1 pound salmon fillet, cut into 3 pieces

3 teaspoons fresh dill, chopped
5 tablespoons fresh lemon juice, divided
Salt and ground black pepper, as required
Directions:
Arrange a steamer trivet in Instant Pot and pour ¼ cup of lemon juice.
Season the salmon with salt and black pepper evenly.
Place the salmon pieces on top of trivet, skin side down and drizzle with remaining lemon juice.Now, sprinkle the salmon pieces with dill evenly.
Close the lid and place the pressure valve to "Seal" position.
Press "Steam" and use the default time of 3 minutes.
Press "Cancel" and allow a "Natural" release.
Open the lid and serve hot.
Nutrition Info: Calories: 20 Fats: 9.6g, Carbs: 1.1g, Sugar: 0.5g, Proteins: 29.7g, Sodium: 74mg

Herring & Veggies Soup

Servings: 5
Cooking Time: 25 Minutes
Ingredients:
2 tablespoons olive oil
1 shallot, chopped
2 small garlic cloves, minced
1 jalapeño pepper, chopped
1 head cabbage, chopped
1 small red bell pepper, seeded and chopped finely
1 small yellow bell pepper, seeded and chopped finely
5 cups low-sodium chicken broth
2 (4-ounce) boneless herring fillets, cubed
¼ cup fresh cilantro, minced
2 tablespoons fresh lemon juice
Ground black pepper, as required
2 scallions, chopped
Directions:
In a large soup pan, heat the oil over medium heat and sauté shallot and garlic for 2-3 minutes.
Add the cabbage and bell peppers and sauté for about 3-4 minutes.
Add the broth and bring to a boil over high heat.Now, reduce the heat to medium-low and simmer for about 10 minutes.
Add the herring cubes and cook for about 5-6 minutes.

Stir in the cilantro, lemon juice, salt and black pepper and cook for about 1-2 minutes.
Serve hot with the topping of scallion.
Meal Prep Tip: Transfer the soup into a large bowl and set aside to cool. Divide the soup into 5 containers evenly. Cover the containersand refrigerate for 1-2 days. Reheat in the microwave before serving.
Nutrition Info: Calories 215 Total Fat 11.2g Saturated Fat 2.1 g Cholesterol 35 mg Total Carbs 14.7 g Sugar 7 g Fiber 4.5 g Sodium 152 mg Potassium 574 mg Protein 15.1 g

Garlicky Clams

Servings: 4
Cooking Time: 5 Minutes
Ingredients:
3 lbs clams, clean
4 garlic cloves
1/4 cup olive oil
1/2 cup fresh lemon juice
1 cup white wine
Pepper
Salt
Directions:
Add oil into the inner pot of instant pot and set the pot on sauté mode.
Add garlic and sauté for 1 minute.
Add wine and cook for 2 minutes.
Add remaining ingredients and stir well.
Seal pot with lid and cook on high for 2 minutes.
Once done, allow to release pressure naturally. Remove lid.
Serve and enjoy.
Nutrition Info: Calories 332 Fat 13.5 g Carbohydrates 40.5 g Sugar 12.4 g Protein 2.5 g Cholesterol 0 mg

Tuna Salad

Servings: 2
Ingredients:
2 (5-ounce) cans water packed tuna, drained
2 tablespoons fat-free plain Greek yogurt
Salt and ground black pepper, as required
2 medium carrots, peeled and shredded
2 apples, cored and chopped
2 cups fresh spinach, torn

Directions:

In a large bowl, add the tuna, yogurt, salt and black pepper and gently, stir to combine.

Add the carrots and apples and stir to combine. Serve immediately.

Meal Prep Tip: Divide tuna mixture in 2 mason jars evenly. Place the remaining ingredients in the layers of, carrots, apples and spinach. Cover each jar with the lid tightly and refrigerate for about 1 day. Shake the jars well just before serving.

Nutrition Info: Calories 306 Total Fat 1.8g Saturated Fat 0 g Cholesterol 63 mg Total Carbs 38 g Sugar 26 g Fiber 7.6 g Sodium 324 mg Potassium 602 mg Protein 35.8 g

Grilled Tuna Salad

Servings: 4

Cooking Time: 15 Minutes

Ingredients:

4 oz. tuna fish, 4 steaks

¾ lb. red potatoes, diced

½ lb. green beans, trimmed

16 kalamata olives, chopped

4 cups of baby spinach leaves

What you will need from the store cupboard:

2 tablespoons canola oil

2 tablespoons red wine vinegar

1/8 teaspoon salt

1 tablespoon water

1/8 teaspoon red pepper flakes

Directions:

Steam the green beans and potatoes to make them tender.

Drain, rinse to shake off the excess water.

Bring together the vinaigrette ingredients in your jar while the vegetables are cooking. Close the lid and shake well. Everything should blend well.

Brush the vinaigrette over your fish.

Coat canola oil on your pan. Heat over medium temperature.

Grill each side of the tuna for 3 minutes.

Now divide the greens on your serving plates.

Arrange the green beans, olives, and potatoes over the greens.

Drizzle the vinaigrette on the salad. Top with tuna.

Nutrition Info: Calories 345, Carbohydrates 26g, Fiber 5g, Cholesterol 40mg, Total Fat 14g, Protein 29g, Sodium 280mg

Mediterranean Fish Fillets

Servings: 4

Cooking Time: 3 Minutes

Ingredients:

4 cod fillets

1 lb grape tomatoes, halved

1 cup olives, pitted and sliced

2 tbsp capers

1 tsp dried thyme

2 tbsp olive oil

1 tsp garlic, minced

Pepper

Salt

Directions:

Pour 1 cup water into the instant pot then place steamer rack in the pot.

Spray heat-safe baking dish with cooking spray.

Add half grape tomatoes into the dish and season with pepper and salt.

Arrange fish fillets on top of cherry tomatoes. Drizzle with oil and season with garlic, thyme, capers, pepper, and salt.

Spread olives and remaining grape tomatoes on top of fish fillets.

Place dish on top of steamer rack in the pot.

Seal pot with a lid and select manual and cook on high for 3 minutes.

Once done, release pressure using quick release. Remove lid.

Serve and enjoy.

Nutrition Info: Calories 212 Fat 11.9 g Carbohydrates 7.1 g Sugar 3 g Protein 21.4 g Cholesterol 55 mg

Herbed Salmon

Servings: 4

Cooking Time: 3 Minutes

Ingredients:

4 (4-ounce) salmon fillets

¼ cup olive oil

2 tablespoons fresh lemon juice

1 garlic clove, minced

¼ teaspoon dried oregano

Salt and ground black pepper, as required

4 fresh rosemary sprigs

4 lemon slices

Directions:

For dressing: in a large bowl, add oil, lemon juice, garlic, oregano, salt and black pepper and beat until well co combined.

Arrange a steamer trivet in the Instant Pot and pour 11/2 cups of water in Instant Pot.

Place the salmon fillets on top of trivet in a single layer and top with dressing.

Arrange 1 rosemary sprig and 1 lemon slice over each fillet.

Close the lid and place the pressure valve to "Seal" position. Press "Steam" and just use the default time of 3 minutes. Press "Cancel" and carefully allow a "Quick" release.

Open the lid and serve hot.

Nutrition Info: Calories 262, Fats 17g, Carbs 0.7g, Sugar 0.2g, Proteins 22.1g, Sodium 91mg

Tarragon Scallops

Servings: 4
Cooking Time: 15 Minutes
Ingredients:
1 cup water
1 lb. asparagus spears, trimmed
2 lemons
1 ¼ lb. scallops
Salt and pepper to taste
1 tablespoon olive oil
1 tablespoon fresh tarragon, chopped
Directions:
Pour water into a pot.
Bring to a boil. Add asparagus spears.
Cover and cook for 5 minutes.
Drain and transfer to a plate.
Slice one lemon into wedges.
Squeeze juice and shred zest from the remaining lemon.
Season the scallops with salt and pepper.
Put a pan over medium heat.
Add oil to the pan.
Cook the scallops until golden brown.
Transfer to the same plate, putting scallops beside the asparagus. Add lemon zest, juice and tarragon to the pan. Cook for 1 minute.
Drizzle tarragon sauce over the scallops and asparagus.
Nutrition Info: Calories 250 g Fat 10 g Carbohydrates 30 g Protein 15 g Cholesterol 24 mg

Sardine Curry

Servings: 2
Cooking Time: 35 Minutes
Ingredients:
5 tins of sardines in tomato
1lb chopped vegetables
1 cup low sodium fish broth
3tbsp curry paste
Directions:
Mix all the ingredients in your Instant Pot.
Cook on Stew for 35 minutes.
Release the pressure naturally.
Nutrition Info: Calories 320; Carbs 8; Sugar 2; Fat 16; Protein GL 3

Grilled Salmon With Ginger Sauce

Servings: 4
Cooking Time: 8 Minutes
Ingredients:
1 tablespoon toasted sesame oil
1 tablespoon fresh cilantro, chopped
1 tablespoon lime juice
1 teaspoon fish sauce
1 clove garlic, mashed
1 teaspoon fresh ginger, grated
1 teaspoon jalapeño pepper, minced
4 salmon fillets
1 tablespoon olive oil
Salt and pepper to taste
Directions:
In a bowl, mix the sesame oil, cilantro, lime juice, fish sauce, garlic, ginger and jalapeño pepper.
Preheat your grill.
Brush oil on salmon.
Season both sides with salt and pepper.
Grill salmon for 6 to 8 minutes, turning once or twice.
Take 1 tablespoon from the oil mixture.
Brush this on the salmon while grilling.
Serve grilled salmon with the remaining sauce.
Nutrition Info: Calories 204 Total Fat 11 g Saturated Fat 2 g Cholesterol 53 mg Sodium 320 mg Total Carbohydrate 2 g Dietary Fiber 0 g Total Sugars 2 g Protein 23 g Potassium 437 mg

Shrimp With Broccoli

Servings: 6
Cooking Time: 12 Minutes
Ingredients:
2 tablespoons olive oil, divided
4 cups broccoli, chopped
2-3 tablespoons filtered water
1½ pounds large shrimp, peeled and deveined
2 garlic cloves, minced
1 (1-inch) piece fresh ginger, minced
Salt and ground black pepper, as required
Directions:
In a large skillet, heat 1 tablespoon of oil over medium-high heatand cook the broccoli for about 1-2 minutes stirring continuously.
Stir in the water and cook, covered for about 3-4 minutes, stirring occasionally.
With a spoon, push the broccoli to side of the pan.
Add the remaining oil and let it heat.
Add the shrimp and cook for about 1-2 minutes, tossing occasionally.
Add the remaining ingredients and sauté for about 2-3 minutes.
Serve hot.
Meal Prep Tip: Transfer the shrimp mixture into a large bowl and set aside to cool. Divide the shrimp mixture into 6 containers evenly. Cover the containers and refrigerate for 1 day. Reheat in the microwave before serving.
Nutrition Info: Calories 197 Total Fat 6.8 g Saturated Fat 1.3 g Cholesterol 239 mg Total Carbs 6.1 g Sugar 1.1 g Fiber 1.6 g Sodium 324 mg Potassium 389 mg Protein 27.6 g

Citrus Salmon

Servings: 4
Cooking Time: 7 Minutes
Ingredients:
4 (4-ounce) salmon fillets
1 cup low-sodium chicken broth
1 teaspoon fresh ginger, minced
2 teaspoons fresh orange zest, grated finely
3 tablespoons fresh orange juice
1 tablespoon olive oil
Ground black pepper, as required
Directions:
In Instant Pot, add all ingredients and mix.

Close the lid and place the pressure valve to "Seal" position.
Press "Manual" and cook under "High Pressure" for about 7 minutes.
Press "Cancel" and allow a "Natural" release.
Open the lid and serve the salmon fillets with the topping of cooking sauce.
Nutrition Info: Calories 190, Fats 10.5g, Carbs 1.8g, Sugar 1g,Proteins 22. Sodium 68mg

Salmon In Green Sauce

Servings: 4
Cooking Time: 12 Minutes
Ingredients:
4 (6-ounce) salmon fillets
1 avocado, peeled, pitted and chopped
1/2 cup fresh basil, chopped
3 garlic cloves, chopped
1 tablespoon fresh lemon zest, grated finely
Directions:
Grease a large piece of foil.
In a large bowl, add all ingredients except salmon and water and with a fork, mash completely.
Place fillets in the center of foil and top with avocado mixture evenly.
Fold the foil around fillets to seal them.
Arrange a steamer trivet in the Instant Pot and pour 1/2 cup of water.
Place the foil packet on top of trivet.
Close the lid and place the pressure valve to "Seal" position.
Press "Manual" and cook under "High Pressure" for about minutes.
Meanwhile, preheat the oven to broiler.
Press "Cancel" and allow a "Natural" release.
Open the lid and transfer the salmon fillets onto a broiler pan.
Broil for about 3-4 minutes.
Serve warm.
Nutrition Info: Calories 333, Fats 20.3g, Carbs 5.5g, Sugar 0.4g, Proteins 34.2g, Sodium 79mg

Blackened Shrimp

Servings: 4
Cooking Time: 5 Minutes
Ingredients:
1 ½ lbs. shrimp, peel & devein
4 lime wedges
4 tbsp. cilantro, chopped

What you'll need from store cupboard:
4 cloves garlic, diced
1 tbsp. chili powder
1 tbsp. paprika
1 tbsp. olive oil
2 tsp Splenda brown sugar
1 tsp cumin
1 tsp oregano
1 tsp garlic powder
1 tsp salt
½ tsp pepper
Directions:
In a small bowl combine seasonings and Splenda brown sugar.
Heat oil in a skillet over med-high heat. Add shrimp, in a single layer, and cook 1-2 minutes per side.
Add seasonings, and cook, stirring, 30 seconds.
Serve garnished with cilantro and a lime wedge.
Nutrition Info: Calories 252 Total Carbs 7g Net Carbs 6g Protein 39g Fat 7g Sugar 2g Fiber 1g

Popcorn Shrimp

Servings: 4
Cooking Time: 8 Minutes
Ingredients:
Cooking spray
½ cup all-purpose flour
2 eggs, beaten
2 tablespoons water
1 ½ cups panko breadcrumbs
1 tablespoon garlic powder
1 tablespoon ground cumin
1 lb. shrimp, peeled and deveined
½ cup ketchup
2 tablespoons fresh cilantro, chopped
2 tablespoons lime juice
Salt to taste
Directions:
Coat the air fryer basket with cooking spray
Put the flour in a dish.
In the second dish, beat the eggs and water.
In the third dish, mix the breadcrumbs, garlic powder and cumin.
Dip each shrimp in each of the three dishes, first in the dish with flour, then the egg and then breadcrumb mixture.
Place the shrimp in the air fryer basket.

Cook at 360 degrees F for 8 minutes, flipping once halfway through.
Combine the rest of the ingredients as dipping sauce for the shrimp.
Nutrition Info: Calories 200 g Fat 25 g Carbohydrates 13.8 g Protein 10 g Cholesterol 21 mg

Tuna Carbonara

Servings: 4
Cooking Time: 25 Minutes
Ingredients:
½ lb. tuna fillet, cut in pieces
2 eggs
4 tbsp. fresh parsley, diced
What you'll need from store cupboard:
½ Homemade Pasta, cook & drain, (chapter 15)
½ cup reduced fat parmesan cheese
2 cloves garlic, peeled
2 tbsp. extra virgin olive oil
Salt & pepper, to taste
Directions:
In a small bowl, beat the eggs, parmesan and a dash of pepper.
Heat the oil in a large skillet over med-high heat. Add garlic and cook until browned. Add the tuna and cook 2-3 minutes, or until tuna is almost cooked through. Discard the garlic.
Add the pasta and reduce heat. Stir in egg mixture and cook, stirring constantly, 2 minutes. If the sauce is too thick, thin with water, a little bit at a time, until it has a creamy texture.
Salt and pepper to taste and serve garnished with parsley.
Nutrition Info: Calories 409 Total Carbs 7g Net Carbs 6g Protein 25g Fat 30g Sugar 3g Fiber 1g

Flavors Cioppino

Servings: 6
Cooking Time: 5 Minutes
Ingredients:
1 lb codfish, cut into chunks
1 1/2 lbs shrimp
28 oz can tomatoes, diced
1 cup dry white wine
1 bay leaf
1 tsp cayenne
1 tsp oregano
1 shallot, chopped

1 tsp garlic, minced
1 tbsp olive oil
1/2 tsp salt
Directions:
Add oil into the inner pot of instant pot and set the pot on sauté mode.
Add shallot and garlic and sauté for 2 minutes.
Add wine, bay leaf, cayenne, oregano, and salt and cook for 3 minutes.
Add remaining ingredients and stir well.
Seal pot with a lid and select manual and cook on low for 0 minutes.
Once done, release pressure using quick release. Remove lid.
Serve and enjoy.
Nutrition Info: Calories 281 Fat 5 g Carbohydrates 10.5 g Sugar 4.9 g Protein 40.7 g Cholesterol 266 mg

Delicious Shrimp Alfredo

Servings: 4
Cooking Time: 3 Minutes
Ingredients:
12 shrimp, remove shells
1 tbsp garlic, minced
1/4 cup parmesan cheese
2 cups whole wheat rotini noodles
1 cup fish broth
15 oz alfredo sauce
1 onion, chopped
Salt
Directions:
Add all ingredients except parmesan cheese into the instant pot and stir well.
Seal pot with lid and cook on high for 3 minutes.
Once done, release pressure using quick release. Remove lid.
Stir in cheese and serve.
Nutrition Info: Calories 669 Fat 23.1 g Carbohydrates 76 g Sugar 2.4 g Protein 37.8 g Cholesterol 190 mg

Salmon & Asparagus

Servings: 2
Cooking Time: 10 Minutes
Ingredients:
2 salmon fillets
8 spears asparagus, trimmed
2 tablespoons balsamic vinegar
1 teaspoon olive oil
1 teaspoon dried dill
Salt and pepper to taste
Directions:
Preheat your oven to 325 degrees F.
Dry salmon with paper towels.
Arrange the asparagus around the salmon fillets on a baking pan.
In a bowl, mix the rest of the ingredients.
Pour mixture over the salmon and vegetables.
Bake in the oven for 10 minutes or until the fish is fully cooked.
Nutrition Info: Calories 150 g Fat 22 g Carbohydrates 13.6 g Protein 7 g Cholesterol 20 mg

Tuna Sweet Corn Casserole

Servings: 2
Cooking Time: 35 Minutes
Ingredients:
3 small tins of tuna
0.5lb sweet corn kernels
1lb chopped vegetables
1 cup low sodium vegetable broth
2tbsp spicy seasoning
Directions:
Mix all the ingredients in your Instant Pot.
Cook on Stew for 35 minutes.
Release the pressure naturally.
Nutrition Info: Calories: 300;Carbs: 6 ;Sugar: 1 ;Fat: 9 ;Protein: ;GL: 2

Tortilla Chip With Black Bean Salad

Servings: 4
Cooking Time: 20 Minutes
Ingredients:
4 oz. white fish fillets and tortilla chips
1/3 cup frozen egg, thawed
¼ red onion, chopped
¼ teaspoon cumin, ground
½ cup cherry tomatoes, halved
What you will need from the store cupboard:
2 teaspoons olive oil
1 tablespoon lemon juice
¼ teaspoon cayenne pepper
½ cup green bell pepper, chopped
¼ teaspoon salt
Cooking spray

Directions:

Preheat your oven to 350 °F. Use a foil to line your baking sheet.

Apply cooking spray on the foil.

Combine the cayenne pepper and tortilla chips in your food processor.

Cover till it is crushed fine. Keep in a dish.

Use paper towels to pat dry.

Pour egg into a second dish. Dip your fish into this and then in your tortilla chips.

Now keep the fish on the baking sheet. Coat it with cooking spray lightly.

Bake for 8 minutes. The fish must flake easily with a fork.

In the meantime, for the salad, bring together the tomatoes, onion, lemon juice, bell pepper, cumin, salt, and oil in your bowl.

Place fish on top of the salad. Sprinkle some cheese on top.

Nutrition Info: Calories 361, Carbohydrates 35g, Fiber 8g, Sugar 0.3g, Cholesterol 46mg, Total Fat 11g, Protein 28g

Crunchy Lemon Shrimp

Servings: 4

Cooking Time: 10 Minutes,

Ingredients:

1 lb. raw shrimp, peeled and deveined

2 tbsp. Italian parsley, roughly chopped

2 tbsp. lemon juice, divided

What you'll need from store cupboard:

⅔ cup panko bread crumbs

2½ tbsp. olive oil, divided

Salt and pepper, to taste

Directions:

Heat oven to 400 degrees.

Place the shrimp evenly in a baking dish and sprinkle with salt and pepper. Drizzle on 1 tablespoon lemon juice and 1 tablespoon of olive oil. Set aside.In a medium bowl, combine parsley, remaining lemon juice, bread crumbs, remaining olive oil, and ¼ tsp each of salt and pepper. Layer the panko mixture evenly on top of the shrimp.

Bake 8-10 minutes or until shrimp are cooked through and the panko is golden brown.

Nutrition Info: Calories 283 Total Carbs 15g Net Carbs 14g Protein 28g Fat 12g Sugar 1g Fiber 1g

Fish Amandine

Servings: 4

Cooking Time: 15 Minutes

Ingredients:

4 oz. frozen or fresh tilapia, halibut or trout fillets (skinless, 1-inch size)

1/8 teaspoon red pepper, crushed

¼ cup almonds, chopped

½ cup bread crumbs

2 tablespoons parsley, chopped

What you will need from the store cupboard:

½ teaspoon dry mustard

¼ cup buttermilk

1 tablespoon melted butter

2 tablespoons Parmesan cheese, grated

¼ teaspoon salt

Directions:

Preheat your oven to 350 °F and grease the baking pan. Keep it aside.

Rinse the fish. Use paper towels to pat dry.

Now pour the buttermilk into a dish.

Take another dish and bring together the parsley, bread crumbs, salt, and dry mustard.

Place fish into the buttermilk. Then into your crumb mix.

Now keep the coated fish in the baking pan.

Sprinkle Parmesan cheese and almonds on the fish.

Drizzle melted butter.

Also, sprinkle the crushed red pepper.

Bake for 4-6 minutes.

Nutrition Info: Calories 209, Carbohydrates 7g, Fiber 1g, Sugar 1g, Cholesterol 67mg, Total Fat 9g, Protein 26g

Shrimp & Veggies Curry

Servings: 6

Cooking Time: 20 Minutes

Ingredients:

2 teaspoons olive oil

1½ medium white onions, sliced

2 medium green bell peppers, seeded and sliced

3 medium carrots, peeled and sliced thinly

3 garlic cloves, chopped finely

1 tablespoon fresh ginger, chopped finely

2½ teaspoons curry powder

1½ pounds shrimp, peeled and deveined

1 cup filtered water

2 tablespoons fresh lime juice

Salt and ground black pepper, as required
2 tablespoons fresh cilantro, chopped
Directions:
In a large skillet, heat oil over medium-high heat and sauté the onion for about 4-5 minutes.
Add the bell peppers and carrot and sauté for about 3-4 minutes.
Add the garlic, ginger and curry powder and sauté for about 1 minute.
Add the shrimp and sauté for about 1 minute.
Stir in the water and cook for about 4-6 minutes, stirring occasionally.
Stir in lime juice and remove from heat.
Serve hot with the garnishing of cilantro.
Meal Prep Tip: Transfer the curry into a large bowl and set aside to cool. Divide the curry into 6 containers evenly. Cover the containers and refrigerate for 1-2 days. Reheat in the microwave before serving.
Nutrition Info: Calories 193 Total Fat 3.8 g Saturated Fat 0.9 g Cholesterol 239 mg Total Carbs 12 g Sugar 4.7 g Fiber 2.3 g Sodium 328 mg Potassium 437 mg Protein 27.1 g

Coconut Clam Chowder

Servings: 6
Cooking Time: 7 Minutes
Ingredients:
6 oz clams, chopped
1 cup heavy cream
1/4 onion, sliced
1 cup celery, chopped
1 lb cauliflower, chopped
1 cup fish broth
1 bay leaf
2 cups of coconut milk
Salt
Directions:
Add all ingredients except clams and heavy cream and stir well.
Seal pot with lid and cook on high for 5 minutes.
Once done, release pressure using quick release. Remove lid.
Add heavy cream and clams and stir well and cook on sauté mode for 2 minutes.
Stir well and serve.
Nutrition Info: Calories 301 Fat 27.2 g Carbohydrates 13.6 g Sugar 6 g Protein 4.9 g Cholesterol 33 mg

Lemon Pepper Salmon

Servings: 4
Cooking Time: 10 Minutes
Ingredients:
3 tbsps. ghee or avocado oil
1 lb. skin-on salmon filet
1 julienned red bell pepper
1 julienned green zucchini
1 julienned carrot
¾ cup water
A few sprigs of parsley, tarragon, dill, basil or a combination
1/2 sliced lemon
1/2 tsp. black pepper
¼ tsp. sea salt
Directions:
Add the water and the herbs into the bottom of the Instant Pot and put in a wire steamer rack making sure the handles extend upwards.
Place the salmon filet onto the wire rack, with the skin side facing down.
Drizzle the salmon with ghee, season with black pepper and salt, and top with the lemon slices.
Close and seal the Instant Pot, making sure the vent is turned to "Sealing".
Select the "Steam" setting and cook for 3 minutes. While the salmon cooks, julienne the vegetables, and set aside.
Once done, quick release the pressure, and then press the "Keep Warm/Cancel" button.
Uncover and wearing oven mitts, carefully remove the steamer rack with the salmon.
Remove the herbs and discard them.
Add the vegetables to the pot and put the lid back on.
Select the "Sauté" function and cook for 1-2 minutes.
Serve the vegetables with salmon and add the remaining fat to the pot.
Pour a little of the sauce over the fish and vegetables if desired.
Nutrition Info: Calories 296, Carbs 8g, Fat 15 g, Protein 31 g, Potassium (K) 1084 mg, Sodium (Na) 284 mg

Tomato Olive Fish Fillets

Servings: 4
Cooking Time: 8 Minutes
Ingredients:
2 lbs halibut fish fillets
2 oregano sprigs
2 rosemary sprigs
2 tbsp fresh lime juice
1 cup olives, pitted
28 oz can tomatoes, diced
1 tbsp garlic, minced
1 onion, chopped
2 tbsp olive oil
Directions:
Add oil into the inner pot of instant pot and set the pot on sauté mode.Add onion and sauté for 3 minutes.Add garlic and sauté for a minute.
Add lime juice, olives, herb sprigs, and tomatoes and stir well.Seal pot with lid and cook on high for 3 minutes.
Once done, release pressure using quick release. Remove lid.
Add fish fillets and seal pot again with lid and cook on high for 2 minutes.
Once done, release pressure using quick release. Remove lid.
Serve and enjoy.
Nutrition Info: Calories 333 Fat 19.1 g Carbohydrates 31.8 g Sugar 8.4 g Protein 13.4 g Cholesterol 5 mg

Almond Crusted Baked Chili Mahi Mahi

Servings: 4
Cooking Time: 15 Minutes
Ingredients:
4 mahi mahi fillets
1 lime
2 teaspoons olive oil
Salt and pepper to taste
½ cup almonds
¼ teaspoon paprika
¼ teaspoon onion powder
¾ teaspoon chili powder
½ cup red bell pepper, chopped
¼ cup onion, chopped
¼ cup fresh cilantro, chopped
Directions:

Preheat your oven to 325 degrees F.
Line your baking pan with parchment paper.
Squeeze juice from the lime.
Grate zest from the peel.
Put juice and zest in a bowl.
Add the oil, salt and pepper.
In another bowl, add the almonds, paprika, onion powder and chili powder.
Put the almond mixture in a food processor.
Pulse until powdery.
Dip each fillet in the oil mixture.
Dredge with the almond and chili mixture.
Arrange on a single layer in the oven.
Bake for 12 to 15 minutes or until fully cooked.
Serve with red bell pepper, onion and cilantro.
Nutrition Info: Calories 322 Total Fat 12 g Saturated Fat 2 g Cholesterol 83 mg Sodium 328 mg Total Carbohydrate 28 g Dietary Fiber 4 g Total Sugars 10 g Protein 28 g Potassium 829 mg

Shrimp Lemon Kebab

Servings: 5
Cooking Time: 4 Minutes
Ingredients:
1 ½ lb. shrimp, peeled anddeveined but with tails intact
⅓cup olive oil
¼ cup lemon juice
2 teaspoons lemon zest
1 tablespoon fresh parsley, chopped
8 cherry tomatoes, quartered
2 scallions, sliced
Directions:
Mix the olive oil, lemon juice, lemon zest and parsley in a bowl.
Marinate the shrimp in this mixture for 15 minutes.
Thread each shrimp into the skewers.
Grill for 4 to 5 minutes, turning once halfway through. Serve with tomatoes and scallions.
Nutrition Info: Calories 180 g Fat 20 g Carbohydrates 15 g Protein 11 g Cholesterol 26 mg

Turkish Tuna With Bulgur And Chickpea Salad

Servings: 4
Cooking Time: 20 Minutes
Ingredients:
16 oz. tuna, 4 steaks

½ cup bulgur
12 oz. chickpeas
4 teaspoons lemon zest, grated
¼ cup Italian parsley, chopped
What you will need from the store cupboard:
¼ cup extra-virgin olive oil
¼ teaspoon ground pepper
½ teaspoon salt
Directions:
Boil water and keep the bulgur in your bowl.
Add 2 inches of the water.Mix your bulgur with 1 tablespoon of oil, pepper, salt, and the lemon zest.Add the chickpeas and parsley.Stir well to combine.Now heat the remaining oil in your skillet over medium heat.
Add the tuna. Sear both sides until they become brown. The tuna should flake easily with your fork. Transfer to a plate.
In the meantime, bring together ¼ teaspoon salt and the remaining lemon zest in a bowl.
Transfer your tuna fish to a serving platter.
Sprinkle lemon zest and serve with the bulgur.
Nutrition Info: Calories 459, Carbohydrates 43g, Fiber 8g, Sugar 0.2g, Cholesterol 44mg, Total Fat 16g, Protein 36g

Cajun Flounder & Tomatoes

Servings: 4
Cooking Time: 15 Minutes
Ingredients:
4 flounder fillets
2 ½ cups tomatoes, diced
¾ cup onion, diced
¾ cup green bell pepper, diced
What you'll need from store cupboard:
2 cloves garlic, diced fine
1 tbsp. Cajun seasoning
1 tsp olive oil
Directions:
Heat oil in a large skillet over med-high heat. Add onion and garlic and cook 2 minutes, or until soft. Add tomatoes, peppers and spices, and cook 2-3 minutes until tomatoes soften.
Lay fish over top. Cover, reduce heat to medium and cook, 5-8 minutes, or until fish flakes easily with a fork. Transfer fish to servingplates and top with sauce.
Nutrition Info: Calories 194 Total Carbs 8g Net Carbs 6g Protein 32g Fat 3g Sugar 5g Fiber 2g

Lemon Sole

Servings: 2
Cooking Time: 5 Minutes
Ingredients:
1lb sole fillets, boned and skinned
1 cup low sodium fish broth
2 shredded sweet onions
juice of half a lemon
2tbsp dried cilantro
Directions:
Mix all the ingredients in your Instant Pot.
Cook on Stew for 5 minutes.
Release the pressure naturally.
Nutrition Info: Calories 230; Carbs Sugar 1; Fat 6; Protein 46; GL 1

Trout Bake

Servings: 2
Cooking Time: 35 Minutes
Ingredients:
1lb trout fillets, boneless
1lb chopped winter vegetables
1 cup low sodium fish broth
1tbsp mixed herbs
sea salt as desired
Directions:
Mix all the ingredients except the broth in a foil pouch.
Place the pouch in the steamer basket your Instant Pot. Pour the broth into the Instant Pot.
Cook on Steam for 35 minutes.
Release the pressure naturally.
Nutrition Info: Calories 310; Carbs 14; Sugar 2; Fat 12; Protein 40; GL 5

Garlic Shrimp & Spinach

Servings: 4
Cooking Time: 10 Minutes
Ingredients:
3 tablespoons olive oil, divided
6 clove garlic, sliced and divided
1 lb. spinach
Salt to taste
1 tablespoons lemon juice
1 lb. shrimp, peeled and deveined
¼ teaspoon red pepper, crushed
1 tablespoon parsley, chopped
1 teaspoon lemon zest

Directions:

Pour 1 tablespoon olive oil in a pot over medium heat.

Cook the garlic for 1 minute.

Add the spinach and season with salt.

Cook for 3 minutes.

Stir in lemon juice.

Transfer to a bowl.

Pour the remaining oil.

Add the shrimp.

Season with salt and add red pepper.

Cook for 5 minutes.

Sprinkle parsley and lemon zest over the shrimp before serving.

Nutrition Info: Calories 226 Total Fat 12 g Saturated Fat 2 g Cholesterol 183 mg Sodium 444 mg Total Carbohydrate 6 g Dietary Fiber 3 g Total Sugars 1 g Protein 26 g Potassium 963 mg

Salmon With Bell Peppers

Servings: 6

Cooking Time: 20 Minutes

Ingredients:

6 (3-ounce) salmon fillets

Pinch of salt

Ground black pepper, as required

1 yellow bell pepper, seeded and cubed

1 red bell pepper, seeded and cubed

4 plum tomatoes, cubed

1 small onion, sliced thinly

½ cup fresh parsley, chopped

¼ cup olive oil

2 tablespoons fresh lemon juice

Directions:

Preheat the oven to 400 degrees F.

Season each salmon fillet with salt and black pepper lightly.

In a bowl, mix together the bell peppers, tomato and onion.

Arrange 6 foil pieces onto a smooth surface.

Place 1 salmon fillet over each foil paper and sprinkle with salt and black pepper.

Place veggie mixture over each fillet evenly and top with parsley and capers evenly.

Drizzle with oil and lemon juice.

Fold each foil around salmon mixture to seal it.

Arrange the foil packets onto a large baking sheet in a single layer.

Bake for about 20 minutes.

Serve hot.

Meal Prep Tip: Transfer the salmon mixture into a large bowl and set aside to cool. Divide the salmon mixture into 6 containers evenly. Cover the containers and refrigerate for 1 day. Reheat in the microwave before serving.

Nutrition Info: Calories 220 Total Fat 14 g Saturated Fat 2 g Cholesterol 38 mg Total Carbs 7.7 g Sugar 4.8 g Fiber 2 g Sodium 74 mg Potassium 647 mg Protein 17.9 g

Tarragon Scallops

Servings: 4

Cooking Time: 15 Minutes

Ingredients:

1 cup water

1 lb. asparagus spears, trimmed

2 lemons

1 ¼ lb. scallops

Salt and pepper to taste

1 tablespoon olive oil

1 tablespoon fresh tarragon, chopped

Directions:

Pour water into a pot.

Bring to a boil.

Add asparagus spears.

Cover and cook for 5 minutes.

Drain and transfer to a plate.

Slice one lemon into wedges.

Squeeze juice and shred zest from the remaining lemon.

Season the scallops with salt and pepper.

Put a pan over medium heat.

Add oil to the pan.

Cook the scallops until golden brown.

Transfer to the same plate, putting scallops beside the asparagus.

Add lemon zest, juice and tarragon to the pan.

Cook for 1 minute.

Drizzle tarragon sauce over the scallops and asparagus.

Nutrition Info: Calories 253 Total Fat 12 g Saturated Fat 2 g Cholesterol 47 mg Sodium 436 mg Total Carbohydrate 14 g Dietary Fiber 5 g Total Sugars 3 g Protein 27 g Potassium 773 mg

Salmon Curry

Servings: 6
Cooking Time: 30 Minutes
Ingredients:
6 (4-ounce) salmon fillets
1 teaspoon ground turmeric, divided
Salt, as required
3 tablespoon olive oil, divided
1 yellow onion, chopped finely
1 teaspoon garlic paste
1 teaspoon fresh ginger paste
3-4 green chilies, halved
1 teaspoon red chili powder
½ teaspoon ground cumin
½ teaspoon ground cinnamon
¾ cup fat-free plain Greek yogurt, whipped
¾ cup filtered water
3 tablespoon fresh cilantro, chopped
Directions:
Season each salmon fillet with ½ teaspoon of the turmeric and salt.
In a large skillet, melt 1 tablespoon of the butter over medium heat and cook the salmon fillets for about 2 minutes per side.
Transfer the salmon onto a plate.
In the same skillet, melt the remaining butter over medium heat and sauté the onion for about 4-5 minutes.
Add the garlic paste, ginger paste, green chilies, remaining turmeric and spices and sauté for about 1 minute.
Now, reduce the heat to medium-low.
Slowly, add the yogurt and water, stirring continuously until smooth.
Cover the skillet and simmer for about 10-15 minutes or until desired doneness of the sauce.
Carefully, add the salmon fillets and simmer for about 5 minutes.
Serve hot with the garnishing of cilantro.
Meal Prep Tip: Transfer the curry into a large bowl and set aside to cool. Divide the curry into 6 containers evenly. Cover the containers and refrigerate for 1-2 days. Reheat in the microwave before serving.
Nutrition Info: Calories 242 Total Fat 14.3 g Saturated Fat 2 g Cholesterol 51 mg Total Carbs 4.1 g Sugar 2 g Fiber 0.8 g Sodium 98 mg Potassium 493 mg Protein 25.4 g

Halibut With Spicy Apricot Sauce

Servings: 4
Cooking Time: 17 Minutes
Ingredients:
4 fresh apricots, pitted
⅓ cup apricot preserves
½ cup apricot nectar
½ teaspoon dried oregano
3 tablespoons scallion, sliced
1 teaspoon hot pepper sauce
Salt to taste
4 halibut steaks
1 tablespoon olive oil
Directions:
Put the apricots, preserves, nectar, oregano, scallion, hot pepper sauce and salt in a saucepan.
Bring to a boil and then simmer for 8 minutes.
Set aside.
Brush the halibut steaks with olive oil.
Grill for 7 to 9 minutes or until fish is flaky.
Brush one tablespoon of the sauce on both sides of the fish.
Serve with the reserved sauce.
Nutrition Info: Calories 304 Total Fat 8 g Saturated Fat 1 g Cholesterol 73 mg Sodium 260 mg Total Carbohydrate 27 g Dietary Fiber 2 g Total Sugars 16 g Protein 29 g Potassium 637 mg

Easy Salmon Stew

Servings: 6
Cooking Time: 8 Minutes
Ingredients:
2 lbs salmon fillet, cubed
1 onion, chopped
2 cups fish broth
1 tbsp olive oil
Pepper
salt
Directions:
Add oil into the inner pot of instant pot and set the pot on sauté mode. Add onion and sauté for 2 minutes. Add remaining ingredients and stir well.
Seal pot with lid and cook on high for 6 minutes.
Once done, release pressure using quick release. Remove lid. Stir and serve.
Nutrition Info: Calories 243 Fat 12.6 g Carbohydrates 0.8 g Sugar 0.3 g Protein 31 g Cholesterol 78 mg

Cilantro Lime Grilled Shrimp

Servings: 6
Cooking Time: 5 Minutes,
Ingredients:
1 ½ lbs. large shrimp raw, peeled, deveined with tails on
Juice and zest of 1 lime
2 tbsp. fresh cilantro chopped
What you'll need from store cupboard:
¼ cup olive oil
2 cloves garlic, diced fine
1 tsp smoked paprika
¼ tsp cumin - 1/2 teaspoon salt
¼ tsp cayenne pepper
Directions:
Place the shrimp in a large Ziploc bag.
Mix remaining Ingredients in a small bowl and pour over shrimp. Let marinate 20-30 minutes.
Heat up the grill. Skewer the shrimp and cook 2-3 minutes, per side, just until they turn pick. Be careful not to overcook them. Serve garnished with cilantro.
Nutrition Info: Calories 317 Total Carbs 4g Protein 39g Fat 15g Sugar 0g Fiber 0g

Cajun Catfish

Servings: 4
Cooking Time: 15 Minutes
Ingredients:
4 (8 oz.) catfish fillets
What you'll need from store cupboard:
2 tbsp. olive oil
2 tsp garlic salt
2 tsp thyme
2 tsp paprika
½ tsp cayenne pepper
½ tsp red hot sauce
¼ tsp black pepper
Nonstick cooking spray
Directions:
Heat oven to 450 degrees. Spray a 9x13-inch baking dish with cooking spray.
In a small bowl whisk together everything but catfish. Brush both sides of fillets, using all the spice mix. Bake 10-13 minutes or until fish flakes easily with a fork. Serve.
Nutrition Info: Calories 366 Total Carbs 0g Protein 35g Fat 24g Sugar 0g Fiber 0g

Halibut With Spicy Apricot Sauce

Servings: 4
Cooking Time: 17 Minutes
Ingredients:
4 fresh apricots, pitted
⅓cup apricot preserves
½ cup apricot nectar
½ teaspoon dried oregano
3 tablespoons scallion, sliced
1 teaspoon hot pepper sauce
Salt to taste
4 halibut steaks
1 tablespoon olive oil
Directions:
Put the apricots, preserves, nectar, oregano, scallion, hot pepper sauce and salt in a saucepan.
Bring to a boil and then simmer for 8 minutes.
Set aside.
Brush the halibut steaks with olive oil.
Grill for 7 to 9 minutes or until fish is flaky.
Brush one tablespoon of the sauce on both sides of the fish.
Serve with the reserved sauce.
Bake in the oven for 10 minutes or until the fish is fully cooked.
Nutrition Info: Calories 150 g Fat 22 g Carbohydrates 13.6 g Protein 7 g Cholesterol 20 mg

Mixed Chowder

Servings: 2
Cooking Time: 35 Minutes
Ingredients:
1lb fish stew mix
2 cups white sauce
3tbsp old bay seasoning
Directions:
Mix all the ingredients in your Instant Pot.
Cook on Stew for 35 minutes.
Release the pressure naturally.
Nutrition Info: Calories 320; Carbs 9; Sugar 2; Fat 16; Protein GL 4

Shrimp With Zucchini

Servings: 4
Cooking Time: 8 Minutes
Ingredients:
3 tablespoons olive oil

1 pound medium shrimp, peeled and deveined
1 shallot, minced
4 garlic cloves, minced
¼ teaspoon red pepper flakes, crushed
Salt and ground black pepper, as required
¼ cup low-sodium chicken broth
2 tablespoons fresh lemon juice
1 teaspoon fresh lemon zest, grated finely
½ pound zucchini, spiralized with Blade C
Directions:
In a large skillet, heat the oil and butter over medium-high heat and cook the shrimp, shallot, garlic, red pepper flakes, salt and black pepper for about 2 minutes, stirring occasionally.
Stir in the broth, lemon juice and lemon zest and bring to a gentle boil.
Stir in zucchini noodles and cook for about 1-2 minutes.
Serve hot.
Meal Prep Tip: Transfer the shrimp mixture into a large bowl and set aside to cool. Divide the shrimp mixture into 4 containers. Coverthe containers and refrigerate for about 1-2 days. Reheat in microwave before serving.
Nutrition Info: Calories 245 Total Fat 12.6 g Saturated Fat 2.2 g Cholesterol 239 mg Total Carbs 5.8 g Sugar 1.2 g Fiber 08 g Sodium 289 mg Potassium 381 mg Protein 27 g

Braised Shrimp

Servings: 4
Cooking Time: 4 Minutes
Ingredients:
1 pound frozen large shrimp, peeled and deveined
2 shallots, chopped
¾ cup low-sodium chicken broth
2 tablespoons fresh lemon juice
2 tablespoons olive oil
1 tablespoon garlic, crushed
Ground black pepper, as required
Directions:
In the Instant Pot, place oil and press "Sauté". Now add the shallots and cook for about 2 minutes.
Add the garlic and cook for about 1 minute.
Press "Cancel" and stir in the shrimp, broth, lemon juice and black pepper.
Close the lid and place the pressure valve to "Seal" position.

Press "Manual" and cook under "High Pressure" for about 1 minute.
Press "Cancel" and carefully allow a "Quick" release.
Open the lid and serve hot.
Nutrition Info: Calories 209, Fats 9g, Carbs 4.3g, Sugar 0.2g, Proteins 26.6g, Sodium 293mg

Salmon Soup

Servings: 4
Cooking Time: 20 Minutes
Ingredients:
1 tablespoon olive oil
1 yellow onion, chopped
1 garlic clove, minced
4 cups low-sodium chicken broth
1 pound boneless salmon, cubed
2 tablespoon fresh cilantro, chopped
Ground black pepper, as required
1 tablespoon fresh lime juice
Directions:
In a large pan heat the oil over medium heat and sauté the onion for about 5 minutes.
Add the garlic and sauté for about 1 minute.
Stir in the broth and bring to a boil over high heat. Now, reduce the heat to low and simmer for about 10 minutes.
Add the salmon, and soy sauce and cook for about 3-4 minutes.
Stir in black pepper, lime juice, and cilantro and serve hot.
Meal Prep Tip: Transfer the soup into a large bowl and set aside to cool. Divide the soup into 4 containers evenly. Cover the containers and refrigerate for 1-2 days. Reheat in the microwave before serving.
Nutrition Info: Calories 208 Total Fat 10.5 g Saturated Fat 1.5 g Cholesterol 50 mg Total Carbs 3.9 g Sugar 1.2 g Fiber 0.6 g Sodium 121 mg Potassium 331 mg Protein 24.4 g

Salmon With Pineapple-cilantro Salsa

Servings: 4
Cooking Time: 15 Minutes
Ingredients:
1 lb. salmon fillets, skinless, 1 inch thick
2 tablespoons parsley or cilantro, chopped
2 cups pineapple, chopped
¼ cup red onion, chopped

½ cup green or red bell pepper, chopped
What you will need from the store cupboard:
¼ teaspoon salt
½ teaspoon chili powder
3 tablespoons lime juice
Lime wedges, optional
Pinch of cayenne pepper
Directions:
Rinse the fish. Use paper towels to pat dry.
For the salsa, bring together the bell pepper, pineapple, lime juice, red onion, and a tablespoon of parsley or cilantro in a bowl. Keep this aside.
Now combine the lime juice, salt, and the remaining parsley or cilantro.
Brush this on both sides of your fish.
Keep fish on your grill and grill for 8 minutes. Turn once.
Cut your fish into 4 serving sizes. Apply salsa on top.
You can serve with lettuce and lime wedges.
Nutrition Info: Calories 257, Carbohydrates 13g, Fiber 2g, Sugar 1g, Cholesterol 66mg, Total Fat 12g, Protein 23g

Italian Tuna Pasta

Servings: 6
Cooking Time: 5 Minutes
Ingredients:
15 oz whole wheat pasta
2 tbsp capers
3 oz tuna
2 cups can tomatoes, crushed
2 anchovies
1 tsp garlic, minced
1 tbsp olive oil
Salt
Directions:
Add oil into the inner pot of instant pot and set the pot on sauté mode.
Add anchovies and garlic and sauté for 1 minute.

Add remaining ingredients and stir well. Pour enough water into the pot to cover the pasta.
Seal pot with a lid and select manual and cook on low for 4 minutes.
Once done, release pressure using quick release. Remove lid.
Stir and serve.
Nutrition Info: Calories 339 Fat 6 g Carbohydrates 56.5 g Sugar5.2 g Protein 15.2 g Cholesterol 10 mg

Baked Salmon With Garlic Parmesan Topping

Servings: 4
Cooking Time: 20 Minutes,
Ingredients:
1 lb. wild caught salmon filets
2 tbsp. margarine
What you'll need from store cupboard:
¼ cup reduced fat parmesan cheese, grated
¼ cup light mayonnaise
2-3 cloves garlic, diced
2 tbsp. parsley
Salt and pepper
Directions:
Heat oven to 350 and line a baking pan with parchment paper.
Place salmon on pan and season with salt and pepper.
In a medium skillet, over medium heat, melt butter. Add garlic and cook, stirring 1 minute.
Reduce heat to low and add remaining Ingredients. Stir until everything is melted and combined.
Spread evenly over salmon and bake 15 minutes for thawed fish or 20 for frozen. Salmon is done when it flakes easily with a fork. Serve.

Nutrition Info: Calories 408 Total Carbs 4g Protein 41g Fat 24g Sugar 1g Fiber 0g

Chapter 13
Beef, Pork & Lamb Recipes

Beef & Broccoli Skillet

Servings: 4
Cooking Time: 10 Minutes
Ingredients:
1 lb. lean ground beef
3 cups cauliflower rice, cooked
2 cups broccoli, chopped
4 green onions, sliced
What you'll need from store cupboard:
1 cup teriyaki sauce (chapter 15)
Directions:
Cook beef in a large skillet over med-high heat until brown. Add the broccoli and white parts of the onion, cook, stirring for 1 minute.
Add the cauliflower and sauce and continue cooking until heated through and broccoli is tender-crisp, about 3-5 minutes. Serve garnished with green parts of the onion.
Nutrition Info: Calories 255 total carbs 9g Net carbs 6g Protein 37g Fat 7g Sugar 3g Fiber 3g

Balsamic Chicken & Vegetable Skillet

Servings: 4
Cooking Time: 20 Minutes
Ingredients:
1 lb. chicken breasts, cut in 1-inch cubes
1 cup cherry tomatoes, halved
1 cup broccoli florets
1 cup baby Bella mushrooms, sliced
1 tbsp. fresh basil, diced
What you'll need from store cupboard:
1/2 recipe homemade pasta, cooked and drain well (chapter 14)
½ cup low sodium chicken broth
3 tbsp. balsamic vinegar
2 tbsp. olive oil, divided
1 tsp pepper
½ tsp garlic powder
½ tsp salt
½ tsp red pepper flakes

Directions:
Heat oil in a large, deep skillet over med-high heat. Add chicken and cook until browned on all sides, 8-10 minutes.
Add vegetables, basil, broth, and seasonings. Cover, reduce heat to medium and cook 5 minutes, or vegetables are tender.
Uncover and stir in cooked pasta and vinegar. Cook until heated through, 3-4 minutes. Serve.
Nutrition Info: Calories 386 Total Carbs 11g Net Carbs 8g Protein 43g Fat 18g Sugar 5g Fiber 3g

Russian Steaks With Nuts And Cheese

Servings: 4
Cooking Time: 20 Minutes
Ingredients:
800g of minced pork
200g of cream cheese
50g peeled walnuts
1 onion
Salt
Ground pepper
1 egg
Breadcrumbs
Extra virgin olive oil
Directions:
Put the onion cut into quarters in the Thermo mix glass and select 5 seconds speed 5.
Add the minced meat, cheese, egg, salt, and pepper. Select 10 seconds, speed 5, turn left.
Add the chopped and peeled walnuts and select 4 seconds, turn left, speed 5.
Pass the dough to a bowl.
Make Russian steaks and go through breadcrumbs. Paint the Russian fillets with extra virgin olive oil on both sides with a brush.
Put in the basket of the air fryer, without stacking the Russianfillets.
Select 1800C, 15 minutes.
Nutrition Info: Calories: 1232Fat: 3.41g Carbohydrates: 0g Protein: 20.99g Sugar: 0gCholesterol: 63mg

Creamy Chicken Tenders

Servings: 4
Cooking Time: 15 Minutes
Ingredients:
1 lb. chicken breast tenders
1 cup half-n-half
4 tbsp. margarine
What you'll need from store cupboard:
2 tsp garlic powder
2 tsp chili powder
Directions:
In a small bowl, stir together seasonings with a little salt if desired. Sprinkle over chicken to coat.
Heat 2 tablespoons margarine in a large skillet over medium heat. Cook chicken until no longer pink, 3-4 minutes per side. Transfer to a plate.
Add half-n-half and stir, scraping up the brown bits from the bottom of the skillet, and cook until it starts to boil. Reduce heat to med-low and simmer until sauce is reduced by half. Stir in remaining margarine and add chicken back to sauce to heat through. Serve.
Nutrition Info: Calories 281 Total Carbs 3g Protein 24g Fat 19g Sugar 0g Fiber 0g

Tangy Balsamic Beef

Servings: 8
Cooking Time: 6 – 8 Hours
Ingredients:
3-4 lb. beef roast, boneless
½ onion, diced fine
What you'll need from store cupboard:
1 can low sodium beef broth
½ cup balsamic vinegar
5 cloves garlic, diced fine

3 tbsp. honey
1 tbsp. lite soy sauce
1 tbsp. Worcestershire sauce
1 tsp red chili flakes
Directions:
Place all Ingredients, except the roast, into the crock pot. Stir well. Add roast and turn to coat. Cover and cook on low 6-8 hours. When the beef is done, remove to a plate and shred, using two forks. Add it back to the sauce and serve.
Nutrition Info: Calories 410 Total Carbs 9g Protein 45g Fat 20g Sugar 7g Fiber 0g

Sirloin Strips & "rice"

Servings: 6
Cooking Time: 30 Minutes
Ingredients:
1 ½ lbs. top sirloin steak, cut in thin strips
3 cup Cauliflower Rice, cook, (chapter 14)
2 onions, slice thin
What you'll need from store cupboard:
14 ½ oz. tomatoes, diced, undrained
½ cup low sodium beef broth
1/3 cup dry red wine
1 clove garlic, diced
1 bay leaf
2 tsp olive oil, divided
1 tsp salt
½ tsp basil
½ tsp thyme
¼ tsp pepper
Directions:
Sprinkle beef strips with salt and pepper.
Heat oil in a large skillet over medium heat. Add steak and cook, stirring frequently, just until browned. Transfer to a plate and keep warm.
Add remaining oil to the skillet along with the onion and cook until tender. Add the garlic and cook 1 minute more.
Stir in remaining Ingredients, except the cauliflower, and bring to a boil. Reduce heat and simmer 10 minutes.
Return the steak back to the skillet and cook 2-4 minutes until heated through and tender. Discard bay leaf and serve over cauliflower rice.
Nutrition Info: Calories 278 Total Carbs 9g Net Carbs 6g Protein 37g Fat 9g Sugar 5g Fiber 3g

Spicy Bbq Beef Brisket

Servings: 14
Cooking Time: 5 Hours
Ingredients:
3 ½ lb. beef brisket
½ cup onion, diced fine
1 tsp lemon juice
What you'll need from store cupboard:
2 cup barbecue sauce, (chapter 15)
1 pkt. Chili seasoning
1 tbsp. Worcestershire sauce
1 tsp garlic, diced fine
Directions:
Cut brisket in half and place in crock pot.
In a small bowl, combine remaining Ingredients, and pour over beef. Cover and cook on high heat 5-6 hours or until beef is fork tender.
Transfer brisket to a bowl. Use two forks and shred. Add the meat back to the crock pot and stir to heat through. Serve as is or on buns.
Nutrition Info: Calories 239 Total Carbs 7g Protein 34g Fat 7g Sugar 4g Fiber 0g

Slow Cooker Lemon Chicken With Gravy

Servings: 4
Cooking Time: 3 Hours
Ingredients:
1 lb. chicken tenderloins
3 tbsp. fresh lemon juice
3 tbsp. margarine, cubed
2 tbsp. fresh parsley, diced
2 tbsp. fresh thyme, diced
1 tbsp. lemon zest
What you'll need from store cupboard:
¼ cup low sodium chicken broth
2 cloves garlic, sliced
2 tsp cornstarch
2 tsp water
½ tsp salt
½ tsp white pepper
Directions:
Add the broth, lemon juice, margarine, zest, garlic, salt and pepper to the crock pot, stir to combine. Add chicken, cover and cook on low heat 2 ½ hours.
Add the parsley and thyme and cook 30 minutes more, or chicken is cooked through.

Remove chicken to a plate and keep warm. Pour cooking liquid into a small saucepan and place over medium heat.
Stir water and cornstarch together until smooth. Add to sauce pan and bring to a boil. Cook, stirring, 2 minutes or until thickened. Serve with chicken.
Nutrition Info: Calories 303 Total Carbs 2g Protein 33g Fat 17g Sugar 0g Fiber 0g

Ritzy Beef Stew

Servings: 6
Cooking Time: 2 Hours
Ingredients:
2 tablespoons all-purpose flour
1 tablespoon Italian seasoning
2 pounds (907 g) top round, cut into ¾-inch cubes
2 tablespoons olive oil
4 cups low-sodium chicken broth, divided
1½ pounds (680 g) cremini mushrooms, rinsed, stems removed, and quartered
1 large onion, coarsely chopped
3 cloves garlic, minced
3 medium carrots, peeled and cut into ½-inch pieces
1 cup frozen peas
1 tablespoon fresh thyme, minced
1 tablespoon red wine vinegar
½ teaspoon freshly ground black pepper
Directions:
Combine the flour and Italian seasoning in a large bowl. Dredge the beef cubes in the bowl to coat well.
Heat the olive oil in a pot over medium heat until shimmering.
Add the beef to the single layer in the pot and cook for 2 to 4 minutes or until golden brown on all sides. Flip the beef cubes frequently.
Remove the beef from the pot and set aside, then add ¼ cup of chicken broth to the pot.
Add the mushrooms and sauté for 4 minutes or until soft. Remove the mushrooms from the pot and set aside.
Pour ¼ cup of chicken broth in the pot. Add the onions and garlic to the pot and sauté for 4 minutes or until translucent.
Put the beef back to the pot and pour in the remaining broth. Bring to a boil.

Reduce the heat to low and cover. Simmer for 45 minutes. Stir periodically.

Add the carrots, mushroom, peas, and thyme to the pot and simmer for 45 more minutes or until the vegetables are soft.

Open the lid, drizzle with red wine vinegar and season with black pepper. Stir and serve in a large bowl.

Nutrition Info: calories: 250 fat: 7.0g protein: 25.0g carbs: 24.0g fiber: 3.0g sugar: 5.0g sodium: 290mg

Pork Trinoza Wrapped In Ham

Servings: 6
Cooking Time: 20 Minutes
Ingredients:
6 pieces of Serrano ham, thinly sliced
454g pork, halved, with butter and crushed
6g of salt
1g black pepper
227g fresh spinach leaves, divided
4 slices of mozzarella cheese, divided
18g sun-dried tomatoes, divided
10 ml of olive oil, divided
Directions:
Place 3 pieces of ham on baking paper, slightly overlapping each other. Place 1 half of the pork in the ham. Repeat with the other half.

Season the inside of the pork rolls with salt and pepper.

Place half of the spinach, cheese, and sun-dried tomatoes on top of the pork loin, leaving a 13 mm border on all sides.

Roll the fillet around the filling well and tie with a kitchen cord to keep it closed.

Repeat the process for the other pork steak and place them in the fridge.

Select Preheat in the air fryer and press Start/Pause.

Brush 5 ml of olive oil on each wrapped steak and place them in the preheated air fryer.

Select Steak. Set the timer to 9 minutes and press Start/Pause.

Allow it to cool for 10 minutes before cutting.

Nutrition Info: Calories: 282 Fat: 23.41 Carbohydrates: 0g Protein: 16.59 Sugar: 0g Cholesterol: 73gm

Mississippi Style Pot Roast

Servings: 8
Cooking Time: 8 Hours
Ingredients:
3 lb. chuck roast
What you'll need from store cupboard:
6-8 pepperoncini
1 envelope au jus gravy mix
1 envelope ranch dressing mix
Directions:
Place roast in crock pot. Sprinkle both envelopes of mixes over top. Place the peppers around the roast.

Cover and cook on low 8 hours, or high 4 hours.

Transfer roast to a large bowl and shred using 2 forks. Add it back to the crock pot and stir. Remove the pepperoncini, chop and stir back into the roast. Serve.

Nutrition Info: Calories 379 Total Carbs 3g Protein 56g Fat 14g Sugar 1g Fiber 0g

Spicy Grilled Turkey Breast

Servings: 14
Cooking Time: 1 ½ Hours
Ingredients:
5 lb. turkey breast, bone in
What you'll need from store cupboard:
1 cup low sodium chicken broth
¼ cup vinegar
¼ cup jalapeno pepper jelly
2 tbsp. Splenda brown sugar
2 tbsp. olive oil
1 tbsp. salt
2 tsp cinnamon
1 tsp cayenne pepper
½ tsp ground mustard
Nonstick cooking spray
Directions:
Heat grill to medium heat. Spray rack with cooking spray. Place a drip pan on the grill for indirect heat. In a small bowl, combine Splenda brown sugar with seasonings.

Carefully loosen the skin on the turkey from both sides with your fingers. Spread half the spice mix on the turkey. Secure the skin to the underneath with toothpicks and spread remaining spice mix on the outside.

Place the turkey over the drip pan and grill 30 minutes.

In a small saucepan, over medium heat, combine broth, vinegar, jelly, and oil. Cook and stir 2 minutes until jelly is completely melted. Reserve ½ cup of the mixture.

Baste turkey with some of the jelly mixture. Cook 1-1 ½ hours, basting every 15 minutes, until done, when thermometer reaches 170 degrees.

Cover and let rest 10 minutes. Discard the skin. Brush with reserved jelly mixture and slice and serve.

Nutrition Info: Calories 314 Total Carbs 5g Protein 35g Fat 14g Sugar 5g Fiber 0g

Stuffed Cabbage And Pork Loin Rolls

Servings: 4
Cooking Time: 25 Minutes
Ingredients:
500g of white cabbage
1 onion
8 pork tenderloin steaks
2 carrots
4 tbsp. soy sauce
50g of olive oil
Salt
8 sheets of rice
Directions:
Put the chopped cabbage in the Thermo mix glass together with the onion and the chopped carrot.
Select 5 seconds, speed 5. Add the extra virgin olive oil. Select 5 minutes, varoma temperature, left turn, spoon speed.
Cut the tenderloin steaks into thin strips. Add the meat to the Thermomix glass. Select 5 minutes, varoma temperature, left turn, spoon speed. Without beaker
Add the soy sauce. Select 5 minutes, varoma temperature, left turn, spoon speed. Rectify salt. Let it cold down.
Hydrate the rice slices. Extend and distribute the filling between them.
Make the rolls, folding so that the edges are completely closed. Place the rolls in the air fryer and paint with the oil.
Select 10 minutes, 1800C.
Nutrition Info: Calories: 120 Fat: 3.41g Carbohydrates: 0g Protein: 20.99g Sugar: 0gCholesterol: 65mg

Cheesy Chicken & Spinach

Servings: 6
Cooking Time: 45 Minutes
Ingredients:
3 chicken breasts, boneless, skinless and halved lengthwise
6 oz. low fat cream cheese, soft
2 cup baby spinach
1 cup mozzarella cheese, grated
What you'll need from store cupboard:
2 tbsp. olive oil, divided
3 cloves garlic, diced fine
1 tsp Italian seasoning
Nonstick cooking spray
Directions:
Heat oven to 350 degrees. Spray a 9x13-inch glass baking dish with cooking spray.
Lay chicken breast cutlets in baking dish. Drizzle 1 tablespoon oil over chicken. Sprinkle evenly with garlic and Italian seasoning. Spread cream cheese over the top of chicken.
Heat remaining tablespoon of oil in a small skillet over medium heat. Add spinach and cook until spinach wilts, about 3 minutes. Place evenly over cream cheese layer. Sprinkle mozzarella over top. Bake 35-40 minutes, or until chicken is cooked through. Serve.
Nutrition Info: Calories 363 Total Carbs 3g Protein 31g Fat 25g Sugar 0g Fiber 0g

Bbq Chicken & Noodles

Servings: 4
Cooking Time: 25 Minutes
Ingredients:
4 slices bacon, diced
1 chicken breast, boneless, skinless, cut into 1-inch pieces
1 onion, diced
1 cup low fat cheddar cheese, grated
½ cup skim milk
What you'll need from store cupboard:
14 ½ oz. can tomatoes, diced
2 cup low sodium chicken broth
¼ cup barbecue sauce, (chapter 15)
2 cloves garlic, diced fine
¼ tsp red pepper flakes
Homemade noodles, (chapter 14)
Salt and pepper, to taste

Directions:

Place a large pot over med-high heat. Add bacon and cook until crispy. Drain fat, reserving 1 tablespoon.

Stir in chicken and cook until browned on all sides, 3-5 minutes.

Add garlic and onion and cook, stirring often, until onions are translucent, 3-4 minutes.

Stir in broth, tomatoes, milk, and seasonings. Bring to boil, cover, reduce heat and simmer 10 minutes.

Stir in barbecue sauce, noodle, and cheese and cook until noodles are done and cheese has melted, 2-3 minutes. Serve.

Nutrition Info: Calories 331 Total Carbs 18g Net Carbs 15g Protein 34g Fat 13g Sugar 10g Fiber 3g

Homemade Flamingos

Servings: 4
Cooking Time: 20 Minutes
Ingredients:
400g of very thin sliced pork fillets c / n
2 boiled and chopped eggs
100g chopped Serrano ham
1 beaten egg
Breadcrumbs
Directions:
Make a roll with the pork fillets. Introduce half-cooked egg and Serrano ham. So that the roll does not lose its shape, fasten with a string or chopsticks.
Pass the rolls through beaten egg and then through the breadcrumbs until it forms a good layer.
Preheat the air fryer a few minutes at 180° C.
Insert the rolls in the basket and set the timer for about 8 minutes at 180o C.
Nutrition Info: Calories: 482 Fat: 23.41 Carbohydrates: 0g Protein: 16.59 Sugar: 0g Cholesterol: 173gm

Pesto Chicken

Servings: 6
Cooking Time: 20 Minutes
Ingredients:
1 ¾ lbs chicken breasts, skinless, boneless, and slice
½ cup mozzarella cheese, shredded
¼ cup pesto

Directions:
Add chicken and pesto in a mixing bowl and mix until well coated.
Place in refrigerator for 2-3 hours.
Grill chicken over medium heat until completely cooked.
Sprinkle cheese over chicken and serve.
Nutrition Info: 303 Fat: 13g Carbohydrates: 1g Protein: 2Sugar: 1gCholesterol: 122mg

Breaded Chicken With Seed Chips

Servings: 4
Cooking Time: 40 Minutes
Ingredients:
12 chicken breast fillets
Salt
2 eggs
1 small bag of seed chips
Breadcrumbs
Extra virgin olive oil
Directions:
Put salt to chicken fillets.
Crush the seed chips and when we have them fine, bind with the breadcrumbs.
Beat the two eggs.
Pass the chicken breast fillets through the beaten egg and then through the seed chips that you have tied with the breadcrumbs.
When you have them all breaded, paint with a brush of extra virgin olive oil.
Place the fillets in the basket of the air fryer without being piled up.
Select 170 degrees, 20 minutes.
Take out and put another batch, repeat temperature and time. So, until you use up all the steaks.
Nutrition Info: Calories: 242 Fat: 13g Carbohydrates: 13.5g Protein: 18gSugar: 0g Cholesterol: 42mg

Turkey Meatballs With Spaghetti Squash

Servings: 4
Cooking Time: 35 Minutes
Ingredients:
1 lb. lean ground turkey
1 lb. spaghetti squash, halved and seeds removed
2 egg whites

1/3 cup green onions, diced fine
¼ cup onion, diced fine
2 ½ tbsp. flat leaf parsley, diced fine
1 tbsp. fresh basil, diced fine
What you'll need from store cupboard:
14 oz. can no-salt-added tomatoes, crushed
1/3 cup soft whole wheat bread crumbs
¼ cup low sodium chicken broth
1 tsp garlic powder
1 tsp thyme
1 tsp oregano
½ tsp red pepper flakes
½ tsp whole fennel seeds
Directions:
In a small bowl, combine bread crumbs, onion, garlic, parsley, pepper flakes, thyme, and fennel.
In a large bowl, combine turkey and egg whites. Add bread crumb mixture and mix well. Cover and chill 10 minutes. Heat the oven to broil.
Place the squash, cut side down, in a glass baking dish. Add 3-4 tablespoons of water and microwave on high 10-12 minutes, or until fork tender.
Make 20 meatballs from the turkey mixture and place on a baking sheet. Broil 4-5 minutes, turn and cook 4 more minutes.
In a large skillet, combine tomatoes and broth and bring to a simmer over low heat. Add meatballs, oregano, basil, and green onions. Cook, stirring occasionally, 10 minutes or until heated through.
Use a fork to scrape the squash into "strands" and arrange on a serving platter. Top with meatballs and sauce and serve.
Nutrition Info: Calories 253 Total Carbs 15g Net Carbs 13g Protein 27g Fat 9g Sugar 4g Fiber 2g

Spicy Lettuce Wraps

Servings: 6
Cooking Time: 5 Minutes
Ingredients:
12 Romaine lettuce leaves
1 lb. ground chicken
1/3 cup green onions, slice thin
2 tsp fresh ginger, grated
What you'll need from store cupboard:
1/3 cup water chestnuts, diced fine
1/3 cup peanuts, chopped
2 cloves garlic, diced fine
3 tbsp. lite soy sauce
1 tbsp. cornstarch

1 tbsp. peanut oil
¼ tsp red pepper flakes
Directions:
In a large bowl, combine chicken, ginger, garlic, and pepper flakes.
In a small bowl, stir together cornstarch and soy sauce until smooth.
Heat oil in a large skillet over med-high heat, Add chicken and cook, stirring, 2-3 minutes, or chicken is cooked through.
Stir in soy sauce and cook, stirring, until mixture starts to thicken, about 30 seconds. Add water chestnuts, green onions, and peanuts and heat through.
Lay lettuce leaves out on a work surface. Divide filling evenly over them and roll up. Filling can also be made ahead of time andreheated as needed. Serve warm with Chinese hot mustard for dipping, (chapter 15).
Nutrition Info: Calories 234 Total Carbs 13g Net Carbs 12g Protein 26g Fat 12g Sugar 6g Fiber 1g

Deconstructed Philly Cheesesteaks

Servings: 4
Cooking Time: 20 Minutes
Ingredients:
1 lb. lean ground beef
5-6 mushrooms, halved
4 slices provolone cheese
3 green bell peppers, quartered
2 medium onions, quartered
What you'll need from store cupboard:
½ cup low sodium beef broth
1-2 tbsp. Worcestershire sauce
1 tsp olive oil
Salt & pepper, to taste
Directions:
Heat oven to 400 degrees.
Place vegetables in a large bowl and add oil. Toss to coat. Dump out onto a large baking sheet and bake 10-15 minutes, or until tender-crisp.
Place beef in a large skillet and cook over med-high heat until no longer pink. Drain off fat.
Add broth and Worcestershire. Cook, stirring occasionally, until liquid is absorbed, about 5 minutes. Salt and pepper beef if desired. Top with sliced cheese, remove from heat and cover until cheese melts.

Divide vegetables evenly between 4 bowls. Top with beef and serve.

Nutrition Info: Calories 388 Total Carbs 15g Net Carbs 12g Protein 44g Fat 16g Sugar 9g Fiber 3g

Bbq Pork Tacos

Servings: 16
Cooking Time: 6 Hours
Ingredients:
2 lb. pork shoulder, trim off excess fat
2 onions, diced fine
2 cups cabbages, shredded
What you'll need from store cupboard:
16 (6-inch) low carb whole wheat tortillas
4 chipotle peppers in adobo sauce, pureed
1 cup light barbecue sauce
2 cloves garlic, diced fine
1 ½ tsp paprika
Directions:
In a medium bowl, whisk together garlic, barbecue sauce and chipotles, cover and chill.
Place pork in the crock pot. Cover and cook on low 8-10 hours, or on high 4-6 hours.
Transfer pork to a cutting board. Use two forks and shred the pork, discarding the fat. Place pork back in the crock pot. Sprinkle with paprika then pour the barbecue sauce over mixture.
Stir to combine, cover and cook 1 hour. Skim off excess fat.
To assemble the tacos: place about ¼ cup of pork on warmed tortilla. Top with cabbage and onions and serve. Refrigerate any leftover pork up to 3 days.
Nutrition Info: Calories 265 Total Carbs 14g Net Carbs 5g Protein 17g Fat 14g Sugar 3g Fiber 9g

Beef Picadillo

Servings: 10
Cooking Time: 3-4 Hour
Ingredients:
1 ½ lbs. lean ground beef
1 onion, diced fine
1 red bell pepper, diced
1 small tomato, diced
¼ cup cilantro, diced fine
What you'll need from store cupboard:
1 cup tomato sauce
3 cloves garlic, diced fine
¼ cup green olives, pitted

2 bay leaves
1 ½ tsp cumin
¼ tsp garlic powder
Salt & pepper, to taste
Directions:
In a large skillet, over medium heat, brown ground beef. Season with salt and pepper. Drain fat. Add onion, bell pepper, and garlic and cook 3-4 minutes.
Transfer to crock pot and add remaining Ingredients. Cover and cook on high 3 hours.
Discard bay leaves. Taste and adjust seasonings as desired. Serve.
Nutrition Info: Calories 255 Total Carbs 6g Net Carbs 5g Protein 35g Fat 9g Sugar 3g Fiber 1g

Citrus Pork Tenderloin

Servings: 4
Cooking Time: 30 Minutes
Ingredients:
¼ cup freshly squeezed orange juice
2 teaspoons orange zest
1 teaspoon low-sodium soy sauce
1 teaspoon honey
1 teaspoon grated fresh ginger
2 teaspoons minced garlic
1½ pounds (680 g) pork tenderloin roast, fat trimmed
1 tablespoon extra-virgin olive oil
Directions:
Combine the orange juice and zest, soy sauce, honey, ginger, and garlic in a large bowl. Stir to mix well. Dunk the pork in the bowl and press to coat well.
Wrap the bowl in plastic and refrigerate to marinate for at least 2 hours.
Preheat the oven to 400°F (205°C).
Remove the bowl from the refrigerator and discard the marinade. Heat the olive oil in an oven-safe skillet over medium-high heatuntil shimmering.Add the pork and sear for 5 minutes. Flip the pork halfway through the cooking time.
Arrange the skillet in the preheated oven and roast the pork for 25 minutes or until well browned. Flip the pork halfway through the cooking time.
Transfer the pork on a plate. Allow to cool before serving.
Nutrition Info: calories: 228 fat: 9.0g protein: 34.0g carbs: 4.0g fiber: 0g sugar: 3.0g sodium: 486mg

Beef Scallops

Servings: 4
Cooking Time: 20 Minutes
Ingredients:
16 veal scallops
Salt
Ground pepper
Garlic powder
2 eggs
Breadcrumbs
Extra virgin olive oil
Directions:
Put the beef scallops well spread, salt, and pepper. Add some garlic powder.
In a bowl, beat the eggs.
In another bowl put the breadcrumbs.
Pass the Beef scallops for beaten egg and then for the breadcrumbs.
Spray with extra virgin olive oil on both sides.
Put a batch in the basket of the air fryer. Do not pile the scallops too much.
Select 1800C, 15 minutes. From time to time, shake the basket so that the scallops move.
When finishing that batch, put the next one and so on until you finish with everyone, usually 4 or 5 scallops enter per batch.
Nutrition Info: Calories: 330 Fat: 3.41g Carbohydrates: 0g Protein: 20.99g Sugar: 0gCholesterol:1 65mg

Chicken Pappardelle

Servings: 4
Cooking Time: 15 Minutes
Ingredients:
¾ lb. chicken breast, sliced lengthwise into 1/8-inch strips
1 small onion, sliced thin
8 cup spinach, chopped fine
4 cup low sodium chicken broth
1 cup fresh basil
What you'll need from store cupboard:
2 quarts water
¼ cup reduced fat parmesan cheese, divided
6 cloves garlic, diced
1 tbsp. walnuts, chopped
¼ tsp cinnamon
¼ tsp paprika
¼ tsp red pepper flakes

Salt
Olive oil cooking spray
Directions:
Bring 2 quarts water to a simmer in a medium pot. Lightly spray a medium skillet with cooking spray and place over med-high heat. Add the garlic and cook until golden brown. Add the cinnamon, paprika, red pepper flakes, basil leaves, and onion. Cook until the onion has softened, about 2 minutes.
Add the spinach and cook until it has wilted and softened, another 2 minutes. Add the broth, bring to a simmer, cover, and cook until tender, about 5 minutes.
Add a pinch of salt to the now-simmering water. Turn off the heat and add the chicken and stir so that all the strips are separated. Cook just until the strips have turned white; they will be half-cooked. Using a slotted spoon, transfer the strips to a plate to cool.
Check the spinach mixture; cook it until most of the broth has evaporated Stir in half the cheese and season with salt to taste. Add the chicken, toss to coat, and continue to cook until the chicken strips have cooked through, about 90 seconds. Spoon the mixtureonto four plates, top with the remaining cheese and serve.
Nutrition Info: Calories 174 Total Carbs 7g Net Carbs 5g Protein 24g Fat 5g Sugar 2g Fiber 2g

One Pot Beef & Veggies

Servings: 10
Cooking Time: 8 Hours
Ingredients:
3 lb. beef roast
1 lb. red potatoes, cubed
¼ lb. mushrooms
1 green bell pepper, diced
1 parsnip, diced
1 red onion, diced
What you'll need from store cupboard:
14 ½ oz. low sodium beef broth
¼ cup water
3 tbsp. cornstarch
¾ tsp salt
¾ tsp oregano
¼ tsp pepper

Directions:

Place the vegetables in a large crock pot. Cut roast in half and place on top of vegetables.

Combine broth, salt, oregano, and pepper, pour over meat.

Cover and cook on low heat 8 hours or until roast is tender.

Remove meat and vegetables to a serving platter, keep warm. Skim fat from cooking liquid and transfer to a small saucepan.

Place pan over medium heat and bring to a boil. Stir water and cornstarch together until smooth. Add to cooking liquid and stir 2 minutes until thickened. Serve with roast.

Nutrition Info: Calories 381 Total Carbs 28g Net Carbs 22g Protein 46g Fat 9g Sugar 12g Fiber 6g

Zesty Chicken & Asparagus Pasta

Servings: 4

Cooking Time: 15 Minutes

Ingredients:

2 chicken breasts, boneless, skinless, cut in 1-inch pieces

1 lb. asparagus, trim ends and cut in 2-inch pieces

½ cup half-n-half

½ cup mozzarella cheese, grated

Juice and zest of one lemon

3 tbsp. margarine

What you'll need from store cupboard:

½ recipe homemade pasta, (chapter 14) cook and drain

2/3 cup reduced fat parmesan cheese

1½ tbsp. olive oil

1½ tbsp. garlic, diced fine

1 tsp garlic powder

½ tsp oregano

½ tsp oregano

¼ tsp thyme

Salt and black pepper, to taste

Directions:

Heat oil in a large skillet, over med-high heat. Add the chicken and salt and pepper to taste. Stir in oregano and cook 5 minutes, stirring occasionally until chicken is cooked through. Add 1 teaspoon diced garlic and cook 1 minute more. Transfer to plate. Add margarine to the skillet and let melt. Add remaining garlic and asparagus and cook 1 minute, or until asparagus starts to turn bright green.

Whisk in the remaining Ingredients. Cook, stirring frequently, until cheese melts and sauce thickens. Add the pasta and chicken, toss to coat and cook until heated through. Serve garnished with more parmesan cheese and chopped parsley if desired.

Nutrition Info: Calories 455 Total Carbs 15g Net Carbs 11g Protein 36g Fat 29g Sugar 6g Fiber 4g

Curried Chicken & Apples

Servings: 4

Cooking Time: 30 Minutes

Ingredients:

1 lb. chicken breasts, boneless, skinless, cut in 1-inch cubes

2 tart apples, peel and slice

1 sweet onion, cut in half and slice

1 jalapeno, seeded and diced

2 tbsp. cilantro, diced

½ tsp ginger, grated

What you'll need from store cupboard:

14 ½ oz. tomatoes, diced and drained

½ cup water

3 cloves garlic, diced

2 tbsp. sunflower oil

1 tsp salt

1 tsp coriander

½ tsp turmeric

¼ tsp cayenne pepper

Directions:

Heat oil in a large skillet over med-high heat. Add chicken and onion, and cook until onion is tender. Add garlic and cook 1 more minute.

Add apples, water and seasonings and stir to combine. Bring to a boil. Reduce heat and simmer 12-15 minutes, or until chicken is cooked through, stirring occasionally.

Stir in tomatoes, jalapeno, and cilantro and serve.

Nutrition Info: Calories 371 Total Carbs 23g Net Carbs 18g Protein 34g Fat 16g Sugar 15g Fiber 5g

Arroz Con Pollo

Servings: 4

Cooking Time: 25 Minutes

Ingredients:

1 onion, diced

1 red pepper, diced

2 cup chicken breast, cooked and cubed

1 cup cauliflower, grated

1 cup peas, thaw

2 tbsp. cilantro, diced
½ tsp lemon zest
What you'll need from store cupboard:
14 ½ oz. low sodium chicken broth
¼ cup black olives, sliced
¼ cup sherry
1 clove garlic, diced
2 tsp olive oil
¼ tsp salt
¼ tsp cayenne pepper
Directions:
Heat oil in a large skillet over med-high heat. Add pepper, onion and garlic and cook 1 minute. Add the cauliflower and cook, stirring frequently, until light brown, 4-5 minutes.
Stir in broth, sherry, zest and seasonings. Bring to a boil. Reduce heat, cover and simmer 15 minutes. Stir in the chicken, peas and olives. Cover and simmer another 3-6 minutes or until heated through. Serve garnished with cilantro.
Nutrition Info: Calories 161 Total Carbs 13g Net Carbs 9g Protein 14g Fat 5g Sugar 5g Fiber 4g

Tasty Harissa Chicken

Servings: 4
Cooking Time: 4 Hours 10 Minutes
Ingredients:
1 lb chicken breasts, skinless and boneless
1/2 tsp ground cumin
1 cup harissa sauce
1/4 tsp garlic powder
1/2 tsp kosher salt
Directions:
Season chicken with garlic powder, cumin, and salt. Place chicken to the slow cooker.
Pour harissa sauce over the chicken.
Cover slow cooker with lid and cook on low for 4 hours. Remove chicken from slow cooker and shred using a fork. Return shredded chicken to the slow cooker and stir well.
Nutrition Info: Calories: 235 Fat: 13g Carbohydrates: 1g Protein: 2Sugar: 1gCholesterol: 130mg

Pork Souvlakia With Tzatziki Sauce

Servings: 4
Cooking Time: 12 Minutes
Ingredients:
¼ cup lemon juice

1 tablespoon dried oregano
¼ teaspoon salt
¼ teaspoon ground black pepper
1 pound (454 g) pork tenderloin, cut into 1-inch cubes
1 tablespoon olive oil
Tzatziki Sauce:
½ cup plain Greek yogurt
1 large cucumber, peeled, deseeded and grated
1 tablespoon fresh lemon juice
4 cloves garlic, minced or grated
¼ teaspoon ground black pepper
Special Equipment:
8 bamboo skewers, soaked in water for at least 30 minutes
Directions:
Combine the lemon juice, oregano, salt, and ground black pepper in a large bowl. Stir to mix well.
Dunk the pork cubes in the bowl of mixture, then toss to coat well. Wrap the bowl in plastic and refrigerate to marinate for 10 minutes or overnight. Preheat the oven to 450°F (235°C) or broil. Grease a baking sheet with the olive oil.
Remove the bowl from the refrigerator. Run the bamboo skewers through the pork cubes. Set the skewers on the baking sheet, then brush with marinade.
Broil the skewers in the preheated oven for 12 minutes or until well browned. Flip skewers at least 3 times during the broiling.
Meanwhile, combine the ingredients for the tzatziki sauce in a small bowl.
Remove the skewers from the oven and baste with the tzatziki sauce and serve immediately.
Nutrition Info: calories: 260 fat: 7.0g protein: 28.0g carbs: 21.0g fiber: 3.0g sugar: 3.0g sodium: 360mg

Salted Biscuit Pie Turkey Chops

Servings: 4
Cooking Time: 20 Minutes
Ingredients:
8 large turkey chops
300 gr of crackers
2 eggs
Extra virgin olive oil
Salt
Ground pepper

Directions:

Put the turkey chops on the worktable, and salt and pepper.

Beat the eggs in a bowl.

Crush the cookies in the Thermo mix with a few turbo strokes until they are made grit, or you can crush them with the blender.

Put the cookies in a bowl.

Pass the chops through the beaten egg and then passed them through the crushed cookies. Press well so that the empanada is perfect.

Paint the empanada with a silicone brush and extra virgin olive oil.

Put the chops in the basket of the air fryer, not all will enter. They will be done in batches.

Select 200 degrees, 15 minutes.

When you have all the chops made, serve.

Nutrition Info: Calories: 126 Fat: 6g Carbohydrates 0gProtein: 18g Sugar: 0g

Cheesy Beef & Noodles

Servings: 4
Cooking Time: 15 Minutes
Ingredients:
1 lb. lean ground beef
1 onion, diced
2 cup mozzarella, grated
½ cup + 2 tbsp. fresh parsley diced
What you'll need from store cupboard:
Homemade Noodles, (chapter 15)
2 tbsp. tomato paste
1 tbsp. extra-virgin olive oil
1 tbsp. Worcestershire sauce
3 cloves garlic, diced fine
1 tsp red pepper flakes
½ tsp pepper
Salt, to taste
Directions:
Heat oil in a large skillet over med-high heat. Add beef and cook, breaking up with a spatula, about 2 minutes.

Reduce heat to medium and season with salt and pepper. Stir in garlic, onion, pepper flakes, Worcestershire, tomato paste, ½ cup parsley, and ½ cup water. Bring to a simmer and cook, stirring occasionally, 8 minutes.

Stir in noodles and cook 2 minutes more. Stir in 1 cup of cheese, sprinkle the remaining cheese over the top and cover with lid, off the heat, until cheese melts. Serve garnished with remaining parsley.

Nutrition Info: Calories 372 Total Carbs 7g Net Carbs 6g Protein 44g Fat 18g Sugar 3g Fiber 1g

Chicken's Liver

Servings: 4
Cooking Time: 30 Minutes
Ingredients:
500g of chicken livers
2 or 3 carrots
1 green pepper
1 red pepper
1 onion
4 tomatoes
Salt
Ground pepper
1 glass of white wine
½ glass of water
Extra virgin olive oil
Directions:
Peel the carrots, cut them into slices and add them to the bowl of the air fryer with a tablespoon of extra virgin olive oil 5 minutes.

After 5 minutes, add the peppers and onion in julienne. Select 5 minutes.

After that time, add the tomatoes in wedges and select 5 more minutes.

Add now the chicken liver clean and chopped.

Season, add the wine and water.

Select 10 minutes.

Check that the liver is tender.

Nutrition Info: 76 Fat: 13g Carbohydrates: 1g Protein: 2Sugar: 1gCholesterol: 130mg

Chutney Turkey Burgers

Servings: 4
Cooking Time: 15 Minutes
Ingredients:
1 lb. lean ground turkey
16 baby spinach leaves
4 slices red onion
2 green onions, diced
½ cup chutney, divided
¼ cup fresh parsley, diced
2 tsp lime juice
What you'll need from store cupboard:
8 Flourless Burger Buns, (chapter 14)
1 tbsp. Dijon mustard

½ tsp salt
¼ tsp pepper
Nonstick cooking spray.
Directions:
Heat grill to med-high heat. Spray rack with cooking spray.
In a small bowl, combine ¼ cup chutney, mustard, and lime juice.
In a large bowl, combine parsley, green onions, salt, pepper, and remaining chutney. Crumble turkey over mixture and mix well. Shape into 4 patties.
Place burgers on the grill and cook 5-7 minutes per side, or meat thermometer reaches 165 degrees.
Serve on buns with spinach leaves, sliced onions and reserved chutney mixture.
Nutrition Info: Calories 275 Total Carbs 15g Net Carbs 13g Protein 28g Fat 11g Sugar 2g Fiber 2g

Chicken Marsala

Servings: 4
Cooking Time: 25 Minutes
Ingredients:
4 boneless chicken breasts
½ lb. mushrooms, sliced
1 tbsp. margarine
What you'll need from store cupboard:
1 cup Marsala wine
¼ cup flour
1 tbsp. oil
Pinch of white pepper
Pinch of oregano
Pinch of basil
Directions:
On a shallow plate, combine flour and seasonings. Dredge the chicken in the flour mixture to coat both sides.
In a large skillet, over medium heat, heat oil until hot. Add chicken and cook until brown on both sides, about 15 minutes. Transfer chicken to a plate.
Reduce heat to low and add mushrooms and ¼ cup of the wine. Cook about 5 minutes. Scrape bottom of pan to loosen any flour. Stir in reserved flour mixture and the remaining wine.
Simmer until mixture starts to thicken, stirring constantly. Add the chicken back to the pan and cook an additional 5 minutes. Serve.
Nutrition Info: Calories 327 Total Carbs 9g Net Carbs 8g Protein 21g Fat 14g Sugar 1g Fiber 1g

Poblano & Cheese Burgers

Servings: 4
Cooking Time: 15 Minutes
Ingredients:
1 lb. lean ground beef
4 slices Monterey jack cheese
2 poblano peppers, seeded and chopped
1 egg
2 tbsp. margarine
What you'll need from store cupboard
2 tbsp. dried minced onion
1 tbsp. liquid smoke
1 tbsp. Worcestershire sauce
Salt & pepper to taste
Directions:
Heat up the grill.
In a large bowl, combine the beef, egg, onion, liquid smoke, Worcestershire, salt and pepper. Form into 6 patties and grill to desired doneness. Top with cheese.
Melt butter in a large skillet over med-high heat. Add pepper and cook until tender and it starts to char.
Place burgers on buns (chapter 14) top with peppers and your favorite burger toppings. Serve.
Nutrition Info: Calories 396 Total Carbs 4g Protein 43g Fat 22g Sugar 2g Fiber 0g

Ham And Cheese Stuffed Chicken Burgers

Servings: 4Cooking Time: 15 Minutes
Ingredients:
⅓ Cup soft bread crumbs
3 tablespoons milk
1 egg, beaten
½ teaspoon dried thyme
Pinch salt
Freshly ground black pepper
1¼ pounds ground chicken
¼ cup finely chopped ham
⅓ cup grated Havarti cheese
Olive oil for misting
Directions:
In a medium bowl, combine the breadcrumbs, milk, egg, thyme, salt, and pepper. Add the chicken and mix gently but thoroughly with clean hands.
Form the chicken into eight thin patties and place on waxed paper.

Top four of the patties with the ham and cheese. Top with remaining four patties and gently press the edges together to seal, so the ham and cheese mixture is in the middle of the burger.Place the burgers in the basket and mist with olive oil. Grill for 13 to 16 minutes or until the chicken is thoroughly cooked to 165°F as measured with a meat thermometer.

Beef, Pork, Lamb Recipes

Nutrition Info: 324 Fat: 13g Carbohydrates: 1g Protein: 2Sugar: 1gCholesterol: 130mg

Turkey Stuffed Peppers

Servings: 8

Cooking Time: 55 Minutes

Ingredients:

1 lb. lean ground turkey

4 green bell peppers, halved and ribs and seeds removed

1 onion, diced

1 ½ cup mozzarella cheese

1 cup cauliflower, grated

1 cup mushrooms, diced

What you'll need from store cupboard:

3 cups spaghetti sauce, (chapter 16)

3 cloves garlic, diced fine

2 tbsp. olive oil

Directions:

Heat the oil in a large skillet over med-high heat. Add the garlic, mushrooms, and onion. Add the turkey, cook, breaking up the turkey with a spatula, until turkey is cooked through, about 10 minutes. Stir in the cauliflower, and cook, stirring frequently, 3-5 minutes.Add the spaghetti sauce and 1 cup mozzarella. Stir to combine and remove from heat. Heat oven to 350 degrees. Place bell peppers in a large baking dish, skin side down. Fill the insides with the turkey mixture, place any extra filling around the peppers. Top each pepper with remaining mozzarella. Bake 40-45 minutes or the peppers are tender. Serve immediately.

Nutrition Info: Calories 214 Total Carbs 14g Net Carbs 10g Protein 20g Fat 11g Sugar 9g Fiber 4g

Sausage & Spinach Frittata

Servings: 6

Cooking Time: 40 Minutes

Ingredients:

8 eggs, beaten

1 1/3 cup sausage

1 ½ cup red bell pepper, diced

¾ cups baby spinach

¼ cup red onion, diced

What you'll need from store cupboard:

Salt and pepper, to taste

Nonstick cooking spray

Directions:

Heat oven to 350 degrees. Spray a 9-inch pie pan with cooking spray.

Cook sausage in a medium skillet until no longer pink. Transfer to a large bowl with a slotted spoon. Add remaining Ingredients and mix well. Pour into prepared pan and bake 30-35 minutes or until the center is completely set and top is starting to brown. Serve immediately.

Nutrition Info: Calories 156 Total Carbs 3g Net Carbs 2g Protein 12g Fat 10g Sugar 2g Fiber 1g

Crust Less Pizza

Servings: 4

Cooking Time: 25 Minutes

Ingredients:

Pepperoni, ham, sausage, mushrooms, or toppings of your choice

8 oz. fat free cream cheese, soft

1 ½ cup mozzarella cheese, grated

2 eggs

What you'll need from store cupboard:

½ cup lite pizza sauce

¼ cup reduced fat parmesan cheese

1 tsp garlic powder

¼ tsp pepper

Directions:

Heat oven to 350 degrees. Spray and 9x13-inch baking dish with cooking spray.

In a large bowl, beat cream cheese, eggs, pepper, garlic powder, and parmesan until combined. Spread in prepared dish and bake 12-15 minutes or until golden brown. Let cool 10 minutes.

Spread pizza sauce over crust. Top with cheese and your favorite pizza toppings. Sprinkle lightly with garlic powder. Bake 8-10 minutes or until cheese melts. Cool 5 minutes before serving.

Nutrition Info: Calories 164 Total Carbs 4g Net Carbs 3g Protein 12g Fat 11g Sugar 1g Fiber 1g

Creamy Turkey & Peas With Noodles

Servings: 4

Cooking Time: 15 Minutes
Ingredients:
1 lb. lean ground turkey
1 lemon, juice and zest
1 ½ cup skim milk
1 cup low fat sharp cheddar cheese, grated
1 cup peas, frozen
¼ cup fresh parsley, diced
1 tbsp. margarine
What you'll need from store cupboard:
Homemade noodles, (chapter 14)
½ cup low sodium chicken broth
3 tbsp. flour
1 tbsp. olive oil
3 cloves garlic, diced fine
½ tsp ground mustard
Pinch of nutmeg
Salt and pepper, to taste
Directions:
Heat oil in a large skillet over med-high heat. Add turkey and season with salt and pepper. Cook, breaking up with a spatula, until no longer pink. Add garlic and cook 1 minute more.
Add the margarine and flour, and cook, stirring, 2 minutes until combined.
Stir in the broth and milk. Bring to a low boil, reduce heat to low and simmer until mixture starts to thicken. Add the cheese and cook, stirring until it melts and combines into the sauce. Add the seasonings and peas, simmer 5 minutes, stirring occasionally. Add the noodles and lemon juice and cook another 2 minutes. Serve garnished with lemon zest and parsley.
Nutrition Info: Calories 427 Total Carbs 18g Net Carbs 16g Protein 40g Fat 22g Sugar 7g Fiber 2g

Classic Stroganoff

Servings: 5 Cooking Time: 20 Minutes
Ingredients:
5 ounces (142 g) cooked egg noodles
2 teaspoons olive oil
1 pound (454 g) beef tenderloin tips, boneless, sliced into 2-inch strips
1½ cups white button mushrooms, sliced
½ cup onion, minced
1 tablespoon all-purpose flour
½ cup dry white wine
1 (14.5-ounce / 411-g) can fat-free, low-sodium beef broth

1 teaspoon Dijon mustard
½ cup fat-free sour cream
¼ teaspoon salt
¼ teaspoon black pepper
Directions:
Put the cooked egg noodles on a large plate.
Heat the olive oil in a nonstick skillet over high heat until shimmering.
Add the beef and sauté for 3 minutes or until lightly browned. Remove the beef from the skillet and set on the plate with noodles.
Add the mushrooms and onion to the skillet and sauté for 5 minutes or until tender and the onion browns.
Add the flour and cook for a minute. Add the white wine and cook for 2 more minutes.
Add the beef broth and Dijon mustard. Bring to a boil. Keep stirring. Reduce the heat to low and simmer for another 5 minutes.
Add the beef back to the skillet and simmer for an additional 3 minutes. Add the remaining ingredients and simmer for 1 minute.
Pour them over the egg noodles and beef, and serve immediately.
Nutrition Info: calories: 275 fat: 7.0g protein: 23.0g carbs: 29.0g fiber: 4.0g sugar: 3.0g sodium: 250mg

Ranch Chicken Casserole

Servings: 8 Cooking Time: 30 Minutes
Ingredients:
2 cup chicken, cooked & diced
½ lb. bacon, cooked & diced
4 eggs
1 cup reduced fat cheddar cheese, grated
½ cup half-n-half
What you'll need from store cupboard:
½ cup fat free Ranch dressing
Nonstick cooking spray
Directions:
Heat oven to 350 degrees. Lightly spray an 8x8-inch or 11x7-inch pan with cooking spray.
Spread chicken and bacon in the bottom of prepared pan. Top with cheese.
Whisk together eggs, half-n-half, and ranch dressing. Pour on topof chicken mixture.
Bake, uncovered, for 30 to 35 minutes.
Nutrition Info: Calories 413 Total Carbs 2g Protein 38g Fat 27g Sugar 1g Fiber 0g

Healthy Turkey Chili

Servings: 4
Cooking Time: 45 Minutes
Ingredients:
1 lb. lean ground turkey
2 carrots, peeled and diced
2 stalks of celery, diced
1 onion, diced
1 zucchini, diced
1 red pepper, diced
What you'll need from store cupboard:
14 oz. can tomato sauce
1 can black beans, drained and rinsed
1 can kidney beans, drained and rinsed
3 cups water
3 garlic cloves, diced fine
1 tbsp. chili powder
1 tbsp. olive oil
2 tsp salt
1 tsp pepper
1 tsp cumin
1 tsp coriander
1 bay leaf
Directions:
Heat oil in a heavy bottom soup pot over med-high heat. Add turkey and onion and cook until no longer pink, 5-10 minutes.
Add the vegetables and cook, stirring occasionally, 5 minutes. Add the garlic and spices and cook, stirring, 2 minutes.
Add the remaining Ingredients and bring to a boil. Reduce heat to low and simmer 30
Nutrition Info: Calories 218 Total Carbs 14g Net Carbs 10g Protein 25g Fat 9g Sugar 6g Fiber 4g

Roasted Vegetable And Chicken Tortillas

Servings: 4
Cooking Time: 20 Minutes
Ingredients:
1 red bell pepper, seeded and cut into 1-inch-wide strips
½ small eggplant, cut into ¼-inch-thick slices
½ small red onion, sliced
1 medium zucchini, cut lengthwise into strips
1 tablespoon extra-virgin olive oil
Salt and freshly ground black pepper, to taste
4 whole-wheat tortilla wraps

2 (8-ounce / 227-g) cooked chicken breasts, sliced
Directions:
Preheat the oven to 400°F (205°C). Line a baking sheet with aluminum foil.
Combine the bell pepper, eggplant, red onion, zucchini, and olive oil in a large bowl. Toss to coat well.
Pour the vegetables into the baking sheet, then sprinkle with salt and pepper.
Roast in the preheated oven for 20 minutes or until tender and charred.
Unfold the tortillas on a clean work surface, then divide the vegetables and chicken slices on the tortillas.
Wrap and serve immediately.
Nutrition Info: calories: 483 fat: 25.0g protein: 20.0g carbs: 45.0g fiber: 3.0g sugar: 4.0g sodium: 730mg

Beer Braised Brisket

Servings: 10
Cooking Time: 8 Hours
Ingredients:
5 lb. beef brisket
1 bottle of lite beer
1 onion, sliced thin
What you'll need from store cupboard:
15 oz. can tomatoes, diced
3 cloves garlic, diced fine
1 tbsp. + 1 tsp oregano
1 tbsp. salt
1 tbsp. black pepper
Directions:
Place the onion on the bottom of the crock pot. Add brisket, fat side up. Add the tomatoes, undrained and beer. Sprinkle the garlic and seasonings on the top.
Cover and cook on low heat 8 hours, or until beef is fork tender.
Nutrition Info: Calories 445 Total Carbs 4g Net Carbs 3g Protein 69g Fat 14g Sugar 2g Fiber 1g

Beef With Sesame And Ginger

Servings: 4-6
Cooking Time: 23 Minutes
Ingredients:
½ cup tamari or soy sauce
3 tbsp. olive oil
2 tbsp. toasted sesame oil

1 tbsp. brown sugar

1 tbsp. ground fresh ginger

3 cloves garlic, minced

1 to 1½ pounds skirt steak, boneless sirloin, or low loin

Directions:

Put together the tamari sauce, oils, brown sugar, ginger, and garlic in small bowl. Add beef to a quarter-size plastic bag and pour the marinade into the bag. Press on the bag as much air as possible and seal it.

Refrigerate for 1 to 1½ hours, turning half the time. Remove the meat from the marinade and discard the marinade. Dry the meat with paper towels. Cook at a temperature of 350°F for 20 to 23 minutes, turning halfway through cooking.

Nutrition Info: Calories: 381 Fat: 5g Carbohydrates: 9.6g Protein: 38g Sugar: 1.8gCholesterol: 0mg

Cheesy Beef Paseíllo

Servings: 15

Cooking Time: 20 Minutes

Ingredients:

1-2 tbsp. olive oil

2 pounds lean ground beef

½ chopped onion

2 cloves garlic, minced

½ tbsp. Adobo seasoning

2 tsp. dried oregano

1 packet of optional seasoning

2 tbsp. chopped cilantro

¼ cup grated cheese

15 dough disks

15 slices of yellow cheese

Directions:

In a large skillet over medium-high heat, heat the oil. Once the oil has warmed, add the meat, onions, and Adobo seasoning.

Brown veal, about 6-7 minutes. Drain the ground beef. Add the remaining seasonings and cilantro. Cook an additional minute. Add grated cheese, if desired. Melt the cheese.

On each dough disk, add a slice of cheese to the center and add 3-4 tablespoons of meat mixture over the slice of cheese. Fold over the dough disk and with a fork, fold the edges and set it aside.

Preheat the air fryer to 3700C for 3 minutes.

Once three minutes have passed, spray the air fryer pan with cooking spray and add 3-4 cupcakes to the basket. Close the basket, set to 3700C, and cook for 7 minutes. After 7 minutes, verify it. Cook up to 3 additional minutes, or the desired level of sharpness, if desired.

Repeat until finished.

Nutrition Info: Calories: 225 Fat: 3.41g Carbohydrates: 0g Protein: 20.99g Sugar: 0gCholesterol: 25mg

Pork Head Chops With Vegetables

Servings: 2-4

Cooking Time: 20 Minutes

Ingredients:

4 pork head chops

2 red tomatoes

1 large green pepper

4 mushrooms

1 onion

4 slices of cheese

Salt

Ground pepper

Extra virgin olive oil

Directions:

Put the four chops on a plate and salt and pepper. Put two of the chops in the air fryer basket.

Place tomato slices, cheese slices, pepper slices, onion slices and mushroom slices. Add some threads of oil.Take the air fryer and select 1800C, 15 minutes.Check that the meat is well made and take out.Repeat the same operation with the other two pork chops.

Nutrition Info: Calories: 106 Fat: 3.41g Carbohydrates: 0g Protein: 20.99g Sugar: 0gCholesterol: 0mg

Easy Lime Lamb Cutlets

Servings: 4

Cooking Time: 8 Minutes

Ingredients:

¼ cup freshly squeezed lime juice

2 tablespoons lime zest

2 tablespoons chopped fresh parsley

Sea salt and freshly ground black pepper, to taste

1 tablespoon extra-virgin olive oil

12 lamb cutlets (about 1½ pounds / 680 g in total)

Directions:

Combine the lime juice and zest, parsley, salt, black pepper, and olive oil in a large bowl. Stir to mix well.

Dunk the lamb cutlets in the bowl of the lime mixture, then toss to coat well. Wrap the bowl in plastic and refrigerate to marinate for at least 4 hours.

Preheat the oven to 450°F (235°C) or broil. Line a baking sheet with aluminum foil.

Remove the bowl from the refrigerator and let sit for 10 minutes,then discard the marinade. Arrange the lamb cutlets on the baking sheet.

Broil the lamb in the preheated oven for 8 minutes or until it reaches your desired doneness. Flip the cutlets with tongs to make sure they are cooked evenly.

Serve immediately.

Nutrition Info: calories: 297 fat: 18.8g protein: 31.0g carbs: 1.0g fiber: 0g sugar: 0g sodium: 100mg

Hot Chicken Salad Casserole

Servings: 6

Cooking Time: 30 Minutes

Ingredients:

3 cup chicken breast, cooked and cut into cubes

6 oz. container plain low-fat yogurt

1 cup celery, diced

1 cup yellow or red sweet pepper, diced

¾ cup cheddar cheese, grated

¼ cup green onions, diced

What you'll need from store cupboard:

1 can reduced-fat and reduced-sodium condensed cream of chicken soup

½ cup cornflakes, crushed

¼ cup almonds, sliced

1 tbsp. lemon juice

¼ teaspoon ground black pepper

Directions:

Heat oven to 400 degrees.In a large bowl, combine chicken, celery, red pepper, cheese, soup, yogurt, onions, lemon juice, and black pepper, stir to combine. Transfer to 2-quart baking dish.In a small bowl stir the cornflakes and almonds together. Sprinkle evenly over chicken mixture.Bake 30 minutes or until heated through. Let rest 10 minutes before serving.

Nutrition Info: Calories 238 Total Carbs 9g Net Carbs 8g Protein 27g Fat 10g Sugar 3g Fiber 1g

Horseradish Meatloaf

Servings: 8Cooking Time: 45 Minutes

Ingredients:

1 ½ lbs. lean ground beef

1 egg, beaten

½ cup celery, diced fine

¼ cup onion, diced fine

¼ cup skim milk

What you'll need from store cupboard:

4 slices whole wheat bread, crumbled

½ cup ketchup, (chapter 15)

¼ cup horseradish

2 tbsp. Dijon mustard

2 tbsp. chili sauce

1 ½ tsp Worcestershire sauce

½ tsp salt

¼ tsp pepper

Nonstick cooking spray

Directions:

Heat oven to 350 degrees. Spray an 11x7-inch baking dish with cooking spray.In a large bowl, soak bread in milk for 5 minutes. Drain.Stir in celery, onion, horseradish, mustard, chili sauce, Worcestershire, egg, salt, and pepper. Crumble beef over mixture and mix well.Shape into loaf in the prepared baking dish. Spread ketchup over the top. Bake 45-50 minutes or a meat thermometer reaches 160 degrees. Let rest 10 minutes before slicing and serving.

Nutrition Info: Calories 213 Total Carbs 8g Net Carbs 7g Protein 29g Fat 7g Sugar 2g Fiber 1g

Beef Tenderloin With Roasted Vegetables

Servings: 10

Cooking Time: 1 Hour

Ingredients:

3 lb. beef tenderloin

1 lb. Yukon gold potatoes, cut in 1-inch wedges

1 lb. Brussel sprouts, halved

1 lb. baby carrots

4 tsp fresh rosemary, diced

What you'll need from store cupboard:

¾ cup dry white wine

¾ cup low sodium soy sauce

3 cloves garlic, sliced

4 tsp Dijon mustard

1 ½ tsp ground mustard

Nonstick cooking spray
Directions:
Place beef in a large Ziploc bag.
In a small bowl combine wine, soy sauce, rosemary, Dijon, ground mustard, and garlic. Pour half the mixture over the beef. Seal the bag and turn to coat. Refrigerate 4 ½ hours, turning occasionally. Cover and refrigerate remaining marinade.
Heat oven to 425 degrees. Spray a 9x13-inch baking dish with cooking spray.
Place the potatoes, Brussel sprouts and carrots in the prepared dish. Add reserved marinade and toss to coat. Cover and bake 30 minutes.
Remove tenderloin and discard marinade. Place over vegetables and bake 30-45 minutes or until meat reaches desired doneness.
Remove been and let stand 15 minutes. Check vegetables, if they are not tender bake another 10-15 minutes until done. Slice36 the beef and serve with vegetables.
Nutrition Info: Calories 356 Total Carbs 13g Net Carbs 10g Protein 43g Fat 13g Sugar 4g Fiber 3g

Ginger Chili Broccoli

Servings: 5
Cooking Time: 25 Minutes
Ingredients:
8 cups broccoli florets
1/2 cup olive oil
2 fresh lime juice
2 tbsp fresh ginger, grated
2 tsp chili pepper, chopped
Directions:
Add broccoli florets into the steamer and steam for 8 minutes.
Meanwhile, for dressing in a small bowl, combine limejuice, oil, ginger, and chili pepper.
Add steamed broccoli in a large bowl then pour dressing over broccoli. Toss well.
Nutrition Info: Calories 239 Fat 20.8 g, Carbohydrates 13.7 g, Sugar 3 g, Protein 4.5 g, Cholesterol 0 mg

Fried Pork Chops

Servings: 2
Cooking Time: 35 Minutes
Ingredients:
3 cloves of ground garlic
2 tbsp. olive oil

1 tbsp. of marinade
4 thawed pork chops
Directions:
Mix the cloves of ground garlic, marinade, and oil. Then apply this mixture on the chops.
Put the chops in the air fryer at 3600C for 35 minute
Nutrition Info: Calories: 118 Fat: 3.41g Carbohydrates: 0g Protein: 20.99g Sugar: 0gCholesterol: 39mg

Southwest Turkey Lasagna

Servings: 8
Cooking Time: 20 Minutes
Ingredients:
1 lb. lean ground turkey
1 onion, diced
1 green bell pepper, diced
1 red pepper, diced
8 oz. fat free cream cheese
1 cup Mexican cheese blend, grated
½ cup fat free sour cream
What you'll need from store cupboard:
6 8-inch low carb whole wheat tortillas
10 oz. enchilada sauce
½ cup salsa, (chapter 16)
1 tsp chili powder
Nonstick cooking spray
Directions:
Heat oven to 400 degrees. Spray a 13x9-inch baking dish with cooking spray.
In a large skillet, over medium heat, cook turkey, onion, and peppers until turkey is no longer pink. Drain fat.
Stir in cream cheese and chili powder.
Pour enchilada sauce into a shallow dish. Dip tortillas in sauce to coat. Place two tortillas in prepared dish. Spread with ½ the turkey mixture and sprinkle 1/3 of the cheese over turkey. Repeat layer. Top with remaining tortillas and cheese.
Cover with foil and bake 20-25 minutes, or until heated through. This can also be frozen up to 3 months.
Let rest 10 minutes before cutting. Serve topped with salsa and sour cream.
Nutrition Info: Calories 369 Total Carbs 36g Net Carbs 17g Protein 27g Fat 22g Sugar 4g Fiber 19g

Stuffed Grilled Pork Tenderloin

Servings: 6
Cooking Time: 25 Minutes
Ingredients:
2 ¾ lb. pork tenderloins
½ tsp fresh ginger, grated
What you'll need from store cupboard:
"Cornbread" Stuffing, (chapter 15)
¾ cup dry red wine
1/3 cup Splenda brown sugar
¼ cup ketchup, (chapter 16)
2 tbsp. low sodium soy sauce
2 cloves garlic, diced
1 tsp curry powder
1/5 tsp pepper
Nonstick cooking spray
Directions:
Slice the tenderloins down the center lengthwise to within ½-inch of the bottom.

In a large Ziploc bag, combine wine, sugar, ketchup, soy sauce, garlic, curry powder, ginger and pepper. Add the pork, seal and turn to coat. Refrigerate 2-3 hours.

Heat the grill to med-high. Spray the grill rack with cooking spray.

Remove the pork from the bag and discard marinade. Open the tenderloins to lie flat, spread stuffing down the center of each. Tie closed with butcher string in 1 ½-inch intervals.

Place tenderloins on the grill, cover and cook 25-40 minutes, or until a meat thermometer reaches 160 degrees. Let rest 5 minutes before slicing and serving.

Nutrition Info: Calories 452 Total Carbs 22g Net Carbs 19g Protein 36g Fat 18g Sugar 14g Fiber 3g

Pasta Bolognese

Servings: 8
Cooking Time: 2 Hours
Ingredients:
1 lb. lean ground beef
4 oz. pancetta, chopped
1 small onion, diced
½ cup celery, diced
½ cup carrots, diced
½ cup half-n-half
¼ cup fresh parsley, diced
1 tbsp. margarine

What you'll need from store cupboard:
2 28 oz. cans tomatoes, crushed
¼ cup white wine
1 bay leaf
Salt & fresh pepper, to taste
Homemade pasta, cook and drain, (chapter 14)
Directions:
Place a heavy, deep saucepan over med-high heat. Add pancetta and cook, stirring occasionally, until fat melts.Add margarine, onions, celery and carrots, reduce heat to med-low and cook until soft, about 5 minutes.Increase heat to med-high, add meat, season with salt and pepper and sauté until browned.

Add wine and cook until it reduces down, about 3-4 minutes.Add tomatoes and bay leaf. Reduce heat to low, cover and simmer, at least 1-1/2 to 2 hours, stirring occasionally.Stir in half & half and parsley, cook 2 minutes longer. Serve over pasta.

Nutrition Info: Calories 421 Total Carbs 23g Net Carbs 16g Protein 41g Fat 18g Sugar 13g Fiber 7g

Tasty Chicken Tenders

Servings: 4
Cooking Time: 25 Minutes
Ingredients:
1 ½ lbs chicken tenders
1 tbsp. extra virgin olive oil
1 tsp. rotisserie chicken seasoning
2 tbsp. BBQ sauce
Directions:
Add all ingredients except oil in a zip-lock bag.
Seal bag and place in the refrigerator for 2-3 hours.
Heat oil in a large pan over medium heat.
Cook marinated chicken tenders in a pan until lightly brown and cooked.

Nutrition Info: Calories 365 Fat 16.1 g, Carbohydrates 2.8 g, Sugar 2 g, Protein 49.2 g, Cholesterol 151 mg

Creole Chicken

Servings: 2
Cooking Time: 25 Minutes
Ingredients:
2 chicken breast halves, boneless and skinless
1 cup cauliflower rice, cooked
1/3 cup green bell pepper, julienned
¼ cup celery, diced
¼ cup onion, diced

What you'll need from store cupboard:
14 ½ oz. stewed tomatoes, diced
1 tsp sunflower oil
1 tsp chili powder
½ tsp thyme
1/8 tsp pepper
Directions:
Heat oil in a small skillet over medium heat. Add chicken and cook 5-6 minutes per side or cooked through. Transfer to plate and keep warm.
Add the pepper, celery, onion, tomatoes, and seasonings. Bring to a boil. Reduce heat, cover, and simmer 10 minutes or until vegetables start to soften.
Add chicken back to pan to heat through. Serve over cauliflower rice.
Nutrition Info: Calories 362 Total Carbs 14g Net Carbs 10g Protein 45g Fat 14g Sugar 8g Fiber 4g

Potatoes With Loin And Cheese

Servings: 4
Cooking Time: 30 Minutes
Ingredients:
1kg of potatoes
1 large onion
1 piece of roasted loin
Extra virgin olive oil
Salt
Ground pepper
Grated cheese
Directions:
Peel the potatoes, cut the cane, wash, and dry.
Put salt and add some threads of oil, we bind well.
Pass the potatoes to the basket of the air fryer and select 1800C,20 minutes.
Meanwhile, in a pan, put some extra virgin olive oil, add the peeled onion, and cut into julienne.
When the onion is transparent, add the chopped loin.
Sauté well and pepper.
Put the potatoes on a baking sheet.
Add the onion with the loin.
Cover with a layer of grated cheese.
Bake a little until the cheese takes heat and melts.
Nutrition Info: Calories: 332 Fat: 3.41g Carbohydrates: 0g Protein: 20.99g Sugar: 0gCholesterol: 0mg

Kielbasa & Lamb Cassoulet

Servings: 6
Cooking Time: 5 Hours 30 Minutes
Ingredients:
12 oz. lamb stew meat, cut into 1-inch cubes
8 oz. kielbasa, cut into 1/4-inch slices
1 eggplant, peeled and chopped
1 green pepper, coarsely chopped
1 tbsp. fresh thyme
What you'll need from store cupboard:
2 cups low sodium beef broth
1 cup dried navy beans, rinsed well
6 oz. can tomato paste
3 cloves garlic, diced fine
1 tbsp. olive oil
1 bay leaf
¼ tsp whole black peppercorn
Salt & pepper, to taste
Directions:
Place beans in a large saucepan. Add enough water to cover by 2 inches. Bring to a boil; reduce heat. Simmer, uncovered, for 10 minutes. Remove from heat. Cover and let stand for 1 hour. Drain and rinse beans.
Heat oil in a large skillet over med-high heat. Add lamb and cook until brown on all sides. Drain off fat. Transfer to a crock pot.
Add beans, broth, kielbasa, thyme, garlic, peppercorns, and bay leaf. Cover and cook on high 4 to 5 hours.
Add the eggplant, pepper and tomato paste, stir well. Cook another 30 minutes until vegetables are tender. Discard bay leaf and serve.
Nutrition Info: Calories 391 Total Carbs 35g Net Carbs 22g Protein 32g Fat 14g Sugar 8g Fiber 13g

Crock Pot Carnitas

Servings: 4
Cooking Time: 6 Hours
Ingredients:
4 lb. pork butt, boneless, trim the fat and cut into 2-inch cubes
1 onion, cut in half
Juice from 1 orange, reserve orange halves
2 tbsp. fresh lime juice
What you'll need from store cupboard:
2 cup water
1 ½ tsp salt

1 tsp cumin
1 tsp oregano
2 bay leaves
¾ tsp pepper
Directions:
Place pork and orange halves in the crock pot. In a medium bowl, combine remaining Ingredients and stir to combine. Pour over pork.

Cover and cook on high 5 hours. Pork should be tender enough to shred with a fork. If not, cook another 60 minutes.

Transfer pork to a bowl. Pour the sauce into a large saucepan and discard the bay leaves and orange halves.

Bring to a boil and cook until it thickens and resembles a syrup.

1.   Use two forks to shred the pork. Add pork to the sauce and stir to coat. Serve.

Nutrition Info: Calories 464 Total Carbs 3g Protein 35g Fat 35g Sugar 1g Fiber 0g

Zucchini Lasagna

Servings: 4
Cooking Time: 1 Hour
Ingredients:
1 lb. lean ground beef
2 medium zucchini, julienned
3 tomatoes, blanch in hot water, remove skins and dice
1 onion, diced
1 serrano chili, remove seeds and dice
1 cup mushrooms, remove stems and dice
½ cup low-fat mozzarella, grated
What you'll need from store cupboard:
2 cloves garlic, diced fine
½ cube chicken bouillon
1 tsp. paprika
1 tsp. dried thyme
1 tsp. dried basil
Salt and pepper
Nonstick cooking spray
Directions:
Lay zucchini on paper towel lined cutting board and sprinkle lightly with salt. Let sit for 10 minutes. Heat oven to broil. Blot zucchini with paper towels and place on baking sheet. Broil 3 minutes. Transfer to paper towels again to remove excess moisture.

Lightly coat a deep skillet with cooking spray and place over med-high heat. Add garlic, onion, and chili and cook 1 minute.

Add the tomatoes and mushrooms and cook, stirring frequently, about 4 minutes. Transfer vegetables to a bowl.

Add the beef to the skillet with the paprika and cook until no longer pink. Add the vegetables and bouillon to the beef along with remaining spices and let simmer over low heat 25 minutes.

Heat oven to 375 degrees. Line a small baking dish with parchment paper and place 1/3 of the zucchini in an even layer on the bottom. Top with 1/3 of the meat mixture. Repeat layers.

Sprinkle cheese over top and bake 35 minutes. Let rest 10 minutes before serving.

Nutrition Info: Calories 272 Total Carbs 11g Net Carbs 8g Protein38g Fat 8g Sugar 6g Fiber 3g

Stuffed Flank Steak

Servings: 6
Cooking Time: 30 Minutes
Ingredients:
1 ½ lb. flank steak
¼ cup fresh parsley, diced fine
¼ cup sun dried tomatoes
What you'll need from store cupboard:
½ cup boiling water
½ cup reduced fat parmesan cheese
1 tbsp. horseradish, drain
2 tsp vegetable oil
1 tsp coarse black pepper
Nonstick cooking spray
Directions:
Heat oven to 400 degrees. Line a shallow roasting pan with foil and spray it with cooking spray.

Place tomatoes in a small bowl and pour boiling water over. Let stand 5 minutes.

Drain the tomatoes and add cheese, parsley, horseradish, and pepper.

Cut steak down the middle, horizontally, to within 1/2-inch of opposite side. Open up to lay flat and flatten to ¼-inch thick.

Spread tomato mixture over steak leaving ½-inch edges. Roll up and tie with butcher string.

Place in prepared pan and cook 30-40 minutes, or until meat reaches desired doneness, 145 degrees on a meat thermometer is med-rare. Let rest 10-15 minutes then slice and serve.

Nutrition Info: Calories 267 Total Carbs 2g Protein 34g Fat 13g Sugar 0g Fiber 0g

Shepherd's Pie

Servings: 8
Cooking Time: 45 Minutes
Ingredients:
1 ½ lbs. ground lamb
3 carrots, grated
1 cauliflower, separated into small florets
1 red onion, diced
4 tbsp. margarine
2 tbsp. half-n-half
¼ cup low fat cheddar cheese, grated
What you'll need from store cupboard:
1 2/3 cups canned tomatoes, diced
4 tbsp. low sodium beef broth
2 cloves garlic, diced fine
1 tbsp. olive oil
Salt & pepper, to taste
Directions:
Heat oven to 350 degrees. Put a large saucepan of water on to boil.
Heat the oil in a large saucepan over med-high heat. Add onion and cook until soft. Add the lamb and cook, stirring occasionally, until brown on all sides.
Stir in the broth, tomatoes, and carrots. Reduce heat, and simmer 10 minutes, or until vegetables are tender and liquid evaporates.
Add the cauliflower to the boiling water and cook until soft, about 8-10 minutes. Drain well. Add the margarine, half-n-half, salt, and pepper and use an immersion blender to puree until smooth.
Pour the meat mixture into a large casserole dish. Top with cauliflower mash and sprinkle cheese over top. Bake 20 minutes, or until cheese is nicely browned. Serve.
Nutrition Info: Calories 262 Total Carbs 9g Net Carbs 6g Protein 27g Fat 13g Sugar 4g Fiber 3g

Lemon Chicken With Basil

Servings: 4
Cooking Time: 1h
Ingredients:
1kg chopped chicken
1 or 2 lemons
Basil, salt, and ground pepper
Extra virgin olive oil

Directions:
Put the chicken in a bowl with a jet of extra virgin olive oil.
Put salt, pepper, and basil.
Bind well and let stand for at least 30 minutes stirring occasionally.
Put the pieces of chicken in the air fryer basket and take the air fryer
Select 30 minutes. Occasionally remove.
Take out and put another batch.
Do the same operation.
Nutrition Info: Calories: 126 Fat: 6g Carbohydrates 0gProtein: 18g Sugar: 0g

Turkey & Pepper Skillet

Servings: 4
Cooking Time: 25 Minutes
Ingredients:
4 turkey cutlets, ¼-inch thick
1 red bell pepper, cut into strips
1 yellow bell pepper, cut into strips
½ large sweet onion, sliced
What you'll need from store cupboard
14 oz. can crushed tomatoes, fire-roasted
2 tbsp. extra-virgin olive oil, divided
2 tsp red wine vinegar
1 tsp salt, divided
½ teaspoon Italian seasoning
¼ teaspoon black pepper
Directions:
Season turkey with ½ teaspoon salt. Heat 1 tablespoon oil in a large skillet over med-high heat. Add turkey, 2 cutlets at a time, and cook 1-3 minutes, then flip and cook until done, 1-2 more minutes. Transfer to a plate and keep warm while you cook the other 2 cutlets.
Add the onion, peppers, and remaining salt to the skillet. Coverand cook, stirring frequently, until vegetables are soft, about 5-7 minutes.
Add seasoning and pepper, and cook, stirring, 30 seconds. Add vinegar, and cook, stirring, until liquid has almost evaporated completely. Add tomatoes and bring to a simmer, stirring frequently. Add the turkey back to the skillet, reduce heat to med-low, and cook, turning cutlets to coat with sauce, 1-2 minutes. Serve garnished with fresh chopped basil if desired.
Nutrition Info: Calories 245 Total Carbs 14g Net Carbs 19g Protein 31g Fat 9g Sugar 9g Fiber 4g

Taco Casserole

Servings: 6
Cooking Time: 40 Minutes
Ingredients:
1 lb. lean ground beef
4 eggs
1 jalapeno, seeded and diced
2 oz. low fat cream cheese
½ cup cheddar cheese, grated
½ cup pepper jack cheese, grated
¼ cup onion, diced
¼ cup half-n-half
What you'll need from store cupboard:
1 pkg. taco seasoning
¼ cup water
¼ cup salsa
1 tbsp. hot sauce
Nonstick cooking spray
Directions:
Heat oven to 350 degrees. Spray an 8x8-inch baking dish with cooking spray.
Place a large skillet over medium heat and cook beef until no longer pink
Add onion and jalapeno and cook until onion is translucent. Drain off fat.
Stir in taco seasoning and water and cook 5 minutes. Add the cream cheese and salsa and stir to combine.
In a medium bowl, whisk the eggs, hot sauce and half-n-half together.
Pour the meat mixture into prepared pan and top with egg mixture. Sprinkle with both cheeses and bake 30 minutes, or until eggs are set.
Let cool 5 minutes before slicing and serving.
Nutrition Info: Calories 307 Total Carbs 6g Net Carbs 5g Protein 34g Fat 15g Sugar 1g Fiber 1g

Spicy Grilled Flank Steak

Servings: 6
Cooking Time: 15 Minutes
Ingredients:
1 ½ lb. flank steak
What you'll need from store cupboard:
3 tbsp. lite soy sauce
3 tbsp. sherry
3 tbsp. red wine vinegar
3 tbsp. Splenda brown sugar
1 tbsp. vegetable oil
1 ½ tsp paprika
1 ½ tsp red pepper flakes
1 ½ tsp chili powder
1 ½ tsp Worcestershire sauce
¾ tsp parsley flakes
¾ tsp garlic powder
¾ tsp salt
Nonstick cooking spray
Directions:
In a small bowl, combine all Ingredients except steak. Pour 1/3 cup marinade into a large Ziploc bag and add steak. Seal and turn to coat. Refrigerate 1-3 hours. Save remaining marinade for basting.
Heat grill to medium heat. Spray rack with cooking spray.
Place steak on the grill and cook 6-8 minutes per side, basting every few minutes. Let rest 10 minutes, then slice against the grainand serve.
Nutrition Info: Calories 271 Total Carbs 7g Protein 35g Fat 9g Sugar 7g Fiber 0g

Creamy And Aromatic Chicken

Servings: 4
Cooking Time: 30 Minutes
Ingredients:
4 (4-ounce / 113-g) boneless, skinless chicken breasts
Salt and freshly ground black pepper, to taste
1 tablespoon extra-virgin olive oil
½ sweet onion, chopped
2 teaspoons chopped fresh thyme
1 cup low-sodium chicken broth
¼ cup heavy whipping cream
1 scallion, white and green parts, chopped
Directions:
Preheat the oven to 375°F (190°C).
On a clean work surface, rub the chicken with salt and pepper.
Heat the olive oil in an oven-safe skillet over medium-high heat until shimmering.
Put the chicken in the skillet and cook for 10 minutes or until well browned. Flip halfway through. Transfer onto a platter and set aside.
Add the onion to the skillet and sauté for 3 minutes or until translucent.
Add the thyme and broth and simmer for 6 minutes or until the liquid reduces in half.

Mix in the cream, then put the chicken back to the skillet.

Arrange the skillet in the oven and bake for 10 minutes.

Remove the skillet from the oven and serve them with scallion.

Nutrition Info: calories: 287 fat: 14.0g protein: 34.0g carbs: 4.0g fiber: 1.0g sugar: 1.0g sodium: 184mg

Orange Chicken

Servings: 6
Cooking Time: 20 Minutes
Ingredients:
1 ½ lbs. chicken breast, cut into ½-inch pieces
1 medium orange, zest then cut in half
½ inch fresh ginger, peel and grate
What you'll need from store cupboard:
1 cup pork rinds
½ cup coconut flour
2 cloves garlic, peeled
4 tbsp. coconut oil, divided
2 tbsp. Swerve confectioners
1 tsp black pepper
1 tsp salt
Directions:
Add the pork rinds, coconut flour and pepper to a food processor. Pulse until the mixture becomes a fine powder. Dump into a medium bowl.

Season the chicken with salt and pepper.

Heat 2 tablespoons oil in a large skillet over med-high heat. Add the chicken to the pork rind mixture and toss to coat. Add to skillet and cook, 2-3 minutes per side, or until browned. This will need to be done in batches. Transfer to paper towel lined plate.

Add remaining oil to a small sauce pan and heat over med-high heat. Add swerve and stir to combine. Once the swerve has dissolved, lower the heat to medium and add zest, garlic, ginger, and the juice from half the orange. Stir and bring to a simmer, stirring occasionally. Remove from heat when it thickens and becomes glossy.

Place the chicken on serving plate. Pour the orange glaze over it, sprinkle with sesame seeds and serve.

Nutrition Info: Calories 377 Total Carbs 10g Net Carbs 9g Protein 37g Fat 23g Sugar 8g Fiber 1g

Cajun Chicken & Pasta

Servings: 4
Cooking Time: 20 Minutes
Ingredients:
3 chicken breasts, boneless, skinless, cut in 1-inch pieces
4 Roma tomatoes, diced
1 green bell pepper, sliced
1 red bell pepper, sliced
½ red onion, sliced
1 cup half-n-half
2 tbsp. margarine
¼ cup fresh parsley, diced
What you'll need from store cupboard:
½ recipe homemade pasta, (chapter 14), cook and drain
2 cup low sodium chicken broth
½ cups white wine
2 tbsp. olive oil
3 tsp Cajun spice mix
3 cloves garlic, diced fine
Cayenne pepper, to taste
Freshly ground black pepper, to taste
Salt, to taste
Directions:
Place chicken in a bowl and sprinkle with 1 ½ teaspoons Cajun spice, toss to coat.

Heat 1 tablespoon oil and 1 tablespoon margarine in a large cast iron skillet over high heat. add chicken, cooking in 2 batches, cook until brown on one side, about 1 minute, flip and brown the other side. Transfer to a plate with a slotted spoon.

Add remaining oil and margarine to the pan. Add peppers, onion, and garlic. Sprinkle remaining Cajun spice over vegetables and salt to taste. Cook, stirring occasionally, until vegetables start to turn black, 3-5 minutes. Add tomatoes and cook another 30 seconds. Transfer vegetables to a bowl with a slotted spoon.

Add wine and broth to the pan and cook, stirring to scrape up brown bits from the bottom, 3-5 minutes. Reduce heat to med-low and add half-n-half, stirring constantly. Cook until sauce starts to thicken. Taste and season with cayenne, pepper and salt, it should be spicy. Add chicken and vegetables to the sauce and cook 1-2 minutes until hot. Stir in pasta and parsley and serve.

Nutrition Info: Calories 475 Total Carbs 21g Net Carbs 17g Protein 38g Fat 25g Sugar 10g Fiber 4g

Breaded Chicken Fillets

Servings: 4
Cooking Time: 25 Minutes
Ingredients:
3 small chicken breasts or 2 large chicken breasts
Salt
Ground pepper
3 garlic cloves
1 lemon
Beaten eggs
Breadcrumbs
Extra virgin olive oil
Directions:
Cut the breasts into fillets.
Put in a bowl and add the lemon juice, chopped garlic cloves and pepper.
Flirt well and leave 10 minutes.
Beat the eggs and put breadcrumbs on another plate. Pass the chicken breast fillets through the beaten egg and the breadcrumbs.
When you have them all breaded, start to fry.
Paint the breaded breasts with a silicone brush and extra virgin olive oil. Place a batch of fillets in the basket of the air fryer and select 10 minutes 180 degrees.
Turn around and leave another 5 minutes at 180 degrees.
Nutrition Info: Calories: 120 Fat: 6g Carbohydrates 0gProtein: 18g Sugar: 0g

Crunchy Grilled Chicken

Servings: 8
Cooking Time: 10 Minutes
Ingredients:
8 chicken breast halves, boneless and skinless
1 cup fat free sour cream
¼ cup lemon juice
Butter flavored spray, refrigerated
What you'll need from store cupboard:
2 cup stuffing mix, crushed
4 tsp Worcestershire sauce
2 tsp paprika
1 tsp celery salt
1/8 tsp garlic powder
Nonstick cooking spray
Directions:
In a large Ziploc bag combine sour cream, lemon juice, Worcestershire, and seasonings. Add

chicken, seal, and turn to coat. Refrigerate 1-4 hours.
Heat grill to medium heat. Spray rack with cooking spray.
Place stuffing crumbs in a shallow dish. Coat both sides of chicken with crumbs and spritz with butter spray.
Place on grill and cook 4-7 minutes per side, or until chicken is cooked through. Serve.
Nutrition Info: Calories 230 Total Carbs 22g Net Carbs 21g Protein 25g Fat 3g Sugar 4g Fiber 1g

Hawaiian Chicken

Servings: 8
Cooking Time: 3 Hours
Ingredients:
8 chicken thighs, bone-in and skin-on
1 red bell pepper, diced
1 red onion, diced
2 tbsp. fresh parsley, chopped
2 tbsp. margarine
What you'll need from store cupboard:
8 oz. can pineapple chunks
8 oz. can crushed pineapple
1 cup pineapple juice
½ cup low sodium chicken broth
¼ cup Splenda brown sugar
¼ cup water
3 tbsp. light soy sauce
2 tbsp. apple cider vinegar
2 tbsp. honey
2 tbsp. cornstarch
1 tsp garlic powder
1 tsp Sriracha
½ tsp ginger
½ tsp sesame seeds
Salt & pepper to taste
Directions:
Season chicken with salt and pepper.
Melt butter in a large skillet over medium heat. Add chicken, skin side down, and sear both side until golden brown. Add chicken to the crock pot.
In a large bowl, combine pineapple juice, broth, Splenda, soy sauce, honey, vinegar, Sriracha, garlic powder, and ginger. Pour over chicken.
Top with kinds of pineapple. Cover and cook on high 2 hours. Baste the chicken occasionally.
Mix the cornstarch and water together until smooth. Stir into chicken and add the pepper and

onion, cook another 60 minutes, or until sauce has thickened. Serve garnished with parsley and sesame seeds.

Nutrition Info: Calories 296 Total Carbs 24g Protein 17g Fat 13g Sugar 18g Fiber 1g

Lamb Ragu

Servings: 8
Cooking Time: 8 Hours
Ingredients:
2 lbs. lamb stew meat
2 onions, diced
1 carrot, peeled and sliced thin
4 sprigs fresh rosemary
3 tbsp. fresh sage
What you'll need from store cupboard
28 oz. can whole plum tomatoes, peeled
2 cups red wine
8 cloves garlic, diced
2 tbsp. olive oil
Salt & pepper, to taste
Directions:
Sprinkle lamb with salt and pepper.
Heat oil in a large skillet over med-high heat. Add lamb and cook until brown on all sides.
Add onion, reduce heat, and cook 10 minutes, until onion is golden brown. Transfer mixture to a crock pot.
Crush the tomatoes with a fork and add to the crock pot with remaining Ingredients. Cover and cook on low 8 hours.
Use two forks to shred any chunks of lamb and stir well. Serve.
Nutrition Info: Calories 331 Total Carbs 11g Net Carbs 9g Protein 34g Fat 12g Sugar 6g Fiber 2g

Turkey Roulade

Servings: 8
Cooking Time: 40 Minutes
Ingredients:
4 8 oz. turkey cutlets
5 oz. spinach, thaw and squeeze dry
1 egg, beaten
1 cup tart apple, peel and dice
1 cup mushrooms, diced
½ cup onion, diced fine
2 tbsp. lemon juice
2 tsp lemon zest
What you'll need from store cupboard:
½ cup bread crumbs
2 tsp olive oil
¾ tsp salt, divided
¼ tsp pepper
1/8 tsp nutmeg
Nonstick cooking spray
Directions:
Heat oven to 375 degrees. Spray 11x7-inch baking pan with cooking spray.
Heat oil in a large skillet over med-high heat. Add apple, mushrooms, and onion and cook until tender.
Remove from heat and stir in spinach, juice, zest, nutmeg, and ¼ teaspoon salt.
Cut the cutlets down the center to within ½ inch of the bottom. Open them so they lay flat and flatten to ¼-inch thickness. Sprinkle with salt and pepper.
Spread spinach mixture over cutlets leaving 1 inch around the edges. Roll up and tie closed with butcher string.
Place bread crumbs in a shallow dish. Dip each roulade in the egg then roll in bread crumbs. Place seam side down in prepared dish.
Bake 40-45 minutes or until turkey is cooked through. Let stand 5 minutes. Cut away the string and serve.
Nutrition Info: Calories 262 Total Carbs 10g Net Carbs 8g Protein 36g Fat 8g Sugar 4g Fiber 2g

Jalapeno Turkey Burgers

Servings: 4
Cooking Time: 10 Minutes
Ingredients:
1 lb. lean ground turkey
4 slices pepper Jack cheese
2 jalapeno peppers, seeded and diced
4 tbsp. lettuce, shredded
4 tbsp. fat free sour cream
2 tbsp. cilantro, diced
2 tbsp. light beer
What you'll need from store cupboard:
4 low carb hamburger buns
2 cloves garlic, diced
4 tbsp. salsa
½ tsp pepper
¼ tsp hot pepper sauce
¼ tsp salt
¼ tsp cayenne pepper

Nonstick cooking spray.

Directions:

Heat grill to medium heat. Spray the grill rack with cookingspray.

In a large bowl, combine jalapenos, cilantro, beer, pepper sauce, garlic, pepper, salt, and cayenne. Crumble turkey over mixture and combine thoroughly. Shape into 4 patties.

Place the burgers on the grill and cook 3-5 minutes per side, or until meat thermometer reaches 165 degrees. Top each with slice of cheese, cover, and cook until cheese melts.

Place patties on buns and top with salsa, sour cream and lettuce.

Nutrition Info: Calories 389 Total Carbs 20g Net Carbs 14g Protein 38g Fat 19g Sugar 4g Fiber 6g

Creamy Braised Oxtails

Servings: 6

Cooking Time: 4-6 Hours

Ingredients:

2 pounds oxtails

1 onion, diced

½ cup half-n-half

1 tsp margarine

What you'll need from store cupboard:

1 cup low sodium beef broth

¼ cup sake

4 cloves garlic, diced

2 tbsp. chili sauce

1 tsp Chinese five spice

Salt & pepper

Directions:

Melt the margarine in a large skillet over med-high heat. Sprinkle oxtails with salt and pepper and cook until brown on all sides, about 3-4 minutes per side. Add onion and garlic and cook another 3-5 minutes. Add the sake to deglaze the skillet and cook until liquid is reduced, 1-2 minutes.

Transfer mixture to the crock pot. Add the broth, chili sauce, and five spice, stir to combine. Cover and cook on low 6 hours, or high 4 hours, or until meat is tender.

Stir in the half-n-half and continue cooking another 30-60 minutes or sauce has thickened. Serve.

Nutrition Info:Calories 447 Total Carbs 4g Protein 48g Fat 24g Sugar 1g Fiber 0g

North Carolina Style Pork Chops

Servings: 2

Cooking Time: 10 Minutes

Ingredients:

2 boneless pork chops

15 ml of vegetable oil

25g dark brown sugar, packaged

6g of Hungarian paprika

2g ground mustard

2g freshly ground black pepper

3g onion powder

3g garlic powder

Salt and pepper to taste

Directions:

Preheat the air fryer a few minutes at 1800C.

Cover the pork chops with oil.

Put all the spices and season the pork chops abundantly, almost as if you were making them breaded.

Place the pork chops in the preheated air fryer.

Select Steak, set the time to 10 minutes.

Remove the pork chops when it has finished cooking. Let it stand for 5 minutes and serve.

Nutrition Info: Calories: 118 Fat: 6.85g Carbohydrates: 0 Protein: 13.12g Sugar: 0gCholesterol: 39mg

Seared Duck Breast With Red Wine & Figs

Servings: 6

Cooking Time: 35 Minutes

Ingredients:

2 duck breasts, with skin still on

¼ onion, diced

1 sprig fresh rosemary

What you'll need from store cupboard:

½ cup red wine

1 tbsp. sugar free fig preServings:

½ tbsp. red wine vinegar

½ clove garlic, diced

1/8 tsp Splenda

Salt & pepper, to taste

1 pinch sugar

Directions:

Heat the oven to 450 degrees. Sprinkle the duck breasts with Splenda, salt and pepper.

Place a cast iron skillet over med-high heat. Place the duck breasts in the pan skin side down. Cook for 3 minutes, moving them around to make sure the skin doesn't burn.

Flip the breasts over and place the pan in the oven. Cook for 5 minutes. Then remove the breasts, and set aside.

Return the skillet to the stove medium heat. Add the onions and cook for 10 minutes. Add the garlic and cook for 1 minute more.

Add the wine, vinegar, fig preserves, and herb sprig. Cook, stirring occasionally, for 15 minutes. Then strain the sauce into a small saucepan.

With five minutes left in cooking the sauce, place the duck breasts back into the oven to warm.

Slice the duck into 1/2-inch thick pieces, and spoon on some of the sauce. Serve.

Nutrition Info: Calories 180 Total Carbs 4g Protein 18g Fat 7g Sugar 3g Fiber 0g

Alfredo Sausage & Vegetables

Servings: 6
Cooking Time: 15 Minutes
Ingredients:

- 1 pkg. smoked sausage, cut in ¼-inch slices
- 1 cup half-and-half
- ½ cup zucchini, cut in matchsticks
- ½ cup carrots, cut in matchsticks
- ½ cup red bell pepper, cut in matchsticks
- ½ cup peas, frozen
- ¼ cup margarine
- ¼ cup onion, diced
- 2 tbsp. fresh parsley, diced
- What you'll need from store cupboard:
- ½ recipe Homemade Pasta, cook & drain, (chapter 15)
- 1/3 cup reduced fat parmesan cheese
- 1 clove garlic, diced fine
- Salt & pepper, to taste

Directions:

1. Melt margarine in a large skillet over medium heat. Add onion and garlic and cook, stirring occasionally, 3-4 minutes or until onion is soft.

2. Increase heat to med-high. Add sausage, zucchini, carrots, and red pepper. Cook, stirring frequently, 5-6 minutes, or until carrots are tender crisp.

3. Stir in peas and half-n-half, cook 1-2 minutes until heated through. Stir in cheese, parsley, salt, and pepper. Add pasta nd toss to mix. Serve.

Nutrition Info: Calories 283 Total Carbs 18g Net Carbs 14g Protein 21g Fat 15g Sugar 8g Fiber 4g

Cheesesteak Stuffed Peppers

Servings: 4
Cooking Time: 35 Minutes
Ingredients:

- 4 slices low-salt deli roast beef, cut into 1/2-inch strips
- 4 slices mozzarella cheese, cut in half
- 2 large green bell peppers, slice in half, remove seeds, and blanch in boiling water 1 minute
- 1 ½ cup sliced mushrooms
- 1 cup thinly sliced onion
- 1 tbsp. margarine
- What you'll need from store cupboard:
- 1 tbsp. vegetable oil
- 2 tsp garlic, diced fine
- ¼ tsp salt
- ¼ tsp black pepper

Directions:

1. Heat oven to 400 degrees. Place peppers, skin side down, in baking dish.

2. Heat oil and margarine in a large skillet over medium heat. Once hot, add onions, mushrooms, garlic, salt, and pepper, and cook, stirring occasionally, 10-12 minutes or mushrooms are tender.

3. Remove from heat and stir in roast beef.

4. Place a piece of cheese inside each pepper and fill with meat mixture. Cover with foil and bake 20 minutes.

5. Remove the foil and top each pepper with remaining cheese. Bake another 5 minutes, or until cheese is melted.

Nutrition Info: Calories 191 Total Carbs 10g Net Carbs 8g Protein 12g Fat 12g Sugar 5g Fiber 2g

Chicken Soup

Servings: 6
Cooking Time: 1 Hour 20 Minutes
Ingredients:

- 4 lbs Chicken, cut into pieces

- 5 carrots, sliced thick
- 8 cups of water
- 2 celery stalks, sliced 1 inch thick
- 2 large onions, sliced

Directions:

1. In a large pot add chicken, water, and salt. Bring to boil.
2. Add celery and onion in the pot and stir well.
3. Turn heat to medium-low and simmer for 30 minutes.
4. Add carrots and cover pot with a lid and simmer for 40 minutes.
5. Remove Chicken from the pot and remove bones and cut Chicken into bite-size pieces.
6. Return chicken into the pot and stir well.

Nutrition Info: Calories: 89 Fat: 6.33gCarbohydrates: 0g Protein: 7.56g Sugar: 0gCholesterol: 0mg

French Onion Chicken & Vegetables

Servings: 10
Cooking Time: 4 Hours
Ingredients:

- 1 lb. chicken breasts, boneless and skinless, cut in 1-inch pieces
- 1 lb. green beans, trim
- 1 lb. red potatoes, quartered
- ½ lb. mushrooms, halved
- ½ cup sweet onion, sliced
- 1 tsp lemon zest
- What you'll need from store cupboard:
- 2 14 ½ oz. cans low sodium chicken broth
- 2 tbsp. onion soup mix
- 1 tbsp. sunflower oil
- 2 tsp Worcestershire sauce
- ½ tsp lemon pepper
- ½ tsp salt
- ½ tsp pepper
- ¼ tsp garlic powder

Directions:

1. Sprinkle chicken with lemon pepper.
2. Heat oil in a large skillet over medium heat. Cook chicken 4-5 minutes or until brown on all sides.

3. Layer the green beans, potatoes, mushrooms, and onion in the crock pot.
4. In a small bowl, combine remaining Ingredients and pour over vegetables. Top with chicken.
5. Cover and cook on low heat 4-5 hours or until vegetables are tender. Serve.

Nutrition Info: Calories 256 Total Carbs 15g Net Carbs 12g Protein 30g Fat 8g Sugar 2g Fiber 3g

Pork On A Blanket

Servings: 4
Cooking Time: 10 Minutes
Ingredients:

- ½ puff pastry sheet, defrosted
- 16 thick smoked sausages
- 15 ml of milk

Directions:

1. Preheat la air fryer to 200°C and set the timer to 5 minutes.
2. Cut the puff pastry into 64 x 38 mm strips.
3. Place a cocktail sausage at the end of the puff pastry and roll around the sausage, sealing the dough with some water.
4. Brush the top (with the seam facing down) of the sausages wrapped in milk and place them in the preheated air fryer.
5. Cook at 200°C for 10 minutes or until golden brown.

Nutrition Info: Calories: 381 Fat: 5g Carbohydrates: 9.6g Protein: 38g Sugar: 1.8gCholesterol: 0mg

Chicken Thighs

Servings: 2
Cooking Time: 20 Minutes
Ingredients:

- 4 chicken thighs
- Salt to taste
- Pepper
- Mustard
- Paprika

Directions:

1. Before using the pot, it is convenient to turn on for 5 minutes to heat it. Marinate the thighs with salt, pepper, mustard and paprika. Put your thighs in the air fryer for 10 minutes at 3800F

2. After the time, turn the thighs and fry for 10 more minutes. If necessary, you can use an additional 5 minutes depending on the size of the thighs so that they are well cooked

Nutrition Info: 72 Fat: 13g Carbohydrates: 1g Protein: 2Sugar: 0gCholesterol: 39mg

Bacon & Cauliflower Casserole

Servings: 6
Cooking Time: 20 Minutes
Ingredients:

- 6 slices bacon, cooked and crumbled, divided
- 3 scallions, sliced thin, divided
- 5 cup cauliflower
- 2 cup cheddar cheese, grated and divided
- 1 cup fat free sour cream
- What you'll need from store cupboard:
- ½ tsp salt
- ¼ tsp fresh cracked pepper
- Nonstick cooking spray

Directions:

1. Heat oven to 350 degrees. Spray casserole dish with cooking spray.
2. Steam cauliflower until just tender.
3. In a large bowl, combine cauliflower, sour cream, half the bacon, half the scallions and half the cheese. Stir in salt and pepper. Place in prepared baking dish and sprinkle remaining cheese over top.
4. Bake 18-20 minutes until heated through. Sprinkle remaining scallions and bacon over top and serve.

Nutrition Info: Calories 332 Total Carbs 15g Net Carbs 11g Protein 21g Fat 20g Sugar 6g Fiber 4g

Beef Tenderloin Steaks With Brandied Mushrooms

Servings: 4
Cooking Time: 20 Minutes
Ingredients:

- 4 beef tenderloin steaks, about ¾ inch thick
- 3 ½ cups Portobello mushrooms, sliced
- 1 tbsp. margarine
- What you'll need from store cupboard:
- ½ cup brandy, divided
- 1 tsp balsamic vinegar

- ½ tsp salt
- ½ tsp coarsely ground pepper
- ½ tsp instant coffee granules
- Nonstick cooking spray

Directions:

1. Heat oven to 200 degrees.
2. Salt and pepper both sides of the steaks and let sit 15 minutes.
3. In a small bowl, mix together coffee, vinegar, all but 1 tablespoon brandy, salt and pepper.
4. Spray a large skillet with cooking spray and place over med-high heat.
5. Spray the mushrooms with cooking spray and add to the hot pan. Cook 5 minutes or until most of the liquid is absorbed. Transfer the mushrooms to a bowl.
6. Add the steaks to the skillet and cook 3 minutes per side. Reduce heat to med-low and cook 2 more minutes or to desired doneness. Place on dinner plates, cover with foil and place in oven.
7. Add the brandy mixture to the skillet and bring to a boil. Boil 1 minute, or until reduced to about ¼ cup liquid. Stir in mushrooms and cook 1-2 minutes, or most of the liquid has evaporated.
8. Remove from heat and stir in remaining 1 tablespoon brandy and the margarine.
9. Spoon evenly over steaks and serve immediately.

Nutrition Info: Calories 350 Total Carbs 1g Protein 44g Fat 12g Sugar 0g Fiber 0g

Turkey Stuffed Poblano Peppers

Servings: 2
Cooking Time: 40 Minutes
Ingredients:

- 2 Poblano peppers, halved lengthwise, cores and seeds removed
- 1 lb. ground turkey
- ½ cup low-fat cheddar cheese, grated
- 1 green onion, diced
- 1 tbsp. cilantro, chopped
- What you'll need from store cupboard:
- 8 oz. can tomato sauce
- 1 tbsp. olive oil
- 1 tsp oregano
- 1 tsp paprika

- 1 tsp ground cumin
- ½ tsp onion powder
- ½ tsp garlic paste or minced garlic
- Salt and pepper

Directions:
1. Heat oven to 350 degrees.
2. Use tongs to roast the skin of the peppers over an open flame until charred and blistered all over. Or place on a cookie sheet underthe broiler until skin is charred.
3. Place peppers in a plastic bag to steam for 15 minutes.
4. In a small bowl, stir together tomato sauce, oregano, paprika, and cumin
5. Heat oil in a large skillet over medium heat. Add turkey, onion powder, and garlic paste. Cook, stirring frequently, until meat has browned. Stir in 2 tablespoons of the sauce and season with salt and pepper.
6. Pour remaining sauce in the bottom of a baking dish.
7. With a butter knife, scrape the charred skin off the peppers, and place on sauce in dish.
8. Divide turkey mixture evenly over the peppers, sprinkle with cheese. Cover and bake 20 minutes.
9. Remove the foil, and bake until cheese starts to brown, about 5-7 minutes. Serve garnished with chopped green onion and cilantro.
Nutrition Info: Calories 665 Total Carbs 12g Net Carbs 9g Protein 71g Fat 36g Sugar 8g Fiber 3g

Hearty Beef Chili

Servings: 4
Cooking Time: 1 Hour
Ingredients:
- 1 lb. lean ground beef
- 1 large bell pepper, diced
- 1 cup onion, diced
- What you'll need from store cupboard:
- 4 oz. can green chilies, diced
- 1 cup tomato sauce
- 1 cup low sodium beef broth
- 1 tbsp. tomato paste
- 2 cloves garlic, diced fine
- 2 tsp chili powder
- 1 tsp salt

- 1 tsp Worcestershire
- 1 tsp cumin
- ½ tsp celery salt
- ¼ tsp pepper

Directions:
1. Heat a large pan over med-high heat. Add beef, onions, bell pepper and garlic and cook, stirring occasionally, until beef is no longer pink. Drain fat.
2. Add remaining Ingredients and bring to a simmer. Reduce heat to med-low and simmer 30 minutes to an hour. Taste and adjust seasonings if needed. Serve.
Nutrition Info: Calories 355 Total Carbs 30g Net Carbs 20g Protein 40g Fat 9g Sugar 18g Fiber 10g

Turkey Sloppy Joes

Servings: 8
Cooking Time: 4 Hours
Ingredients:
- 1 lb. lean ground turkey
- 1 onion, diced
- ½ cup celery, diced
- ¼ cup green bell pepper, diced
- What you'll need from store cupboard:
- 8 Flourless Burger Buns, (chapter 14)
- 1 can no salt added condensed tomato soup
- ½ cup ketchup, (chapter 14)
- 2 tbsp. yellow mustard
- 1 tbsp. Splenda brown sugar
- ¼ tsp pepper

Directions:
1. In a large saucepan, over medium heat, cook turkey, onion, celery, and green pepper until turkey is no longer pink. Transfer to crock pot.Add remaining Ingredients and stir to combine. Cover, and cook on low heat 4 hours. Stir well and serve on buns.
Nutrition Info: Calories 197 Total Carbs 12g Net Carbs 11g Protein 17g Fat 8g Sugar 8g Fiber 1g

Chestnut Stuffed Pork Roast

Servings: 15
Cooking Time: 1 Hour 35 Minutes
Ingredients:
- 5 lb. pork loin roast, boneless, double tied
- ½ lb. ground pork

- ½ cup celery, diced fine
- ½ cup onion, diced fine
- 2 tbsp. fresh parsley, diced, divided
- 1 tbsp. margarine
- What you'll need from store cupboard:
- 15 oz. can chestnuts, drained
- 2 cup low sodium chicken broth
- 3 tbsp. flour
- 2 tbsp. brandy, divided
- ½ tsp salt
- ½ tsp pepper
- 1/8 tsp allspice
- Salt & black pepper, to taste

Directions:
1. Heat oven to 350 degrees.
2. Untie roast, open and pound lightly to even thickness.
3. Melt margarine in a skillet over med-high heat. Add celery and onion and cook until soft.
4. In a large bowl, combine ground pork, 1 tablespoon parsley, 1 tablespoon brandy and seasonings. Mix in celery and onion. Spread over roast.
5. Lay a row of chestnuts down the center. Roll meat around filling and tie securely with butcher string. Roast in oven 1 ½ hours or until meat thermometer reaches 145 degrees. Remove and let rest 10 minutes.
6. Measure out 2 tablespoons of drippings, discard the rest, into a saucepan. Place over medium heat and whisk in flour until smooth. Add broth and cook, stirring, until mixture thickens. Chop remaining chestnuts and add to gravy along with remaining brandy and parsley. Season with salt and pepper if desired. Slice the roast and serve topped with gravy.

Nutrition Info: Calories 416 Total Carbs 15g Protein 48g Fat 16g Sugar 0g Fiber 0g

Honey Bourbon Pork Chops

Servings: 4
Cooking Time: 4 Hours
Ingredients:
- 4 pork chops, cut thick
- What you'll need from store cupboard:
- 5 tbsp. honey
- 2 tbsp. lite soy sauce
- 2 tbsp. bourbon
- 2 cloves garlic, diced fine

Directions:
1. In a small bowl, whisk together honey, soy sauce and bourbon. Stir in garlic.
2. Place pork chops in crock pot and top with sauce. Turn to make sure the pork chops are coated.
3. Cover and cook on low heat for 4 hours, or until the chops reach desired doneness. Serve.

Nutrition Info: Calories 231 Total Carbs 24g Protein 23g Fat 3g Sugar 20g Fiber 0g

Pork Rind

Servings: 4
Cooking Time: 1h
Ingredients:
- 1kg of pork rinds
- Salt
- ½ tsp. black pepper coffee

Directions:
1. Preheat the air fryer. Set the time of 5 minutes and the temperature to 2000C.
2. Cut the bacon into cubes - 1 finger wide.
3. Season with salt and a pinch of pepper.
4. Place in the basket of the air fryer. Set the time of 45 minutes and press the power button.
5. Shake the basket every 10 minutes so that the pork rinds stay golden brown equally.
6. Once they are ready, drain a little on the paper towel so they staydry. Transfer to a plate and serve.

Nutrition Info: (Nutrition per Serving):Calories: 282 Fat: 23.41 Carbohydrates: 0g Protein: 16.59 Sugar: 0g Cholesterol: 73gm

Korean Chicken

Servings: 6
Cooking Time: 3-4 Hours
Ingredients:
- 2 lbs. chicken thighs, boneless and skinless
- 2 tbsp. fresh ginger, grated
- What you'll need from store cupboard:
- 4 cloves garlic, diced fine
- ¼ cup lite soy sauce

- ¼ cup honey
- 2 tbsp. Korean chili paste
- 2 tbsp. toasted sesame oil
- 2 tsp cornstarch
- Pinch of red pepper flakes

Directions:
1.   Add the soy sauce, honey, chili paste, sesame oil, ginger, garlic and pepper flakes to the crock pot, stir to combine. Add the chicken and turn to coat in the sauce.
2.   Cover and cook on low 3–4 hours or till chicken is cooked through.
3.   When the chicken is cooked, transfer it to a plate.
4.   Pour the sauce into a medium saucepan. Whisk the cornstarch and ¼ cup cold water until smooth. Add it to the sauce. Cook over medium heat, stirring constantly, about 5 minutes, or until sauce is thick and glossy.
5.   Use 2 forks and shred the chicken. Add it to the sauce and stir to coat. Serve.

Nutrition Info: Calories 397 Total Carbs 18g Protein 44g Fat 16g Sugar 13g Fiber 0g

Dry Rub Chicken Wings

Servings: 4Cooking Time: 30 Minutes
Ingredients:
- 9g garlic powder
- 1 cube of chicken broth, reduced sodium
- 5g of salt
- 3g black pepper
- 1g smoked paprika
- 1g cayenne pepper
- 3g Old Bay seasoning, sodium free
- 3g onion powder
- 1g dried oregano
- 453g chicken wings
- Nonstick Spray Oil
- Ranch sauce, to serve

Directions:
1.   Preheat the air fryer. Set the temperature to 180 °C.
2.   Put ingredients in a bowl and mix well.
3.   Season the chicken wings with half the seasoning mixture and sprinkle abundantly with oil spray.

4.   Place the chicken wings in the preheated air fryer.
5.   Select Chicken, set the timer to 30 minutes.
6.   Shake the baskets halfway through cooking.
7.   Transfer the chicken wings to a bowl and sprinkle them with the other half of the seasonings until they are well covered. Servings with ranch sauce

Nutrition Info: Calories: 120 Fat: 6g Carbohydrates 0gProtein: 18g Sugar: 0g

Tandoori Lamb

Servings: 6Cooking Time: 30 Minutes
Ingredients:
- 1 leg of lamb, butterflied
- ½ cup plain Greek yogurt
- What you'll need from store cupboard:
- 1 tbsp. paprika
- 1 tsp cumin
- 1 tsp coriander
- 1 tsp onion powder
- 1 tsp garlic paste
- 1 tsp ginger paste
- Salt & pepper, to taste

Directions:
1.   In a large Ziploc bag, combine yogurt and spices. Zip closed and squish to mix Ingredients. Add the lamb and massage the marinade into the meat. Chill 1 hour or overnight.
2.   Heat oven to 325 degrees. Transfer lamb to a baking sheet. Season with salt and pepper and roast 30 minutes, or until lamb is medium rare.
3.   Remove from oven and let rest 5 minutes. Slice and serve.

Nutrition Info: Calories 448 Total Carbs 2g Protein 68g Fat 17g Sugar 1g Fiber 0g

Turkey & Mushroom Casserole

Servings: 8
Cooking Time: 50 Minutes
Ingredients:
- 1 lb. cremini mushrooms, washed and sliced
- 1 onion, diced
- 6 cup cauliflower, grated
- 4 cup turkey, cooked and cut in bite size pieces
- 2 cup reduced fat Mozzarella, grated, divided

- 1 cup fat free sour cream
- What you'll need from store cupboard:
- ½ cup lite mayonnaise
- ¼ cup reduced fat parmesan cheese
- 2 tbsp. olive oil, divided
- 2 tbsp. Dijon mustard
- 1 ½ tsp thyme
- 1 ½ tsp poultry seasoning
- Salt and fresh-ground black pepper to taste
- Nonstick cooking spray

Directions:

1.   Heat oven to 375 degrees. Spray a 9x13-inch baking dish with cooking spray.
2.   In a medium bowl, stir together sour cream, mayonnaise, mustard, ½ teaspoon each thyme and poultry seasoning, 1 cup of the mozzarella, and parmesan cheese.
3.   Heat 2 teaspoons oil in a large skillet over med-high heat. Add mushrooms and sauté until they start to brown and all liquid is evaporated. Transfer them to the prepared baking dish.
4.   Add 2 more teaspoons oil to the skillet along with the onion and sauté until soft and they start to brown. Add the onions to the mushrooms.
5.   Add another 2 teaspoons oil to the skillet with the cauliflower. Cook, stirring frequently, until it starts to get soft, about 3-4 minutes. Add the remaining thyme and poultry seasoning and cook 1 more minute.
6.   Season with salt and pepper and add to baking dish. Place the turkey over the vegetables and stir everything together.
7.   Spread the sauce mixture over the top and stir to combine. Sprinkle the remaining mozzarella over the top and bake 40 minutes, or until bubbly and cheese is golden brown. Let cool 5 minutes, then cut and serve.

Nutrition Info: Calories 351 Total Carbs 13g Net Carbs 10g Protein 37g Fat 16g Sugar 5g Fiber 3g

Meatloaf Reboot

Servings: 2
Cooking Time: 9 Minutes
Ingredients:

- 4 slices of leftover meatloaf, cut about 1-inch thick.

Directions:

1.   Preheat your air fryer to 350 degrees.
2.   Spray each side of the meatloaf slices with cooking spray. Add the slices to the air fryer and cook for about 9 to 10 minutes. Don't turn the slices halfway through the cooking cycle, because they may break apart. Instead, keep them on one side to cook to ensure they stay together

Nutrition Info: Calories: 201 Fat: 5g Carbohydrates: 9.6g Protein: 38g Sugar: 1.8gCholesterol: 10mg

Pork Loin With Onion Beer Sauce

Servings: 6
Cooking Time: 3 Hours
Ingredients:

- 1 ½ lb. pork loin
- 1 ½ cup dark beer
- 1 large onion, sliced
- What you'll need from store cupboard:
- 2 cloves garlic, diced fine
- 3 tbsp. water
- 2 tbsp. cornstarch
- 1 tbsp. olive oil
- 1 tbsp. Dijon mustard
- 2 bay leaves

Directions:

1.   Heat oil in a large skillet over med-high heat. Add onions and cook until tender. Add the pork and brown on all sides. Transfer to the crock pot.
2.   Add the beer, mustard, garlic, and bay leaves. Cover and cook on high 3 hours, or until pork is tender.
3.   Transfer pork to a plate. Whisk together the corn starch and water and add to the crock pot, stir well. Let cook until sauce thickens, about 30 minutes.
4.   Slice the pork and serve topped with sauce.

Nutrition Info: Calories 342 Total Carbs 7g Protein 31g Fat 18g Sugar 1g Fiber 0g

Mediterranean Stuffed Chicken

Servings: 6
Cooking Time: 45 Minutes
Ingredients:

- 6 chicken breast halves, boneless and skinless

- 10 oz. spinach, thaw and squeeze dry
- 4 green onions, slice thin
- 1 cup feta cheese, crumbled
- ½ cup sun dried tomatoes
- What you'll need from store cupboard:
- 1 cup boiling water
- 1 clove garlic, diced
- ¼ cup Greek olives, diced
- ¼ tsp salt
- ¼ tsp pepper
- Nonstick cooking spray

Directions:
1. Heat oven to 350 degrees. Spray 13x9-inch baking dish with cooking spray.
2. Place tomatoes in a bowl and add boiling water. Let set for 5 minutes.
3. In a medium bowl, combine spinach, cheese, onions, olive and garlic. Drain the tomatoes and chop, add to spinach mixture.
4. Flatten chicken to ¼-inch thick and sprinkle with salt and pepper.
5. Spread spinach mixture over chicken and roll up, secure with toothpicks. Place in prepared dish and cover with foil.
6. Bake 30 minutes. Uncover, and bake 15-20 minutes, or until chicken is cooked through. Remove toothpicks before serving.

Nutrition Info: Calories 221 Total Carbs 6g Net Carbs 4g Protein 27g Fat 10g Sugar 1g Fiber 2g

Cajun Smothered Pork Chops

Servings: 4
Cooking Time: 25 Minutes
Ingredients:
- 4 pork chops, thick-cut
- 1 small onion, diced fine
- 1 cup mushrooms, sliced
- 1 cup fat free sour cream
- 2 tbsp. margarine
- What you'll need from store cupboard:
- 1 cup low sodium chicken broth
- 3 cloves garlic, diced fine
- 1 tbsp. Cajun seasoning
- 2 bay leaves
- 1 tsp smoked paprika
- Salt & pepper to taste

Directions:
1. Melt margarine in a large skillet over medium heat. Sprinkle chops with salt and pepper and cook until nicely browned, about 5 minutes per side. Transfer to a plate.
2. Add onions and mushrooms and cook until soft, about 5 minutes. Add garlic and cook one minute more.
3. Add broth and stir to incorporate brown bits on bottom of the pan. Add a dash of salt and the bay leaves. Add pork chops back to sauce. Bring to a simmer, cover, and reduce heat. Cook 5-8 minutes, or until chops are cooked through.
4. Transfer chops to a plate and keep warm. Bring sauce to a boil and cook until it has reduced by half, stirring occasionally.
5. Reduce heat to low and whisk in sour cream, Cajun seasoning, and paprika. Cook, stirring frequently, 3 minutes. Add chops back to the sauce and heat through. Serve.

Nutrition Info: Calories 323 Total Carbs 13g Net Carbs 12g Protein 24g Fat 18g Sugar 5g Fiber 1g

Pork Liver

Servings: 4
Cooking Time: 15 Minutes
Ingredients:
- 500g of pork liver cut into steaks
- Breadcrumbs
- Salt
- Ground pepper
- 1 lemon
- Extra virgin olive oil

Directions:
1. Put the steaks on a plate or bowl.
2. Add the lemon juice, salt, and ground pepper.
3. Leave a few minutes to macerate the pork liver fillets.
4. Drain well and go through breadcrumbs, it is not necessary to pass the fillets through beaten egg because the liver is very moist, the breadcrumbs are perfectly glued.
5. Spray with extra virgin olive oil. If you don't have a sprayer, paint with a silicone brush.
6. Put the pork liver fillets in the air fryer basket.
7. Program 1800C, 10 minutes.

8. Take out if you see them golden to your liking and put another batch. You should not pile the pork liver fillets, which are well extended so that the empanada is crispy on all sides.

Nutrition Info: Calories: 120 Fat: 3.41g Carbohydrates: 0g Protein: 20.99g Sugar: 0gCholesterol: 65mg

French Onion Casserole

Servings: 8Cooking Time: 55 Minutes
Ingredients:

- 1 lb. lean ground beef
- 6 eggs
- 2 cup skim milk
- 1 cup Swiss cheese, grated
- ½ cup onion, diced
- What you'll need from store cupboard:
- 10 oz. can condensed French onion soup
- 6 oz. pkg. herb stuffing mix
- 1 tbsp. Worcestershire sauce
- 1 tbsp. olive oil
- 1 tbsp. chili sauce
- 2 tsp thyme
- Nonstick cooking spray

Directions:

1. Heat oven to 350 degrees. Spray a 13x9-inch baking dish with cooking spray.
2. Heat oil in a large skillet over medium heat. Add beef and cook, breaking up with spatula, until no longer pink.Add onion, Worcestershire, and chili sauce, and cook 3-5 minutes, until onions are soft.
3. In a large bowl, beat eggs, soup, milk, ½ cup cheese, and 1 teaspoon thyme. Add the dry stuffing mix and beef. Stir well, making sure to coat the stuffing mixture.
4. Transfer to prepared baking dish. Sprinkle with remaining cheeseand thyme and let rest 15 minutes. Bake 45 minutes or until a knife inserted in center comes out clean. Serve.

Nutrition Info: Calories 327 Total Carbs 23g Net Carbs 22g Protein 30g Fat 12g Sugar 7g Fiber 1g

Cheesy Stuffed Chicken

Servings: 4Cooking Time: 20 Minutes
Ingredients:

- 1 lb. chicken breasts, boneless and butterflied

- 2 cups fresh spinach, chopped
- 4 oz. low fat cream cheese, soft
- ¼ cup mozzarella cheese, grated
- What you'll need from store cupboard:
- ¼ cup reduced fat Parmesan cheese
- 1 tbsp. garlic, diced fine
- 1 tbsp. olive oil
- 1 tsp chili powder
- 1 tsp Italian seasoning
- ¾ tsp black pepper, divided
- ½ tsp salt

Directions:

1. In a medium bowl, combine spinach, cream cheese, parmesan, mozzarella, garlic, ½ teaspoon salt and ½ teaspoon pepper, stir to combine.
2. In a small bowl, stir together the chili powder, Italian seasoning, salt, and pepper, use it to season both sides of the chicken. Spoon ¼ of the cheese mixture into the middle of the chicken and fold over to seal it inside.
3. Heat oil in a large skillet over med-high heat. Add the chicken, cover and cook 9-10 minutes per side, or until cooked through. Serve.

Nutrition Info: Calories 256 Total Carbs 2g Net Carbs 1g Protein 29g Fat 14g Sugar 0g Fiber 1g

Middle East Chicken Skewers

Servings: 6
Cooking Time: 15 Minutes
Ingredients:

- 2 ½ lbs. chicken thighs, boneless, skinless, cut in large pieces
- 1 red onion, cut in wedges
- Zest & juice of 1 lemon
- 1 cup plain Greek yogurt
- What you'll need from store cupboard:
- 5 cloves garlic, diced
- 2 tbsp. olive oil
- 2 tsp paprika
- 1 ¾ tsp salt
- 1 tsp red pepper flakes
- ½ tsp pepper
- ½ tsp cumin
- 1/8 tsp cinnamon
- Nonstick cooking spray

Directions:

1. In a medium bowl, combine the yogurt, olive oil, paprika, cumin, cinnamon, red pepper flakes, lemon zest, lemon juice, salt, pepper and garlic.

2. Thread the chicken onto metal skewers, folding if the pieces are long and thin, alternating occasionally with the red onions. Place the kebabs on a baking sheet lined with aluminum foil. Spoon or brush the marinade all over the meat, coating well. Cover and refrigerate at least eight hours or overnight.

3. Heat the grill to medium-high heat. Spray the rack with cooking spray. Grill the kebabs until golden brown and cooked through, turning skewers occasionally, 10 to 15 minutes. Transfer the skewers to a platter and serve.

Nutrition Info: Calories 474 Total Carbs 14g Net Carbs 13g Protein 64g Fat 18g Sugar 12g Fiber 1g

Chicken Tuscany

Servings: 4

Cooking Time: 15 Minutes

Ingredients:

- 1½ lbs. chicken breasts, boneless, skinless and sliced thin –
- 1 cup spinach, chopped
- 1 cup half-n-half
- What you'll need from store cupboard:
- ½ cup reduced fat parmesan cheese
- ½ cup low sodium chicken broth
- ½ cup sun dried tomatoes
- 2 tbsp. olive oil - 1 tsp Italian seasoning
- 1 tsp garlic powder

Directions:

1. Heat oil in a large skillet over med-high heat. Add chicken and cook 3-5 minutes per side, or until browned and cooked through. Transfer to a plate.

2. Add half-n-half, broth, cheese and seasonings to the pan. Whisk constantly until sauce starts to thicken. Add spinach and tomatoes and cook, stirring frequently, until spinach starts to wilt, about 2-3 minutes.

3. Add chicken back to the pan and cook just long enough to heat through.

Nutrition Info: Calories 462 Total Carbs 6g Net Carbs 5g Protein 55g Fat 23g Sugar 0g Fiber 1g

Ritzy Jerked Chicken Breasts

Servings: 4

Cooking Time: 15 Minutes

Ingredients:

- 2 habanero chile peppers, halved lengthwise, seeded - ½ sweet onion, cut into chunks
- 1 tablespoon minced garlic
- 1 tablespoon ground allspice
- 2 teaspoons chopped fresh thyme
- ¼ cup freshly squeezed lime juice
- ½ teaspoon ground nutmeg
- ¼ teaspoon ground cinnamon
- 1 teaspoon freshly ground black pepper
- 2 tablespoons extra-virgin olive oil
- 4 (5-ounce / 142-g) boneless, skinless chicken breasts - 2 cups fresh arugula
- 1 cup halved cherry tomatoes

Directions:

1. Combine the habaneros, onion, garlic, allspice, thyme, lime juice, nutmeg, cinnamon, black pepper, and olive oil in a blender. Pulse to blender well.

2. Transfer the mixture into a large bowl or two medium bowls, then dunk the chicken in the bowl and press to coat well.

3. Put the bowl in the refrigerator and marinate for at least 4 hours.

4. Preheat the oven to 400°F (205°C).

5. Remove the bowl from the refrigerator, then discard the marinade.

6. Arrange the chicken on a baking sheet, then roast in the preheated oven for 15 minutes or until golden brown and lightly charred. Flip the chicken halfway through the cooking time.

7. Remove the baking sheet from the oven and let sit for 5 minutes. Transfer the chicken on a large plate and serve with arugula and cherry tomatoes.

Nutrition Info: calories: 226 fat: 9.0g protein: 33.0g carbs: 3.0g fiber: 0g sugar: 1.0g sodium: 92mg

Lemon Chicken

Servings: 4

Cooking Time: 10 Minutes

Ingredients:

- 3 large boneless, skinless chicken breasts, cut into strips

- ¼ cup red bell pepper, cut into 2 inch strips
- ¼ cup green bell pepper, cut into 2 inch strips
- ¼ cup snow peas
- ¼ cup fresh lemon juice
- 1 tsp fresh ginger, peeled and diced fine
- What you'll need from store cupboard:
- ¼ cup + 1 tbsp. low sodium soy sauce, divided
- ¼ cup low-fat, low-sodium chicken broth
- 1 tbsp. Splenda
- 1 tbsp. vegetable oil
- 2 cloves garlic, diced fine
- 2 tsp cornstarch

Directions:

1. In a medium bowl, whisk together 1 teaspoon cornstarch and 1 tablespoon soy sauce. Add chicken, cover and chill about 10 minutes.
2. In a separate medium mixing bowl, stir together lemon juice, ¼ cup soy sauce, broth, ginger, garlic, Splenda, and remaining cornstarch until thoroughly combined.
3. Heat oil in a large skillet over med-high heat. Add chicken and cook, stirring frequently, 3-4 minutes or just until chicken is no longer pink.
4. Add sauce, peppers and peas. Cook 2 more minutes or until sauce thickens and vegetables are tender-crisp. Serve.

Nutrition Info: Calories 242 Total Carbs 9g Net Carbs 8g Protein 27g Fat 10g Sugar 5g Fiber 1g

Teriyaki Turkey Bowls

Servings: 4
Cooking Time: 15 Minutes
Ingredients:

- 1 lb. lean ground turkey
- 1 medium head cauliflower, separated into small florets
- What you'll need from store cupboard:
- 1 cup water, divided
- ¼ cup + 1 tbsp. soy sauce
- 2 tbsp. Hoisin sauce
- 2 tbsp. honey
- 1 ½ tbsp. cornstarch
- 1 tsp crushed red pepper flakes
- 1 tsp garlic powder
- Salt

Directions:

1. In a medium nonstick skillet, cook turkey over med-high heat until brown.
2. In a medium saucepan, combine ¾ cup water, ¼ cup soy sauce, hoisin, pepper flakes, honey, and garlic powder and cook over medium heat, stirring occasionally, until it starts to bubble.
3. In a small bowl whisk together ¼ cup water and cornstarch and add to the saucepan. Bring mixture to a full boil, stirring occasionally. Once it starts to boil, remove from heat and the turkey. Stir to combine.
4. Place the cauliflower florets in a food processor and pulse until it resembles rice.
5. Spray a nonstick skillet with cooking spray and add the cauliflower and 1 tablespoon soy sauce and cook until cauliflower starts to get soft, about 5-7 minutes.
6. To serve, spoon cauliflower evenly into four bowls, top with turkey mixture and garnish with

Nutrition Info: Calories 267 Total Carbs 24g Net Carbs 20g Protein 26g Fat 9g Sugar 15g Fiber 4g

Garlic Honey Pork Chops

Servings: 6
Cooking Time: 10 Minutes
Ingredients:

- 6 boneless pork loin chops, trim excess fat
- What you'll need from store cupboard:
- ¼ cup lemon juice
- ¼ cup honey
- ¼ cup low sodium soy sauce
- ¼ cup dry white wine
- 2 tbsp. garlic, diced fine
- 1 tbsp. vegetable oil
- ¼ tsp black pepper

Directions:

1. Combine lemon juice, honey, soy sauce, wine, garlic, and pepper in a 9x13 baking dish. Mix well.
2. Add pork chops, turning to coat. Cover and refrigerate at least 4 hours, or overnight, turning chops occasionally.
3. Heat oil in a large skillet over med-high heat. Add chops and cook 2-3 minutes per side.
4. Pour marinade over chops and bring to a boil. Reduce heat to low and simmer 2-3 minutes,

or chops are desired doneness. Servetopped with sauce.
Nutrition Info: Calories 436 Total Carbs 14g Protein 26g Fat 30g Sugar 12g Fiber 0g

Chicken Stuffed With Mushrooms

Servings: 4
Cooking Time: 3 Hours
Ingredients:
- 4 thin chicken breasts, boneless and skinless
- What you'll need from store cupboard:
- 1 small can mushrooms, drain and slice
- ½ cup + 2 tbsp. low sodium chicken broth
- ½ cup fine bread crumbs
- 1 tbsp. dry white wine
- 1 tbsp. cornstarch
- ½ tsp sage
- ½ tsp garlic powder
- ¼ tsp marjoram
- Salt & pepper to taste
Directions:
1. Place chicken between 2 sheets of plastic wrap and pound to 1/8-inch thick, working from the center to the edges.
2. In a small bowl, combine mushrooms, bread crumbs, 2 tablespoons broth and seasonings. Spoon one fourth stuffing mix onto short end of chicken breast. Fold long sides in and roll up. Secure with toothpick.
3. Place chicken in crock pot and add the ½ cup broth. Cover and cook on high 3 hours, or until chicken is cooked through. Transfer chicken to a plate and tent with foil to keep warm.
4. Strain cooking liquid through a sieve into a small saucepan. Place over medium heat. In a small bowl, whisk together the wine and cornstarch. Add to the saucepan and cook, stirring constantly, until sauce is bubbly and thick. Cook 2 minutes more. Spoon sauce over chicken and serve.
Nutrition Info: Calories 181 Total Carbs 13g Net Carbs 12g Protein 28g Fat 2g Sugar 1g Fiber 1g

Chicken Zucchini Patties With Salsa

Servings: 8
Cooking Time: 10 Minutes
Ingredients:
- 2 cup chicken breast, cooked, divided
- 1 zucchini, cut in ¾-inch pieces
- ¼ cup cilantro, diced
- What you'll need from store cupboard:
- 1/3 cup bread crumbs
- 1/3 cup lite mayonnaise
- 2 tsp olive oil
- ½ tsp salt
- ¼ tsp pepper
- Roasted Tomato Salsa, (chapter 15)
Directions:
1. Place 1 ½ cups chicken and zucchini into a food processor. Cover and process until coarsely chopped. Add bread crumbs, mayonnaise, pepper, cilantro, remaining chicken, and salt. Cover and pulse until chunky.
2. Heat oil in a large skillet over med-high heat. Shape chicken mixture into 8 patties and cook 4 minutes per side, or until golden brown. Serve topped with salsa.
Nutrition Info: Calories 146 Total Carbs 10g Net Carbs 8g Protein 12g Fat 7g Sugar 5g Fiber 2g

Roast Turkey & Rosemary Gravy

Servings: 18Cooking Time: 1 ¾ Hours
Ingredients:
- 6 lb. turkey breast, bone in
- 2 apples, sliced
- 1 ½ cup leek, sliced, white parts only
- 3 tbsp. margarine
- 2 tsp fresh rosemary, diced, divided
- What you'll need from store cupboard:
- 2 ¼ cup low sodium chicken broth
- ¼ cup flour
- 1 tbsp. sunflower oil
Directions:
1. Heat oven to 325 degrees.
2. Place apples and leeks in the bottom of a large roasting pan, and pour in 1 cup of broth. Place turkey on top.
3. In a small bowl, combine oil and 1 ½ teaspoons rosemary. Loosen skin over turkey and rub rosemary mixture over the turkey. Secure skin to underside of turkey with toothpicks.
4. Bake 1 ¾-2 ¼ hours, basting every 30 minutes, until turkey is cooked through. If turkey starts to get too brown, cover with foil.

5. Once turkey is done, cover and let rest 15 minutes before slicing. Discard apples and leeks. Save ¼ cup cooking liquid.

6. Melt margarine in a small saucepan over medium heat. Add flour and remaining rosemary and cook, stirring, until combined. Skim fat off the reserved cooking liquid and add to saucepan with remaining broth. Bring to a boil, cook, stirring, 1 minute until thickened. Serve with turkey.

Nutrition Info: Calories 306 Total Carbs 6g Net Carbs 5g Protein 33g Fat 14g Sugar 3g Fiber 1g

Beef Goulash

Servings: 6 Cooking Time: 1 Hour
Ingredients:
- 2 lb. chuck steak, trim fat and cut into bite-sized pieces
- 3 onions, quartered
- 1 green pepper, chopped
- 1 red pepper, chopped
- 1 orange pepper, chopped
- What you'll need from store cupboard:
- 3 cups water
- 1 can tomatoes, chopped
- 1 cup low sodium beef broth
- 3 cloves garlic, diced fine
- 2 tbsp. tomato paste
- 1 tbsp. olive oil
- 1 tbsp. paprika
- 2 tsp hot smoked paprika
- 2 bay leaves
- Salt & pepper, to taste

Directions:
1. Heat oil in a large soup pot over med-high. Add steak and cook until browned, stirring frequently.
2. Add onions and cook 5 minutes, or until soft. Add garlic and cook another minute, stirring frequently.
3. Add remaining Ingredients. Stir well and bring to a boil. Reduce heat to med-low and simmer 45-50 minutes, stirring occasionally. Goulash is done when steak is tender. Stir well before serving.

Nutrition Info: Calories 413 Total Carbs 14g Protein 53g Fat 15g Sugar 8g Fiber 3g

Herbed Chicken And Artichoke Hearts

Servings: 4
Cooking Time: 20 Minutes
Ingredients:
- 2 tablespoons olive oil, divided
- 4 (6-ounce / 170-g) boneless, skinless chicken breast halves
- ½ teaspoon dried thyme, divided
- 1 teaspoon crushed dried rosemary, divided
- ½ teaspoon ground black pepper, divided
- 2 (14-ounce / 397-g) cans water-packed, low-sodium artichoke hearts, drained and quartered
- ½ cup low-sodium chicken broth
- 2 garlic cloves, chopped
- 1 medium onion, coarsely chopped
- ¼ cup shredded Parmesan cheese
- 1 lemon, cut into 8 slices
- 2 green onions, thinly sliced

Directions:
1. Preheat the oven to 375°F (190°C). Grease a baking sheet with 1 teaspoon of olive oil.
2. Place the chicken breasts on the baking sheet and rub with ¼ teaspoon of thyme, ½ teaspoon of rosemary, ¼ teaspoon of black pepper, and 1 tablespoon of olive oil.
3. Combine the artichoke hearts, chicken broth, garlic, onion, andremaining thyme, rosemary, black pepper, and olive oil. Toss to coat well.
4. Spread the artichoke around the chicken breasts, then scatter with Parmesan and lemon slices.
5. Place the baking sheet in the preheated oven and roast for 20 minutes or until the internal temperature of the chicken breasts reaches at least 165°F (74°C).
6. Remove the sheet from the oven. Allow to cool for 10 minutes, then serve with green onions on top.

Nutrition Info: calories: 339 fat: 9.0g protein: 42.0g carbs: 18.0g fiber: 1.0g sugar: 2.0g sodium: 667mg

Mediterranean Lamb Meatballs

Servings: 4
Cooking Time: 40 Minutes
Ingredients:
- 454g ground lamb

- 3 cloves garlic, minced
- 5g of salt
- 1g black pepper
- 2g of mint, freshly chopped
- 2g ground cumin
- 3 ml hot sauce - 1g chili powder
- 1 scallion, chopped
- 8g parsley, finely chopped
- 15 ml of fresh lemon juice
- 2g lemon zest - 10 ml of olive oil

Directions:

1. Mix the lamb, garlic, salt, pepper, mint, cumin, hot sauce, chili powder, chives, parsley, lemon juice and lemon zest until well combined.
2. Create balls with the lamb mixture and cool for 30 minutes.
3. Select Preheat in the air fryer and press Start/Pause.
4. Cover the meatballs with olive oil and place them in the preheated fryer.
5. Select Steak, set the time to 10 minutes and press Start/Pause.

Nutrition Info: (Nutrition per Serving):Calories: 282 Fat: 23.41 Carbohydrates: 0g Protein: 16.59 Sugar: 0g Cholesterol: 73gm

Italian Pork Medallions

Servings: 2
Cooking Time: 15 Minutes
Ingredients:

- ½ lb. pork tenderloin
- ¼ cup onion, diced
- What you'll need from store cupboard:
- 1 clove garlic, diced
- 2 tbsp. Italian bread crumbs
- 1 tbsp. reduced fat parmesan cheese
- 2 tsp olive oil
- ¼ tsp salt
- 1/8 tsp pepper

Directions:

1. Slice the tenderloin into 4 equal pieces. Flatten each piece to ¼-inch thick.
2. In a large Ziploc bag, combine bread crumbs, cheese, salt, and pepper.

3. Heat oil in a large skillet over medium heat. Add pork to the Ziploc bag, one piece at a time, and turn to coat.
4. Add the pork to the skillet and cook 2-3 minutes per side, or until no longer pink. Transfer to a plate and keep warm.
5. Add onion to the skillet and cook, stirring, until tender. Add garlic and cook 1 minute more. Serve pork topped with onions.

Nutrition Info: Calories 244 Total Carbs 7g Net Carbs 6g Protein 31g Fat 10g Sugar 1g Fiber 1g

Pork Diane

Servings: 4
Cooking Time: 20 Minutes
Ingredients:

- 2 teaspoons Worcestershire sauce
- 1 tablespoon freshly squeezed lemon juice
- ¼ cup low-sodium chicken broth
- 2 teaspoons Dijon mustard
- 4 (5-ounce / 142-g) boneless pork top loin chops, about 1 inch thick
- Sea salt and freshly ground black pepper, to taste
- 1 teaspoon extra-virgin olive oil
- 2 teaspoons chopped fresh chives
- 1 teaspoon lemon zest

Directions:

1. Combine the Worcestershire sauce, lemon juice, broth, and Dijon mustard in a bowl. Stir to mix well.
2. On a clean work surface, rub the pork chops with salt and ground black pepper.
3. Heat the olive oil in a nonstick skillet over medium-high heat until shimmering.
4. Add the pork chops and sear for 16 minutes or until well browned. Flip the pork halfway through the cooking time. Transfer to a plate and set aside.
5. Pour the sauce mixture in the skillet and cook for 2 minutes or until warmed through and lightly thickened. Mix in the chives and lemon zest.
6. Baste the pork with the sauce mixture and serve immediately.

Nutrition Info: calories: 200 fat: 8.0g protein: 30.0g carbs: 1.0g fiber: 0g sugar: 1.0g sodium: 394mg

Turkey Noodle Casserole

Servings: 4
Cooking Time: 45 Minutes
Ingredients:

- 2 cup turkey breast, cooked and cubed
- 10 oz. spinach, thaw and squeeze dry
- 1 cup fat free cottage cheese
- ¾ cup mozzarella cheese, grated
- What you'll need from store cupboard:
- Homemade Noodles, (chapter 15)
- 1 can low fat condensed cream of chicken soup
- 1/8 tsp garlic salt
- 1/8 tsp rosemary
- 1/8 tsp paprika
- Nonstick cooking spray

Directions:

1.	Heat oven to 350 degrees. Spray a 2-quart casserole dish with cooking spray.
2.	In a large bowl combine turkey, soup, and seasonings.
3.	In a separate bowl combine spinach, cottage cheese, and half the mozzarella cheese.
4.	Place ½ the noodles in the prepared dish. Add half the turkey mixture and half the spinach mixture. Repeat.
5.	Cover with foil and bake 35 minutes. Uncover and sprinkle remaining cheese over top. Bake 10-15 minutes longer until edges are lightly browned.
6.	Let rest 5 minutes before sprinkling with paprika. Serve.

Nutrition Info: Calories 267 Total Carbs 12g Net Carbs 10g Protein 26g Fat 8g Sugar 4g Fiber 2g

Cheesy Chicken & "potato" Casserole

Servings: 6
Cooking Time: 40 Minutes
Ingredients:

- 4 slices bacon, cooked and crumbled
- 3 cups cauliflower
- 3 cups chicken, cooked and chopped
- 3 cups broccoli florets
- 2 cups reduced fat cheddar cheese, grated
- 1 cup fat free sour cream
- 4 tbsp. margarine, soft
- What you'll need from store cupboard

- 1 tsp salt
- ½ tsp black pepper
- ½ tsp garlic powder
- ½ tsp paprika
- Nonstick cooking spray

Directions:

1.	In a large saucepan add 4-5 cups of water and bring to a boil. Addthe cauliflower and cook about 4-5 minutes, or until it is tender drain well. Repeat with broccoli.
2.	Heat oven to 350 degrees. Spray a baking dish with cooking spray.
3.	In a medium bowl, mash the cauliflower with the margarine, sour cream and seasonings. Add remaining Ingredients, saving ½ the cheese, and mix well.
4.	Spread mixture in prepared baking dish and sprinkle remaining cheese on top. Bake 20-25 minutes, or until heated through and cheese has melted. Serve.

Nutrition Info: Calories 346 Total Carbs 10g Net Carbs 8g Protein 28g Fat 15g Sugar 4g Fiber 2g

Beef & Veggie Quesadillas

Servings: 4
Cooking Time: 10 Minutes
Ingredients:

- ¾ lb. lean ground beef
- 2 tomatoes, seeded and diced
- 1 onion, diced
- 1 zucchini, grated
- 1 carrot, grated
- ¾ cup mushrooms, diced
- ½ cup mozzarella cheese, grated
- ¼ cup cilantro, diced
- What you'll need from store cupboard:
- 4 8-inch whole wheat tortillas, warmed
- 2 cloves garlic, diced
- 2 tsp chili powder
- ¼ tsp salt
- ¼ tsp hot pepper sauce
- Nonstick cooking spray

Directions:

1.	Heat oven to 400 degrees. Spray a large baking sheet with cooking spray.

2. Cook beef and onions in a large nonstick skillet over medium heat, until beef is no longer pink, drain fat. Transfer to a bowl andkeep warm.

3. Add the mushrooms, zucchini, carrot, garlic, chili powder, salt and pepper sauce to the skillet and cook until vegetables are tender.

4. Stir in the tomatoes, cilantro and beef.

5. Lay the tortillas on the prepared pan. Cover half of each with beef mixture, and top with cheese. Fold other half over filling. Bake 5 minutes. Flip over and bake 5-6 minute more or until cheese has melted. Cut into wedges and serve.

Nutrition Info: Calories 319 Total Carbs 31g Net Carbs 26g Protein 33g Fat 7g Sugar 5g Fiber 5g

Sumptuous Lamb And Pomegranate Salad

Servings: 8
Cooking Time: 30 Minutes
Ingredients:
- 1½ cups pomegranate juice

- 4 tablespoons olive oil, divided
- 1 tablespoon ground cinnamon
- 1 teaspoon cumin
- 1 tablespoon ground ginger
- 3 cloves garlic, chopped
- Salt and freshly ground black pepper, to taste
- 1 (4-pound / 1.8-kg) lamb leg, deboned, butterflied, and fat trimmed
- 2 tablespoons pomegranate balsamic vinegar
- 2 teaspoons Dijon mustard
- ½ cup pomegranate seeds
- 5 cups baby kale
- 4 cups fresh green beans, blanched
- ¼ cup toasted walnut halves
- 2 fennel bulbs, thinly sliced
- 2 tablespoons Gorgonzola cheese
Directions:
1. Mix the pomegranate juice, 1 tablespoon of olive oil, cinnamon, cumin, ginger, garlic, salt, and black pepper in a large bowl. Stir to mix well.
2. Dunk the lamb leg in the mixture, press to coat well. Wrap thebowl in plastic and refrigerate to marinate for at least 8 hours.

3. Remove the bowl from the refrigerate and let sit for 20 minutes. Pat the lamb dry with paper towels.

4. Preheat the grill to high heat.

5. Brush the grill grates with 1 tablespoon of olive oil, then arrange the lamb on the grill grates.

6. Grill for 30 minutes or until the internal temperature of the lamb reaches at least 145°F (63°C). Flip the lamb halfway through the cooking time.

7. Remove the lamb from the grill and wrap with aluminum foil. Let stand for 15 minutes.

8. Meanwhile, Combine the vinegar, mustard, salt, black pepper, and remaining olive oil in a separate large bowl. Stir to mix well.

9. Add the remaining ingredients and lamb leg to the bowl and toss to combine well. Serve immediately.

Nutrition Info: calories: 380 fat: 21.0g protein: 32.0g carbs: 16.0g fiber: 5.0g sugar: 6.0g sodium: 240mg

Mediterranean Grilled Chicken

Servings: 4
Cooking Time: 10 Minutes
Ingredients:
- 4 chicken breasts, boneless, skinless
- What you'll need from store cupboard:
- 6 oz. pesto
- ¼ cup olive oil
- ¼ cup lemon juice
- 2 tbsp. red wine vinegar
- 2 tsp garlic, diced fine
Directions:
1. In a large freezer bag or a container mix together the olive oil, lemon juice, red wine vinegar, minced garlic and pesto. Add chicken and toss to coat. Place in refrigerator and marinate for 6 to 8 hours.
2. Heat grill to med-high. Cook chicken, 3-4 minutes per side, or until cooked through. Or, you can bake it in a 400 degree oven until no longer pink, about 30 minutes. Serve.

Nutrition Info: Calories 378 Total Carbs 2g Protein 36g Fat 25gSugar 2g Fiber 0g

Air Fried Meatloaf

Servings: 2
Cooking Time: 20 Minutes
Ingredients:

- ½ lb. ground beef
- ½ lb. ground turkey
- 1 onion, chopped
- ¼ cup panko bread crumbs
- 3 Tbsp. ketchup
- ¼ cup brown sugar
- 1 egg, beaten
- Salt and pepper to taste

Directions:
1.   Preheat air fryer to 400 degrees.
2.   Let the ground beef and ground turkey sit on the counter for 10 to 15 minutes, as it will be easier to hand mix without being chilled from the refrigerator.
3.   Combine all the ingredients.
4.   Form into a loaf in a dish and place the dish in the frying basket. Spritz the top with a little olive oil. Bake for 25 minutes, or until well browned. Let settle for about 10 minutes before serving.
Nutrition Info: Calories: 381 Fat: 5g Carbohydrates: 9.6g Protein: 38g Sugar: 1.8g Cholesterol: 0mg

Honey Garlic Chicken

Servings: 6
Cooking Time: 6 Hours
Ingredients:

- 6 chicken thighs
- What you'll need from store cupboard:
- 2 tbsp. sugar free ketchup
- 2 tbsp. honey
- 2 tbsp. lite soy sauce
- 3 cloves garlic, diced fine

Directions:
1.   Add everything, except chicken, to the crock pot. Stir to combine.
2.   Lay chicken, skin side up, in a single layer. Cover and cook on low 6 hours, or high for 3 hours.
3.   Place chicken in a baking dish and broil 2-3 minutes to caramelize the outside. Serve.
Nutrition Info: Calories 57 Total Carbs 7g Protein 4g Fat 2g Sugar 6g Fiber 0g

Potatoes With Bacon, Onion And Cheese

Servings: 4
Cooking Time: 15 Minutes
Ingredients:

- 200g potatoes
- 150g bacon
- 1 onion
- Slices of cheese
- Extra virgin olive oil
- Salt

Directions:
1.   Peel the potatoes, cut into thin slices, and wash them well.
2.   Drain and dry the potatoes, put salt and a few strands of extra virgin olive oil.
3.   Stir well and place in the basket of the air fryer.
4.   Cut the onion into julienne, put a little oil, and stir, place on the potatoes.
5.   Finally, put the sliced bacon on the onion.
6.   Take the basket to the air fryer and select 20 minutes, 1800C.
7.   From time to time, remove the basket.
8.   Take all the contents of the basket to a source and when it is still hot, place the slices of cheese on top.
9.   You can let the heat of the potatoes melt the cheese or you can gratin a few minutes in the oven.
Nutrition Info: Calories: 120 Fat: 3.41g Carbohydrates: 0g Protein: 20.99g Sugar: 0gCholesterol: 65mg

Crock Pot Beef Roast With Gravy

Servings: 10
Cooking Time: 5 ½ Hours
Ingredients:

- 3 lb. beef sirloin tip roast
- What you'll need from store cupboard:
- ¼ cup lite soy sauce
- ¼ cup water
- 3 tbsp. balsamic vinegar
- 2 tbsp. cornstarch
- 2 tbsp. coarse ground pepper
- 1 tbsp. Worcestershire sauce

- 2 tsp ground mustard
- 1 ½ tsp garlic, diced fine

Directions:

1. Rub roast with garlic and pepper. Cut in half and place in crock pot.
2. Combine soy sauce, vinegar, Worcestershire, and mustard, pour over roast.
3. Cover and cook on low heat 5 ½-6 hours or until beef is tender.
4. Remove roast and keep warm. Strain juices into a small sauce pan, skim off fat. Heat over medium heat.
5. Stir water and cornstarch together until smooth. Stir into beef juices. Bring to a boil, and cook, stirring, 2 minutes or until thickened. Serve with roast.

Nutrition Info: Calories 264 Total Carbs 3g Protein 37g Fat 12g Sugar 0g Fiber 0g

Pork Paprika

Servings: 6
Cooking Time: 40 Minutes
Ingredients:

- 1 lb. pork loin, trim fat and cut into 1-inch cubes
- 1 onion, diced fine
- 1 cup mushrooms, sliced thick
- 2/3 cup fat free sour cream
- What you'll need from store cupboard:
- 1 can petite tomatoes, diced
- ½ cup low sodium chicken broth
- 2 tbsp. olive oil
- 2 tbsp. sweet paprika, divided
- 1 tbsp. garlic, diced fine
- ½ tsp thyme
- ½ tsp caraway seeds, ground
- Salt & pepper to taste

Directions:

1. Place pork in large bowl and sprinkle 1 tablespoon paprika, salt and pepper over meat, toss to coat.
2. Heat 1 tablespoon oil in a large, deep skillet over med-high heat. Add pork and cook, stirring frequently until brown on all sides, about 5-6 minutes. Transfer to a plate.
3. Add remaining tablespoon of oil to skillet and the mushrooms. Cook, stirring, till browned

and no more liquid remains in the pan, about 5 minutes. Add the mushrooms to the pork.
4. Add more oil if needed and the onion. Cook about 3-5 minutes, or they just start to brown. Add garlic and spices and cook another 1-2 minutes. Add tomatoes with juice and broth, cook, stirring frequently, until mixture starts to thicken, about 5 minutes.
5. Stir the pork and mushrooms into the sauce. Reduce heat, cover, and simmer 15 minutes, or until pork is tender. Serve.

Nutrition Info: Calories 267 Total Carbs 8g Net Carbs 7g 23g Protein 15g Fat Sugar 3g Fiber 1g

Asian Roasted Duck Legs

Servings: 4
Cooking Time: 90 Minutes
Ingredients:

- 4 duck legs
- 3 plum tomatoes, diced
- 1 red chili, deseeded and sliced
- ½ small Savoy cabbage, quartered
- 2 tsp fresh ginger, grated
- What you'll need from store cupboard:
- 3 cloves garlic, sliced
- 2 tbsp. soy sauce
- 2 tbsp. honey
- 1 tsp five-spice powder

Directions:

1. Heat oven to 350 degrees.
2. Place the duck in a large skillet over low heat and cook until brown on all sides and most of the fat is rendered, about 10 minutes. Transfer duck to a deep baking dish. Drain off all but 2 tablespoons of the fat.
3. Add ginger, garlic, and chili to the skillet and cook 2 minutes until soft. Add soy sauce, tomatoes and 2 tablespoons water and bring to a boil.
4. Rub the duck with the five spice seasoning. Pour the sauce over the duck and drizzle with the honey. Cover with foil and bake 1 hour. Add the cabbage for the last 10 minutes.

Nutrition Info: Calories 211 Total Carbs 19g Net Carbs 16g Protein 25g Fat 5g Sugar 14g Fiber 3g

Chicken & Spinach Pasta Skillet

Servings: 4
Cooking Time: 15 Minutes
Ingredients:
- 1 lb. chicken, boneless, skinless, cut into 1-inch pieces
- 10 cup fresh spinach, chopped
- 1 lemon, juiced and zested
- What you'll need from store cupboard:
- ½ recipe homemade pasta, (chapter 14) cook and drain
- ½ cup dry white wine
- 4 cloves garlic, diced fine
- 4 tbsp. reduced fat parmesan cheese, divided
- 2 tbsp. extra-virgin olive oil
- ½ tsp salt
- ¼ tsp ground pepper

Directions:
1. Heat oil in a large, deep skillet over med-high heat. Add chicken, salt and pepper. Cook, stirring occasionally, until just cooked through, 5-7 minutes.
2. Add garlic and cook, stirring, until fragrant, about 1 minute.
3. Stir in wine, lemon juice and zest; bring to a simmer. Remove from heat. Stir in spinach and pasta. Cover and let stand until the spinach is just wilted. Divide among 4 plates and top each serving with 1 tablespoon Parmesan.

Nutrition Info: Calories 415 Total Carbs 12g Net Carbs 9g Protein 40g Fat 19g Sugar 4g Fiber 3g

Short Ribs

Servings: 6
Cooking Time: 6 Hours
Ingredients:
- 4 lbs. lean beef short ribs
- 1 tablespoon canola oil
- ¼ cup onion, chopped
- ½ cup celery, chopped
- 3 garlic cloves, minced
- 8 oz. can tomato sauce
- ¼ teaspoon paprika
- ½ teaspoon black pepper

Directions:
1. Heat oil in a skillet over high heat. Add ribs, cook and brown all sides. Add ribs to a slow cooker.
2. Mix the remaining ingredients in a bowl and add over the ribs. Cover and cook for 6 hours on high heat. Serve.

Nutrition Info: Calories: 769 Fat: 3.41g Carbohydrates: 0g Protein: 20.99g Sugar: 0g

Turkey Meatball And Vegetable Kabobs

Servings: 6
Cooking Time: 20 Minutes
Ingredients:
- 20 ounces (567 g) lean ground turkey (93% fat-free)
- 2 egg whites
- 2 tablespoons grated Parmesan cheese
- 2 cloves garlic, minced
- ½ teaspoon salt, or to taste
- ¼ teaspoon ground black pepper
- 1 tablespoon olive oil
- 8 ounces (227 g) fresh cremini mushrooms, cut in half to make 12 pieces
- 24 cherry tomatoes
- 1 medium onion, cut into 12 pieces
- ¼ cup balsamic vinegar
- Special Equipment:
- 12 bamboo skewers, soaked in water for at least 30 minutes

Directions:
1. Mix the ground turkey, egg whites, Parmesan, garlic, salt, and pepper in a large bowl. Stir to combine well.
2. Shape the mixture into 12 meatballs and place on a baking sheet. Refrigerate for at least 30 minutes.
3. Preheat the oven to 375°F (190°C). Grease another baking sheet with 1 tablespoon of olive oil.
4. Remove the meatballs from the refrigerator. Run the bamboo skewers through 2 meatballs, 1 mushroom, 2 cherry tomatoes, and 1 onion piece alternatively.

5.   Arrange the kabobs on the greased baking sheet and brush with balsamic vinegar.

6.   Grill in the preheated oven for 20 minutes or until an instant-read thermometer inserted in the middle of the meatballs reads at least 165°F (74°C). Flip the kabobs halfway through the cooking time.

7.   Allow the kabobs to cool for 10 minutes, then serve warm.

Nutrition Info: calories: 200 fat: 8.0g protein: 22.0g carbs: 7.0g fiber: 1.0g sugar: 4.0g sodium: 120mg

Roasted Duck Legs With Balsamic Mushrooms

Servings: 4
Cooking Time: 1 Hour
Ingredients:
- 4 bone-in, skin-on duck legs
- 1/2 lb. cremini mushrooms, remove stems and cut caps into thick slices
- 1 green onion, sliced thin
- 1 small shallot, sliced thin
- 3-4 fresh thyme sprigs, crushed lightly
- What you'll need from store cupboard:
- 5 Tbs. extra-virgin olive oil
- 5 Tbs. balsamic vinegar
- 2 cloves garlic, sliced thin
- ½ tsp fresh thyme, chopped
- Kosher salt and freshly ground pepper

Directions:
1.   Rinse duck and pat dry with paper towels.
2.   In a shallow glass bowl, large enough to hold the duck, combine 3 tablespoons oil, 3 tablespoons vinegar, garlic, shallot, thyme sprigs, ½ teaspoon salt and some pepper. Add the duck, turning to coat. Cover and chill 3-4 hours turning legs once or twice.
3.   Remove the duck from the marinade. Pour the marinade into a saucepan and bring to a boil over high heat. Remove from heat.
4.   Place a footed rack on the bottom of a large pot, tall enough that the duck legs can stand 2 inches from the bottom. Add about 1 inch of water. Place the duck, skin side up on the rack. Cover and bring to a boil over med-high heat. Let steam until the skin is translucent, about 20 minutes.

5.   While duck is steaming, heat the oven to 450 degrees. Line a roasting pan large enough to hold the duck with foil. Place a flat rack in the pan.
6.   When the duck is ready, transfer it skin side up to the prepared rack. Brush the skin with the glaze and roast, until skin is brown and crisp, about 20 minutes. Remove from oven and glaze the duck again. Let rest for 5 minutes.
7.   In a large skillet, over med-high heat, heat the remaining oil. Add mushrooms and green onions and cook, stirring frequently about 2 minutes. Add the remaining vinegar, chopped thyme, salt and pepper to taste. Cook until mushrooms are soft and most of the liquid has evaporated.
8.   To serve, place duck leg on a plate and spoon mushrooms over.

Nutrition Info: Calories 374 Total Carbs 4g Net Carbs 3g Protein 26g Fat 28g Sugar 1g Fiber 1g

South Of The Border Chicken Casserole

Servings: 10
Cooking Time: 30 Minutes
Ingredients:
- 1 lb. chicken breast, cooked and shredded
- 1 red bell pepper, diced
- 1 onion, diced
- 1 cup pepper Jack cheese, grated
- ½ cup fat free sour cream
- ¼ cup half-n-half
- 2 tbsp. cilantro, diced fine
- What you'll need from store cupboard:
- 1 cup salsa
- 2 tbsp. olive oil
- 1 tbsp. chili powder
- 1 tbsp. cumin
- 2 tsp oregano
- 2 tsp salt
- 1 tsp pepper

Directions:
1.   Heat oven to 350 degrees.
2.   Heat the oil in a large skillet over med-high heat. Add the pepper, onion, salt and pepper and cook until soft.

3.   In a large bowl, stir together chili powder, cumin, and oregano. Add sour cream, salsa, veggies, and chicken and mix well.

4.   Pour mixture into a 9x13-inch baking dish. Pour the half-n-half evenly over the top and sprinkle with the cheese. Bake 30 minutes, or until heated through and cheese is starting to brown. Serve garnished with cilantro.

Nutrition Info: Calories 240 Total Carbs 8g Net Carb 7g Protein 20g Fat 14g Sugar 3g Fiber 1g

Swedish Beef Noodles

Servings: 4
Cooking Time: 20 Minutes
Ingredients:

- 1 lb. lean ground beef
- 8 oz. cremini mushrooms, sliced
- 1 cup onion, sliced thin
- ½ cup sour cream
- What you'll need from store cupboard:
- 3 ½ cup low sodium beef broth
- 1 tsp garlic salt
- 1 tsp caraway seed
- Homemade noodles, (chapter 14)
- Nonstick cooking spray

Directions:

1.   Spray a large pot with cooking spray and heat over med-high heat. Add beef and cook, breaking up with spatula, 2 minutes. Add onions and mushrooms and cook until beef is browned and onions are soft.

2.   Add the garlic salt, caraway seeds, and broth. Bring to a boil. Cover, reduce heat and simmer 10 minutes. Add noodles and cook another 3-5 minutes or noodles are done.

3.   Stir in sour cream until blended and serve.

Nutrition Info: Calories 368 Total Carbs 12g Net Carbs 11g Protein 46g Fat 13g Sugar 5g Fiber 1g

Grilled Cajun Beef Tenderloin

Servings: 12
Cooking Time: 1 Hour
Ingredients:

- 3 lb. beef tenderloin
- What you'll need from store cupboard:
- 1 tbsp. paprika
- 4 tsp salt

- 2 ¼ tsp onion powder
- 2 tsp cayenne pepper
- 1 ½ tsp garlic powder
- 1 ½ tsp white pepper
- 1 ½ tsp black pepper
- 1 tsp basil
- ½ tsp chili powder
- 1/8 tsp thyme
- 1/8 tsp ground mustard
- Dash of cloves
- Nonstick cooking spray.

Directions:

1.   Heat grill to medium heat. Spray rack with cooking spray.

2.   In a small bowl combine spices.

3.   Tie tenderloin with butcher string in 2-inch intervals. Rub outside of beef with spice mixture.

4.   Place on the grill, cover and cook 50 minutes, or to desired doneness. Or roast in 425 degree oven 45-60 minutes.

5.   Let rest 10 minutes before slicing and serving.

Nutrition Info: Calories 234 Total Carbs 2g Protein 33g Fat 10g Sugar 0g Fiber 0g

Cashew Chicken

Servings: 4
Cooking Time: 10 Minutes
Ingredients:

- 1 lb. skinless boneless chicken breast, cut in cubes
- 1/2 onion, sliced
- 2 tbsp. green onion, diced
- ½ tsp fresh ginger, peeled and grated
- What you'll need from store cupboard:
- 1 cup whole blanched cashews, toasted
- 1 clove garlic, diced fine
- 4 tbsp. oil
- 2 tbsp. dark soy sauce
- 2 tbsp. hoisin sauce
- 2 tbsp. water
- 2 tsp cornstarch
- 2 tsp dry sherry
- 1 tsp Splenda
- 1 tsp sesame seed oil

Directions:

1. Place chicken in a large bowl and add cornstarch, sherry, and ginger. Stir until well mixed.

2. In a small bowl, whisk together soy sauce, hoisin, Splenda, and water stirring until smooth.

3. Heat the oil in a wok or a large skillet over high heat. Add garlic and onion and cook, stirring until garlic sizzles, about 30 seconds.

4. Stir in chicken and cook, stirring frequently, until chicken is almost done, about 2 minutes.

5. Reduce heat to medium and stir in sauce mixture. Continue cooking and stirring until everything is blended together. Add cashews and cook 30 seconds.

6. Drizzle with sesame oil, and cook another 30 seconds, stirring constantly. Serve immediately garnished with green onions.

Nutrition Info: Calories 483 Total Carbs 19g Net Carbs 17g Protein 33g Fat 32g Sugar 6g Fiber 2g

Pork Chops With Creamy Marsala Sauce

Servings: 4
Cooking Time: 20 Minutes
Ingredients:

- 4 thin boneless pork loin chops, (about 1 pound), trimmed
- 4 thin slices prosciutto, (2 ounces), chopped
- 1 small onion, halve and slice thin
- 1 cup low-fat milk
- 3 tsp fresh oregano, chopped fine
- 3 tsp fresh chives, chopped fine
- What you'll need from store cupboard:
- ½ cup Marsala, (see Note), divided
- ¼ cup flour
- 2 tsp cornstarch
- 2 tsp extra-virgin olive oil
- ¼ tsp kosher salt
- ¼ tsp freshly ground pepper

Directions:

1. Mix 2 tablespoons of the wine with cornstarch, set aside.

2. Place flour in a shallow dish. Sprinkle chops with salt and pepper then coat in flour.

3. Heat oil in nonstick skillet over med-high heat. Once it gets hot, reduce heat to medium and

add pork. Cook until browned on both sides, 2 minutes per side. Transfer to a plate.

4. Add prosciutto to the pan and cook, stirring constantly, about 1minute, until browned. Add onion and cook, stirring frequently, 2-3 minutes until it starts to get soft.

5. Add remaining wine, oregano, and 1 ½ teaspoons chives to the pan and bring to a boil. Add milk and cornstarch mix and adjust heat to make sure mixture stays at a simmer. Stir occasionally until sauce has thickened and reduced slightly, about 4-6 minutes.

6. Add pork chops to the sauce, turning to coat, and cook until heated through. Serve topped with sauce and garnished with remaining chives.

Nutrition Info: Calories 499 Total Carbs 14g Net Carbs 13g Protein 32g Fat 32g Sugar 5g Fiber 1g

Chicken Skewers With Yogurt

Servings: 2-4
Cooking Time: 10 Minutes
Ingredients:

- 123g of plain whole milk Greek yogurt
- 20 ml of olive oil
- 2g of paprika
- 1g cumin
- 1g crushed red pepper
- 1 lemon, juice and zest of the peel
- 5g of salt
- 1g freshly ground black pepper
- 4 cloves garlic, minced
- 454g chicken thighs, boneless, skinless, cut into 38 mm pieces - 2 wooden skewers, cut in half
- Nonstick Spray Oil

Directions:

1. Mix the yogurt, olive oil, paprika, cumin, red paprika, lemon juice, lemon zest, salt, pepper, and garlic in a large bowl.

2. Add the chicken to the marinade and marinate in the fridge for at least 4 hours.

3. Select Preheat and press Start/Pause.

4. Cut the marinated chicken thighs into 38 mm pieces and spread them on skewers.

5. Place the skewers in the preheated air fryer.

6. Cook at 200°C for 10 minutes.

Nutrition Info: Calories: 113 Fat: 3.4Carbohydrates: 0g Protein: 20.6g

Provencal Ribs

Servings: 4
Cooking Time: 1h 20 Minutes
Ingredients:

- 500g of pork ribs
- Provencal herbs
- Salt - Ground pepper
- Oil

Directions:

1. Put the ribs in a bowl and add some oil, Provencal herbs, salt, and ground pepper.
2. Stir well and leave in the fridge for at least 1 hour. Put the ribs in the basket of the air fryer and select 2000C, 20 minutes.
3. From time to time, shake the basket and remove the ribs.

Nutrition Info: Calories: 296 Fat: 3.41g Carbohydrates: 0g Protein: 20.99g Sugar: 0gCholesterol: 90mg

Garlic Butter Steak

Servings: 4Cooking Time: 8 Minutes
Ingredients:

- 1 lb. skirt steak
- 1/4 cup fresh parsley, diced, divided
- 5 tbsp. margarine
- What you'll need from store cupboard:
- 6 tsp garlic, diced fine - 1 tbsp. olive oil
- Salt and pepper for taste

Directions:

1. Cut the steak into 4 pieces. Pat dry then season both sides with salt and pepper
2. Heat oil in a large, heavy skillet over med-high heat. Add steak and sear both sides, 2-3 minutes for medium rare, until it reaches desired doneness. Transfer to plate and cover with foil to keep warm.
3. Melt the margarine in a separate skillet over low heat. Add garlic and cook, stirring, until garlic is a light golden brown.
4. Pour the garlic mixture into a bowl and season with salt to taste. Slice the steak against the grain and place on plates. Sprinkle parsley over steak then drizzle with garlic mixture. Serve immediately.

Nutrition Info: Calories 365 Total Carbs 2g Protein 31g Fat 25g Sugar 0g Fiber 0g

Blue Cheese Crusted Beef Tenderloin

Servings: 4
Cooking Time: 15 Minutes
Ingredients:

- 4 beef tenderloin steaks
- 2 tbsp. blue cheese, crumbled
- 4 ½ tsp fresh parsley, diced
- 4 ½ tsp chives, diced
- 1 ½ tsp butter
- What you'll need from store cupboard:
- ½ cup low sodium beef broth
- 4 ½ tsp bread crumbs
- 1 tbsp. flour
- 1 tbsp. Madeira wine
- ¼ tsp pepper
- Nonstick cooking spray

Directions:

1. Heat oven to 350 degrees. Spray a large baking sheet with cooking spray.
2. In a small bowl, combine blue cheese, bread crumbs, parsley, chives, and pepper. Press onto one side of the steaks.
3. Spray a large skillet with cooking spray and place over med-high heat.
4. Add steaks and sear 2 minutes per side. Transfer to prepared baking sheet and bake 6-8 minutes, or steaks reach desired doneness.
5. Melt butter in a small saucepan over medium heat. Whisk in flour until smooth. Slowly whisk in broth and wine. Bring to a boil, cook, stirring, 2 minutes or until thickened.
6. Plate the steaks and top with gravy. Serve.

Nutrition Info: Calories 263 Total Carbs 4g Protein 36g Fat 10g Sugar 0g Fiber 0g

Turkey Enchiladas

Servings: 8
Cooking Time: 35 Minutes
Ingredients:

- 3 cup turkey, cooked and cut in pieces
- 1 onion, diced
- 1 bell pepper, diced
- 1 cup fat free sour cream
- 1 cup reduced fat cheddar cheese, grated
- What you'll need from store cupboard:
- 8 6-inch flour tortillas

• 14 ½ oz. low sodium chicken broth
• ¾ cup salsa - 3 tbsp. flour
• 2 tsp olive oil
• 1 ¼ tsp coriander
• ¼ tsp pepper
• Nonstick cooking spray

Directions:

1. Spray a large saucepan with cooking spray and heat oil over med-high heat. Add onion and bell pepper and cook until tender.

2. Sprinkle with flour, coriander and pepper and stir until blended. Slowly stir in broth. Bring to a boil and cook, stirring, 2 minutes or until thickened. Remove from heat and stir in sour cream and ¾ cup cheese. Heat oven to 350 degrees. Spray a 13x9-inch pan with cooking spray.

3. In a large bowl, combine turkey, salsa, and 1 cup of cheese mixture. Spoon 1/3 cup mixture down middle of each tortilla and roll up. Place seam side down in prepared dish.

4. Pour remaining cheese mixture over top of enchiladas. Cover and bake 20 minutes. Uncover and sprinkle with remaining cheese. Bake another 5-10 minutes until cheese is melted and starts to brown.

Nutrition Info: Calories 304 Total Carbs 29g Net Carbs 27g Protein 23g Fat 10g Sugar 5g Fiber 2g

Easy Carbonara

Servings: 2
Cooking Time: 10 Minutes
Ingredients:
• 1 slice bacon, thick cut
• 1 egg
• ½ tbsp. fresh parsley, diced
• What you'll need from store cupboard:
• Homemade Noodles, chapter 15
• ¼ cup reduced fat parmesan cheese
• Black pepper, to taste

Directions:

1. Bring a large pot of salted water to a boil. Add the noodles and cook 1-2 minutes.

2. In a small bowl, beat the egg and parmesan cheese together. Cook the bacon in a large pan until crispy. Remove the bacon (turn off the heat and leave the fat in the pan) and drain on a paper towel before cutting it into small pieces.

3. Once the noodles have boiled add them to the pan with the bacon fat. Pour the egg mixture over the hot pasta and toss together quickly (the heat from the pasta will cook the egg).

4. Add the chopped parsley, bacon and black pepper and continue tossing until combined. Serve.

Nutrition Info: Calories 237 Total Carbs 2g Protein 17g Fat 18g Sugar 0g Fiber 0g

Chicken Cordon Bleu

Servings: 8
Cooking Time: 25 Minutes
Ingredients:
• 8 chicken breast halves, boneless and skinless
• 8 slices ham
• 1 ½ cup mozzarella cheese, grated
• 2/3 cup skim milk
• ½ cup fat free sour cream
• What you'll need from store cupboard:
• 1 can low fat condensed cream of chicken soup
• 1 cup corn flakes, crushed
• 1 tsp lemon juice
• 1 tsp paprika - ½ tsp pepper
• ½ tsp garlic powder
• ¼ tsp salt
• Nonstick cooking spray

Directions:

1. Heat oven to 350 degrees. Spray a 13x9-inch baking dish with cooking spray.

2. Flatten chicken to ¼-inch thick. Sprinkle with pepper and top with slice of ham and 3 tablespoons of cheese down the middle. Roll up, tuck ends under and secure with a toothpick.

3. Pour milk into a shallow bowl. In a separate shallow bowl, combine corn flakes and seasonings. Dip chicken in milk then roll in corn flake mixture and place in prepared dish. Bake 25-30 minutes or until chicken is cooked through.

4. In a small saucepan, whisk together soup, sour cream, and lemon juice until combined. Cook over medium heat until hot.

5. Remove toothpicks from chicken and place on plates, top with sauce and serve.

Nutrition Info: Calories 382 Total Carbs 9g Net Carbs 8g Protein 50g Fat 14g Sugar 2g Fiber 1g

Chapter 14
Other Favorite Recipes

Grilled Avocado Hummus Paninis

Servings: 4
Cooking Time: 10 Minutes
Ingredients:
4 whole-wheat sandwich thins, split in half
1/3 cup roasted red pepper hummus
½ medium avocado, pitted and sliced thin
Fresh ground pepper
1 cup fresh baby spinach, chopped
2 ounces feta cheese
Directions:
Lay the sandwich thins out flat.
Spread the hummus evenly on both sides of each sandwich thin.
Layer the avocado slices on the bottom of each sandwich thin and season with fresh ground black pepper.
Top each sandwich with ¼ cup spinach and ½ ounce cheese.
Add the top to each sandwich and press down lightly.
Grease a large skillet with cooking spray and heat over medium heat.
Add one or two sandwiches and place a heavy skillet on top.
Cook for 2 minutes or until the bottoms are toasted.
Flip the sandwiches and repeat on the other side.
Cut in half to serve.
Nutrition Info: Calories 230, Total Fat 11.2g, Saturated Fat 3.2g, Total Carbs 27.8g, Net Carbs 19.2g, Protein 8.5g, Sugar 3.5g, Fiber 8.6g, Sodium 508mg

Cauliflower Muffin

Servings: 4
Cooking Time: 30 Minutes
Ingredients:
2,5 cup cauliflower
2/3 cup ham
2,5 cups of cheese
2/3 cup champignon
1,5 tbsp. flaxseed
3 eggs
1/4 tsp. salt
1/8 tsp. pepper
Directions:
Preheat oven to 375 F.
Put muffin liners in a 12-muffin tin.
Combine diced cauliflower, ground flaxseed, beaten eggs, cup diced ham, grated cheese, and diced mushrooms, salt, pepper.
Divide mixture rightly between muffin liners.
Bake 30 Minutes.
This is a great lunch for the whole family.
Nutrition Info: Calories 116 / Protein 10 g / Fat 7 g / Carbs 3 g

Bok Choy Soup

Servings: 4Cooking Time: 25 Minutes
Ingredients:
2 tablespoons coconut oil, melted
1-pound bok choy, torn
2 shallots, chopped

4 cups chicken stock
1 cup heavy cream
1 tablespoon cilantro, chopped
A pinch of salt and black pepper
½ teaspoon nutmeg, ground
Directions:
Heat up a pot with the oil over medium heat, add the shallots and sauté for 5 minutes.
Add the bok choy and the other ingredients, bring to a simmer and cook over medium heat for 20 minutes.
Blend the soup using an immersion blender, divide into bowls and serve.
Nutrition Info: calories 194 fat 18.4 fiber 1.4 carbs 5.4 protein 3.2

Stuffed Mushrooms

Servings: 4
Cooking Time: 20 Minutes
Ingredients:
4 Portobello Mushrooms, large
1/2 cup Mozzarella Cheese, shredded
1/2 cup Marinara, low-sugar
Olive Oil Spray
Directions:
Preheat the oven to 375 F.
Take out the dark gills from the mushrooms with the help of a spoon.
Keep the mushroom stem upside down and spoon it with two tablespoons of marinara sauce and mozzarella cheese.
Bake for 18 minutes or until the cheese is bubbly.
Nutrition Info: Calories – 113kL; Fat – 6g; Carbohydrates – 4g; Protein – 7g; Sodium – 14mg

Roasted Salmon With Lemon

Servings: 6
Cooking Time: 25 Minutes
Ingredients:
1 salmon whole-side fillet, skin on
2 T. lemon juice
1 bunch fresh dill, chopped
4 T. butter
2 T. white wine
1/2 tsp. kosher salt
1/4 tsp. freshly ground black pepper
Directions:
Allow salmon to come to room temperature before baking. Preheat oven to 425°F. Mix dill and lemon juice in a small bowl. Lay fillet skin-side down on a parchment-lined baking sheet and cover with lemon-dill mixture. Top with butter, white wine, salt, and pepper. Bake uncovered until the fish flakes easily with a fork, about 20-25 minutes.
Nutrition Info: Calories: 146.7 Fat: 10.9g Cholesterol: 49.1mg Sodium: 237.3mg Potassium: 269.5mg Carbohydrates: 0.8g Dietary Fiber: 0.1g Sugars: 0.2g Protein: 10.3g

White Spinach Pizza With Cauliflower Crust

Servings: 1 10-inch Pizza
Cooking Time: 25 Minutes
Ingredients:
1 head cauliflower, trimmed and chopped
2 eggs, beaten
2 c. shredded mozzarella cheese, divided
1/4 c. grated Parmesan cheese
2 tsp. Italian seasoning
3 T. extra virgin olive oil
1/2 c. shredded provolone cheese
3/4 c. whole milk ricotta cheese
3 cloves garlic, minced
1/4 c. thinly sliced red onion
1 c. baby spinach, washed
Directions:
To make the crust, pulse cauliflower florets in a food processor until they resemble rice. Microwave, covered loosely, for 5 minutes. Drain cauliflower in paper towel or cheesecloth, wringing out the towel to remove as much moisture as possible. Mix drained cauliflower with eggs, 1/2 cup of the mozzarella, Parmesan, and Italian seasoning. Press into a 10-inch round (or 10x15-inch rectangle) and bake at 425°F for 10-15 minutes. Brush crust with olive oil and top with remaining mozzarella, provolone, ricotta, garlic, red onion, and spinach.
Bake for an additional 10 minutes or until the cheese is melted. This crust recipe will work with any toppings.
Nutrition Info: Calories: 350.3 Fat: 25.6g Cholesterol: 116.7mg Sodium: 558.7mg Potassium: 415.8mg Carbohydrates: 9.3g Dietary Fiber: 2.8g Sugars: 0.8g Protein: 22.4g

Chickpea, Tuna, And Kale Salad

Servings: 1Cooking Time: None
Ingredients:
2 ounces fresh kale
2 tablespoons fat-free honey mustard dressing
1 (3-ounce) pouch tuna in water, drained
1 medium carrot, shredded
Salt and pepper
Directions:
Trim the thick stems from the kale and cut into bite-sized pieces.
Toss the kale with the dressing in a salad bowl.
Top with tuna, chickpeas, and carrots. Season with salt and pepper to serve.
Nutrition Info: Calories 215, Total Fat 0.6g, Saturated Fat 0g, Total Carbs 28.1g, Net Carbs 23.6g, Protein 22.5g, Sugar 16g, Fiber 4.5g, Sodium 1176mg

Tomato Risotto

Servings: 4Cooking Time: 30 Minutes
Ingredients:
1 cup shallots, chopped
cups cauliflower rice
tablespoons olive oil
cups veggie stock
1 cup tomatoes, crushed
¼ cup cilantro, chopped
½ teaspoon chili powder
1 teaspoon cumin, ground
1 teaspoon coriander, ground
Directions:
Heat up a pan with the oil over medium heat, add the shallots and sauté for 5 minutes.
Add the cauliflower rice, tomatoes and the other ingredients, toss, cook over medium heat for 25 minutes more, divide between plates and serve.
Nutrition Info: Calories 200 Fat 4 Fiber 3 Carbs 6 Protein 8

Oats Coffee Smoothie

Servings: 2
Cooking Time: 5 Minutes
Ingredients:
1 cup Oats, uncooked & grounded
2 tbsp. Instant Coffee
3 cup Milk, skimmed
2 Banana, frozen & sliced into chunks
2 tbsp. Flax Seeds, grounded
Directions:
Place all of the ingredients in a high-speed blender and blend for 2 minutes or until smooth and luscious.
Serve and enjoy.
Nutrition Info: Calories: 251Kcal; Carbs 10.9g; Proteins: 20.3g; Fat: 15.1g; Sodium: 102mg

Premium Roasted Baby Potatoes

Servings: 4
Cooking Time: 35 Minutes
Ingredients:
2 pounds' new yellow potatoes, scrubbed and cut into wedges
2 tablespoons extra virgin olive oil
2 teaspoons fresh rosemary, chopped
1 teaspoon garlic powder
1 teaspoon sweet paprika
½ teaspoon sea salt
½ teaspoon freshly ground black pepper
Directions:
Pre-heat your oven to 400 degrees Fahrenheit.
Line baking sheet with aluminum foil and set it aside.
Take a large bowl and add potatoes, olive oil, garlic, rosemary, paprika, sea salt and pepper.
Spread potatoes in single layer on baking sheet and bake for 35 minutes.
Serve and enjoy!
Nutrition Info: Calories: 225 Fat: 7g Carbohydrates: 37g Protein: 5g

Chicken, Strawberry, And Avocado Salad

Cooking Time: 5 Minutes
Ingredients:
1,5 cups chicken (skin removed)
1/4 cup almonds
2 (5-oz) pkg salad greens
1 (16-oz) pkg strawberries
1 avocado
1/4 cup green onion
1/4 cup lime juice
3 tbsp. extra virgin olive oil
2 tbsp. honey
1/4 tsp. salt
1/4 tsp. pepper

Directions:

Toast almonds until golden and fragrant.

Mix lime juice, oil, honey, salt, and pepper.

Mix greens, sliced strawberries, chicken, diced avocado, and sliced green onion and sliced almonds; drizzle with dressing. Toss to coat.

Yummy!

Nutrition Info: Calories 150 / Protein 15 g / Fat 10 g / Carbs 5 g

Lemony Brussels Sprout

Servings: 2Cooking Time: 7 Minutes

Ingredients:

½ pound Brussels sprouts, halved

1 tablespoon olive oil

1 garlic clove, minced

½ teaspoon red pepper flakes, crushed

Salt and ground black pepper, as required

1 tablespoon fresh lemon juice

Directions:

Heat the olive oil in a large skillet over medium heat and cook the garlic and red pepper flakes for about 1 minute, stirring continuously.

Stir in the Brussels sprouts, salt and black pepper and sauté for about 4-5 minutes.

Stir in lemon juice and sauté for about 1 minute more.

Serve hot.

Meal Prep Tip: Transfer the Brussels sprouts into a large bowl and set aside to cool completely. Divide the Brussels sprouts into 2 containers evenly. Cover the containers and refrigerate for about 1-2 days. Reheat in the microwave before serving.

Nutrition Info: Calories 114 Total Fat 7.5 g Saturated Fat 1.2 g Cholesterol 0 mg Total Carbs 11.2 g Sugar 2.7 g Fiber 4.4 g Sodium 108 mg Potassium 465 mg Protein 4.1 g

Easy Egg Salad

Servings: 4

Cooking Time: 15 To 20 Minutes

Ingredients:

6 Eggs, preferably free-range

¼ tsp. Salt

2 tbsp. Mayonnaise

1 tsp. Lemon juice

1 tsp. Dijon mustard

Pepper, to taste

Lettuce leaves, to serve

Directions:

Keep the eggs in a saucepan of water and pour cold water until it covers the egg by another 1 inch.

Bring to a boil and then remove the eggs from heat.

Peel the eggs under cold running water.

Transfer the cooked eggs into a food processor and pulse them until chopped.

Stir in the mayonnaise, lemon juice, salt, Dijon mustard, and pepper and mix them well.

Taste for seasoning and add more if required.

Serve in the lettuce leaves.

Nutrition Info: Calories – 166kcal; Fat – 14g; Carbohydrates - 0.85g; Proteins – 10g; Sodium: 132mg

Cherry Tomato Salad

Servings: 6

Cooking Time: None

Ingredients:

40 cherry tomatoes, halved

1 cup mozzarella balls, halved

1 cup green olives, sliced

1 can (6 oz) black olives, sliced

2 green onions, chopped

3 oz roasted pine nuts

Dressing:

½ cup olive oil

2 tbsp red wine vinegar

1 tsp dried oregano

Salt and pepper to taste

Directions:

In a salad bowl, combine the tomatoes, olives and onions.

Prepare the dressing by combining olive oil with red wine vinegar, dried oregano, salt and pepper.

Sprinkle with the dressing and add the nuts.

Let marinate in the fridge for 1 hour.

Nutrition Info: Carbohydrates: 10.7 g Protein: 2.4 g Total sugars: 3.6 g

Spaghetti Squash Mash

Servings: 4

Cooking Time: 1 Hour

Ingredients:

Spaghetti squash (halved, seeds removed) - 1

Olive oil: 2 tablespoon

Garlic powder: 1 teaspoon

Dried rosemary: 1 teaspoon

Dried parsley: 1 teaspoon
Dried thyme: 1 teaspoon
Sage: ½ teaspoon
Salt: 1 teaspoon
Cracked pepper: ½ teaspoon
Directions:
Put a little water in a baking pan and place the squash halves in it, cut side down.
Roast in an oven preheated to 350 degrees Fahrenheit for 45 minutes to an hour.
Remove, leave to cool and then scoop out all the flesh.
Place the squash in a bowl and mix in the rest of the ingredients.
Place in the oven and cook for 15 minutes more.
Nutrition Info: 91 Cal, 7 g total fat, 5.5 g net carb., 1.5 g fiber, 3 g protein.

Quick Zucchini Bowl

Servings: 4
Cooking Time: 10 Minutes
Ingredients:
½ pound of pasta
2 tablespoons of olive oil
6 crushed garlic cloves
1 teaspoon of red chili
2 finely sliced spring onions
3 teaspoons of chopped rosemary
1 large zucchini cut up in half, lengthways and sliced
5 large portabella mushrooms
1 can of tomatoes
4 tablespoons of Parmesan cheese
Fresh ground black pepper
Directions:
Cook the pasta in boiling water until Al Dente.
Take a large-sized frying pan and place over medium heat.
Add oil and allow the oil to heat up.
Add garlic, onion and chili and sauté for a few minutes until golden.
Add zucchini, rosemary and mushroom and sauté for a few minutes.
Increase the heat to medium-high and add tinned tomatoes to the sauce until thick.
Drain your boiled pasta and transfer to a serving platter.
Pour the tomato mix on top and mix using tongs.

Garnish with Parmesan cheese and freshly ground black pepper.
Enjoy!
Nutrition Info:Calories: 361 Fat: 12g Carbohydrates: 47g Protein: 14g

Blueberry Smoothie

Servings: 2
Cooking Time: 2 Minutes
Ingredients:
1 tbsp. Lemon Juice
1 ¾ cup Coconut Milk, full-fat
1/2 tsp. Vanilla Extract
3 oz. Blueberries, frozen
Directions:
Combine coconut milk, blueberries, lemon juice, and vanilla extract in a high-speed blender.
Blend for 2 minutes for a smooth and luscious smoothie.
Serve and enjoy.
Nutrition Info: Calories: 417cal; Carbohydrates: 9g; Proteins: 4g; Fat: 43g; Sodium: 35mg

Beef Chili

Servings: 4
Cooking Time: 20 Minutes
Ingredients:
1/2 tsp. Garlic Powder
1 tsp. Coriander, grounded
1 lb. Beef, grounded
1/2 tsp. Sea Salt
1/2 tsp. Cayenne Pepper
1 tsp. Cumin, grounded
1/2 tsp. Pepper, grounded
1/2 cup Salsa, low-carb & no-sugar
Directions:
Heat a large-sized pan over medium-high heat and cook the beef in it until browned.
Stir in all the spices and cook them for 7 minutes or until everything is combined.
When the beef gets cooked, spoon in the salsa.
Bring the mixture to a simmer and cook for another 8 minutes or until everything comes together.
Take it from heat and transfer to a serving bowl.
Nutrition Info: Calories: 229Kcal; Fat: 10g; Carbohydrates: 2g; Proteins: 33g; Sodium: 675mg

Avocado Turmeric Smoothie

Servings: 1
Cooking Time: 2 Minutes
Ingredients:
1/2 of 1 Avocado
1 cup Ice, crushed
¾ cup Coconut Milk, full-fat
1 tsp. Lemon Juice
¼ cup Almond Milk
1/2 tsp. Turmeric
1 tsp. Ginger, freshly grated
Directions:
Place all the ingredients excluding the crushed ice in a high-speed blender and blend for 2 to 3 minutes or until smooth.
Transfer to a serving glass and enjoy it.
Nutrition Info: Calories: 232cal; Carbs: 4.1g; Proteins: 1.7g; Fat: 22.4g; Sodium: 25mg

Fried Okra

Servings: 4
Cooking Time: 15 Minutes
Ingredients:
2 teaspoons Cajun seasoning, divided
1 cup buttermilk
8 oz. okra
½ cup white whole-wheat flour
½ cup cornstarch
⅓ cup oil
Salt to taste
Directions:
Mix half of the Cajun seasoning and buttermilk in a bowl.
Add the okra.
Mix well.
Let sit for 10 minutes.
In another bowl, blend the remaining Cajun seasoning, flour and cornstarch.
Drain the okra.
Dip each okra in the flour mixture.
Pour the oil in a pan over medium high heat.
Cook the okra until golden on all sides.
Season with salt before serving.
Nutrition Info: Calories 106 Total Fat 5 g Saturated Fat 0 g Cholesterol 0 mg Sodium 75 mg Total Carbohydrate 14 g Dietary Fiber 2 g Total Sugars 1 g Protein 2 g Potassium 195 mg

Cinnamon Roll Smoothie

Servings: 1
Cooking Time: 0 Minutes
Ingredients:
1 tsp. Flax Meal or oats, if preferred
1 cup Almond Milk
1/2 tsp. Cinnamon
2 tbsp. Protein Powder
1 cup Ice
¼ tsp. Vanilla Extract
4 tsp. Sweetener of your choice
Directions:
Pour the milk into the blender, followed by the protein powder, sweetener, flax meal, cinnamon, vanilla extract, and ice.
Blend for 40 seconds or until smooth.
Serve and enjoy.
Nutrition Info: Calories: 145cal; Carbs: 1.6g; Proteins: 26.5g; Fat: 3.25g; Sodium: 30mg

Cobb Salad

Servings: 1
Cooking Time: 5 Minutes
Ingredients:
4 Cherry Tomatoes, chopped
¼ cup Bacon, cooked & crumbled
1/2 of 1 Avocado, chopped
2 oz. Chicken Breast, shredded
1 Egg, hardboiled
2 cups Mixed Green salad
1 oz. Feta Cheese, crumbled
Directions:
Toss all the ingredients for the Cobb salad in a large mixing bowl and toss well.
Serve and enjoy it.
Nutrition Info: Calories: 307Kcal; Carbohydrates: 3g; Proteins: 27g; Fat: 20g; Sodium: 522mg

Garlic Sautée D Spinach

Servings: 4
Cooking Time: 10 Minutes
Ingredients:
1 1/2 tablespoons olive oil
4 cloves minced garlic
6 cups fresh baby spinach
Salt and pepper

Directions:

Heat the oil in a large skillet over medium-high heat. Add the garlic and cook for 1 minute.

Stir in the spinach and season with salt and pepper. Sauté for 1 to 2 minutes until just wilted. Serve hot.

Nutrition Info: Calories 60, Total Fat 5.5g, Saturated Fat 0.8g, Total Carbs 2.6g, Net Carbs 1.5g, Protein 1.5g, Sugar 0.2g, Fiber 1.1g, Sodium 36mg

Garlic Bread

Servings: 4-5

Cooking Time: 15 Minutes

Ingredients:

2 stale French rolls

4 tbsp. crushed or crumpled garlic

1 cup of mayonnaise

Powdered grated Parmesan

1 tbsp. olive oil

Directions:

Preheat the air fryer. Set the time of 5 minutes and the temperature to 2000C.

Mix mayonnaise with garlic and set aside.

Cut the baguettes into slices, but without separating them completely.

Fill the cavities of equals. Brush with olive oil and sprinkle with grated cheese. Place in the basket of the air fryer. Set the timer to 10 minutes, adjust the temperature to 1800C and press the power button.

Nutrition Info: Calories: 340 Fat: 15g Carbohydrates: 32g Protein: 15g Sugar: 0g Cholesterol: 0mg

Tuna Avocado Salad

Servings: 4

Cooking Time: 0 Minutes

Ingredients:

1 avocado, pit removed and sliced

1 lemon, juiced

1 tablespoon chopped onion

5 ounces cooked or canned tuna

Salt and pepper to taste

Directions:

In a mixing bowl, combine the avocado and lime juice. Mash the avocado and add the tuna.

Season with salt and pepper to taste.

Serve chilled.

Nutrition Info: Calories: 695.5g Fat: 50.7 g Protein: 41.5 g Carbs: 18.3 g

French Toast In Sticks

Servings: 4

Cooking Time: 10 Minutes

Ingredients:

4 slices of white bread, 38 mm thick, preferably hard

2 eggs

60 ml of milk

15 ml maple sauce

2 ml vanilla extract

Nonstick Spray Oil

38g of sugar

3ground cinnamon

Maple syrup, to serve

Sugar to sprinkle

Directions:

Cut each slice of bread into thirds making 12 pieces. Place sideways

Beat the eggs, milk, maple syrup and vanilla.

Preheat the air fryer, set it to 175C.

Dip the sliced bread in the egg mixture and place it in the preheated air fryer. Sprinkle French toast generously with oil spray.

Cook French toast for 10 minutes at 175C. Turn the toast halfway through cooking.

Mix the sugar and cinnamon in a bowl.

Cover the French toast with the sugar and cinnamon mixture when you have finished cooking.

Serve with Maple syrup and sprinkle with powdered sugar

Nutrition Info: Calories 128 Fat 6.2 g, Carbohydrates 16.3 g, Sugar 3.3 g, Protein 3.2 g, Cholesterol 17 mg

Strawberry Salsa

Servings: 4

Cooking Time: 5 Minutes;

Ingredients:

4 tomatoes, seeded and chopped

1-pint strawberry, chopped

1 red onion, chopped

2 tablespoons of juice from a lime

1 jalapeno pepper, minced

What you will need from the store cupboard:

1 tablespoon olive oil

2 garlic cloves, minced

Directions:

Bring together the strawberries, tomatoes, jalapeno, and onion in the bowl.

Stir in the garlic, oil, and lime juice.

Refrigerate. Serve with separately cooked pork or poultry.

Nutrition Info: Calories 19, Carbs 3g, Fiber 1g, Sugar 0.2g, Cholesterol 0mg, Total Fat 1g, Protein 0g

Southwestern Bean-and-pepper Salad

Servings: 4

Cooking Time: 0 Minutes

Ingredients:

1 (15-ounce) can pinto beans, drained and rinsed

2 bell peppers, cored and chopped

1 cup corn kernels (cut from 1 to 2 ears or frozen and thawed)

Salt

Freshly ground black pepper

Juice of 2 limes

1 tablespoon olive oil

1 avocado, chopped

Directions:

In a large bowl, combine beans, peppers, corn, salt, and pepper. Squeeze fresh lime juice to taste and stir in olive oil. Let the mixture stand in the refrigerator for 30 minutes.

Add avocado just before serving.

Budget-saver tip avocado prices can vary dramatically depending on their availability. In addition, while avocado in your salad can really add flavor and satiety, for an equally delicious salad you could add a cup of cooked and chopped sweet potatoes with 1 to 2 tablespoons of sunflower seeds.

Nutrition Info: Total calories: 245 Total fat: 11g Saturated fat: 2g Cholesterol: 0mg Sodium: 97mg Potassium: 380mg Total carbohydrate: 32g Fiber: 10g Sugars: 4g Protein: 8g.

Sautéed Turkey Bowl

Servings: 1

Cooking Time: 10 Minutes

Ingredients:

4 ounces boneless, skinless turkey breast

1 teaspoon olive oil

1 ½ teaspoons balsamic vinegar

½ teaspoon dried basil

¼ teaspoon dried thyme

Salt and pepper

¼ cup instant brown rice

Directions:

Toss the turkey with the olive oil, balsamic vinegar, basil, and thyme.

Season lightly with salt and pepper then cover and chill for 20 minutes.

Bring ¼ cup of water to boil in a small saucepan. Stir in the brown rice then simmer for 5 minutes and remove from heat, covered.

Meanwhile, heat a small skillet over medium heat and grease lightly with cooking spray.

Add the marinated turkey and sauté for 6 to 8 minutes until cooked through. Spoon the turkey over the brown rice and serve hot.

Nutrition Info: Calories: 200, Total Fat 6.8g, Saturated Fat 1.1g, Total Carbs 13.3g, Net Carbs 12.1g, Protein 20.4g, Sugar 4g, Fiber 1.2g, Sodium 1152mg

Cauliflower & Apple Salad

Servings: 4

Cooking Time: 0 Minutes

Ingredients:

3 Cups Cauliflower, Chopped into Florets

2 Cups Baby Kale

1 Sweet Apple, Cored & Chopped

¼ Cup Basil, Fresh & Chopped

¼ Cup Mint, Fresh & Chopped

¼ Cup Parsley, Fresh & Chopped

1/3 Cup Scallions, Sliced Thin

2 Tablespoons Yellow Raisins

1 Tablespoon Sun Dried Tomatoes, Chopped

½ Cup Miso Dressing, Optional

¼ Cup Roasted Pumpkin Seeds, Optional

Directions:

Combine everything together, tossing before serving. Interesting Facts: This vegetable is an extremely high source of vitamin A, vitamin B1, B2 and B3.

Nutrition Info: Calories: 198 Protein: 7 Grams Fat: 8 Grams Carbs: 32 Grams

Zucchini Risotto

Servings: 4

Cooking Time: 30 Minutes

Ingredients:

½ cup shallots, chopped

tablespoons olive oil
garlic cloves, minced
cups cauliflower rice
cup zucchinis, cubed
cups veggie stock
½ cup white mushrooms, chopped
½ teaspoon coriander, ground
A pinch of salt and black pepper
¼ teaspoon oregano, dried
tablespoons parsley, chopped
Directions:
Heat up a pan with the oil over medium heat, add the shallots, garlic, mushrooms, coriander and oregano, stir and sauté for 10 minutes.
Add the cauliflower rice and the other ingredients, toss, cook for 20 minutes more, divide between plates and serve.
Nutrition Info: Calories 231 fat 5 fiber 3 carbs 9 protein 12

Peanut Butter Mousse

Servings: 2Cooking Time: 10 Minutes
Ingredients:
1 tbsp. peanut butter
1 tsp. vanilla extract
1 tsp. stevia
1/2 cup heavy cream
Directions:
Add all ingredients into the bowl and whisk until soft peak forms.
Spoon into the serving bowls and enjoy.
Nutrition Info: Calories 157 Fat 15.1 g, Carbohydrates 5.2 g, Sugar 3.6 g, Protein 2.6 g, Cholesterol 41 mg

Peanut Butter Banana Smoothie

Servings: 1Cooking Time: 2 Minutes
Ingredients:
¼ cup Greek Yoghurt, plain
1/2 tbsp. Chia Seeds
1/2 cup Ice Cubes
1/2 of 1 Banana
1/2 cup Water
1 tbsp. Peanut Butter
Directions:
Place all the ingredients needed to make the smoothie in a high-speed blender and blend to get a smooth and luscious mixture.

Transfer the smoothie to a serving glass and enjoy it.
Nutrition Info: Calories: 202cal; Carbohydrates: 14g; Proteins: 10g; Fat: 9g; Sodium: 30mg

Salmon With Asparagus

Servings: 3
Cooking Time: 10 Minutes
Ingredients:
1 lb. Salmon, sliced into fillets
1 tbsp. Olive Oil
Salt & Pepper, as needed
1 bunch of Asparagus, trimmed
2 cloves of Garlic, minced
Zest & Juice of 1/2 Lemon
1 tbsp. Butter, salted
Directions:
Spoon in the butter and olive oil into a large pan and heat it over medium-high heat.
Once it becomes hot, place the salmon and season it with salt and pepper.
Cook for 4 minutes per side and then cook the other side.
Stir in the garlic and lemon zest to it.
Cook for further 2 minutes or until slightly browned.
Off the heat and squeeze the lemon juice over it.
Serve it hot.
Nutrition Info: Calories: 409Kcal; Carbohydrates: 2.7g; Proteins: 32.8g; Fat: 28.8g; Sodium: 497mg

Roasted Tomatoes

Servings: 4
Cooking Time: 25 Minutes
Ingredients:
1-pound tomatoes, halved
A pinch of salt and black pepper
2 tablespoons olive oil
1 teaspoon rosemary, dried
1 teaspoon basil, dried
1 tablespoon chives, chopped
Directions:
In a roasting pan combine the tomatoes with the oil and the other ingredients, toss gently and bake at 390 degrees F for 25 minutes.
Divide the mix between plates and serve.
Nutrition Info: calories 124 fat 14 fiber 4 carbs 4 protein 14

Crispy Radishes

Servings: 4
Cooking Time: 20 Minutes
Ingredients:
Cooking spray
15 radishes, sliced
Salt and black pepper to the taste
1 tablespoon chives, chopped
Directions:
Arrange radish slices on a lined baking sheet and spray them with cooking oil.
Season with salt and pepper and sprinkle chives, introduce in the oven at 375 degrees F and bake for 10 minutes.
Flip them and bake for 10 minutes more.
Serve them cold.
Enjoy!
Nutrition Info: calories 34 fat 4 fiber 0.4 carbs 4 protein 0.1

Edamame Salad

Servings: 1
Cooking Time: 0 Minutes
Ingredients:
¼ Cup Red Onion, Chopped
1 Cup Corn Kernels, Fresh
1 Cup Edamame Beans, Shelled & Thawed
1 Red Bell Pepper, Chopped
2-3 Tablespoons Lime Juice, Fresh
5-6 Basil Leaves, Fresh & Sliced
5-6 Mint Leaves, Fresh & Sliced
Sea Salt & Black Pepper to Taste
Directions:
Place everything into a Mason jar, and then seal the jar tightly. Shake well before serving.
Interesting Facts: Whole corn is a fantastic source of phosphorus, magnesium, and B vitamins. It also promotes healthy digestion and contains heart-healthy antioxidants. It is important to seek out organic corn in order to bypass all of the genetically modified product that is out on the market.
Nutrition Info: Calories: 299 Protein: 20 Grams Fat: 9 Grams Carbs: 38 Grams

Summer Chickpea Salad

Servings: 4
Cooking Time: 15 Minutes
Ingredients:
1 ½ Cups Cherry Tomatoes, Halved
1 Cup English Cucumber, Slices
1 Cup Chickpeas, Canned, Unsalted, Drained & Rinsed
¼ Cup Red Onion, Slivered
2 Tablespoon Olive Oil
1 ½ Tablespoons Lemon Juice, Fresh
1 ½ Tablespoons Lemon Juice, Fresh
Sea Salt & Black Pepper to Taste
Directions:
Mix everything together, and toss to combine before serving.
Nutrition Info: Calories: 145 Protein: 4 Grams Fat: 7.5 Grams Carbs: 16 Grams

Herbed Risotto

Servings: 4
Cooking Time: 25 Minutes
Ingredients:
cups cauliflower rice
scallions, chopped
tablespoons avocado oil
cups veggie stock
Juice of 1 lime
1 tablespoon parsley, chopped
1 tablespoon cilantro, chopped
1 tablespoon basil, chopped
1 tablespoon oregano, chopped
1 teaspoon sweet paprika
A pinch of salt and black pepper
Directions:
Heat up a pan with the oil over medium heat, add the scallions and sauté for 5 minutes.
Add the cauliflower rice, the stock and the other ingredients, toss, cook over medium heat for 20 minutes, divide between plates and serve as a side dish.
Nutrition Info: Calories 182 fat 4 fiber 2 carbs 8 protein 10

Roasted Radish With Fresh Herbs

Servings: 4
Cooking Time: 30 Minutes
Ingredients:
1 tbsp. coconut oil
1 bunch radishes
2 tbsps. Minced chives
1 tbsp. minced rosemary
1 tbsp. minced thyme

Directions:

Wash the radishes, then remove the tops and stems. Cut them into quarters and reserve.

Add the oil to a cast iron pan, then heat to medium.

Add the radishes, then season with salt and pepper.

Cook on medium heat for 6-8 minutes, until almost tender, then add the herbs and cook through.

The radishes can be served warm with meats or chilled with salads.

Nutrition Info: Net carbs: 1.8g, Protein: .9g, Fat: 13g, Calories: 133kcal.

Rib Eyes With Broccoli

Servings: 4

Cooking Time: 15 Minutes

Ingredients:

4 ounces butter

¾ pound Ribeye steak, sliced

9 ounces broccoli, chopped

1 yellow onion, sliced

1 tablespoon coconut aminos

1 tablespoon pumpkin seeds

Salt and pepper to taste

Directions:

Slice steak and the onions

Chop broccoli, including the stem parts

Take a frying pan and place it over medium heat, add butter and let it melt

Add meat and season accordingly with salt and pepper

Cook until both sides are browned

Transfer meat to a platter

Add broccoli and onion to the frying pan, add more butter if needed

Brown

Add coconut aminos and return the meat

Stir and season again

Serve with a dollop of butter with a sprinkle of pumpkin seeds

Enjoy!

Nutrition Info: Calories: 875 Fat: 75g Carbohydrates: 8g Protein: 40g

Salmon, Quinoa, And Avocado Salad

Servings: 4

Cooking Time: 20 Minutes

Ingredients:

½ cup quinoa

1 cup water

4 (4-ounce) salmon fillets

1-pound asparagus, trimmed

1 teaspoon extra-virgin olive oil, plus 2 tablespoons

½ teaspoon salt, divided

½ teaspoon freshly ground black pepper, divided

¼ teaspoon red pepper flakes

1 avocado, chopped

¼ cup chopped scallions, both white and green parts

¼ cup chopped fresh cilantro

1 tablespoon minced fresh oregano

Juice of 1 lime

Directions:

In a small pot, combine the quinoa and water, and bring to a boil over medium-high heat. Cover, reduce the heat, and simmer for 15 minutes.Preheat the oven to 425°F. Line a large baking sheet with parchment paper.

Arrange the salmon on one side of the prepared baking sheet.Toss the asparagus with 1 teaspoon of olive oil, and arrange on the other side of the baking sheet. Season the salmon and asparagus with ¼ teaspoon of salt, ¼ teaspoon of pepper, and the red pepper flakes. Roast for 12 minutes until browned and cooked through.

While the fish and asparagus are cooking, in a large mixing bowl, gently toss the cooked quinoa, avocado, scallions, cilantro, and oregano. Add the remaining 2 tablespoons of olive oil and the lime juice, and season with the remaining ¼ teaspoon of salt and ¼ teaspoon of pepper.

Break the salmon into pieces, removing the skin and any bones, and chop the asparagus into bite-sized pieces. Fold into the quinoa and serve warm or at room temperature.

Nutrition Info: Calories: 397 Total Fat: 22g Protein: 29g Carbohydrates: 23g Sugars: 3g Fiber: 8g Sodium: 292mg

Orange Scallions And Brussels Sprouts

Servings: 4

Cooking Time: 25 Minutes

Ingredients:

pound Brussels sprouts, trimmed and halved

1 cup scallions, chopped

Zest of 1 lime, grated

tablespoon olive oil

¼ cup orange juice

tablespoons stevia

A pinch of salt and black pepper

Directions:

Heat up a pan with the oil over medium heat, add the scallions and sauté for 5 minutes.

Add the sprouts and the other ingredients, toss, cook over medium heat for 20 minutes more, divide the mix between plates and serve.

Nutrition Info: Calories 193 Fat 4 Fiber 1 Carbs 8 Protein 10

Carrot Ginger Soup

Servings: 4

Cooking Time: 20 Minutes

Ingredients:

1 tablespoon olive oil

1 medium yellow onion, chopped

3 cups fat-free chicken broth

1 pound carrots, peeled and chopped

1 tablespoon fresh grated ginger

¼ cup fat-free sour cream

Salt and pepper

Directions:

Heat the oil in a large saucepan over medium heat.Add the onions and sauté for 5 minutes until softened.Stir in the broth, carrots, and ginger then cover and bring to a boil

Reduce heat and simmer for 20 minutes.

Stir in the sour cream then remove from heat.

Blend using an immersion blender until smooth and creamy.Season with salt and pepper to taste then serve hot.

Nutrition Info: Calories 125, Total Fat 3.6g, Saturated Fat 0.5g, Total Carbs 17.2g, Net Carbs 13.6g, Protein 6.4g, Sugar 7.8g, Fiber 3.6g, Sodium 385mg

Shrimp And Black Bean Salad

Servings: 6

Cooking Time: None

Ingredients:

¼ cup apple cider vinegar

3 tablespoons olive oil

1 teaspoon ground cumin

½ teaspoon chipotle chili powder

¼ teaspoon salt

1 pound cooked shrimp, peeled and deveined

1 (15-ounce) can black beans, rinsed and drained

1 cup diced tomatoes

1 small green pepper, diced

¼ cup sliced green onions

¼ cup fresh chopped cilantro

Directions:

Whisk together the vinegar, olive oil, cumin, chili powder, and salt in a large bowl.

Chop the shrimp into bite-sized pieces then add to the bowl. Toss in the beans, tomatoes, bell pepper, green onion, and cilantro until well combined.

Cover and chill until ready to serve.

Nutrition Info: Calories 405, Total Fat 9.5g, Saturated Fat 1.7g, Total Carbs 47.8g, Net Carbs 36.2, Protein 33.1, Sugar 2.8g, Fiber 11.6g, Sodium 291mg

Spinach & Orange Salad

Servings: 6Cooking Time: 0 Minutes

Ingredients:

¼ -1/3 Cup Vegan Dressing

3 Oranges, Medium, Peeled, Seeded & Sectioned

¾ lb. Spinach, Fresh & Torn

1 Red Onion, Medium, Sliced & Separated into Rings

Directions:

Toss everything together, and serve with dressing.

Interesting Facts: Spinach is one of the most superb green veggies out there. Each serving is packed with 3 grams of protein and is a highly encouraged component of the plant-based diet.

Nutrition Info: Calories: 99 Protein: 2.5 Grams Fat: 5 Grams Carbs: 13.1 Grams

Bacon And Blue Cheese Salad

Servings: 2

Cooking Time: 5-7 Minutes

Ingredients:

2 and ½ ounces fresh spinach

1 red onion, sliced

3-4 tablespoons blue cheese, crumbled

2 ounces almond nibs

5 ounces bacon strips

Directions:

Fry bacon for 2-3 minutes each side, cut the bacon and keep it onthe side

Take your salad plate and place spinach leaves on the bottomAdd sliced onion, cheese, baconTop with almond nibsUse your desired Keto-Friendly salad dressing if neededToss and enjoy it!

Nutrition Info: Calories: 420 Fat: 35g Carbohydrates: 2g Protein: 24g

Baked Salmon Cakes

Servings: 4
Cooking Time: 20 Minutes
Ingredients:
15 ounces canned salmon, drained
1 large egg, whisked
2 teaspoons Dijon mustard
1 small yellow onion, minced
1 ½ cups whole-wheat breadcrumbs
¼ cup low-fat mayonnaise
¼ cup nonfat Greek yogurt, plain
1 tablespoon fresh chopped parsley
1 tablespoon fresh lemon juice
2 green onions, sliced thin
Directions:
Preheat the oven to 450°F and line a baking sheet with parchment. Flake the salmon into a medium bowl then stir in the egg and mustard. Mix in the onions and breadcrumbs by hand, blending well, then shape into 8 patties.
Grease a large skillet and heat it over medium heat. Add the patties and fry for 2 minutes on each side until browned.
Transfer the patties to the baking sheet and bake for 15 minutes or until cooked through. Meanwhile, whisk together the remaining ingredients. Serve the baked salmon cakes with the creamy herb sauce.
Nutrition Info: Calories 240, Total Fat 12.2g, Saturated Fat 1.4g, Total Carbs 9.3g, Net Carbs 7.8g, Protein 25g, Sugar 1.8g, Fiber 1.5g, Sodium 241mg

Lighter Shrimp Scampi

Servings: 4
Cooking Time: 15 Minutes
Ingredients:
11/2 pounds large peeled and deveined shrimp
¼ teaspoon salt
1/8 teaspoon freshly ground black pepper
2 tablespoons olive oil
1 shallot, chopped
2 garlic cloves, minced
¼ cup cooking white wine
Juice of 1/2 lemon (1 tablespoon)
1/2 teaspoon sriracha
2 tablespoons unsalted butter, at room temperature
¼ cup chopped fresh parsley

4 servings (6 cups) zucchini noodles with lemon vinaigrette
Directions:
Season the shrimp with the salt and pepper.
In a medium saucepan over medium heat, heat the oil. Add the shallot and garlic, and cook until the shallot softens and the garlic is fragrant, about 3 minutes. Add the shrimp, cover, and cook until opaque, 2 to 3 minutes on each side. Using a slotted spoon, transfer the shrimp to a large plate. Add the wine, lemon juice, and sriracha to the saucepan, and stir to combine. Bring the mixture to a boil, then reduce the heat and simmer until the liquid is reduced by about half, 3 minutes. Add the butter and stir until melted, about 3 minutes. Return the shrimp to the saucepan and toss to coat. Add the parsley and stir to combine.
Into each of 4 containers, place 11/2 cups of zucchini noodles with lemon vinaigrette, and top with ¾ cup of scampi.
Nutrition Info: calories: 364; total fat: 21g; saturated fat: 6g; protein: 37g; total carbs: 10g; fiber: 2g; sugar: 6g; sodium: 557mg

Onion And Bacon Pork Chops

Servings: 4
Cooking Time: 45 Minutes
Ingredients:
2 onions, peeled and chopped
6 bacon slices, chopped
½ cup chicken stock
Salt and pepper to taste
4 pork chops
Directions:
Heat up a pan over medium heat and add bacon
Stir and cook until crispy
Transfer to bowl
Return pan to medium heat and add onions, season with salt and pepper. Stir and cook for 15 minutes
Transfer to the same bowl with bacon
Return the pan to heat (medium-high) and add pork chops. Season with salt and pepper and brown for 3 minutes. Flip and lower heat to medium. Cook for 7 minutes more
Add stock and stir cook for 2 minutes
Return the bacon and onions to the pan and stir cook for 1 minute. Serve and enjoy!
Nutrition Info: Calories: 325 Fat: 18g Carbohydrates: 6g Protein: 36g

Chapter 15
Dessert and Smoothie Recipes

Mango Bowls

Prep time: 10 minutes
Cook time: 0 minutes
Servings: 4
Ingredients:
2 bananas, peeled and sliced
2 mangoes, peeled and cubed
1 tablespoon walnuts, chopped
1 tablespoon lime juice
Directions:
In a bowl, combine the bananas with the mangoes and the other ingredients, toss and serve.
Nutrition: calories 165, fat 2, fiber 4.4, carbs 38.8, protein 2.5

Watermelon Cream

Prep time: **2 hours**
Cook time: 0 minutes
Servings: 6
Ingredients:
1 watermelon, peeled and cubed
1 teaspoon vanilla extract
½ teaspoon cinnamon powder
2 mangoes, peeled and cubed
Directions:
In a blender, combine the watermelon with the mango and the other ingredients, pulse well, divide into bowls and keep in the fridge for 2 hours before serving.
Nutrition: calories 75, fat 0.5, fiber 1.9, carbs 18.4, protein 1

Almond Banana Mix

Prep time: 10 minutes
Cook time: 0 minutes
Servings: **4**
Ingredients:
1 cup dates, chopped
2 bananas, peeled and sliced
1 cup almond milk
2 tablespoons cocoa powder

1 tablespoon honey
Directions:
In a bowl, combine the dates with the bananas and the other ingredients, toss and serve cold.
Nutrition: calories 338, fat 15, fiber 7.2, carbs 56, protein 3.6

Coconut Apple Bowls

Prep time: 10 minutes
Cook time: 0 minutes
Servings: 2
Ingredients:
2 big green apples, cored and roughly cubed
1 tablespoon honey
1 cup coconut cream
1 teaspoon cinnamon powder
Directions:
In a bowl, combine the apples with the cream and the other ingredients, toss and serve.
Nutrition: calories 100, fat 1, fiber 4, carbs 12, protein 4

Pineapple Cream

Prep time: 10 minutes
Cook time: 20 minutes
Servings: 6
Ingredients:
1 cup pineapple, peeled and cubed
½ cup walnuts, chopped
1 tablespoon honey
1 cup coconut cream
1 egg, whisked
¼ cup coconut oil, melted
Directions:
In a blender, combine the pineapple with the walnuts and the other ingredients, pulse well, divide into 6 ramekins and bake at 370 degrees F for 20 minutes.
Serve cold.
Nutrition: calories 200, fat 3, fiber 4, carbs 12, protein 8

Coconut Apple Bars

Prep time: 10 minutes
Cook time: 25 minutes
Servings: 6
Ingredients:
½ cup coconut cream
1 cup apples, peeled, cored and chopped
½ cup maple syrup
1 teaspoon vanilla extract
½ cup almond flour
2 eggs, whisked
1 teaspoon baking powder
Directions:
In a blender, combine the cream with the apples and the other ingredients and pulse well.
Pour this into a baking dish lined with parchment paper, bake in the oven at 370 degrees F for 25 minutes, cool down, cut into bars and serve.
Nutrition: calories 200, fat 3, fiber 4, carbs 12, protein 11

Avocado and Orange Bowl

Prep time: 10 minutes
Cook time: 0 minutes
Servings: 6
Ingredients:
3 oranges, peeled and cut into segments
1 avocado, peeled, pitted and cubed
3 tablespoons raw honey
½ teaspoon vanilla extract
1 teaspoon orange zest, grated
Directions:
In a bowl, combine the oranges with the avocado and the other ingredients, toss and serve.
Nutrition: calories 211, fat 3, fiber 4, carbs 8, protein 7

Honey Apples

Prep time: 10 minutes
Cook time: 30 minutes
Servings: 4
Ingredients:
2 apples, cored and halved
1 tablespoon ginger, grated
1 tablespoon turmeric powder
¼ cup raw honey
1 tablespoon ginger, grated

Directions:
Arrange the apples in a baking dish, add the ginger and the other ingredients, and bake at 390 degrees F for 30 minutes. Divide the apples mix between dessert plates and serve.
Nutrition: calories 90, fat 2, fiber 1, carbs 2, protein 5

Lemon Avocado Cream

Prep time: **2 hours**
Cook time: 0 minutes
Servings: 4
Ingredients:
2 cups coconut cream
1 watermelon, peeled and chopped
2 avocados, peeled, pitted and chopped
1 tablespoon honey - 2 teaspoons lemon juice
Directions:
In a blender, combine the watermelon with the cream and the other ingredients, pulse well, divide into bowls and keep in the fridge for 2 hours before serving.
Nutrition: calories 121, fat 2, fiber 2, carbs 6, protein 5

Orange Berry Sorbet

Prep time: **2 hours**
Cook time: 0 minutes
Servings: **6**
Ingredients:
1 pound strawberries, halved and frozen
1 cup orange juice
1 tablespoon orange zest, grated
1 tablespoon honey
Directions:
In a blender, combine the strawberries with the orange zest and the other ingredients, pulse well, divide into bowls and keep in the freezer for 2 hours before serving.
Nutrition: calories 121, fat 1, fiber 2, carbs 2, protein 4

Vanilla Pineapple Bowl

Prep time: 10 minutes
Cook time: 0 minutes
Servings: 4
Ingredients:
2 tablespoons almonds, chopped

1 tablespoon walnuts, chopped
2 cups pineapple, peeled and roughly cubed
1 tablespoon lemon juice
Zest of 1 lemon, grated
½ teaspoon vanilla extract
A pinch of cinnamon powder
Directions:
In a bowl, combine the pineapple with the nuts and the other ingredients, toss and serve.
Nutrition: calories 215, fat 3, fiber 4, carbs 12, protein 8

Almond Chia Pudding

Prep time: 30 minutes
Cook time: 0 minutes
Servings: 4
Ingredients:
2 cups almond milk
2 tablespoon honey
1 cup chia seeds
A pinch of cardamom powder
1 tablespoon lemon zest, grated
Directions:
In a bowl, mix the chia seeds with the almond milk and the other ingredients, toss, leave aside for 30 minutes, divide into small bowls and serve.
Nutrition: calories 199, fat 2, fiber 3, carbs 7, protein 5

Orange Mango Smoothie

Prep time: 10 minutes
Cook time: 0 minutes
Servings: 2
Ingredients:
2 cups mango, peeled and c hopped
1 cup orange juice
1 tablespoon ginger, grated
1 teaspoon turmeric powder
Directions:
In your blender, combine the mango with the juice and the other ingredients, pulse well, divide into 2 glasses and serve cold.
Nutrition: calories 100, fat 1, fiber 2, carbs 4, protein 5

Vanilla Chocolate Cream

Prep time: 2 hours
Cook time: 0 minutes
Servings: 4
Ingredients:
2 cups coconut milk
2 tablespoons ginger, grated
2 tablespoons honey
1 cup dark chocolate, chopped and melted
½ teaspoon cinnamon powder
1 teaspoon vanilla extract
Directions:
In a blender, combine the coconut milk with the ginger and the other ingredients, pulse well, divide into bowls and keep in the fridge for 2 hours before serving.
Nutrition: calories 200, fat 3, fiber 5, carbs 12, protein 7

Coconut Avocado Smoothie Bowl

Prep time: 10 minutes
Cook time: 0 minutes
Servings: 4
Ingredients:
2 avocados, peeled, pitted and cut into wedges
1 teaspoon cardamom, ground
½ cup coconut butter
1 cup coconut cream
1 teaspoon vanilla extract
Directions:
In your food processor, combine the avocados with the cream and the other ingredients, pulse well, divide into bowls and serve cold.
Nutrition: calories 211, fat 2, fiber 4, carbs 11, protein 7

Lime Strawberries Mix

Prep time: 10 minutes
Cook time: 20 minutes
Servings: 4
Ingredients:
1 pound strawberries, halved
2 tablespoons almonds, chopped
2 tablespoons coconut oil, melted
2 tablespoons lime juice
1 teaspoon vanilla extract
1 teaspoon honey

Directions:
Arrange the strawberries on a baking sheet lined with parchment paper, add the almonds and the other ingredients, toss and bake at 390 degrees F for 20 minutes.
Divide the strawberries mix into bowls and serve.
Nutrition: calories 220, fat 2, fiber 3, carbs 8, protein 2

Apple Compote

Prep time: 10 minutes
Cook time: 20 minutes
Servings: 4
Ingredients:
Juice of 1 lime
1 pound apples, cored and cut into wedges
1 tablespoon honey
1 and ½ cups water
Directions:
In a pan, combine the apples with the lime juice and the other ingredients, toss, bring to a simmer and cook over medium heat fro 20 minutes.
Divide the mix into bowls and serve cold.
Nutrition: : calories 108, fat 1, fiber 2, carbs 4, protein 7

Lime Berries Mix

Prep time: 10 minutes
Cook time: 0 minutes
Servings: 4
Ingredients:
1 cup blackberries
1 cup blueberries
2 teaspoons lime zest, grated
1 tablespoon raw honey
½ teaspoon vanilla extract
1 cup almond milk
Directions:
In your blender, combine the berries with the lime zest and the other ingredients, pulse well, divide into bowls and serve.
Nutrition: calories 217, fat 7, fiber 8, carbs 10, protein 8

Coconut Berries Mix

Prep time: 10 minutes
Cook time: 15 minutes
Servings: 4

Ingredients:
2 cups coconut milk
1 cup strawberries
¼ teaspoon vanilla extract
1/3 cup pure maple syrup
Directions:
In a small pot, combine the coconut milk with the berries and the other ingredients, toss, cook over medium heat for 15 minutes, divide into bowls and serve cold.
Nutrition: calories 176, fat 4, fiber 2, carbs 7, protein 6

Papaya and Nuts Salad

Prep time: 4 minutes
Cook time: 0 minutes
Servings: 4
Ingredients:
2 apples, cored and cut into wedges
1 cup papaya, roughly cubed
½ teaspoon vanilla extract
2 tablespoons almonds, chopped
1 tablespoon walnuts, chopped
2 tablespoons lemon juice
Directions:
In a bowl, combine the papaya with the apples and the other ingredients, toss, divide into smaller bowls and serve.
Nutrition: calories 140, fat 1, fiber 2, carbs 3, protein 5

Orange Coconut Bars

Prep time: **2 hours**
Cook time: 0 minutes
Servings: 4
Ingredients:
1/3 cup natural coconut butter, melted
1 and ½ tablespoons coconut oil
2 tablespoons orange juice
½ teaspoon orange zest, grated
1 tablespoons honey
Directions:
In a bowl, combine the coconut butter with the oil and the other ingredients, stir well, scoop into a square pan, spread well, cut into bars, keep in the freezer for 2 hours and serve.
Nutrition: calories 72, fat 4, fiber 2, carbs 8, protein 6

Chia Bowls

Prep time: 10 minutes
Cook time: 0 minutes
Servings: 4
Ingredients:
¼ cup chia seeds
1 cup almond milk
2 mangos, peeled and cubed
2 teaspoons vanilla extract
¼ cup coconut, shredded
1 tablespoon honey
Directions:
In a bowl, combine the chia seeds with the mango, the milk and the other ingredients, toss, leave aside for 10 minutes, divide into small bowls and serve.
Nutrition: calories 287, fat 17.2, fiber 5.1, carbs 34.6, protein 3.2

Pomegranate Bowls

Prep time: 2 hours
Cook time: 0 minutes
Servings: 4
Ingredients:
½ cup coconut cream
1 orange, peeled and cut into wedges
1 teaspoon vanilla extract
½ cup almonds, chopped
1 cup pomegranate seeds
1 tablespoon orange zest, grated
Directions:
In a bowl, combine the orange with the pomegranate seeds and the other ingredients, toss and keep in the fridge for 2 hours before dividing into smaller bowls and serving.
Nutrition: calories 68, fat 5.1, fiber 4, carbs 6, protein 1

Maple Berries Bowls

Prep time: 10 minutes
Cook time: 0 minutes
Servings: 4
Ingredients:
½ cup dates, pitted
½ teaspoon vanilla extract
1 cup almonds, chopped
1 cup blackberries
1 tablespoon maple syrup
1 tablespoon coconut oil, melted

Directions:
In a bowl, combine the berries with the almonds and the other ingredients, toss, divide into small cups and serve.
Nutrition: calories 130, fat 5, fiber 5, carbs 12, protein 4

Mint Apple Cream

Prep time: 10 minutes
Cook time: 0 minutes
Servings: **4**
Ingredients:
1 pounds apples, peeled, cored and cubed
2 cups coconut cream
1 tablespoon mint, chopped
Directions:
In your blender, combine the apples with the cream and mint, pulse well, divide into small cups and serve cold.
Nutrition: calories 70, fat 9, fiber 3, carbs 4.4, protein 3

Almond Rhubarb Pudding

Prep time: 10 minutes
Cook time: 20 minutes
Servings: 6
Ingredients:
2 cups rhubarb, sliced
2 tablespoons maple syrup - 3 eggs
2 tablespoons coconut oil, melted
1 cup almond milk
½ teaspoon baking powder
Directions:
In a blender, combine the rhubarb with the oil and maple syrup and pulse well.
In a bowl, combine the rhubarb puree with the other ingredients, whisk, divide into 6 ramekins and bake at 350 degrees F for 20 minutes.
Serve the pudding cold.
Nutrition: calories 220, fat 12, fiber 3, carbs 7, protein 8

Dates and Pears Cake

Prep time: 10 minutes
Cook time: 30 minutes
Servings: 6
Ingredients:
2 pears, cored, peeled and chopped

2 cups coconut flour
1 cup dates, pitted
2 eggs, whisked
1 teaspoon vanilla extract
1 teaspoon baking soda
½ cup coconut oil, melted
½ teaspoon cinnamon powder
Directions:
In a bowl, combine the pears with the flour and the other ingredients, whisk well, pour into a cake pan and bake at 360 degrees F for 30 minutes.
Cool down, slice and serve.
Nutrition: calories 160, fat 7, fiber 4, carbs 8, protein 4.

Pears Cream

Prep time: 10 minutes
Cook time: 0 minutes
Servings: **4**
Ingredients:
2 teaspoons lime juice
1 pound pears, cored, peeled and chopped
1 pound strawberries, chopped
1 cup coconut cream
Directions:
In a blender, combine the pears with strawberries and the other ingredients, pulse well, divide into bowls and serve.
Nutrition: calories 100, fat 2, fiber 3, carbs 8, protein 5

Orange Bowls

Prep time: 10 minutes
Cook time: 0 minutes
Servings: 4
Ingredients:
2 oranges, peeled and cut into segments
1 cantaloupe, peeled and cubed
2 tablespoons honey
1 cup orange juice
1 teaspoon vanilla extract
Directions:
In a bowl, combine the oranges with the cantaloupe and the other ingredients, toss and serve. Enjoy!
Nutrition: calories 110, fat 2, fiber 3, carbs 6, protein 6

Chicory Cherry Cream

Prep time: 10 minutes
Cook time: 15 minutes
Servings: **6**
Ingredients:
1 pound cherries, pitted and chopped
Juice of 1 lime
Zest of 1 lime, grated
2 tablespoons chicory root powder
¼ teaspoon vanilla extract
Directions:
In a pot, mix the cherries with the lime juice and the other ingredients, toss, simmer over medium heat for 15 minutes, blend using an immersion blender, divide into cups and serve cold.
Nutrition: calories 120, fat 2, fiber 2, carbs 3, protein 6

Cinnamon Apple Mix

Prep time: 10 minutes
Cook time: 20 minutes
Servings: 6
Ingredients:
3 apples, cored and roughly cut into wedges
3 pears, cored and cut into wedges
4 tablespoons chicory root powder
2 teaspoons cinnamon powder
Directions:
In a roasting pan, combine the apples with the pears and the other ingredients, toss and cook at 380 degrees F for 20 minutes.
Divide the mix between dessert plates and serve.
Nutrition: calories 110, fat 2, fiber 3, carbs 5, protein 5

Mango Bowls

Prep time: 10 minutes
Cook time: 20 minutes
Servings: **4**
Ingredients:
2 mangoes, peeled and cubed
1 tablespoon ginger, grated
1 tablespoon cinnamon powder
1 teaspoon vanilla extract
1 cup water

Directions:

In a small pot, combine the mango with the cinnamon and the other ingredients, toss, simmer over medium heat for 20 minutes, divide into bowls and serve.

Nutrition: calories 140, fat 2, fiber 2, carbs 8, protein 9

Lime Watermelon Bowls

Prep time: 10 minutes
Cook time: 15 minutes
Servings: **4**
Ingredients:
2 tablespoons lime juice
2 cups watermelon, peeled and cubed
1 tablespoon chicory root powder
2 tablespoons flax meal mixed with 4 tablespoons water
Directions:

In a small pot, combine the watermelon with the other ingredients, toss, simmer over medium heat for 15 minutes, divide into bowls and serve cold.

Nutrition: calories 161, fat 4, fiber 2, carbs 8, protein 5

Coconut Pudding

Prep time: 10 minutes
Cook time: 20 minutes
Servings: **4**
Ingredients:
2 cups coconut milk
1 pear, cored, peeled and cubed ½ cup maple syrup
3 tablespoons coconut oil, melted
3 tablespoons flax meal mixed with 6 tablespoons water
1 cup coconut cream
Directions:

In your blender, mix the pear with the coconut milk and the other ingredients, pulse well and divide into 4 ramekins. Place the ramekins in a baking dish, add the water to the dish, introduce in the oven, cook at 350 degrees F for 20 minutes and serve cold.

Nutrition: calories 171, fat 5, fiber 2, carbs 6, protein 8

Coconut Grapes Bowls

Prep time: 10 minutes
Cook time: 15 minutes
Servings: **4**
Ingredients:
2 cups coconut cream
1 cup grapes, halved
2 cups rolled oats
1 teaspoon vanilla extract
½ cup walnuts, chopped
Directions:

In a small pot, combine the grapes with the cream and the other ingredients, stir, bring to a simmer over medium heat, cook for 15 minutes, divide into bowls and serve cold.

Nutrition: calories 142, fat 3, fiber 3, carbs 7, protein 4

Nutmeg Grapes Cake

Prep time: 10 minutes
Cook time: 35 minutes
Servings: **4**
Ingredients:
2 cups stevia - 2 cups coconut flour
2 cups grapes, chopped
3 eggs, whisked
2 teaspoon baking powder
1 teaspoon vanilla extract
1 teaspoon nutmeg powder
Directions:

In a bowl, combine the stevia with the flour and the other ingredients, whisk well, pour into a cake pan and cover with tin foil.

Introduce in the oven, bake at 350 degrees F for 35 minutes, cool it down, slice and serve.

Nutrition: calories 300, fat 11, fiber 4, carbs 8, protein 4

Quinoa Pudding

Prep time: 10 minutes
Cook time: 35 minutes
Servings: **4**
Ingredients:
3 cups almond milk
2 tablespoons chicory root powder

1 cup quinoa

2 apples, cored and cubed

1 tablespoon cinnamon powder

Directions:

In a pot, combine the milk with the quinoa and the other ingredients, toss, bring to a simmer over medium-low heat, cook for 35 minutes, divide into bowls and serve cold.

Nutrition:

calories 629, fat 45.7, fiber 9.6, carbs 52.6, protein 10.6

Rice Pudding

Prep time: 10 minutes

Cook time: 30 minutes

Servings: **6**

Ingredients:

1 tablespoon coconut oil, melted

1 cup brown rice

3 cups almond milk

1 cup grapes, chopped

½ teaspoon vanilla extract

Directions:

In a small pot, combine the rice with the almond milk and the other ingredients, stir well, bring to a simmer over medium heat, cook for 30 minutes, divide into bowls and serve cold.

Nutrition: calories 172, fat 4, fiber 1, carbs 14, protein 8

Peach Compote

Prep time: 10 minutes

Cook time: 20 minutes

Servings: **6**

Ingredients:

3 peaches, peeled and roughly cubed

2 tablespoons chicory root powder

1 teaspoon vanilla extract - 3 cups water

Directions:

In a small pot, mix the peaches the other ingredients, stir, bring to a simmer over medium heat, cook for 20 minutes, divide into cups and serve cold.

Nutrition: calories 122, fat 4, fiber 2, carbs 8, protein 2

Lime Coconut Pudding

Prep time: 10 minutes

Cook time: 25 minutes

Servings: **6**

Ingredients:

2 cups coconut cream

1 teaspoon vanilla extract

4 eggs, whisked

1 teaspoon lime juice

½ teaspoon nutmeg powder

Directions:

In a bowl, combine the cream with the eggs and the other ingredients, whisk well, and divide into small ramekins.

Bake at 350 degrees F for 25 minutes, and serve cold

Nutrition: calories 200, fat 5, fiber 2, carbs 8, protein 8

Apricot Cream

Prep time: 10 minutes

Cook time: 0 minutes

Servings: **4**

Ingredients:

12 ounces apricots, chopped

2 tablespoons chia seeds

2 cups coconut cream

2 avocados, peeled, pitted and cubed

2 tablespoons maple syrup

2 tablespoons chicory root powder

1 tablespoon vanilla extract

Directions:

In a blender, combine the apricots with the chia seeds and the other ingredients, pulse well, divide into bowls and serve really cold.

Nutrition: calories 140, fat 2, fiber 2, carbs 10, protein 7

Lime Berry Compote

Prep time: 10 minutes

Cook time: 20 minutes

Servings: **4**

Ingredients:

2 cups strawberries, halved

2 cups water

2 tablespoons chicory root powder
1 tablespoon lime juice
½ teaspoon vanilla extract
Method:
In a pan, combine the strawberries with the water and the other ingredients, toss, bring to a simmer and cook over medium heat for 20 minutes.
Divide the mix into bowls and serve cold.
Nutrition: calories 200, fat 2, fiber 3, carbs 5, protein 10

Honey Berry Curd

Prep time: 10 minutes
Cook time: 10 minutes
Servings: **4**
Ingredients:
2 cups blackberries
¼ cup lime juice
2 tablespoons honey
2 teaspoons lime zest, grated
4 tablespoons coconut oil, melted
3 egg yolks, whisked
Directions:
Heat up a small pan over medium heat, add the berries and lime juice, stir, bring to a simmer, cook for 5 minutes, strain this into a heatproof bowl and mash a bit.
Put some water into a pan, bring to a simmer over medium heat, add the bowl with the berries on top, also add the rest of the ingredients, stir well, cook for 5 minutes more, divide into small cups and serve cold.
Nutrition: calories 140, fat 3, fiber 3, carbs 6, protein 8

Coconut Avocado Pie

Prep time: 30 minutes
Cook time: 40 minutes
Servings: **8**
Ingredients:
2 cups coconut flour
6 tablespoons coconut butter
5 tablespoons water

For the filling:
2 avocados, peeled, pitted and cubed
3 tablespoons chicory root powder
3 tablespoons almond flour
½ teaspoon vanilla extract
2 eggs, whisked
1 tablespoon coconut oil, melted
2 tablespoons coconut milk
Directions:
In a bowl, mix the coconut flour with the coconut butter and the water, stir until you obtain a firm dough, transfer the dough to a floured working surface, knead it, shape a flattened disk, wrap in plastic, keep in the fridge for 30 minutes, roll a circle and arrange in a pie pan.
In a bowl, mix the avocados with the chicory root powder and the other ingredients for the filling, stir well, pour into the pie pan, introduce in the oven at 370 degrees F, bake for 40 minutes, cut and serve.
Nutrition: calories 200, fat 6.3, fiber 3, carbs 11.6, protein 9

Coconut Carrot Cake

Prep time: 10 minutes
Cook time: 35 minutes
Servings: **6**
Ingredients:
2 cups coconut milk
½ cup coconut oil, melted
Chicory root powder to the taste
4 eggs, whisked
2 carrots, grated
2 teaspoons vanilla extract
2 cups almond flour
1 teaspoon baking soda
Directions:
In a bowl, combine the milk with the coconut oil and the other ingredients, stir well, pour into a cake pan, bake in the oven at 350 degrees F 35 minutes, slice, divide between plates and serve.
Nutrition: calories 170, fat 4, fiber 5, carbs 6, protein 2

Quinoa Pudding

Prep time: 5 minutes
Cook time: 20 minutes
Servings: **4**
Ingredients:
1 cup quinoa
2 cups almond milk
3 tablespoons coconut butter
¼ cup almonds, chopped
1 tablespoon chicory root powder
½ cup pomegranate seeds
Directions:
In a pot, combine the quinoa with the almond milk and the other ingredients, bring to a simmer and cook over medium heat for 20 minutes.
Divide into bowls and serve cold.
Nutrition: calories 176, fat 6.4, fiber 5, carbs 9, protein 8

Banana Salad

Prep time: 10 minutes
Cook time: 0 minutes
Servings: **4**
Ingredients:
4 bananas, peeled and chopped
1 cup blackberries - 1 cup strawberries
Juice of 1 lime - 1 tablespoon coconut oil, melted
2 tablespoons chicory root powder
Directions:
In a bowl, combine the bananas with the berries and the other ingredients, toss and serve.
Nutrition: calories 370, fat 7, fiber 5, carbs 11, protein 8

Honey Orange Salad

Prep time: 10 minutes
Cook time: 0 minutes
Servings: **2**
Ingredients:
2 tablespoons raw honey
2 oranges, peeled, and cut into medium segments
1 cup coconut cream
1 tablespoon mint leaves, chopped

Directions:
In a bowl, combine the oranges with the cream and the other ingredients, toss, divide into small bowls and serve.
Nutrition: calories 150, fat 2, fiber 5, carbs 10, protein 11

Green Tea Pudding

Prep time: 10 minutes
Cook time: 15 minutes
Servings: **4**
Ingredients:
3 cups almond milk
½ cup coconut cream
2 tablespoons green tea powder
1 teaspoon vanilla extract
3 tablespoons chicory root powder
Directions:
In a pot, combine the almond milk with the cream and the other ingredients, whisk, bring to a simmer and cook over medium heat for 15 minutes.
Divide the mix into bowls and serve.
Nutrition: calories 220, fat 3, fiber 3, carbs 7, protein 5

Blackberry Cream

Prep time: 5 minutes
Cook time: 0 minutes
Servings: **4**
Ingredients:
1 cup blackberries
1 cup pineapple, peeled and cubed
1 tablespoon coconut oil, melted
¾ cup coconut cream
2 tablespoons maple syrup
Directions:
In your blender, combine the berries with the pineapple and the other ingredients, pulse well, divide into bowls and serve cold.
Nutrition: calories 120, fat 3, fiber 3, carbs 6, protein 8

Strawberries Pudding

Prep time: 10 minutes
Cook time: 25 minutes
Servings: **4**
Ingredients:
2 cups almond milk - 1 cup black rice
½ cup strawberries
2 tablespoons chicory root powder
1 teaspoon cinnamon powder
Directions:
Heat up a pan with the milk over medium heat, add the rice and the other ingredients, cook for 25 minutes stirring often, divide into bowls and serve cold.
Nutrition: calories 130, fat 1, fiber 3, carbs 4, protein 2

Coconut Pudding

Prep time: 10 minutes
Cook time: 12 minutes
Servings: **4**
Ingredients:
2 cups almond milk
½ cup coconut, unsweetened and shredded
1 tablespoon cinnamon powder
1 teaspoon allspice, ground
1 tablespoon chicory root powder
2 teaspoons ginger, ground
2 tablespoons pumpkin seeds
1 tablespoon chia seeds
1 teaspoon green tea powder
Directions:
Heat up a pan with the milk over medium heat, add the coconut, cinnamon and the other ingredients, whisk, cook over medium heat for 12 minutes, divide into bowls and serve cold.
Nutrition: calories 150, fat 4, fiber 2, carbs 6, protein 3

Coconut Grapes Bowls

Prep time: 10 minutes
Cook time: 25 minutes
Servings: **4**
Ingredients:
2 cups coconut milk

½ cup coconut cream
½ cup black tea
1 teaspoon vanilla extract
1 cup grapes, halved
1 tablespoon chicory root powder
1 tablespoon maple syrup
Directions:
Heat up a pan with the coconut milk over medium heat, add the cream, the grapes and the other ingredients, bring to a simmer and cook over medium heat for 25 minutes.
Divide into bowls and serve cold.
Nutrition: calories 140, fat 4, fiber 2, carbs 6, protein 5

Lemon Coconut Cream

Prep time: 30 minutes
Cook time: 0 minutes
Servings: 4
Ingredients:
2 cups coconut cream
Juice of 1 lemon
Zest of 1 lemon, grated
1 teaspoon vanilla extract
2 tablespoons chicory root powder
Directions:
In a bowl, combine the cream with the lemon juice and the other ingredients, whisk, divide into bowls and keep in the fridge for 30 minutes before serving.
Nutrition: calories 279, fat 28.6, fiber 2.6, carbs 6.8, protein 2.8

Cinnamon Rice Pudding

Prep time: 10 minutes
Cook time: 30 minutes
Servings: **4**
Ingredients:
2 cup coconut milk
1 cup black rice
3 tablespoons chicory root powder
2 teaspoons green tea powder
1 teaspoon cinnamon powder

Directions:

In a pan, combine the milk with the rice and the other ingredients, whisk, bring to a simmer and cook over medium heat for 30 minutes.

Divide the pudding into bowls and serve.

Nutrition: calories 276, fat 28.6, fiber 2.6, carbs 6.7, protein 2.8

Walnuts Cream

Prep time: 10 minutes

Cook time: 10 minutes

Servings: **6**

Ingredients:

2 tablespoons chicory root powder

2 cups coconut milk

1 cup coconut cream

¼ cup walnuts, chopped

½ cup dark chocolate, chopped

Directions:

Put the milk in a pan, heat up over medium heat, add the cream, chocolate and the other ingredients and cook for 10 minutes stirring often.

Transfer this bowls and serve warm.

Nutrition: calories 204, fat 15, fiber 4, carbs 10, protein 5

Mango and Banana Bowls

Prep time: 10 minutes

Cook time: 0 minutes

Servings: **4**

Ingredients:

1 avocado, peeled, pitted and chopped

1 big banana, peeled and chopped

1 mango, peeled and cubed

1 tablespoon honey

½ cup grapes, halved

1 tablespoon lime juice

2 teaspoons lime zest, grated

Directions:

In a bowl, combine the avocado with the banana and the other ingredients, toss, divide into small bowls and serve.

Nutrition: calories 207, fat 10.3, fiber 5.8, carbs 31.1, protein 2.1

Banana Cake

Prep time: 10 minutes

Cook time: 30 minutes

Servings: **6**

Ingredients:

2 tablespoons green tea powder

2 cups coconut milk

4 eggs, whisked

2 bananas, peeled and chopped

2 teaspoons vanilla extract

2 cups almond flour

1 teaspoon baking soda

Directions:

In a bowl, combine the coconut milk with the green tea powder and the other ingredients, stir well, pour into a cake pan, introduce in the oven and bake at 350 degrees F for 30 minutes.

Slice and serve cold.

Nutrition: calories 490, fat 39.9, fiber 7.1, carbs 21.8, protein 14.3

Chia Cream

Prep time: **2 hours**

Cook time: 0 minutes

Servings: **4**

Ingredients:

2 cups almond milk - 1 cup coconut cream

2 tablespoons chia seeds

2 tablespoons coconut, unsweetened and shredded

1 tablespoon chicory root powder

1 teaspoon cocoa powder

Directions:

In a bowl, combine the almond milk with the cream, chia seeds and the other ingredients, whisk well, divide into smaller bowls and keep in the fridge for 2 hours before serving.

Nutrition: calories 493, fat 48.2, fiber 9.2, carbs 16.6, protein 6.6

Cantaloupe Salad

Prep time: 5 minutes

Cook time: 0 minutes

Servings: **2**

Ingredients:

1 cup cantaloupe, peeled and cubed

1 cup grapes, halved
2 tablespoons mint, chopped
1 tablespoon honey
1 teaspoon nutmeg, ground
1 teaspoon vanilla extract
1 tablespoon lemon juice
Directions:
In a bowl, combine the cantaloupe with the grapes, mint and the other ingredients, toss, divide into smaller bowls and serve.
Nutrition: calories 105, fat 0.8, fiber 1.8, carbs 24.4, protein 1.3

Dandelion Avocado Smoothie

Preparation Time : 15 minutes
Cooking Time : 0
Servings : 1
Ingredients :
One cup of Dandelion
One Orange (juiced)
Coconut water
One Avocado
One key lime (juice)
Directions :
In a high-speed blender until smooth, blend Ingredients.
Nutrition : Calories: 160; Fat: 15 g; Carbohydrates: 9 g; Protein: 2 g

Amaranth Greens and Avocado Smoothie

Preparation Time : 15 minutes
Cooking Time : 0
Servings : 1
Ingredients :
One key lime (juice).
Two sliced apples (seeded).
Half avocado. - Two cupsful of amaranth greens.
Two cupsful of watercress.
One cupful of water.
Directions :
Add the whole recipes together and transfer them into the blender. Blend thoroughly until smooth.
Nutrition : Calories: 160; Fat: 15 g; Carbohydrates: 9 g; Protein: 2 g

Lettuce, Orange and Banana Smoothie

Preparation Time : 15 minutes
Cooking Time : 0
Servings : 1
Ingredients :
One and a half cupsful of fresh lettuce.
One large banana.
One cup of mixed berries of your choice.
One juiced orange.
Directions :
First, add the orange juice to your blender.
Add the remaining recipes and blend thoroughly.
Enjoy the rest of your day.
Nutrition : Calories: 252.1; Protein: 4.1 g

Delicious Elderberry Smoothie

Preparation Time : 15 minutes
Cooking Time : 0
Servings : 1
Ingredients :
One cupful of Elderberry
One cupful of Cucumber
One large apple
A quarter cupful of water
Directions :
Add the whole recipes together into a blender. Grind very well until they are uniformly smooth and enjoy.
Nutrition : Calories: 106; Carbohydrates: 26.68

Peaches Zucchini Smoothie

Preparation Time : 15 minutes
Cooking Time : 0
Servings : 1
Ingredients :
A half cupful of squash.
A half cupful of peaches.
A quarter cupful of coconut water.
A half cupful of Zucchini.
Directions :
Add the whole recipes together into a blender and blend until smooth and serve.
Nutrition : 55 Calories; 0g Fat; 2g Of Protein; 10mg Sodium; 14 G Carbohydrate; 2g Of Fiber

Ginger Orange and Strawberry Smoothie

Preparation Time : 15 minutes

Cooking Time : 0

Servings : 1

Ingredients :

One cup of strawberry.

One large orange (juice)

One large banana.

Quarter small sized ginger (peeled and sliced).

Directions :

Transfer the orange juice to a clean blender.

Add the remaining recipes and blend thoroughly until smooth.

Enjoy. Wow! You have ended the 9th day of your weight loss and detox journey.

Nutrition : 32 Calories; 0.3g Fat; 2g Of Protein; 10mg Sodium; 14g Carbohydrate; Water; 2g Of Fiber.

Kale Parsley and Chia Seeds Detox Smoothie

Preparation Time : 15 minutes

Cooking Time : 0

Servings : 1

Ingredients :

Three tbsp. chia seeds (grounded).

One cupful of water.

One sliced banana.

One pear (chopped).

One cupful of organic kale.

One cupful of parsley.

Two tbsp. of lemon juice.

A dash of cinnamon.

Directions :

Add the whole recipes together into a blender and pour the water before blending. Blend at high speed until smooth and enjoy.

You may or may not place it in the refrigerator depending on how hot or cold the weather appears.

Nutrition : 75 calories; 1g fat; 5g protein; 10g fiber

Watermelon Limenade

Preparation Time : 5 Minutes

Cooking Time : 0 minutes

Servings : 6

When it comes to refreshing summertime drinks, lemonade is always near the top of the list. This Watermelon "Limenade" is perfect for using up leftover watermelon or for those early fall days when stores and farmers are almost giving them away. You can also substitute 4 cups of ice for the cold water to create a delicious summertime slushy.

Ingredients:

4 cups diced watermelon

4 cups cold water

2 tablespoons freshly squeezed lemon juice

1 tablespoon freshly squeezed lime juice

Directions:

In a blender, combine the watermelon, water, lemon juice, and lime juice, and blend for 1 minute. Strain the contents through a fine-mesh sieve or nut-milk bag. Serve chilled. Store in the refrigerator for up to 3 days.

SERVING TIP: Slice up a few lemon or lime wedges to serve with your Watermelon Limenade, or top it with a few fresh mint leaves to give it an extra-crisp, minty flavor.

Nutrition : Calories: 60

Bubbly Orange Soda

Preparation Time : 5 Minutes

Cooking Time : 0 minutes

Servings : 4

Soda can be one of the toughest things to give up when you first adopt a WFPB diet. That's partially because refined sugars and caffeine are addictive, but it can also be because carbonated beverages are fun to drink! With sweetness from the orange juice and bubbliness from the carbonated water, this orange "soda" is perfect for assisting in the transition from SAD to WFPB.

Ingredients:

4 cups carbonated water

2 cups pulp-free orange juice (4 oranges, freshly squeezed and strained)

Directions:

For each serving, pour 2 parts carbonated water and 1-part orange juice over ice right before serving.

Stir and enjoy.

SERVING TIP: This recipe is best made right before drinking. The amount of fizz in the carbonated water will decrease the longer it's open, so if you're going to make it ahead of time, make sure it's stored in an airtight, refrigerator-safe container.

Nutrition: Calories: 56

Creamy Cashew Milk

Preparation Time : 5 Minutes

Cooking Time : 0 minutes

Servings : 8

Learning how to make your own plant-based milks can be one of the best ways to save money and ditch dairy for good. This is one of the easiest milk recipes to master, and if you have a high-speed blender, you can skip the straining step and go straight to a refrigerator-safe container. Large mason jars work great for storing plant-based milk, as they allow you to give a quick shake before each use.

Ingredients:

4 cups water

¼ cup raw cashews, soaked overnight

Directions:

In a blender, blend the water and cashews on high speed for 2 minutes.

Strain with a nut-milk bag or cheesecloth, then store in the refrigerator for up to 5 days.

VARIATION TIP: This recipe makes unsweetened cashew milk that can be used in savory and sweet dishes. For a creamier version to put in your coffee, cut the amount of water in half. For a sweeter version, add 1 to 2 tablespoons maple syrup and 1 teaspoon vanilla extract before blending.

Nutrition: Calories: 18

Homemade Oat Milk

Preparation Time : 5 Minutes

Cooking Time : 0 minutes

Servings : 8

Oat milk is a fantastic option if you need a nut-free milk or just want an extremely inexpensive plant-based milk. Making a half-gallon jar at home costs a fraction of the price of other plant-based or dairy milks. Oat milk can be used in both savory and sweet dishes.

Ingredients:

1 cup rolled oats

4 cups water

Directions:

Put the oats in a medium bowl, and cover with cold water. Soak for 15 minutes, then drain and rinse the oats.

Pour the cold water and the soaked oats into a blender. Blend for 60 to 90 seconds, or just until the mixture is a creamy white color throughout. (Blending any further may over blend the oats, resulting in a gummy milk.)

Strain through a nut-milk bag or colander, then store in the refrigerator for up to 5 days.

Nutrition: Calories: 39

Lucky Mint Smoothie

Preparation Time : 5 Minutes

Cooking Time : 0 minutes

Servings : 2

As spring approaches and mint begins to take over the garden once again, "Irish"-themed green shakes begin to pop up as well. In contrast to the traditionally high-fat, sugary shakes, this smoothie is a wonderful option for sunny spring days. So next time you want to sip on something cool and minty, do so with a health-promoting Lucky Mint Smoothie.

Ingredients:

2 cups plant-based milk (here or here)

2 frozen bananas, halved

1 tablespoon fresh mint leaves or ¼ teaspoon peppermint extract

1 teaspoon vanilla extract

Directions :

In a blender, combine the milk, bananas, mint, and vanilla. Blend on high for 1 to 2 minutes, or until the contents reach a smooth and creamy consistency, and serve.

VARIATION TIP: If you like to sneak greens into smoothies, add a cup or two of spinach to boost the health benefits of this smoothie and give it an even greener appearance.

Nutrition: Calories: 152

Paradise Island Smoothie

Preparation Time : 5 Minutes
Cooking Time : 0 minutes
Servings : 2

Ingredients :

2 cups plant-based milk (here or here)
1 frozen banana
½ cup frozen mango chunks
½ cup frozen pineapple chunks
1 teaspoon vanilla extract

Directions :

In a blender, combine the milk, banana, mango, pineapple, and vanilla. Blend on high for 1 to 2 minutes, or until the contents reach a smooth and creamy consistency, and serve.

LEFTOVER TIP: If you have any leftover smoothie, you can put it in a jar with some rolled oats and allow the mixture to soak in the refrigerator overnight to create a tropical version of overnight oats.

Nutrition: Calories: 176

21-Day Meal Plan

Day	Breakfast	First Course	Second Course	Dessert
1	Blueberry Breakfast Cake	Blueberry and Chicken Salad	Cauliflower Rice with Chicken	Peanut Butter Cups
2	Whole-Grain Pancakes	Beef and Red Bean Chili	Turkey with Fried Eggs	Fruit Pizza
3	Buckwheat Grouts Breakfast Bowl	Berry Apple Cider	Sweet Potato, Kale, And White Bean Stew	Choco Peppermint Cake
4	Peach Muesli Bake	Brunswick Stew	Slow Cooker Two-Bean Sloppy Joes	Roasted Mango
5	Steel-Cut Oatmeal Bowl with Fruit and Nuts	Buffalo Chicken Salads	Lighter Eggplant Parmesan	Roasted Plums
6	Whole-Grain Dutch Baby Pancake	Cacciatore Style Chicken	Coconut-Lentil Curry	Figs with Honey & Yogurt
7	Mushroom, Zucchini, And Onion Frittata	Carnitas Tacos	Stuffed Portobello With Cheese	Flourless Chocolate Cake
8	Spinach and Cheese Quiche	Chicken Chili	Lighter Shrimp Scampi	Lava Cake
9	Spicy Jalapeno Popper Deviled Eggs	Chicken Vera Cruz	Maple-Mustard Salmon	Cheese Cake
10	Lovely Porridge	Chicken and Cornmeal Dumplings	Chicken Salad with Grapes and Pecans	Orange Cake
11	Salty Macadamia Chocolate Smoothie	Chicken and Pepperoni	Roasted Vegetables	Madeleine
12	Basil and Tomato Baked Eggs	Chicken and Sausage Gumbo	Millet Pilaf	Waffles
13	Cinnamon and Coconut Porridge	Chicken, Barley, And Leek Stew	Sweet and Sour Onions	Pretzels
14	An Omelet of Swiss Chard	Cider Pork Stew	Sautéed Apples and Onions	Cheesy Taco Bites
15	Cheesy Low-Carb Omelet	Creamy Chicken Noodle Soup	Zucchini Noodles with Portabella Mushrooms	Nut Squares
16	Yogurt and Kale Smoothie	Cuban Pulled Pork Sandwich	Grilled Tempeh with Pineapple	Pumpkin & Banana Ice Cream
17	Bacon and Chicken Garlic Wrap	Gazpacho	Courgettes in Cider Sauce	Brulee Oranges
18	Grilled Chicken Platter	Tomato and Kale Soup	Baked Mixed Mushrooms	Frozen Lemon & Blueberry
19	Parsley Chicken Breast	Comforting Summer Squash Soup with Crispy Chickpeas	Spiced Okra	Peanut Butter Choco Chip Cookies
20	Mustard Chicken	Curried Carrot Soup	Lemony Salmon Burgers	Watermelon Sherbet
21	Balsamic Chicken	Thai Peanut, Carrot, And Shrimp Soup	Caprese Turkey Burgers	Strawberry & Mango Ice Cream

Printed in Great Britain
by Amazon